Windows® 98 Registry Handbook

Windows® 98 Registry Handbook

 201 West 103rd Street,
Indianapolis, Indiana 46290

Jerry Honeycutt

Windows® 98 Registry Handbook

Copyright © 1998 by Que

All rights reserved. No part of this book shall be reproduced, stored in a retrieval system, or transmitted by any means, electronic, mechanical, photocopying, recording, or otherwise, without written permission from the publisher. No patent liability is assumed with respect to the use of the information contained herein. Although every precaution has been taken in the preparation of this book, the publisher and author assume no responsibility for errors or omissions. Neither is any liability assumed for damages resulting from the use of the information contained herein. International Standard Book Number: 0-7897-1947-9

Library of Congress Catalog Card Number: 98-88299

Printed in the United States of America

First Printing: *December 1998*

00 99 98   4   3   2   1

Executive Editor
Brad Koch
Acquisitions Editor
Dustin Sullivan
Development Editor
Tom Dinse
Managing Editor
Brice Gosnell
Project Editor
Sara Bosin
Indexer
Kelly Talbot
Proofreader
Benjamin Berg
Technical Editor
Curtis Knight
Interior Design
Ruth Lewis
Production
Ben Hart
Louis Porter, Jr.

Contents

About the Author

Jerry Honeycutt provides business-oriented technical leadership to the Internet community, software development industry, and end-user community. He has served companies such as the Travelers, IBM, Nielsen North America, IRM, Howard Systems International, and NCR. He continues to serve a variety of organizations via consulting, speaking, training, and so on.

Having published 18 books through various publishers, Jerry is a leading author in the operating system and Internet categories. Many of Jerry's books are international best-sellers and have been translated into a variety of languages. Jerry keeps busy in other types of media, too. He is a regular speaker at Windows World, Comdex, and other industry trade shows on topics related to the Windows product family and the Internet. He writes a bimonthly column for Frisco Style Magazine and has contributed to Computer Language magazine. Jerry also maintains a Web site at http://www.honeycutt.com, where he speaks to a variety of issues confronting all readers, individual and corporate.

Jerry graduated from the University of Texas at Dallas in 1992 with a BS degree in Computer Science. He currently lives in the Dallas suburb of Frisco, Texas with Bones, his loyal Jack Russell Terrier; and has a passion for golf, fine photography, and international travel. Feel free to contact Jerry on the Internet at jerry@honeycutt.com.

Dedication

For the boys, Corky and Turbo, I miss you already!

Acknowledgments

To do a book right takes a lot of time and a lot of effort from a lot of people. Some of those people deserve special mention. Otherwise, make sure you flip over a few pages to see a full list of people who contributed to this book.

Probably the most deserving of a pat or two is Dustin Sullivan who, after a few ups and downs, managed to show patience that bewilders and astonishes most of us. Such patience comes more from vision than anything his mother taught him. Producing a best-of-breed book being his number one goal meant that he was able to keep his feet off my dog long enough to let that happen.

I'd also like to thank Macmillan's editorial department for sticking with it—Brad Koch for his infinite wisdom, and Tom Dinse for his great attitude.

My Web hosting service, Data Return, didn't help publish this book. Still, I must acknowledge them since they pick up where Macmillan leaves off, providing a service that makes supporting you via my companion Web site and mailing list easy and affordable. Thanks Mike. If interested in a Web hosting service, visit `http://www.datareturn.com` to learn more about Data Return.

Tell Us What You Think!

As the reader of this book, *you* are our most important critic and commentator. We value your opinion and want to know what we're doing right, what we could do better, what areas you'd like to see us publish in, and any other words of wisdom you're willing to pass our way.

As the executive editor for the Operating Systems team at Macmillan Computer Publishing, I welcome your comments. You can fax, email, or write me directly to let me know what you did or didn't like about this book—as well as what we can do to make our books stronger.

Please note that I cannot help you with technical problems related to the topic of this book, and that due to the high volume of mail I receive, I might not be able to reply to every message.

When you write, please be sure to include this book's title and author as well as your name and phone or fax number. I will carefully review your comments and share them with the author and editors who worked on the book.

Fax: 317-581-4663

Email: opsys@mcp.com

Mail: Executive Editor
           Operating Systems
           Macmillan Computer Publishing
           201 West 103rd Street
           Indianapolis, IN 46290 USA

Introduction

The Registry contains most of the configuration data used by Windows 98. It's the central repository for your configuration data, tying all the different parts of the operating system together so that it operates seamlessly. One of the biggest technologies made possible by the Registry is Plug and Play. Other advantages are less spectacular but equally important. The Registry allows applications to integrate with Windows 98, for instance, making it tough to determine where the operating system ends and the application begins.

As a tool, the Windows 98 Registry is useful to three types of users. Administrators gain the most from the Registry, using it as a remote administration tool. Power users use the Registry to customize their computers. Programmers must learn how to write code that stores configuration data in the Registry. You'll learn more about how this book helps each type of user a bit later in this introduction.

What's New

Outwardly, Microsoft has made few changes to the Windows 98 Registry. The organization is roughly the same as with Windows 95, but it does contain a number of new settings. The Registry Editor is unchanged. Most of the changes to the Registry are technological:

- The Registry uses less memory, allowing Windows 98 to start faster and providing an across-the-board performance improvement.

- Microsoft has improved the Registry's caching so that looking up values takes less time. This is another across-the-board performance improvement.

- Windows 98 automatically detects a variety of Registry errors and repairs them. You're less likely to see Registry errors when you start the computer.

- Windows 98 includes a new backup and repair utility that does for the Registry what ScanDisk does for the file system.

How to Use This Book

This is not a tell-all book about Windows. It doesn't cover the entire breadth and depth of Windows like *Special Edition Using Windows 98*. However, it does cover the Registry in more detail than you are likely to find in any other source. It provides many useful tips for personalizing Windows and overcoming some of Windows' more annoying quirks. In short, this book contains the secrets you're looking for.

No matter what type of user you are—administrator or power user—read all of Part A, "Starting Out," before you continue with the rest of this book. The information in these chapters shows you how to protect yourself from accidents, get around the Registry, and use the Registry Editor. After you've read these chapters, take a look at the following sections to learn which parts of this book might be most valuable to you.

Administrators

Sometimes Microsoft just can't win. According to the August 26, 1996 issue of *PC Week* magazine, 55 percent of IT managers surveyed said that their support costs didn't decrease after they deployed Windows 95. *PC Week* goes on to report that "several Windows 95 features that might reduce client support costs have been largely ignored by administrators." Only 16 percent of the managers they surveyed said that they use policies to restrict a user's privileges. Likewise, only 33 percent use the Registry to remotely administer a user's computer.

If you want to make a difference in your organization, help reduce support costs by learning how to remotely administer and control the computers. You can start by diving into Part D, "Administering the Windows 98 Registry." This part shows you how to remotely edit a user's Registry; how to work with script, REG, and INF files; and how to use policies to control what a user can do.

Power Users

If you're a power user who wants to learn more about Windows, personalize or troubleshoot Windows, or protect yourself from the many problems the Registry creates, you're reading the right book. Here are some suggestions to get you started:

- If you want to dive right in and learn more about Windows through the Registry, start with Part B, "Exploring the Registry."
- If you want to change how Windows looks, works, or performs, skim the table of contents for Part C, "Customizing and Troubleshooting," to find a place to jump to.
- If you're reading this book because you have a specific problem that you think you can fix using the Registry, read Chapter 10, "Fixing Common Problems via the Registry." You'll learn how to fix some of the more common problems that involve the Registry.
- If you're getting all sorts of strange error messages about a bad or corrupted Registry, keep your hands off the keyboard until you read Chapter 4, "Troubleshooting the Registry."

How This Book Is Organized

The Windows 98 Registry Handbook covers the Windows Registry in depth. It has four parts, 15 chapters, and an index. You learn the basics of the Registry in the first two parts. Part C shows you how to customize and troubleshoot Windows using the Registry. Part D is for administrators, but power users will also find these chapters useful. You'll find more information about how this book is organized in the rest of this section.

Part A: Starting Out with the Registry

Chapter 1, "Inside the Windows 98 Registry," is Registry 101. You learn the basics in this chapter, such as working with the Registry files and backing up the Registry. You also get a brief overview of the Registry's organization.

Chapter 2, "Backing Up and Restoring the Registry," shows you how to protect your data. It also describes Windows 98's new Registry Checker, which is the only program you need to back up and restore the Registry.

Chapter 3, "Using the Windows 98 Registry Editor," shows you how to use the Registry Editor.

Chapter 4, "Troubleshooting the Registry," is the Registry's little instruction book. This chapter shows you how to get out of trouble when you find that something's not quite right with the Registry.

Part B: Exploring the Regsitry

This portion of the book explains the contents of the Registry in detail. You find four chapters in Part B, each of which covers a specific portion of the Registry:

Chapter 5, "HKEY_CLASSES_ROOT"

Chapter 6, "HKEY_LOCAL_MACHINE"

Chapter 7, "HKEY_USERS and HKEY_CURRENT_USER"

Chapter 8, "HKEY_CURRENT_CONFIG and HKEY_DYN_DATA"

Part C: Customizing and Troubleshooting

Chapter 9, "Customizing the Windows 98 Desktop," is like the TV show *Inside Edition*—for Windows. It exposes some of Windows's deepest secrets so that you can personalize it just the way you want.

Windows is a complex operating system. You might have problems that have annoyed you for months, and maybe even problems you don't yet know about. Chapter 10, "Fixing Common Problems via the Registry," shows you how to fix them.

You can find many freeware and shareware programs that help you and the Registry live together peacefully. Chapter 11, "Tweak UI and Other Registry Programs," shows you where to find them and how to use them.

Chapter 12, "Tracking Down Registry Settings," shows you how to locate changes in the Registry. It introduces you to products such as ConfigSafe and shows you how to compare before and after versions of the Registry to locate changes.

Part D: Administering the Registry

Chapter 13, "Security and Remote Administration," shows you how to tighten up Windows 98 security a bit and how to install Windows 98 so that it supports remote Registry administration.

Chapter 14, "Profiles, System Policies, and the Registry," introduces you to two of the most useful tools for administrators: user profiles and system policies. Too bad that they're also the most underutilized tools.

REG and INF files let you write a script for changing the Registry that you can pass around to your users—perhaps in an email message. Chapter 15, "Script, REG, and INF Files," shows you how to create these types of files.

Special Features in This Book

This book has some special features designed to help you get the information you need—fast. These features are described in this section.

Chapter Roadmaps

Each chapter begins with a brief list of the topics that are covered. You know what you'll be reading about before you start. You can think of the roadmap as my commitment to cover those topics in the chapter.

Tips, Notes, Cautions

Notes, tips, cautions, and so on give you useful information that applies to the passage you're reading. You'll find a sample of each element below. Each sample describes the type of information you'll find it that element.

> TIP: Tips enhance your experience with Windows 95 by providing hints and tricks you won't find elsewhere.

> NOTE: Notes provide useful information that's not necessarily essential to the discussion. They usually contain more technical information, but can also contain interesting but non-vital technical or non-technical information.

> CAUTION: Cautions warn you that a particular action can cause severe harm to your configuration. Given the consequences of editing your Registry, you shouldn't skip the cautions in this book.

> **Troubleshooting**
> *I need help with a particular problem.* Troubleshooting elements anticipate the problems you might have and provide a solution.

> **Sidebars Are Interesting Nuggets of Information**
> Sidebars are detours from the main text. They usually provide background or interesting information that is relevant but not essential reading. You might find information that's a bit more technical than the surrounding text, or you might find a brief diversion into the historical aspects of the text..

SEE ALSO
➤ Cross-references point you to a chapter where you can learn more about the topic under discussion.

Conventions

In addition to the special features that help you find what you need, this book uses some special conventions that make it easier to understand. The following sections describe the keyboard, mouse, typographical, and other conventions you find in this book.

Keyboard

The keyboard conventions listed here help you better understand what the instructions are telling you to do. For example, they help you understand the key combinations and menu commands that you are supposed to type or choose.

Element	Convention
Hot keys	Hot keys are underlined in this book, just as they appear on Windows 98 menus. For example, the F in **File** is a hot key. To use a hot key, press Alt and the underlined letter to make that menu appear.
Key combinations	Key combinations are separated by plus signs. For example, "Press Ctrl+Alt+D" means that you press and hold down the Ctrl and Alt keys simultaneously and then press and release the D key. Always press and release, rather than hold down, the last key in a key combination.
Menu commands	A comma is used to separate the parts of a pull-down menu command. For example, "Choose **File**, **New**" means to open the **File** menu and click the **New** command.

In most cases, special-purpose keys are referred to by the text that actually appears on them on a standard 101-key keyboard. For example, you'll see "Press Esc" or "Press F1" or "Press Enter." However, some of the keys on your keyboard don't have words on them. Here are the conventions used for those keys:

Backspace key

Up-, down-, left-, or right-arrow key

Mouse

In this book, the following phrases tell you how to operate the mouse within Windows:

Click

Double-click

Drag

Drop

Typeface

This book uses some special typeface conventions that make it easier to read:

Element	Convention
Italic	Italic text indicates new terms. It also indicates placeholders (words that stand for what you actually type) in commands, addresses, and code listings.
Bold	Bold is used for menu commands and options in dialog boxes.
`Monospace`	Monospace is used for text you see onscreen, Registry keys, code listings, and any text you're asked to type. It also represents URLs (Web page addresses).

Other

When a line of code is too long to fit on one line of this book, it is broken at a convenient place and continued to the next line. The continuation of the line is preceded by a code continuation character (➡).

Other Books of Interest

This book focuses on the Windows 98 Registry. Macmillan Publishing publishes books that focus on other specific areas, as well as more general books about Windows 98. Here are some you might find interesting:

- *Special Edition Using Windows 98* covers just about every facet of Windows 98. If you buy only one more book about Windows 98, this should be it.

- *Special Edition Using Microsoft Office 97 with Windows 98* provides equally wide coverage for using Microsoft Word, Excel, and PowerPoint. Macmillan Publishing also publishes books focused on each individual part of Office, including *Special Edition Using Microsoft Word 97, Best Seller Edition; Special Edition Using Microsoft Excel 97, Best Seller Edition;* and *Special Edition Using Microsoft PowerPoint 97.*

- *Special Edition Using the Internet, Fourth Edition,* shows you how to get connected to the Internet and how to use it like a pro. It also points you to some of the more useful resources on the Internet and shows you how to use the World Wide Web, UseNet newsgroups, mailing lists, and so on.

A

Starting Out

Inside the Windows 98 Registry

In this chapter:

- What's the Registry?
- Registry Files on Disk: *.DAT
- Keys, Subkeys, Values, and Other Bits
- Registry Organization and Content
- The Role of INI Files in Windows 98
- Warning: Follow These Rules
- Your Choice of Registry Tools

What's the Registry?

Microsoft calls Windows 98's Registry the central repository for configuration data. I prefer to think of it as simply the configuration database. Indeed, the Registry is a database—a hierarchical database. This means that data is stored in a hierarchy—much like an outline or a company's organizational chart. There is little or no relationship between data in one branch of the database and data in another branch unless it was explicitly created by the data stored in it. This organization just brings a measure of structure to all the data so that you can locate it easily using a simple notation that's similar to paths in the MS-DOS file system. Each piece of data in the database is stored as an ordered pair with a name and a value. This is much like how a bank associates an account number (the name) with an account balance (the value).

The Registry serves dozens of innovative purposes, allowing features that were difficult at best in previous versions of Windows. It keeps track of the software you install on the computer and how each program interrelates. With few exceptions, all 32-bit Windows programs store their configuration data as well as your preferences in the Registry, while most 16-bit Windows programs and MS-DOS programs don't, favoring the outdated INI files instead. The Registry contains the computer's hardware configuration, which includes Plug and Play devices with their automatic configuration and legacy devices. It allows the operating system to keep multiple hardware configurations and multiple users with individual preferences. It allows programs to extend the desktop with such items as shortcut menus and property sheets. It supports remote administration via the network. And the list goes on.

A Bed of Roses It Isn't

The Registry isn't a bed of roses. Most of its problems result from a lack of information. Microsoft scarcely says a word about the Registry, forgetting that the Registry is a powerful tool when placed in the right hands. Windows 98 Help provides a few short lines on using the Registry Editor. The *Microsoft Windows 98 Resource Kit*, published by Microsoft Press, does say a bit more in a handful of pages dedicated to the Registry, but it leaves you with plenty of unanswered questions. How do I optimize the Registry? How do I distribute Registry updates in a user's login script? How do I import DWORD values via an INF file? How do I customize Windows 98? How do I use the Registry to eliminate the operating system's irritating features?

Misinformation knows few boundaries. My favorite example is that Windows 98 has an error message that says you must reinstall the operating system, when freeing up a few megabytes for a backup copy of the Registry will do the job nicely. Microsoft is infamous for stating how the Registry makes the operating system easier to use and maintain, but they leave you in the dark when common problems occur, such as a corrupted Registry, a haywire file association, or a corrupted hardware configuration. When these problems occur, the operating system is anything but easy to use if you don't know how to fix the problems in the Registry. Given that I use over 500 pages to adequately explain the Registry, I suppose I can't fault Microsoft for not making the same information available.

NOTE: Real mode and protected mode are two different modes in which a processor can address memory. In real mode, programs aren't protected from one another, and they're limited to 1 MB of memory using 16-bit segmented addresses. In protected mode, the processor protects each program's address space, and each program can access up to 4 GB of memory using 32-bit linear addresses.

What's New for Windows 98

Outwardly, little has changed in the Registry between Windows 95 and Windows 98. The organization is the same. The Registry Editor is the same. The API looks the same.

The underlying code is new, though. Microsoft optimized it, improving the overall performance of the operating system ever so slightly. The API now uses less real and protected mode memory. It also has improved caching. Both improvements make access to the Registry faster and allow the operating system to start faster.

The Windows 98 Registry is also a bit more reliable than in Windows 95. This isn't due to changes in the Registry itself—it's the operating system. The operating system automatically watches for errors in the Registry, and if it detects a problem, it uses Registry Checker to scan and fix the problem. It also uses Registry Checker to automatically back up the Registry once a day. The Registry Checker is new to Windows 98, combining a number of different tools for which you used to have to look elsewhere. You use it to back up the Registry, scan and fix problems in the Registry, and optimize the Registry so that it requires less disk space.

➤ Chapter 2, "Backing Up and Restoring the Registry," describes how Registry Checker automatically backs up the Registry every day when you start your computer. You also learn how to manually back up the Registry.

➤ Chapter 4, "Troubleshooting the Registry," shows you how to fix a plethora of problems that you might encounter with the Windows 98 Registry. This chapter also contains a list of all the Registry-related error messages you might see and tells you what to do about them.

What the Registry Means to You

With all this mumbo jumbo about the technological advantages of the Registry, you might feel a bit left out. What does the Registry do for you? That very topic is what this book is all about. You can customize the heck out of Windows 98. You can make the user interface snappier, add commands to shortcut menus, slim down the Start menu, and more. Chapter 9, "Customizing the Windows 98 Desktop," describes an abundance of customizations that you can use to make Windows 98 fit your needs.

NOTE: The single biggest Registry-related improvement you find in Windows 98 is Registry Checker. This utility makes backing up, fixing, and optimizing the Registry easier. More importantly, its automatic daily backups ensure that you'll always have a working configuration. You'll learn more about this utility in Chapter 4, "Troubleshooting the Registry."

Mastering the Registry allows you to prevent configuration problems by backing up. Since the Registry contains the whole of the computer's configuration, making a backup copy of the Registry protects your computer's entire configuration. Chapter 2, "Backing Up and Restoring the Registry," tells you more. Sometimes restoring a backup copy of the Registry isn't the best idea, because you might lose any configuration changes since your last backup. In those cases, you can fix a variety of common problems whose solutions are rooted in the Registry. The biggest example is a file association that's gone awry; that's easy to fix in the Registry. Other examples include fixing broken property sheets or replacing commands that are missing from shortcut menus. Chapter 10, "Fixing Common Problems Via the Registry," tells you more.

Administrators get the best deal when it comes to the Registry. The Registry enables remote administration. In other words, the administrator can sit at his computer and edit settings on a remote computer. It even allows the administrator to control what the user can do where and when. Chapter 13, "Security and Remote Administration," describes how to enable remote administration and how to take control over the workstations on your network.

Registry Files on Disk: *.DAT

Windows 98 stores the entire contents of the Registry in two files: System.dat and User.dat. These are binary files that you can't view using a text editor, as you can with INI files. Windows 98 also turns on the read-only, system, and hidden attributes of System.dat and User.dat so that you can't accidentally replace, change, or delete them. System.dat contains computer-specific configuration data, and User.dat contains user-specific data.

Take a look; both files are in C:\Windows. You must show hidden and system files in order to see them by selecting **Show all files** on the View tab of Windows Explorer's Folder Options dialog box.

The location of User.dat is different on a computer that has user profiles enabled. Windows creates a new system folder called C:\Windows\Profiles, under which you'll find a folder for each user who logs onto the machine. Each user's profile folder contains an individual copy of User.dat (and a mess of other files and folders). You'll still find a User.dat file in C:\Windows, which Windows uses as the default for new users. Just remember that you see C:\Windows\Profiles*Name* for each user who logs onto that computer. Chapter 14, "Profiles, System Policies, and the Registry," shows you how to enable profiles and what other files and folders you find within each user's profile folder.

> **NOTE:** The one word that describes what understanding the Registry means to you is *control*. You control the computer's configuration. You control whether or not the computer succumbs to some silly configuration error. Learning about the Registry is similar to learning how to give your car a tune-up.

One other file, Config.pol, affects the settings you see in the Registry, but it's not actually part of the Registry. Unlike System.dat and User.dat, Config.pol is an optional part of Windows 98's configuration. You open a policy template in the System Policy editor, choose the settings you want to enforce, save the results to Config.pol, and place this file on the network. When a user logs onto a Windows 98 computer, the operating system applies any settings it finds in Config.pol to the user's Registry. There is little a user can do to circumvent the settings you put in this file, as long as he logs onto the network, so it's a good way to enforce restrictions throughout the network. Chapter 14, "Profiles, System Policies, and the Registry," shows where on the network you place this file.

The following list summarizes the files that comprise the Registry:

User.dat   The following list describes how Windows 98 determines the folder from which it loads User.dat.

- **C:\Windows** Windows 98 always loads User.dat into the Registry from this folder and uses it for the default user, even if profiles are enabled, meaning that the operating system might load two different User.dat files at once.

- **C:\Windows\Profiles*Name*** Windows 98 loads User.dat from this folder if profiles are enabled and the operating system doesn't find a more recent User.dat file in the user's network home folder.

- **\\Server*Home* or \\Server*Mailfolder*** Windows 98 loads User.dat from the network server if the user has a home folder and a profile in it that's more current than the files in C:\Windows\Profiles*Name*.

System.dat   For the most part, Windows 98 always loads System.dat from C:\Windows. If you're using a diskless workstation, the operating system might load System.dat from the network, but this situation is so rare that I don't discuss it in this book.

Config.pol   Windows 98 loads Config.pol from two different places, depending on which network server is designated as the primary network logon:

- The Client for Microsoft Networks looks for Config.pol in \\Server\Netlogon.

- The Client for NetWare Networks looks for Config.pol in SYS:PUBLIC.

NOTE: Profiles allow multiple users to log onto a single computer with their own familiar settings (Start menu, desktop, and so on). You enable profiles using the Enable Multi-users Settings Wizard, which you access by opening Users in the Control Panel. Alternatively, open the Passwords icon in the Control Panel and use the Passwords Properties dialog box.

SEE ALSO

➤ Chapter 2, "Backing Up and Restoring the Registry," shows you how to preserve the Registry files. Remember that Windows 98 automatically backs up these files once a day and will also restore them if it detects a problem with the Registry.

➤ Chapter 13, "Security and Remote Administration," describes how to enable remote administration. Remote administration isn't required in order to use user profiles or system policies, but if you're going to use either one, you might as well go for the whole enchilada. What remote administration does allow you to do is edit another computer's Registry across the network.

➤ Chapter 14, "Profiles, System Policies, and the Registry," tells you more about user profiles. Aside from enabling user profiles, this chapter shows you how to create mandatory profiles as well as establish system policies for groups and users.

Keys, Subkeys, Values, and Other Bits

Figure 1.1 shows what the Windows 98 Registry looks like in the Registry Editor. In the left pane, called the *Key pane,* you see all of the Registry's folders. At the top, you see My Computer. This represents the local computer, whose Registry you're viewing. When viewing a remote computer in the Registry Editor, you see an additional item at the same level as My Computer whose name is the name of the remote computer.

> NOTE: Two files exist in Windows 95 but not in Windows 98. System.da0 and User.da0 were backup copies of the Registry that Windows 95 made every time the operating system started successfully. Since Windows 98 uses Registry Checker to make backup copies in CAB files, these DA0 files are no longer necessary.

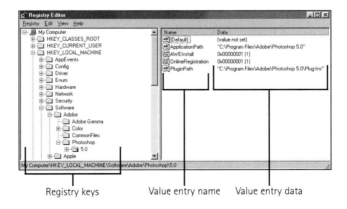

Registry keys   Value entry name   Value entry data

Figure 1.1 The Registry Editor is a simple program that packs a lot of power, providing access to the entire configuration.

Under My Computer, you see a number of folders organized somewhat like an outline or an upside-down tree. Each folder in the Key pane is called a *key*. Again, keys are analogous to folders in Windows Explorer. As such, they can contain any number of subfolders, called *subkeys*. Subkeys can contain more subkeys, and so on. You see subkeys in Registry Editor's Key pane, so don't look for them in the right pane. If you need to know whether a key contains subkeys, look for a plus or minus sign next to the key's name. Note that the six keys you see directly under My Computer are called *root keys*. Key names can be any combination of alphabetic, numeric, or symbol characters (except backslashes) and spaces. If all this seems a bit much to remember, occasionally refer to the sidebar called "Registry Terminology" to refresh your memory.

Registry Terminology

Registry   Physically, the Registry is the two files System.dat and User.dat. Logically, the Registry is the configuration data that you see in the Registry Editor.

Registry Editor   The program you use to edit the Registry. It shows the Registry as a single unit even though Windows 98 stores the Registry in two files.

HKEY   Windows 98 divides the Registry into six sections called HKEY_*Name*. Programmers will know that HKEY means *handle* to a *key*. Another name for these is *root key*.

key   Similar to a folder in Windows Explorer. It can contain additional folders and one or more values.

subkey   A *child* that appears underneath another key, the *parent*. This concept is similar to folders and subfolders in Windows Explorer.

branch   Represents a particular subkey and everything it contains. A branch can start at the very top of the Registry, but it usually describes a key and all its contents.

value entry   An *ordered pair* with a name and a value. Value entries are analogous to files in Windows Explorer.

default value   Every key has a default value that may or may not contain data. The default value in each key is called (Default) in the Registry Editor.

TIP: I use the terms *key* and *subkey* interchangeably. In particular, the first time I refer to a child key, or a key underneath the key being discussed, I call it a subkey. From then on, I'll simply refer to it as a key. Also, in most cases throughout this book, I start the discussion by presenting the fully qualified key name, starting from the root key. When the path to a subkey is obvious based on the context, I'll just use its name.

In Registry Editor's right pane, called the *Contents pane,* you see all the configuration data for the selected key. Each key, besides containing any number of subkeys, can contain any number of value entries. *Value entries*—sometimes just called *values*—are analogous to files in Windows Explorer. Each value entry has three parts:

- **Name**   Each name can be any combination of alphabetic, numeric, and symbol characters, including spaces. You can't use backslashes. The name uniquely identifies the value entry within a key. You might find the same name used in other Registry keys, but not within the same key.

- **Data type**   Whereas INI files store only string configuration data, the Registry stores a variety of different types of data in a value entry. Table 1.1 describes the types of data that you'll find in the Windows 98 Registry.

- **Data**   Value data can be up to 64 KB in size in Windows 98. An important concept you need to understand is that of an empty value entry. There's no such thing. If Windows or some other program has never assigned a value to a value entry, the value entry contains the *null* value. This is very different from assigning an empty string to a value entry, which is a string of characters that just happens to be of zero length.

Table 1.1   **Windows 98 Data Types**

Type	Example	Description
String	"Hello World"	Text. Words. Phrases. The Registry always displays strings within quotation marks.
Binary	F03D990000BC	Binary values of unlimited size represented as hexadecimal. They're similar to DWORDs, except they're not limited to 4 bytes.
DWORD	0x12345678	32-bit binary values in hexadecimal format (double words). The Registry displays DWORDs as 8-digit hexadecimal numbers.

Every key contains at least one value entry, called (Default). I usually just call it the default value for a key. The default value is always a string value. Windows provides it for compatibility with the Windows 3.1 Registry and older 16-bit applications. In many cases, the default value is null. In other cases, when a program needs to store only one value, the default value entry is the only data stored in that key.

> NOTE: As you learn in this section, value entries associate a value with a name. This makes them an ordered pair. Every value data also has a data type that indicates whether the value is a string, binary, or DWORD value.

Registry Organization and Content

You find six root keys in the Windows 98 Registry (as shown in Figure 1.1). Windows 98 stores HKEY_LOCAL_MACHINE in System.dat and each branch of HKEY_USERS in the appropriate User.dat file.

The remaining root keys are aliases. *Aliases* are shortcuts to branches within HKEY_LOCAL_MACHINE or HKEY_USERS that make accessing a particular set of configuration data easier. For instance, HKEY_CURRENT_USER is an alias for HKEY_USERS*Name*, where *Name* represents the username of the current user. This branch contains all the user's settings. An alias for HKEY_LOCAL_MACHINE\\Software\\Classes is HKEY_CLASSES_ROOT, making it easier to access file associations in the Registry. Think of an alias as containing a temporary copy of a branch in either HKEY_LOCAL_MACHINE or HKEY_USERS. If you change a value in the alias, the original branch reflects that change. The opposite applies, too. Figure 1.2 shows you this concept better than words alone.

SEE ALSO

➤ Chapter 5, "HKEY_CLASSES_ROOT"

➤ Chapter 6, "HKEY_LOCAL_MACHINE"

➤ Chapter 7, "HKEY_USERS and HKEY_CURRENT_USER"

➤ Chapter 8, "HKEY_CURRENT_CONFIG and HKEY_DYN_DATA"

Registry Paths

You must get acquainted with the notation used in this book and other sources to describe the location of a value in the Registry. It's called a *path*, similar to file paths in the MS-DOS file system.

Remember that the Registry is a hierarchical database. You can therefore describe the location of any value by showing its path like this: *key1**key2**key3*. This means open *key1*, then, underneath that, open *key2*, followed by *key3*. An example is regfile\\shell\\open, which means to open the key called regfile, open its subkey called shell, and then open shell's subkey called open. A *fully qualified path* always starts with the root key so that you can find the value relative to the top of the Registry.

The value's name is never given as part of the path. It's always named separately, like this: "Open MyValue in HKEY_LOCAL_MACHINE\\MyKey" or "Open HKEY_LOCAL_MACHINE\\MyKey and change MyValue to Howdy." When discussing a key's default value entry, you'll see something like this: "Change the default value of MyKey" or "Open MyKey and change the default value to Howdy."

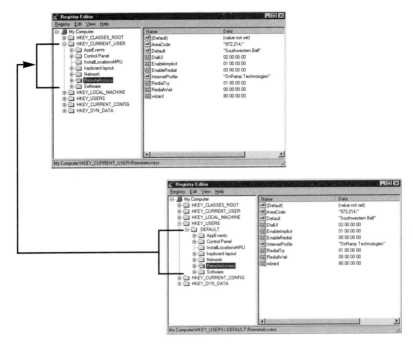

Figure 1.2   HKEY_CURRENT_USER is an alias for HKEY_USERS\.DEFAULT.

HKEY_USERS

HKEY_USERS contains all the user-specific configuration data for the computer. Under this root key, you find one or two keys. If you see a single subkey called .DEFAULT, profiles are not enabled on the computer, and Windows 98 loads .DEFAULT from the User.dat file in C:\Windows. If you see two subkeys, one is .DEFAULT, and the other is *Username*, where *Username* is the name of the current user. Again, .DEFAULT comes from the User.dat file in C:\Windows, while *Username* comes from the User.dat file found in C:\Windows\Profiles*Username* or from the user's home folder on the network.

The following list describes the subkeys you typically find under each subkey of HKEY_USERS:

AppEvents   This subkey associates the sounds that Windows 98 produces with events generated by the operating system and other programs. You'll find subkeys called EventLabels, which describes each sound event, and Schemes\Apps, which assigns sound files to each event.

`Control Panel`	This subkey contains settings that the user can change using the Control Panel, such as Display and Accessibility options. Many of the settings in Control Panel were migrated from the Windows 3.1 Win.ini and Control.ini files.
`InstallLocationsMRU`	This itty-bitty subkey contains the last several paths from which you've installed Windows components. That is, every time you open the Add/Remove Programs Properties dialog box from the Control Panel and click Have Disk on the Windows Setup tab to install an extension, Windows 98 records the path of the INF file in `InstallLocationsMRU`.
`Keyboard Layout`	This subkey defines the language used for the current keyboard layout. You change these values in the Keyboard icon in the Control Panel.
`Network`	Windows 98 stores persistent network connections in `HKEY_CURRENT_USER\Network\Persistent`. Each subkey represents a mapped drive letter (D, E, F, and so on). Under each drive letter's subkey, you'll find a handful of value entries that describe the connection, such as `Provider Name`, `RemotePath`, and `UserName`.
`Software`	`Software` is by far the most interesting subkey in this branch. It contains software settings that are specific to each user. Windows stores each user's desktop preferences under this subkey. As well, each program installed on the computer installs user-specific preferences in this subkey. This subkey is organized just like the similarly named subkey in `HKEY_LOCAL_MACHINE`.

NOTE: The Registry has an order of precedence. Often, Windows 98 or other programs will store duplicate data in both HKEY_USERS and HKEY_LOCAL_MACHINE. In these cases, the configuration data stored in HKEY_USERS has precedence over the data stored in HKEY_LOCAL_MACHINE. Windows does this so that individual user preferences will override computer-specific settings.

HKEY_LOCAL_MACHINE

HKEY_LOCAL_MACHINE contains configuration data that describes the hardware and software installed on the computer, such as device drivers, security data, and computer-specific software settings such as uninstall information. This information is specific to the computer itself rather than to any one user who logs on to it. Thus, the operating system uses the settings stored in HKEY_LOCAL_MACHINE regardless of who logs onto the computer.

The following list describes the contents of each subkey immediately under HKEY_LOCAL_MACHINE:

Config	This subkey contains information about multiple hardware configurations for the computer, also known as hardware profiles. It contains groups of individual hardware settings from which Windows 98 may choose automatically or that you can choose when you start the computer. Each subkey under HKEY_LOCAL_MACHINE\Config (numbered 0001, 0002, and so on) represents an individual hardware profile. HKEY_LOCAL_MACHINE\System\ CurrentControlSet\Control\IDConfigDB contains the name and identifier of the hardware profile that Windows 98 is currently using.
Enum	This subkey contains information about each device installed on the computer. Each subkey under Enum represents a particular type of bus (BIOS, ESDI, PCI, PCMCIA, SCSI, and so on). Under each hardware class, you'll find one or more subkeys that in turn contain subkeys that identify a single piece of hardware. The organization of this branch and its contents depends largely on the devices you install on the computer and how the manufacturer organizes its settings.
Hardware	Windows 98 doesn't do much with this subkey, because it provides Hardware for compatibility with Windows NT.
Network	This subkey contains information about the user who is currently logged on to the computer. Each time a user logs on to the computer, Windows stores details about the current network session, such as the user's logon name, in Network\Logon.

Security

This subkey contains information about the computer's network security provider, administrative shares (for remote administration), and public shares. Windows 98 keeps track of all open network connections that other users have on your computer in `Security\Access`; you find a single subkey for each connection.

Software

This and the next subkey are the heart and soul of `HKEY_LOCAL_MACHINE`. Programs store settings that are specific to the computer in this subkey. These programs store their settings in branches that look like `HKEY_LOCAL_MACHINE\ Software\CompanyName\ ProductName\Version`, where `CompanyName` is the name of the company, `ProductName` is the name of the product, and `Version` is the current version number of the product. You find many Windows-specific settings in this subkey, too, which you find under `Software\Microsoft\Windows\CurrentVersion`.

System

Windows 98 maintains *control sets,* each of which determines exactly which device drivers and services the operating system loads and how it configures them when it starts. For example, a control set provides the various parameters Windows needs when it starts, such as the computer's network name and the current hardware profile. A control set also controls which device drivers and file systems Windows loads and provides the parameters that Windows needs in order to configure each driver.

NOTE: The single largest branch in the Registry is `HKEY_LOCAL_MACHINE\Software\Classes`. This subkey describes all the associations between documents and programs, as well as information about COM (*Component Object Model*) classes, and is therefore very large. You can also get to this branch through the alias `HKEY_CLASSES_ROOT`.

Aliases: *HKEY_CURRENT_USER* and So On

Even though the Registry Editor shows six root keys, there are really only two: HKEY_LOCAL_MACHINE and HKEY_USERS. As you learned, the remaining root keys are aliases that refer to branches within the other two root keys. In other words, aliases are a bit like shortcuts in Explorer: If you change a value in one of the aliases, that value is actually changed in the original location.

The following table lists each alias and the branch to which it points. HKEY_CLASSES_ROOT points to a branch within HKEY_LOCAL_MACHINE that contains the associations between file extensions and programs. HKEY_CURRENT_USER points to the subkey of HKEY_USERS that belongs to the current user; without user profiles, it always points to HKEY_USER\.DEFAULT. HKEY_CURRENT_CONFIG is an alias for HKEY_LOCAL_MACHINE\Config\ *Profile*, where *Profile* is 0001, 0002, and so on. It contains the computer's current hardware configuration.

Alias	Branch
HKEY_CLASSES_ROOT	HKEY_LOCAL_MACHINE\Software\Classes
HKEY_CURRENT_USER	HKEY_USERS*Username*
HKEY_CURRENT_CONFIG	HKEY_LOCAL_MACHINE\Config*Profile*

HKEY_DYN_DATA isn't actually an alias. It's a dynamic key that contains dynamic information about the current status of the computer. As with aliases, this root key isn't stored to disk; the operating system rebuilds it every time you restart the computer.

The Windows 98 Configuration Manager

The Configuration Manager is at the heart of Plug and Play. It is responsible for managing the configuration process on the computer. It identifies each bus on your computer (PCI, SCSI, ISA) and all of the devices on each bus. It notes the configuration of each device, making sure that each device is using unique resources (IRQ, I/O address).

The Configuration Manager uses three key components to make all of this happen: *bus enumerators, arbitrators,* and *device drivers.* Here's a summary of the purpose of each component:

Bus enumerators	These are responsible for building the *hardware tree.* They query each device or each device driver for configuration information.
Arbitrators	These assign resources to each device in the hardware tree. That is, they dole out IRQs, I/O addresses, and such to each device, resolving conflicts as they arise.
Device drivers	The Configuration Manager loads a device driver for each device in the hardware tree and communicates the device's configuration to the driver.

The Role of INI Files in Windows 98

Remember INI files? Windows 98 isn't quite finished with them. When I search my hard disk for INI files, I find 54. And that's after a clean installation and after installing a handful of 32-bit applications such as Microsoft Office. The operating system still uses Win.ini and System.ini, too. Some of those settings are duplicated in the Registry and are only provided in the INI files for compatibility with applications that require them.

Recall that INI files are text files that you can edit with Notepad. In fact, Windows 98 associates INI files with Notepad so that you can easily open them for editing. Open Win.ini in Notepad, and you'll see something similar to Listing 1.1. An INI file is separated into sections, with each section name appearing between brackets. In Listing 1.1, for example, [windows] and [Desktop] are sections. Following each section name you see a number of items, each with a name and a value separated by an equal sign. As with the Registry, this is an ordered pair that allows a program to retrieve the value from the INI file by providing the value's name in addition to the name of the section that contains it.

Listing 1.1 **Win.ini**

```
[windows]
load=
run=
NullPort=None
device=HP LaserJet 5,PCL5EMS,\\SERVER\LaserJet

[Desktop]
Wallpaper=(None)
TileWallpaper=1
WallpaperStyle=0
Pattern=(None)
```

Two INI files are of special interest. Win.ini typically contains data used to specify user preferences: desktop settings, wallpaper, and so on. Windows 98 stores these values in the Registry now, but the operating system still reflects these settings in Win.ini for compatibility with old Windows applications.

System.ini contains system settings. The [boot] section contains drivers that Windows 98 needs when it starts. The [386Enh] section loads any virtual device drivers that the operating system requires when it starts. This section is smaller than in previous versions of Windows since the operating system loads most of its VXD files from the \Iosubsys and \Vmm32 folders within C:\Windows\System, eliminating the need to explicitly list these files in System.ini. Note that if Windows 98 recognizes a device when you upgrade, it removes that device's settings from System.ini and stores them in the Registry. Otherwise, it might leave those settings in System.ini.

Warning: Follow These Rules

Changing the Registry is risky but not the most dangerous thing in the world; thus, I promise this is the only time you'll see these annoying warnings in this book. The worst-case scenario after making a mistake is that Windows 98 will no longer start. The best-case scenario after making an error is that you won't notice anything, but certain applications or devices might behave improperly. No damage is irreparable if you back up the Registry using the methods discussed in Chapter 2, "Backing Up and Restoring the Registry," or if you stick to the plan you'll learn about in this section.

Beware of the Registry-editing pitfalls that can claim your soul if you're not careful. First of all, the Registry Editor does not have an Undo feature. It doesn't validate your changes, either, and it doesn't know what is or isn't valid for a particular value. As a result, the Registry Editor allows you to put anything you want in any value in the Registry, regardless of what the application using that value expects from it. Another pitfall is that the operating system frequently maintains relationships between one portion of the Registry and another; if you're clueless about these relationships, you might change a value in one part of the Registry without changing the related value in the other part of the Registry. One last caveat is about how programs store data in the Registry. I call it Jerry's Rule: Two different programs will tend to store the exact same type of data in two totally different formats. You can't rely on programs to store a Boolean flag the same way, for example. One might store it as a DWORD value, while the other will store it as a string. One program might store a date in string format, while another will store a date in binary format. This fact hinders your ability to decipher the data you find in the Registry and make accurate changes to it.

> **NOTE:** When you export the Registry to a REG file, the file contains HKEY_LOCAL_MACHINE and HKEY_USERS. It doesn't contain entries from the four remaining aliases, because exporting an alias is redundant.

Abbreviations for Root Keys

You'll frequently see abbreviations for the root keys used in many publications. I don't use these abbreviations in this book so that the Registry paths you see here will more closely match what you see in the Registry Editor. The following table describes the abbreviations commonly used for each root key:

Abbreviation	Root Key	Alias For
HKCR	HKEY_CLASSES_ROOT	HKEY_LOCAL_MACHINE\Software\Classes
HKCU	HKEY_CURRENT_USER	HKEY_USERS*Username*
HKLM	HKEY_LOCAL_MACHINE	
HKU	HKEY_USERS	
HKCC	HKEY_CURRENT_CONFIG	HKEY_LOCAL_MACHINE\Config*Profile*
HKDD	HKEY_DYN_DATA	

Even with all these pitfalls, you can learn to make changes to and experiment with the Registry without risk. After writing three books on the Registry and throughout endless tinkering, I've made only one change that I couldn't fix. Make sure your experience with the Registry is just as good by making a plan before diving in headfirst. To that end, here's a sample plan that you can change to suit your own needs:

- Back up the Registry before you make any change. You'll learn many techniques for backing up the Registry in Chapter 2, "Backing Up and Restoring the Registry." Most of them are quick and painless.

- Make only one change at a time. If you make too many changes in one sitting, you're not as likely to figure out what went wrong if Windows 98 fails.

- Don't delete data from the Registry until you're sure of the impact. Rename data so as to hide it; this will have the same effect as deleting it. When you're sure everything is okay, delete the data.

- Don't make changes to a setting until you're sure of the impact. Make a copy of the setting in a new temporary entry, and then make your change. If everything works, remove the temporary value. If nothing else, write down the original value so that you can easily recall it if things don't work out.

SEE ALSO

➤ Chapter 2, "Backing Up and Restoring the Registry," shows you how to protect your computer from Registry problems.

➤ Chapter 4, "Troubleshooting the Registry," describes how to fix problems once they occur.

INI Files and the Registry

INI files serve the same purpose as the Registry. Unlike the Registry, which contains settings from the operating system and a variety of applications, each INI file is typically unique to a single application. Remember too that keys in the Registry can contain subkeys and values. The sections in an INI file can contain only values, however; they can't contain subsections. A common work-around for this problem, used by clever programmers, is to have an item within a section that points to a different INI file.

Windows 98 keeps a variety of other INI files, aside from System.ini and Win.ini, using them partially. When an INI file doesn't contain all the settings you expect or that it used to contain in previous versions of Windows, you should suspect that those settings are now in the Registry. Even if you do see settings in an INI file, you should suspect that the operating system reflects all or a portion of its contents in the Registry.

CAUTION: You wouldn't expect the Registry to be in peril when you install a new program, because you don't change any settings yourself. Regardless, my experience suggests that you should back up the Registry before installing programs with which you're unfamiliar so that you can easily recover from a wayward setup program's faux pas.

Your Choice of Registry Tools

You use a variety of tools to work with the Registry. Some types of tools are required, and others are just niceties. A registry editor is a must-have. You use it to change values in the Registry. You can use the Registry Editor that comes with Windows 98, or you can use a third-party registry editor such as Norton Registry Editor or ShellWizard Registry Editor.

The nicety variety includes customization utilities and troubleshooting tools. Customization utilities are programs that help you make changes to the Registry via a well-defined user interface, which typically uses checkboxes to enable or disable options. An example of a customization utility is the Registry Power Tools program that you can download from http://www.honeycutt.com. Another example is Tweak UI, which you'll learn about in Chapter 11, "Tweak UI and Other Registry Programs." Chapter 11 also tells you about dozens of other programs. Troubleshooting tools include programs that help you fix the Registry after it gets screwed up. These include programs such as Norton WinDoctor, which fixes a whole host of common Registry problems, and REGCLEAN, which fixes problems specific to several Microsoft products.

Windows 98 Versus Windows NT

The Windows 98 and Windows NT Registries are identical where it counts: file associations and software settings. In other words, HKEY_CLASSES_ROOT and the Software branches of HKEY_LOCAL_MACHINE and HKEY_CURRENT_USER are organized the same in both operating systems.

Both Registries are radically different when you look at the binary files on disk, though. The NT Registry stores HKEY_LOCAL_MACHINE in separate files called *hive files,* one for each subkey of HKEY_LOCAL_MACHINE, which you find in \Winnt\System32\Config. As well, each user's configuration is in Ntuser.dat rather than User.dat. Given that Windows NT's file system is secure, you can't copy or remove these files while the operating system is running, so backing up the Registry isn't a simple matter of copying the files.

Security is another difference between the two Registries. Windows 98 has none. The Windows NT Registry does have security, however, allowing the administrator to control exactly which keys and values a user can access. Not only that, but the administrator can audit the user's usage of the Registry to see what he's been doing.

The Windows NT Registry is different in a variety of other ways, too. It supports more data types than the Windows 98 Registry. The organization of hardware data is different in the NT Registry, owing to the fact that NT doesn't fully support the Plug and Play specification. NT also comes with its own Registry Editor, Regedt32, in addition to the Registry Editor you see in Windows 98.

You'll learn about a huge variety of Registry tools in this book. The following sections give you a brief overview of most of them. I'm going to take a definitive position, though, and recommend some specific programs that you should include in your toolbox. Here's your shopping list:

- **ConfigSafe** has a good name. It locks your configuration in a safe place so that you can restore any portion of it if things go wrong.

- **Norton Utilities** comes with two really great Registry programs, Norton Registry Editor and Norton WinDoctor, and one so-so program called Norton Registry Tracker.

- **Registry Monitor** allows you to watch what's going on in the Registry in real time. In other words, you can observe changes to the Registry as they occur. The best part is that Registry Monitor is free.

- **Registry Checker** comes with Windows 98. It is the best program to use for automatically backing up and restoring the Registry and fixing the most common problems with the Registry.

- **Registry Power Tools** provides an easy method to use most of the customizations discussed in this book.

Registry Editor

Windows 98 comes with the Registry Editor. You'll learn about it in Chapter 3, "Using the Windows 98 Registry Editor." This program lets you make the usual types of changes. You can add and remove keys and values. You can change values. You can export entire branches of the Registry to a REG file and then import that REG file at a later time.

The Registry Editor is good enough to tackle most jobs, and it's relatively bug-free, but it lacks the advanced features that power users require. My biggest beef with the Registry Editor is that opening the Registry to the same key repeatedly is inconvenient. You must navigate to that same location by opening each parent key and click, click, click until you finally reach the target. Other Registry Editors, such as Norton Registry Editor, solve this problem by allowing you to bookmark keys and then return to them by choosing the name from a menu. Other features that are missing include the ability to undo changes you make, to search and replace values, to make shortcuts to branches within the Registry, and to back up the Registry from within the editor. The Norton Registry Editor has all of these capabilities.

TIP: Often, the best tools for the job aren't programs at all; they're scripts, INF, and REG files. You use these files to specify changes to the Registry. When you run, install, or import these files, the operating system implements the changes you described in the file. These are particularly hardworking tools for administrators since they allow the administrator to distribute changes to users all across the network.

SEE ALSO

➤ Chapter 3, "Using the Windows 98 Registry Editor," shows you how to use Windows 98's Registry Editor and introduces you to Norton Registry Editor.

Norton Utilities

If you intend to become a certified Registry guru, you must have Norton Utilities. It fills all those voids left by the Registry tools that come with Windows 98. You read about Norton Registry Editor in the preceding section and now know that it provides all those advanced features that a guru-wannabe needs.

It has a few other Registry programs, too, that make the entire suite megabyte-worthy. Norton Rescue helps you start the computer in the event of system failure. It can even help you recover from startup problems caused by Registry errors. Registry Tracker isn't the sharpest program in the suite, but it does help you track changes to the Registry. However, other programs, such as ConfigSafe, are better at this task. One of the most useful programs in the suite is Norton WinDoctor, which helps you fix a whole host of Registry problems, including orphans. Last, Norton Optimization Wizard helps you optimize the Registry, logically and physically, with the aim of improving your computer's performance.

SEE ALSO

➤ Chapter 2, "Backing Up and Restoring the Registry," discusses recovering a system with Norton Rescue.

➤ Chapter 3, "Using the Windows 98 Registry Editor," shows you how to use Norton Registry Editor.

➤ Chapter 4, "Troubleshooting the Registry," shows you how to repair the Registry using Norton WinDoctor.

➤ Chapter 12, "Tracking Down Registry Settings," describes how to use Norton Registry Tracker to uncover changes to the Registry.

NOTE: You can purchase Norton Utilities from any computer retailer. You can even get it from most consumer electronics stores, such as Best Buy and Circuit City. If you want more immediate gratification, download an evaluation copy from `http://www.symantec.com` or order a copy from `http://www.software.net`.

Registry Monitor

Registry Monitor is a freeware program that you use to monitor changes to the Registry as they occur. It gives you insight into how the operating system and other programs use the Registry. You can monitor Windows Explorer's Registry access as you open the Folder Options dialog box to see where the program stores each option in the Registry. If you're curious about the changes that a setup program makes to the Registry, monitor the setup program and filter Registry Monitor's output so that it displays only changes.

SEE ALSO

➤ Chapter 11, "Tweak UI and Other Registry Programs," shows you how to download and install Registry Monitor. It also introduces you to an extension of this program called RegMonEx, which has a more powerful but more confusing filtering feature.

➤ Chapter 12, "Tracking Down Registry Settings," shows you how to use Registry Monitor to track down changes to the Registry.

Registry Checker

Registry Checker comes with Windows 98. Finally, Microsoft ships a useful Registry program with the operating system! This program fulfills several purposes:

- Backs up and restores the Registry
- Scans and fixes a variety of Registry errors
- Optimizes the unused space of the Registry

The best part about Registry Checker is that it largely does its own thing. Windows 98 starts Registry Checker every time you boot the operating system. Registry Checker then backs up the Registry to CAB files that you find in C:\Windows\Sysbckup. It also scans the Registry for errors. If it finds any, Windows 98 restarts the computer in MS-DOS mode and runs Registry Checker to automatically restore a good backup copy of the Registry or fix those errors.

SEE ALSO

➤ Chapter 2, "Backing Up and Restoring the Registry," describes Registry Checker.

➤ Chapter 4, "Troubleshooting the Registry," shows you how to repair the Registry using Registry Checker.

ConfigSafe

ConfigSafe periodically makes a backup copy of your configuration. Each backup is called a *snapshot*. Each snapshot contains any portion of your configuration that you specify.

You can compare any two snapshots, and ConfigSafe neatly displays the differences. Did you install a program on Wednesday? Compare snapshots taken on Tuesday and Thursday to figure out what changed. You can also compare any snapshot to your current configuration. If you find a change that doesn't sit well with you, for instance, or if your computer isn't working correctly, compare your current configuration to the most recent snapshot and restore the original settings necessary to fix the problem.

> SEE ALSO
> ➤ Chapter 12, "Tracking Down Registry Settings," describes how to use ConfigSafe. It also shows you how to download an evaluation copy.

REGCLEAN

REGCLEAN is a freeware utility from Microsoft that repairs a number of problems common to Microsoft products. This utility isn't nearly as useful as Norton WinDoctor, but it serves the needs of many users.

> SEE ALSO
> ➤ Chapter 4, "Troubleshooting the Registry," shows you how to use REGCLEAN.

Tweak UI

The one customization utility you should install, other than the Registry Power Tools, is Microsoft Tweak UI. Microsoft developers built this tool to help users use the most popular customizations without actually having to edit the Registry. This program didn't come with Windows 95; you had to download it from the Internet. It *does* come with Windows 98.

> SEE ALSO
> ➤ Chapter 11, "Tweak UI and Other Registry Programs," describes how to use Microsoft's Tweak UI, a customization program. It also describes dozens of other shareware Registry programs, many of which you'll find on my Web site at http://www.honeycutt.com.

NOTE: ConfigSafe isn't a substitute for Registry Checker, and vice versa. ConfigSafe is more like a version control system for your configuration, allowing you to undo individual changes to your configuration. Registry Checker can restore an entire backup of the Registry but not individual settings. ConfigSafe can't repair a broken Registry, but Registry Checker can fix common problems.

Registry Power Tools

Registry Power Tools, shown in Figure 1.3, is available from my Web site: http://www.honeycutt.com. It allows you to implement most of the customizations you'll read about in this book, including those discussed in Chapter 9, "Customizing the Windows 98 Desktop."

Microsoft Windows 98 Resource Kit

The *Microsoft Windows 98 Resource Kit,* published by Microsoft, comes with three MS-DOS Registry utilities that aren't available on the Windows 98 CD-ROM. Look in \Reskit\Registry.

Compreg.exe allows you to compare branches from two different Registries and list the differences. For example, you can compare a branch in the local Registry to the same branch in a remote Registry, and locate differences that might help you solve a problem. Reg.exe provides a plethora of functions in a neatly wrapped MS-DOS program. You can query, add, update, delete, copy, save, back up, restore, load, and unload keys and values. Srchreg.exe allows you to search for keys, value names, and value data in the Registry. It displays each item it finds, but it doesn't allow you to replace values.

Other Files and Programs

Chapter 11, "Tweak UI and Other Registry Programs," describes dozens of shareware Registry programs you can use to edit, customize, and troubleshoot the Registry. Some of them are terrific programs, but others aren't worth the money the author is asking. One good example of a shareware Registry program is ShellWizard's Registry Editor. If you don't already own Norton Utilities, ShellWizard's editor is close competition for Norton's Registry Editor. It has most of the same features and adds a few more. My favorite feature is that you can record notes for each Registry key. I prefer Norton Registry Editor, because ShellWizard's editor is a bit buggy, but if you don't already have the utilities, ShellWizard's Registry Editor is a good alternative.

> **TIP:** The *Microsoft Windows 98 Resource Kit* comes with the three Registry programs in \Reskit\Registry: Compreg.exe, Reg.exe, and Srchreg.exe. You can learn how to use each of these programs by running each from the MS-DOS command line using the /? command line option.
>
> **NOTE:** One shareware Registry program deserves special mention for administrators. It's called Multi-Remote Registry Change, and it doesn't get enough notice. Too bad. This is a great product that lets an administrator change a Registry value across any number of computers on the network. You can't beat convenience like this when you need a quick fix.

Figure 1.3 Registry Power Tools includes most of the customizations you'll learn about in this book.

Three important types of files you should add to your arsenal aren't programs; they're scripts, INF files, and REG files. Windows 98 includes the Windows Scripting Host, an interpreter that understands JavaScript and VBScript script files and allows those scripts to access the object model exposed by the Windows operating system. INF and REG files are very similar. They both allow you to script changes to the Registry. You can use INF files to add, remove, and change values. The notation is simple and easy to write. REG files only allow you to add and change values, not remove them. They're also not as clean to write as INF files, but you can easily create them by exporting branches from within the Registry Editor.

All three types of files have the benefit of being easy to distribute via the network. You can post them to a Web site and allow users to launch them. You can email them to a user for the same purpose. You can also put them in the user's login script so that the operating system automatically launches them. Chapter 15, "Script, REG, and INF Files," shows you how to distribute these files using all three methods. Distributing INF files via login scripts is a bit more complicated than just launching scripts or REG files, so pay close attention to the advice in Chapter 15 regarding Rundll32.exe.

SEE ALSO

➤ Chapter 11, "Tweak UI and Other Registry Programs," describes a whole host of Registry programs. Most of them are shareware, which means that you can try them first and then pay for them after you decide to keep them.

➤ Chapter 15, "Script, REG, and INF Files," shows you how to write all three types of files and how to distribute them to users via the network.

2

Backing Up and Restoring the Registry

Karanjit S. Siyan, Ph.D

In this chapter:

- The Backup Plan
- Easy Backups with Registry Checker
- Alternative Methods for Manual Backups
- Norton Utilities Rescue Disk
- System.1st as a Last Resort

The Backup Plan

All users have two different backup needs: the quick, intermittent backup that ensures the system can be repaired if an immediate task goes wrong, and the occasional full system backup that preserves the entire system in the event of total failure. This chapter doesn't discuss the latter; it focuses on the intermittent backups. More specifically, this chapter focuses on intermittent backups of the Registry that make sure the user can recover from problems such as an errant setup program, a configuration error, or a bad customization.

The only thing you need to know about making intermittent backup copies of the Registry is the new Windows 98 utility called Registry Checker, which you'll learn about in the following section. This is a big improvement over the Registry backup utilities provided for Windows 95. In most cases, it works in the background so silently that you don't even know it's doing its job. Registry Checker makes regular, daily backups of the Registry. If you want to be more cautious, you can force Registry Checker to make additional backup copies of the Registry before you make a significant configuration change. Thus, other than Registry Checker, you can safely ignore every backup method you'll learn about in this chapter.

With all that said, here's a shot at a backup plan that you can use to make sure you always have a good backup copy of the Registry available. It takes into account both user needs mentioned at the beginning of this chapter, but remember that we only discuss intermittent backups in this chapter. Follow this plan and mold it to suit your needs:

1. Allow Registry Checker to make its daily backups. If nothing else, you can always revert to the previous day's Registry backup, and you'll only lose the configuration changes that you've made in the last day.

2. Force Registry Checker to make a Registry backup before you make any significant change to your configuration. This includes installing new programs, adding new hardware, or trying out one of the customization tips you'll learn in Chapter 9, "Customizing the Windows 98 Desktop."

3. Use a backup program such as Microsoft Backup or a network backup agent such as Cheyenne to make full system backups on a regular basis—weekly if possible. Remember to back up any changed files on a more regular basis.

Easy Backups with Registry Checker

Windows 98 provides two different versions of Registry Checker: a Windows version and a DOS-based version. The Windows version, whose filename is Scanregw.exe, scans the Registry for errors but doesn't fix them. It also determines whether the Registry requires optimization but doesn't perform the optimization itself. Finally, it backs up the Registry files to CAB files that are found in \Windows\Sysbckup. You'll read more about this later.

If SCANREGW detects an error or that the Registry must be optimized, it prompts you to restart the computer. The DOS-based version, whose filename is Scanreg.exe (without the w), attempts to fix the Registry. It tries to restore the previous backup first, repairing the Registry only if it can't find a good backup. If SCANREGW determines that the Registry requires optimization, SCANREG optimizes the Registry the next time you start Windows 98. This is a bit much to remember, so look at Table 2.1; it summarizes all this so you can remember the differences between SCANREGW and SCANREG.

> **NOTE:** If you want to store backup copies of the Registry somewhere other than your computer's disk, you might still need to consider the alternative backup methods in this chapter. You can copy the Registry files to a network drive, for example, or use Norton's Repair Disk to create a backup copy of the Registry on a ZIP disk.

Table 2.1 **SCANREGW Versus SCANREG**

Feature	SCANREGW	SCANREG
Runs automatically	Yes	Yes, if problem detected
Backs up the Registry	Yes	Yes
Compresses backups	Yes	No
Operating environment	Windows	MS-DOS
Repairs the Registry	No	Yes
Restores the Registry	No	Yes
Runs in Safe Mode	Yes	No
Scans the Registry	Yes	Yes

SCANREGW and SCANREG support similar command line options, all of which are listed in Table 2.2. /backup and /comment work in both versions of Registry Checker. /opt, /restore and /fix are available only with SCANREG. /autorun and /scanonly are available only with SCANREGW.

Table 2.2 **SCANREGW and SCANREG Command Lines**

Switch	Description
/autorun	Automatically scans the Registry, but backs it up only once a day. You see this switch used in the Run key of HKEY_LOCAL_MACHINE.
/backup	Backs up the Registry without prompting the user. Backups are stored in CAB files that you find in \Windows\Sysbckup.
"/comment=x"	Associates a comment with the backup. Use this switch with /backup and be sure to enclose the entire switch in quotation marks.
/fix	Repairs the Registry.
/opt	Stands for "optimize." Compresses unused space.
/restore	Allows you to choose from a list of backup configurations that you can restore.
/scanonly	Scans the Registry and returns an error code that you can test from within a batch file. It doesn't back up or repair the Registry.

SEE ALSO

➤ Chapter 4, "Troubleshooting the Registry," describes how to scan, fix, and optimize the Registry using Registry Checker.

Backing Up the Registry

Windows 98 automatically backs up the Registry for you. Once each day, it uses the Windows-based Registry Checker, SCANREGW, to back up the Registry to CAB files that it puts in C:\Windows\Sysbckup, a hidden folder. The first backup is named RB000.cab, the second is RB001.cab, and so on. The file with the highest number is the most recent backup file; thus, RB004.cab is more recent than RB002.cab. This folder might contain dozens of other configuration files that the operating system copies to this folder when a setup program replaces them with more recent versions.

Right-click one of the CAB files, presumably the most recent, and choose **View** to examine its contents. You'll find four files in it: System.dat, System.ini, User.dat, and Win.ini. As described in the section "Configuring Registry Checker," you can specify additional files to back up into each CAB file. Once you open a CAB file in Windows Explorer, you can drag any file from the CAB file to any folder on the computer. You can restore Win.ini, for instance, by dragging it from an open CAB file to C:\Windows.

By default, Windows Registry Checker keeps only five copies of the Registry, but you can increase that number by changing the MaxBackupCopies entry in Scanreg.ini to a higher number—perhaps 10.

Create a Startup Disk

If you're in a pinch and can't start Windows 98, you'll be very glad that you created a *startup disk*. This disk gets your computer going when it won't start from the hard drive. You'll also find a handful of utilities on the disk that you might be able to use to fix your computer. *It doesn't contain the Registry files, however, so don't use the startup disk as a Registry backup.* Here's how to create the startup disk:

1. Open the Add/Remove Programs icon in the Control Panel.

2. Click the Startup Disk tab in the Add/Remove Programs Properties dialog box.

3. Click the **Create Disk** button and follow the onscreen instructions. Windows 98 will likely ask you for your Windows 98 CD-ROM (or diskettes).

4. After Windows 98 finishes creating your startup disk, click **OK** to close the Add/Remove Programs Properties dialog box.

5. Label your Emergency Startup Disk and keep it in a safe place just in case you encounter problems starting Windows 98.

Windows 98 puts CD-ROM drivers on the startup disk, but not network drivers. Double-check to make sure the CD-ROM drivers that the operating system puts on the disk do indeed provide access to the CD-ROM drive. To do so, boot using the startup disk and try to access a disk in the CD-ROM. These drivers don't work with SCSI drives, incidentally. If you need access to the network when you start from the startup disk, copy the 16-bit network drivers to the disk and edit the Config.sys and Autoexec.bat files so that they load properly.

I strongly recommend that you do this, because many configuration errors can go for days without detection, and if you have only five days' worth of backup copies, you're out of luck. You can also force Registry Checker to make additional backup copies of the Registry even if it has already made its daily backup:

1. Run Scanregw.exe. You find it in C:\Windows. After scanning the Registry for errors, it asks you if you want to make another backup of the Registry.

2. Click **Yes**. Windows Registry Checker backs up the Registry to another CAB file and displays a dialog box telling you it's finished.

3. Click **OK** to close the Windows Registry Checker.

Restoring the Registry

You can't restore a backup using the Windows-based version of Registry Checker. You must use the real mode version, Scanreg.exe, which you find in C:\Windows\Command:

1. Start Windows in MS-DOS mode. To do so, select **Command Prompt Only** from Windows 98's boot menu, or choose **Start**, **Shut Down**, select **Restart in MS-DOS mode**, and press Enter.

2. Type scanreg /restore at the command prompt and press Enter to start Registry Checker.

3. Select a backup from the list provided. Registry Checker displays the date, status, and filename of each backup. Ideally, pick the most recent backup. If you know it doesn't work, pick the next most recent backup.

4. Press Enter. Registry Checker restores the backup to your computer.

5. Press Enter to restart your computer.

Configuring Registry Checker

Both versions of Registry Checker, SCANREGW and SCANREG, load settings from Scanreg.ini. Table 2.3 describes the settings you can change in this file. The most interesting settings include MaxBackupCopies and Files. The first controls the number of backups that Registry Checker keeps. The first backup is the first one to be deleted. The default value for this setting is 5, which is a bit small if you want to make sure you can always recover from configuration problems. Sometimes you can go several days before noticing that Windows 98 has a problem. By then, Registry Checker has already replaced the last good backup copy of your configuration with a broken copy.

> **TIP:** Registry Checker does the same thing as Microsoft's CFGBACK, but it does a better job. CFGBACK didn't work well, and Microsoft even warned users not to use it.

Table 2.3 **Settings in Scanreg.ini**

Setting	Description
Backup=[0¦1]	Specifies whether to run SCANREGW each time Windows 98 starts, backing up the Registry. The default value is 1, meaning that Registry Checker backs up the Registry once each day.
	0 = don't run SCANREGW at startup 1 = Run SCANREGW at startup
Optimize=[0¦1]	Specifies whether to automatically optimize the Registry. The default value is 1, meaning that Registry Checker optimizes the Registry as required.
	0 = Don't automatically optimize 1 = Automatically optimize
MaxBackupCopies=x	Specifies the maximum number of backup copies to make of the Registry each time Windows 98 starts. The default value is 5, meaning that Registry Checker keeps only five backup copies. Possible values are 0 to 99.
BackupDirectory=x	Specifies the location in which to store the CAB files containing the configuration backup. The default value is \Windows\Sysbckup. If you use this setting, you must provide a full path starting from the root folder.
Files=[code,]f1,f2	Specifies additional files to include in the configuration backup. You can include this setting as many times as required. Table 2.4 describes the directory codes you can use for code.

Files allows you to specify additional configuration files that you want to include in each backup. By default, Registry Checker backs up System.ini and Win.ini, but what if you want to include Protocol.ini or Autoexec.bat? The syntax looks like this:

```
Files=[dir code,]file1,file2,file3
```

dir code is one of the codes listed in Table 2.4. These codes indicate the location of the configuration file. Note that code 31 is useful only if you're using Registry Checker on a computer with compressed volumes. To back up Protocol.ini from \Windows, for example, you would write a line like this:

```
Files=10,protocol.ini
```

You can include more than one file in each statement, each separated by a comma.

Table 2.4 **Values for** `dir code`

Code	Directory	Example
10	Windows installation folder	\Windows
11	Windows system folder	\Windows\System
30	Boot drive	C:\
31	Boot host folder	H:\

Alternative Methods for Manual Backups

Windows Registry Checker is the preferred method for backing up the Registry. You really don't need to use any other method to safely back up and restore the Registry. There are alternative methods that might suit your needs better, however:

- Windows Explorer
- Registry Editor
- Microsoft Backup
- Emergency Repair Utility

You'll learn about them in the following sections.

Not one of these methods is suitable for a regular daily backup of the Registry. They do have special purposes, however. Backing up the Registry files using Windows Explorer or batch files isn't really suitable for any purpose, considering how easy it is to back up with the Registry Checker, but I've included them in this chapter for the sake of completeness. Backing up the Registry using Microsoft Backup is suitable when you're backing up your complete system. Backing up a Registry branch using the Registry Editor is suitable when you're working in a specific portion of the Registry. The Emergency Repair Utility does almost the same thing as Registry Checker but gets the job done a bit sloppier.

Windows Explorer

The absolute easiest way to back up the contents of the Registry is to copy the files that contain the Registry to a safe place. You can even do this in Windows Explorer:

1. Create a folder on your computer to hold the backup copy of the Registry: C:\Windows\Registry.

2. Make sure that you can view hidden files in Windows Explorer. Select **View**, **Folder Options**, click the View tab, select **Show all files**, and click **OK**.

NOTE: Even though I present several alternative methods for backing up the Registry, don't ever consider replacing Registry Checker with them. Registry Checker is the most effective way to safeguard your computer's configuration, and it shouldn't be thrown out in exchange for inferior methods.

3. Copy System.dat from C:\Windows to the backup folder. Copy User.dat from C:\Windows or your profile folder to the backup folder.

4. Don't forget to restore Windows Explorer so that it hides system files. Choose **View**, **Options**, click the View tab, select **Do not show hidden or system files**, and click **OK**.

If you'd rather do this more or less automatically, create a batch file that does the same thing. Then, all you have to do is execute the batch file to copy System.dat and User.dat to a safe place. The following batch file copies both files (System.dat and User.dat):

```
xcopy %WinDir%\system.dat %WinDir%\Registry\ /H /R
xcopy %WinDir%\user.dat %WinDir%\Registry\ /H /R
```

It uses the xcopy command with the /H and /R switches. The /H switch copies files with hidden and system attributes. You use this switch in lieu of changing the files' attributes with the attrib command. The /R switch replaces read-only files. That way, xcopy will be able to write over previous backup copies of the Registry. %WinDir% expands to the location of your Windows folder when the batch file runs. You find this file on my Web site, http://www.honeycutt.com, in a file called Backup.bat.

To restore a backup copy of the Registry that you made using Windows Explorer or the batch file you just read about, follow these steps:

1. Make sure that you can view hidden files in Windows Explorer. Choose **View**, **Folder Options**, click the View tab, select **Show all files**, and click **OK**.

2. Copy your backup copy of System.dat to C:\Windows. Copy User.dat to C:\Windows or your profile folder.

3. Don't forget to restore Windows Explorer so that it hides system files. Choose **View**, **Folder Options**, click the View tab, select **Do not show hidden or system files**, and click **OK**.

4. Restart your computer.

You can create a batch file that automatically restores your backup copies of System.dat and User.dat. Then all you have to do is execute the batch file to restore them. The following batch file restores your backup files:

```
Xcopy %WinDir%\Registry\System.dat %WinDir%\System.dat /R /H
Xcopy %WinDir%\Registry\User.dat %WinDir%\User.dat /R /H
```

NOTE: Some programs make backup copies of the Registry files when you install them. Norton Utilities copies the Registry files to System.nu3 and User.nu3, for instance, and other programs do similar things. You can locate all of these backup files by showing hidden files in Windows Explorer and then searching the root and Windows folders for any files that begin with *System* or *User*. If you don't have a good backup copy of the Registry handy, one of these backups might make a suitable replacement.

It uses the xcopy command with the /H and /R switches. The /H switch copies hidden and system files. The /R switch replaces read-only files. That way, xcopy will be able to overwrite the current copies of System.dat and User.dat. %WinDir% expands to the location of your Windows folder when the batch file runs. You find this batch file on my Web site, http://www.honeycutt.com, in a file called Restore.bat.

SEE ALSO

➤ Chapter 1, "Inside the Windows 98 Registry," describes the files that comprise the Registry.

➤ Chapter 14, "Profiles, System Policies, and the Registry," better describes how enabling user profiles affects the Registry files on disk.

Registry Editor

As you'll learn in Chapter 3, "Using the Windows 98 Registry Editor," you can export any portion of the Registry into a REG file. In the Windows-based Registry Editor, choose **Registry**, **Export Registry File**. Using the real mode Registry Editor, type

```
REGEDIT [/L:system] [/R:user] /E filename
```

Backing up the Registry with Profiles

If you configured Windows 98 to use user profiles, you'll need to tweak the batch files to make them pick up the correct User.dat file. In particular, you need to change the second line of both batch files so that they copy these files to and from your profile folder rather than the Windows folder. You can also enhance this batch file so that it copies User.dat for all users on the computer by copying the second line for each user, making sure to copy each user's User.dat file into a separate folder.

When to do a Manual Backup

Most folks don't back up the Registry when they should. Since doing so is easy, you should consider backing up the Registry at the following events:

- Immediately after installing Windows 98
- Before installing or removing any program
- Before making a significant change to your configuration, such as adding new devices
- Before changing policies via the System Policy Editor that might lock you out of the Registry
- Before editing the Registry with any tool

at the command prompt and press Enter. *system* is the path and filename of the System.dat file, *user* is the path and filename of the User.dat file, and *filename* is the path and filename of the REG file. With a full backup copy of the Registry in a REG file, you can import it into the Registry at a later time. You can't import a REG file containing the entire Registry while Windows 98 is running, though, because the Registry Editor can't replace keys that are open. You need to start your computer in MS-DOS mode and then use the Registry Editor in real mode to import the Registry:

1. Start Windows in MS-DOS mode. To do so, select **Command Prompt Only** from Windows 98's boot menu, or choose **Start, Shut Down**, select **Restart in MS-DOS mode**, and press Enter.

2. Type the following at the command prompt:
   ```
   regedit /L:system /R:user /C regfile
   ```

   system is the path and filename of System.dat. *user* is the path and filename of User.dat. Normally, this points to the User.dat file in C:\Windows, but if you're using profiles, this might point to a User.dat file within a profile folder in C:\Windows\Profiles. /C instructs the real mode Registry Editor to replace the entire Registry with the contents of *regfile*, which is the filename of the REG file containing the backup.

3. Restart your computer.

SEE ALSO

➤ Chapter 3 describes the differences between the Windows-based Registry Editor and the real mode Registry Editor. It also describes each command line option you can use with the real mode Registry Editor.

CAUTION: Don't rely on a REG file as your only backup. Microsoft reports problems such as Windows 98 not correctly updating all Registry data when you restore a backup using this method. The best use of a REG file is backing up a portion of the Registry in which you're making changes. That way, if something goes awry, you can easily restore that branch by importing the REG file.

NOTE: Norton Registry Editor has a backup feature. To use it, choose Eile, Backup Entire Registry. Note that this feature does nothing more than export the entire Registry to a REG file, which you can do easily with the Registry Editor, which is faster. You can try using Norton Registry Editor's archive feature, but this feature archives the Registry into a proprietary format that other programs, including Windows 98, can't read. Thus, using the archive feature for Registry backups isn't a good idea.

Microsoft Backup

Windows 98 comes with a tape backup utility that you can use as part of your regular backup strategy. Windows 98 Setup doesn't install it by default, but you can use the Add/Remove Programs Properties dialog box in the Control Panel to install it. After you install it, choose **Start**, **Programs**, **Accessories**, **System Tools**, **Backup** to run it. By default, Microsoft Backup doesn't back up the Registry. Thus, to back up the Windows 98 Registry, follow these steps before starting the backup:

1. Choose **Job**, **Options** to display the Backup Job Options dialog box, shown in Figure 2.1, and click the Advanced tab .

2. Select **Back up Windows Registry**.

3. Click **OK** to save your changes.

4. Continue performing your backup as normal.

As with backing up the Registry using Microsoft Backup, you must specifically configure the program to restore the Registry:

1. Choose **Job**, **Options** and click the Advanced tab.

2. Select **Restore the Registry**.

3. Click **OK** to save your changes.

4. Continue restoring the backup as usual.

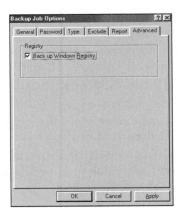

Figure 2.1 By default, Microsoft Backup doesn't back up the Registry.

NOTE: Using Microsoft Backup to back up and restore the Registry is a method better suited to a full backup. In other words, if you restore the Registry from a backup tape, you should also restore the entire system from the same tape. Doing so ensures that the files on your computer match the settings found in the Registry. If you restore just the Registry from an older tape, chances are good that your computer won't work properly, because the configuration data in the Registry doesn't match the remaining files on your computer.

Emergency Repair Utility

The Emergency Repair Utility (ERU) is a tool you can use to back up important configuration files. You can't back up to a floppy disk, which is ERU's default choice, since the configuration files usually won't fit on a floppy. By default, ERU backs up the following files, but you can change the list, as you'll learn later in this section:

Autoexec.bat

Command.com

Config.sys

Io.sys

Msdos.sys

Protocol.ini

System.dat

System.ini

User.dat

Win.ini

Windows 98 doesn't include ERU, as Windows 95 did. You can find it on the CD-ROM that comes with the *Microsoft Windows 98 Resource Kit,* published by Microsoft, in the following path: \Tools\Misc\Eru. You can download it from the following URL and run it to unzip the files:
http://www.microsoft.com/windows/download/eruzip.exe. Copy all four files to a folder on your computer, and then add a shortcut to your Start menu by dragging Eru.exe onto the Start button. After copying ERU to your computer, use these steps to back up your configuration files, including the Registry:

1. Start ERU by choosing it from the Start menu or double-clicking Eru.exe in Windows Explorer.

2. Click **Next** after ERU appears. You see a dialog box that lets you choose between backing up to a floppy or to another folder.

3. Choose **Drive A:** if you want to back up your configuration files to disk, or choose **Other Directory** to back up your configuration files to another folder on your hard drive. Click **Next** to continue.

4. If you're backing up your configuration files to another folder on your computer, type the path of the folder in the space provided. Then click **Next** to continue. Otherwise, insert a formatted disk in drive A:, and click **OK** to continue. You see a list of files that ERU is backing up, as shown in Figure 2.2.

5. Click **Next**. ERU backs up your configuration files to the destination you chose.

6. ERU displays a dialog box that explains how to restore your configuration in the event that something bad happens to them. Click **OK** to close it.

To restore your configuration using the backup files created by ERU, follow these steps:

1. Start your computer in MS-DOS mode.

2. Change to the folder to which you backed up your configuration files. If you backed up your configuration files to a disk, put it in the drive, and change to it.

3. Run Erd.exe. It's mixed in with all the backup copies of your configuration files.

4. Select the files that you want to recover. Highlight a configuration file using the arrow keys, and press the Enter key to select it.

5. Once you've selected the configuration files you want to recover, select **Start Recovery**, and press the Enter key.

Norton Utilities Rescue Disk

Norton's Repair Disk is better than Windows 98's startup disk because it includes more useful utilities across more disks, and it makes a backup copy of the Registry. *Basic Rescue* is a set of floppy disks. It can also back up the files to a ZIP disk and create a bootable floppy disk that you can use to start the computer and access the ZIP drive. This is called *Zip Rescue*.

Start Repair Disk by choosing **Start**, **Programs**, **Norton Utilities**, **Rescue Disk**. Click **Options** to specify additional files that you want the program to include on your rescue disk set. This opens the Options dialog box, which allows you to view the files to be included on the disks, including their original locations and destination. Click **Create** to make a new rescue disk set, or click **Update** to update an existing set. Make sure that you keep your rescue disk set current. If you let the disk set get out of date, it will be of no use to you at all. Norton System Doctor has an indicator that alerts you when it thinks your configuration has changed enough to warrant updating the disk set.

Figure 2.2 Click Custom to change the files that ERU includes in the backup.

Here's a list of the information that Rescue Disk puts on each rescue disk set:

Config.sys

Autoexec.bat

Msdos.sys

Autoexec.dos

Config.dos

CMOS Information

Boot Record Information

Partition Information

Registry Backup

Rescue.exe

Rescued.hlp

Diskedit.exe

Ndd.exe

Format.com

Sys.com

Fdisk.exe

Unerase.exe

Unformat.exe

At the time this chapter was written, the Rescue Disk program that comes with Norton Utilities doesn't work properly. Windows 98 reports a compatibility problem when you run Rescue Disk, saying that the Zip Rescue feature doesn't work. If you continue running the program, Rescue Disk reports the same compatibility problem but lets you go ahead and create a Basic Rescue. You can expect Symantec to update this program, however. You should frequently check for the update by opening LiveUpdate from the Control Panel. Follow the onscreen instructions to update your copy of Norton Utilities with the latest software from Symantec's Web site.

TIP: You can add files to the list that ERU backs up. Open Eru.inf in your favorite text editor (Notepad, perhaps) and follow the instructions that you see at the top of the file.

NOTE: Norton's Rescue Disk can get your computer up and running in the event of a disaster. It makes backup copies of all the important files required to start the computer, including the Registry. If things go awry, put the first disk of the rescue disk set in the drive A: and restart the computer.

NOTE: What's missing from the default rescue disk set that Rescue Disk creates is INI files. In particular, it doesn't back up Win.ini or System.ini. Add these and other important INI files by clicking the **Options** button in Rescue Disk's main window.

SEE ALSO

➤ Chapter 3 shows you how to use Norton Registry Editor.

➤ Chapter 4 shows you how to use Norton WinDoctor, which is a great utility that can fix most problems.

System.1st as a Last Resort

If all else fails, you'll find one more backup copy of the Registry on your computer. System.1st is a read-only, hidden, system file in the root folder of your boot drive. This is a backup copy of System.dat that Windows 98 made after you successfully installed and started Windows 98. It doesn't contain any custom settings, nor does it include any information added by the programs you've installed. This file just gets your computer running again if all else fails. Read Chapter 4 before you give up and restore System.1st.

Here's how to restore System.1st:

1. Start your computer in MS-DOS mode.

2. Copy your C:\System.1st to C:\Windows\System.dat. In other words, type

   ```
   Xcopy C:\system.1st C:\windows\system.dat /H /R
   ```

   at the command prompt, and press Enter.

3. Restart your computer.

SEE ALSO

➤ Chapter 4 shows you how to recover from a variety of problems. Read this chapter before restoring System.1st.

NOTE: Use this method as a last resort only. All the configuration changes you've made to your computer since you first installed Windows 98 will be gone after you restore this file.

3

Using the Windows 98 Registry Editor

Karanjit S. Siyan, Ph.D

In this chapter:

- Introducing the Registry Editor
- Starting the Registry Editor
- Getting Around the Registry Editor
- Working with Keys and Values
- Importing and Exporting Registry Entries
- Using the Real Mode Registry Editor
- Using the Norton Registry Editor

Introducing the Registry Editor

Microsoft's attitude about the Windows 98 Registry Editor is that if you don't know about it, you'll never miss it. Setup doesn't copy a Registry Editor shortcut to the Start menu when you install Windows 98, and Microsoft doesn't tell you much about it. For that matter, you'll find barely a handful of help screens in Windows 98 that describe how to use the Registry Editor, and the *Microsoft Windows 98 Resource Kit* contains one measly chapter describing the entire Registry. It's probably just as well. Microsoft wants to prevent inexperienced users from accidentally harming their computer systems by tampering with the Registry, so they don't provide any encouragement by over-documenting it.

Administrators and power users can't avoid the Registry Editor, however. It's your window into the computer's configuration, allowing you to fix many problems and customize Windows 98 in a variety of ways. You'd use the Registry Editor to customize a desktop object's icon, for example, and you can use it to customize a file's shortcut menu. Many of the solutions in Microsoft's Knowledge Base also require you to use the Registry Editor to make subtle changes to the computer's configuration.

The Registry Editor is a powerful but simple program. It doesn't have a toolbar; its menus are fairly straightforward. It displays the organization of the Registry on the left side of the window and the actual configuration data on the right side—not too complicated. This is the program you will learn how to use in this chapter. You will also learn a variety of helpful tips that come from my own agonizing experiences with the Registry Editor.

Starting the Registry Editor

The Registry Editor isn't on your Start menu, but it is in your Windows folder. The filename is Regedit.exe. Choose **Start, Programs**, **Run**, type regedit, and press Enter. Since the Windows folder is usually in the PATH environment variable, you don't have to specify a path on the command line. You can also drag Regedit.exe from your Windows folder to the Start button to create a shortcut for it. If you're using the Microsoft Management Console that comes with the *Microsoft Windows 98 Resource Kit,* published by Microsoft Press, consider adding the Registry Editor to the snap-ins already shown in it, keeping all your administrative tools in one convenient place.

If you don't find Regedit.exe in \Windows and you installed Windows 98 from shared source files on the network, the administrator might have prevented the Setup program from copying it to your computer. You can ask the administrator for a copy of the program, or you can extract it from Win98_42.cab, which you find on the Windows 98 CD-ROM in \Win98. Right-click the CAB file and choose **View** to open the CAB file in a folder, and then drag the file from the CAB file to \Windows. Likewise, the administrator can prevent you from gaining access to the Registry using the System Policy Editor, in which case you see a message that says Registry editing has been disabled by your administrator when you try to open the Registry Editor. If you want to use the Registry Editor to change values in the Registry, you'll have to plead your case to the administrator for permission to change the Registry.

NOTE: If you think the Windows 98 Registry Editor sounds too simplistic, you might consider using one of the alternative Registry editors you'll learn about in this chapter. The Norton Registry Editor comes with Norton Utilities and offers a variety of enhancements over the Windows 98 Registry Editor. The ShellWizard Registry Editor is a shareware editor that provides even more features than the Norton Registry Editor.

SEE ALSO

➤ Chapter 4, "Troubleshooting the Registry," shows you how to gain access to the Registry when system policies prevent access. See the section called "Removing Restrictions That Prevent Registry Editor."

➤ Chapter 13, "Security and Remote Administration," discusses protecting a Windows 98 workstation as well as the Registry. In particular, you learn about a policy called **Disable Registry Editing Tools**.

Getting Around the Registry Editor

Figure 3.1 shows what the Registry Editor looks like when you open it on your desktop. You see the Registry Editor's menu bar across the top of the window and its status line across the bottom. The status line displays the fully qualified path of the selected Registry key. You should already be familiar with the controls in the Registry Editor's title bar.

Within the window, you see two panes, which the Registry Editor separates by a divider that you can drag to change the size of either pane. The left pane contains the Registry's hierarchy, and the right pane displays the value entries for the selected Registry key. Throughout this book, I call the left pane the *Key* pane and the right pane the *Contents* pane. The following sections describe the contents of each pane in more detail.

The Key Pane: Registry Organization

The Key pane shows the organization of the Registry—its hierarchy. Even though Windows 98 stores the Registry in two files, System.dat and User.dat, the Registry Editor displays the entire Registry as one logical unit. When you update a key in the Registry Editor, it automatically updates the appropriate Registry file, storing changes to HKEY_USERS in User.dat and changes to HKEY_LOCAL_MACHINE to System.dat. However, the location of User.dat varies, depending on whether you enable user profiles on the computer, as you learned in Chapter 1, "Inside the Windows 98 Registry."

> CAUTION: Is the Registry safe from tampering? No, it's not. In Chapter 13, "Security and Remote Administration," you'll learn how to prevent the user from starting the Registry Editor. This policy requires the cooperation of the Registry editing program, however. The Registry Editor cooperates; other programs probably won't. What's more, even if you prevent access to the Registry editing tools by using system policies, the user can still modify it by creating and importing a REG or INF file. Thus, you can never be sure that the Windows 98 Registry is safe from tampering.

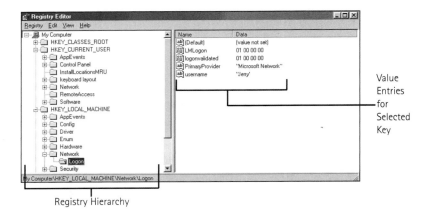

Registry Hierarchy

Figure 3.1 The left pane of the Registry Editor works much like
the left pane of Windows Explorer.

The first entry is My Computer. It contains several root keys that the Registry Editor represents as folders. Each root key contains subkeys, which are also represented as folders. Click the plus sign to expand a branch, or click a minus sign to collapse a branch. If you'd rather use the keyboard, you can use the keystrokes listed in Table 3.1 to move around the Registry Editor. These key combinations are often the quickest way to navigate, because you don't flop around with the mouse. You can collapse an entire branch by pressing the left arrow, for example, and press the left arrow again to select the parent key.

> **TIP:** If the left pane isn't big enough for you to easily tell which key is selected, look at the Registry Editor's status bar to see the key's fully qualified name. You can also drag the divider to the right to make the left pane bigger.

> **TIP:** If you don't want the Registry Editor to "remember" which subkeys are open below a folder after you collapse it, press F5 to refresh it. If you collapse a branch and then expand it, for instance, the Registry Editor restores the branch as it was before you collapsed it. If you want to expand a key so that you see only the subkeys immediately below it, press F5 before expanding it.

Table 3.1 **REGEDIT Keystrokes**

Key	Description
SEARCHING	
Ctrl+F	Searches the Registry.
F3	Repeats the previous search.
MISCELLANEOUS	
F1	Displays online help.
F2	Renames the selected key or value.
F5	Refreshes the Registry Editor's contents.
F10	Opens the Registry Editor's main menu.
Shift+F10	Displays the context menu (right-click) for the selected key or value.
Alt+F4	Closes the Registry Editor.
NAVIGATION	
Keypad +	Expands the selected folder one level.
Keypad –	Collapses the selected folder one level.
Keypad ★	Expands all levels of the selected folder.
Up arrow	Selects the previous open key.
Down arrow	Selects the next open key.
Right arrow	Expands the selected key if it's collapsed; otherwise, selects the first subkey.
Left arrow	Collapses the selected key if it's expanded; otherwise, selects the parent key.
Home	Selects the first entry in the outline.
End	Selects the last open key in the outline.
Page Up	Moves up one screen in the list.
Page Down	Moves down one screen in the list.
F6	Toggles between the Key and Contents panes.
Tab	Toggles between the Key and Contents panes.

TIP: If you don't want the Registry Editor to "remember" which subkeys are open below a folder after you collapse it, press F5 to refresh it. If you collapse a branch and then expand it, for instance, the Registry Editor restores the branch as it was before you collapsed it. If you want to expand a key so that you see only the subkeys immediately below it, press F5 before expanding it.

The Contents Pane: Value Entries for the Selected Key

The Contents pane shows the value entries for the key you've selected in the Key pane. Each row in the Contents pane represents a single value entry. The Name column contains the value's name. The Data column contains the actual value data for each. You can resize each column by dragging the divider you see between each heading.

The first value entry is always (Default). This is a string value entry that represents the default value for that Registry key. You learned about default value entries in Chapter 1, "Inside the Windows 98 Registry." All Registry keys contain this value entry, but some keys don't contain any additional value entries. Aside from (Default), therefore, each key can contain zero or more value entries that have both a name and data. To edit any value entry, double-click its name in the Contents pane. Note too that you can right-click any key or value name to open a shortcut menu from which you can choose a variety of commands.

Notice that different value entries in the Contents pane of the Registry Editor window have different icons. These icons represent the different types of data that the Registry can store, as described in Table 3.2. The first row represents string value entries, and the second represents DWORD and binary value entries.

Table 3.2   **Icons Representing Data Types**

Icon	Description
[ab]	String values that you can read (text)
[binary]	Binary values (hexadecimal strings or DWORDs)

Working with Keys and Values

The following sections show you how to use the Registry Editor to search for, add, change, and delete configuration data. You'll find tips for doing all these things as safely as possible, too. Some of these sections contain real-world examples that you'll apply in Chapter 9, "Customizing the Windows 98 Desktop," so that you can exercise what you learn. Before you continue, however, remember the advice in Chapter 1, "Inside the Windows 98 Registry":

- Back up the Registry before you change it.
- Make sure that you have a plan for making changes so that you can fix any problems you encounter.

The "plan" involves making sure you can get out of a bad situation if one arises. You do that by setting up the situation where you can restore a value's original data if necessary, whether you deleted or changed it. Exporting the key is one approach; copying a value's data to the Clipboard is sometimes a simpler method. Continue reading this chapter to learn about both.

Searching the Registry

When you search the Registry, the Registry Editor looks for keys, value names, and value data that matches the text for which you're searching. It scans the name of each key, the name of each value entry, and the actual data from each value entry for a match. You can use the search feature to find entries relating to a specific product, find all the entries that contain a reference to a file on your computer, or locate entries related to a particular hardware device. Here's how to search the Registry for keys, value names, and value data that contain a particular string:

1. Select **Edit**, **Find**. The Registry Editor displays the dialog box shown in Figure 3.2.

2. Type the text for which you want to search. If you're searching for a number in a string value entry, try both the decimal and hexadecimal notations, because both formats are common in the Registry.

3. Click **Find Next**, and the Registry Editor searches for a match. This can sometimes take quite a while—up to several minutes on slower machines. If the Registry Editor finds a matching key, it selects that key in the left pane. If the Registry Editor finds a matching value entry, it opens the key that contains it in the left pane and selects the value entry in the right pane.

4. If the result isn't exactly what you had in mind, press F3 to continue searching. When the Registry Editor reaches the bottom of the Registry, it displays a dialog box telling you that it has finished searching.

You can hasten the Registry Editor's search if you know what portion of the Registry contains the string you're searching for: keys, value entry names, or value entry data. As just mentioned, deselect **Keys**, **Values**, or **Data** if you don't think the Registry Editor will find the string in one or more of those places. If you're pretty certain that the string you're finding is in a value entry's name, for example, deselect **Keys** and **Data** to limit the Registry Editor to value entry names, thus speeding up the search.

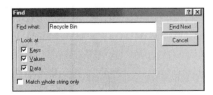

Figure 3.2 Deselect the parts of the Registry in which you don't want REGEDIT to search: Keys, Values, and Data.

Neither the Windows 98 Registry Editor nor the Norton Registry Editor provides the ability to search binary and DWORD value entry data. You can't simply search for 0x000000001 and expect the Registry Editor to find any matching DWORD values. You can still locate these values, however, by exporting the Registry to a text file and searching the text file with your favorite editor. See the later section "Importing and Exporting Registry Entries" to learn how to export the Registry to a REG file. What you need to know is how those values look in a REG file so you can search for them using a text editor. The following table shows you the format of each type in the REG file. For example, if you were searching for the DWORD value 0xA0B0C0D0, you

> **TIP:** Incremental searching makes for an easy way to locate an exposed key in the Registry Editor window, which is particularly valuable when locating a subkey in HKEY_CLASSES_ROOT, a monstrous branch of the Registry. If you click anywhere in the Registry Editor's Key pane and start typing the name of a Registry key, the Registry Editor selects the key that best matches what you've typed thus far. For example, expand HKEY_CLASSES_ROOT. Then press ., and REGEDIT selects .386; press b, and it selects .bat; press m, and it selects .bmp. Note that if you pause between keystrokes, the Registry Editor starts the *incremental search* over with the next keystroke.

Techniques for Searching the Registry

After using the Registry Editor for a time, you should be able to predict where to find a certain key or value. With that knowledge, you can position the cursor somewhere near where you think you'll find the item and then use the Search feature to find it. This takes much less time than searching the entire Registry for the item.

Here's an example. If you're searching for a file extension, open HKEY_CLASSES_ROOT and do an incremental search to locate it faster. Note that you can locate the *program identifier* associated with a file extension, which defines the commands available for the file, by looking at the file extension's default value entry.

Finding a program's configuration data is straightforward, too, because most programs store the same types of configuration data in the same places. You find the program's file associations in HKEY_CLASSES_ROOT. The program probably stores configuration data in \Software*Vendor**AppName**Version* under HKEY_LOCAL_MACHINE and HKEY_CURRENT_USER, where *Vendor* is the name of the company that produced the software, *AppName* is the name of the application, and *Version* is the version number of the program or CurrentVersion.

Remember that computer-specific data goes in HKEY_LOCAL_MACHINE, while user-specific data goes in HKEY_CURRENT_USER. Use that information to your advantage. If you're relatively certain that the data you're searching for is computer-specific, select HKEY_LOCAL_MACHINE before beginning the search. You'd search for any information about a particular device in this root key, for example. Otherwise, if you're certain the data is user-specific, select HKEY_CURRENT_USER before beginning the search.

would search the REG file for dword:A0B0C0D0. If you were searching for the binary value 05 20 59 02 14 65, you would search the REG file for the string hex:05,20,59,02,14,65.

Shown in Type	Format in Registry Editor	Exported REG File
DWORD	`0x00000054`	`dword:00000054`
Binary	`A0 00 00 00`	`hex:a0,00,00,00`

Renaming a Key or Value Entry

Renaming a key or value entry in the Registry Editor works much like renaming a file in Windows Explorer, except that you can't rename it by clicking the name. Instead, select the key or value name that you want to rename, choose **Edit**, **Rename**, type over the name to change it, and press Enter. Alternatively, select the name and press F2, and then type over the name and press Enter.

Renaming a key or value entry has practical value. It's a good way to hide a key or value entry prior to permanently deleting it. Hiding the item under some obscure name has the same effect as removing it. If things go awry, however, you can restore the item's original name to undelete it. For example, assume you want to remove the `IsShortcut` value entry from the `lnkfile` program identifier, which prevents Windows 98 from displaying the shortcut overlay on shortcuts. Instead of deleting the value, rename it to something like `MyIsShortcut` to test the change. Then permanently remove `MyIsShortcut` once you're satisfied that everything works okay.

Changing a Key or Value Entry

To change a value entry, double-click its name, or select it and choose **Edit**, **Modify**. Then change the value and click **OK** to save your changes.

Recall from Chapter 1, "Inside the Windows 98 Registry," that a value entry can be a string, DWORD, or binary data. Thus, when you change a value entry, the Registry Editor presents a different dialog box, depending on the type of data stored in the value. Figures 3.3, 3.4, and 3.5 show you what the dialog boxes look like for String, DWORD, and binary values, respectively. Here's the rundown on each one:

String   Editing a string value entry is uneventful. You type the new string in the Edit String dialog box, shown in Figure 3.3. Remember, though, that you don't add the quotation marks that the Registry Editor displays around a string value. They appear automatically. You must still add any quotation marks that you want to embed in the string.

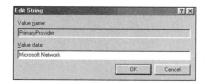

Figure 3.3 The Edit String dialog box shows you the original data before you start editing.

DWORD   The Registry Editor presents the Edit DWORD Value dialog box,
              shown in Figure 3.4, when you double-click a DWORD value in
              the Contents pane. If you know the hexadecimal value, type it in
              the space provided. Otherwise, select **Decimal** and type the value in
              decimal notation.

Binary   Figure 3.5 shows the Edit Binary Value dialog box, which the
              Registry Editor presents when you double-click a binary value in
              the Contents pane. You can type each hexadecimal byte on the left
              side of this dialog box, or you can type ASCII characters from the
              keyboard on the right side. To choose the side in which you want to
              type, click that area of the dialog box.

The following example shows you how to change the text you see below the
Recycle Bin icon on your desktop. You can make it a bit more personal, for example,
by changing it to something like "Jerry's Trashcan." Here's how:

1. Open HKEY_CLASSES_ROOT\CLSID\{645FF040-5081-101B-9F08-00AA002F954E} in
   the Registry Editor.

2. In the Contents pane, double-click the default value entry, (Default).

3. In the Edit String dialog box, type the text you want to see below the Recycle
   Bin icon on your desktop.

4. Click **OK** to save your changes, and minimize the Registry Editor so that you
   can see the desktop.

5. Click any open area of the desktop and press F5. This causes the desktop to
   refresh itself.

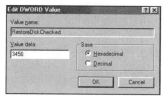

Figure 3.4 Choose Decimal if your hexadecimal math is a bit rusty.
The Registry Editor will convert the value to binary.

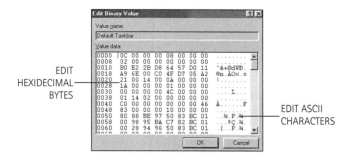

EDIT
HEXIDECIMAL
BYTES

EDIT ASCII
CHARACTERS

Figure 3.5 You can use the Windows calculator (in Scientific mode) to convert decimal values to hexadecimal values for use with this dialog box.

Creating a Key or Value Entry

Creating a new key or value entry is generally harmless and equally as useless—unless, of course, you know for sure that either Windows 98 or another program will use your new key. For example, the Microsoft Knowledge Base might instruct you to create a new Registry key to fix a problem.

When you create a new key, the Registry Editor creates a key called New_Key #1 and highlights the name so that you can rename it. When you create a new value entry, the Registry Editor creates a value called New_Value #1 and also highlights the name so that you can rename it. The Registry Editor sets the initial value of a new value entry to a null string for string values, a null binary string for binary values, or zero for DWORD values. You must change the value as described in the preceding section to set its value.

> **CAUTION:** Use a bit of caution when changing a value. The later sidebar "Protecting Yourself from Errant Edits" provides some good tips for backing up the portion of the Registry in which you're working. Doing so helps you recover from any problems that your edits might cause. The best tip I can offer when editing a value is to make a backup copy of it by giving the original value an obscure name. Then add a new value that has the original name and value. If things go awry, you can remove the new value and restore the original from the backup.

> **NOTE:** Changes that you make to the Registry may not be reflected immediately in Windows or the programs that are currently running. The only way to make sure is to restart Windows or log off and back on again after closing the Registry Editor. In particular, if you change a value in HKEY_LOCAL_MACHINE, you might have to restart the computer in order for the change to take effect. If you change a value in HKEY_USERS, you might have to log off and back on again in order for the change to take effect.
>
> In case you're wondering, the old trick of holding down the Shift key as you confirm that you want to restart Windows no longer works. Windows 98 doesn't confirm that you want to shut down or restart the operating system.

To create new key or value entry, do one of the following:

New Key   Select an existing key under which you want your new subkey to appear. Select **Edit**, **New**, **Key**, type the name of your key, and press Enter.

New Value   Select an existing key under which you want your new value entry to appear. Select **Edit**, **New** and then choose **String Value**, **Binary Value**, or **DWORD** Value. Type the name of your new value entry and press Enter. You can edit your key as described in the preceding section.

Deleting a Key or Value Entry

Be very careful about deleting keys and value entries from the Registry. You'll likely prevent Windows from working properly if you carelessly delete configuration data. To remove a key or value entry, follow these steps:

1. Highlight the key or value you want to delete.
2. Press Delete. The Registry Editor prompts you to confirm that you want to delete the item.
3. Click **Yes** to delete the key or value.

Techniques Using the Clipboard

When using the Registry Editor, use the Clipboard extensively to make your job easier. You can copy to and paste from the Clipboard whenever you edit a name or data, for example. Thus, consider these different ways to use the Clipboard in the Registry Editor:

- To copy the fully qualified name of a Registry key to the Clipboard, select the key and choose **Edit**, **Copy Key Name**.

- To copy a value entry's data to the Clipboard, open the value entry for editing, select the data, and press Ctrl+C to copy the data to the Clipboard.

- To paste data from the Clipboard into a value entry, open the value entry for editing, select the data you want to replace, and press Ctrl+V.

- To copy a key or value entry's name to the Clipboard, right-click the item in the Registry Editor, choose **Rename**, and press Ctrl+C.

NOTE: The second item in the list tells you how to copy a value entry's data to the Clipboard. Use this to back up a value entry before changing it. Copy the value's data to the Clipboard and paste that data into a new bogus value entry. If you want to restore the original value, copy the backup data to the Clipboard and paste it into the value.

TIP: Before deleting a key, give it an obscure name such as MyDeletedKey. This hides it from Windows and your applications. Restart your computer and test things. If everything works okay, go ahead and permanently delete the key.

Printing a Key

Some people think that printing the Registry is useful as a backup or for reading the Registry to better understand it. Considering that a full printout of the entire Registry would occupy hundreds of pages and that you can't import a printout back into the Registry, this position is nonsense.

Printing a small subkey does have merit, however—for two reasons. First, it serves as a useful backup when you're working within a small portion of the Registry. You can restore the original data if you mess things up. Second, it is sometimes helpful to print a small portion of the Registry that you need as a reference when working in another part of the Registry. This is particularly true since you can't open two copies of the Registry Editor to view two portions of the Registry at the same time.

To print a branch, select it in the Key pane, choose **Registry**, **Print**, and click **OK**. The Registry Editor sends the print job to the spooler. The resulting output looks similar to a REG file, as shown in Listing 3.1. Note that the format of each value is slightly different from a REG file, however. The Registry Editor doesn't put quotation marks around string values, for instance. It also doesn't prefix a binary value with the string hex:. The most notable difference is that it writes DWORD values as binary values, reversing the bytes as required in a little endian architecture (see Chapter 15, "Script, REG, and INF Files"). The following mini-table describes how the Registry Editor formats each data type when it prints it:

Shown in Type	Format in Registry Editor	Printed Output
String	`"This is a string"`	`This is a string`
DWORD	`0x00000054`	`54,00,00,00`
Binary	`A0 00 00 00 01 23`	`A0,00,00,00,01,23`

Listing 3.1 **Registry Editor Printer Output**

```
[HKEY_CURRENT_USER\Control Panel\Desktop]
DragFullWindows=1
FontSmoothing=1
UserPreferencemask=a0,00,00,00
ScreenSaveUsePassword=00,00,00,00
SmoothScroll=01,00,00,00
MenuShowDelay=400

[HKEY_CURRENT_USER\Control Panel\Desktop\WindowMetrics]
MenuWidth=-270
MenuHeight=-270
MinAnimate=0
```

continues

Listing 3.1 **Continued**

```
Shell Icon Size=32
IconTitleWrap=0
test=01,00,00,00

[HKEY_CURRENT_USER\Control Panel\Desktop\WindowsMetrics]
MinAnimate=1
```

Importing and Exporting Registry Entries

Exporting the Registry creates a text file with a REG extension, which you can edit using any text editor. This file contains all the information required to describe the keys and values in the exported branch.

Up to this point, you've used the Registry Editor to work with the Registry. You can also export the Registry to a REG file and edit it using a text editor such as WordPad (the file is too big for Notepad). If you export the Registry to a REG file, you can use the editor's search-and-replace features to make massive changes to it. Be careful doing this, however, because you can inadvertently change a value you didn't mean to change. Then you can import the REG file with all its changes by right-clicking it and choosing **Merge**.

Aside from editing the Registry with a text editor, exporting the Registry to a text file has a more practical purpose. You can export as a backup any branch of the Registry in which you're making many changes. If you get confused, or changes get out of hand, you can import that file back into the Registry to restore your settings. You can also export a key or a branch that contains a useful Registry hack. Then you can share that REG file with other people so they can implement the same hack by importing the REG file you provide (all they have to do is double-click the file).

Exporting to a REG File

To export your entire Registry or just a specific branch, follow these steps:

1. Select the key in the Key pane that represents the branch you want to export.

2. Choose **Registry**, **Export Registry File**. The Registry Editor displays the dialog box shown in Figure 3.6.

> **CAUTION:** Nothing prevents you from importing a Windows NT 4.0 REG file into Windows 98, and vice versa. Be careful to avoid doing this, however, because it might prevent either operating system from working properly.

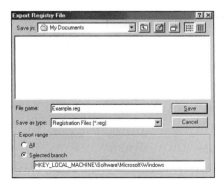

Figure 3.6 If you don't type a file extension, REGEDIT uses the default file extension (REG).

3. If you're exporting the entire Registry, select **All**. Otherwise, choose **Selected branch**. The Registry Editor automatically fills in the key you selected in step 1.

4. Type the filename into the **File name** box in which you want to export the Registry, and click **Save**.

Importing a REG File

In Windows Explorer, right-click a REG file and choose **Merge**. Windows updates your Registry with the contents of the REG file, replacing existing items and adding new ones. When you merge a REG file into the Registry, Windows 98 doesn't remove keys and value entries that exist in the Registry but not in the REG file. As an alternative to merging a REG file from Windows Explorer, you can import a REG file from within the Registry Editor as described here:

1. Choose **Registry**, **Import Registry File**. The Registry Editor displays Import Registry File dialog box.

2. Type the path and filename of the REG file in the space provided, or browse your hard disk to locate it.

3. Click **Open**. The Registry Editor imports the REG file, displaying a message that says `Information in filename has been successfully entered into the registry`.

> **NOTE:** Make sure that you use clear 8.3 filenames for the REG files you export. Clear names help you find these files at the MS-DOS command prompt, and 8.3 filenames help make sure that you can easily specify the name to the real mode Registry Editor on the command line. See "Using the Real Mode Registry Editor" later in this chapter for more information.

Be careful not to accidentally double-click a REG file. Windows will automatically merge it with the Registry because **Merge** is the default command for REG files. Note that you can change the default command for REG files, as described in Chapter 9, "Customizing the Windows 98 Desktop." You can also use a file extension other than REG for exported Registry files, which prevents the user from accidentally merging them. And consider storing all your REG files in their own folder, too, so that you're more inclined to be careful when working with files in that folder.

.reg
⇓
.rey

Reading a REG File

The resulting file looks very much like a classic INI file. Open the REG file in Notepad by right-clicking it and choosing **Edit** (Notepad will offer to open the file in WordPad if it's larger than 64 KB). The first line always contains REGEDIT4, which identifies the file as a Registry file. The remainder of the file contains the keys and value entries that the Registry Editor exported.

Listing 3.2 shows what a REG file looks like. The file is split into multiple sections, with each Registry key in its own section. The name of the key appears between brackets, and it is the fully qualified name of that key in the Registry file. In other words, you see the entire name of the branch, including the name of the root key. Each value entry for a key is listed in that key's section. The value entry's name is in quotation marks, except for default value entries, which the Registry Editor represents with the at sign . The value entry's data looks different depending on its type, as shown in Table 3.3.

Listing 3.2   **A Sample REG File**

```
REGEDIT4

[HKEY_CURRENT_USER\Control Panel\Desktop]
"DragFullWindows"="1"
"FontSmoothing"="1"
"wallpaper"=""
"TileWallpaper"="0"
"UserPreferencemask"=hex:a0,00,00,00
"WallpaperStyle"="0"
"ScreenSaveLowPowerActive"="1"
"ScreenSavePowerOffActive"="0"
"ScreenSaveActive"="0"
"ScreenSaveTimeOut"="60"
"ScreenSaveUsePassword"=dword:00000000
```

NOTE: You must remember that importing a REG file only replaces or adds keys and values to the Registry. This action never removes a key or value that's in the Registry but not in the REG file. If you want to do this sort of thing, remove the key you want to replace from the Registry and then import the REG file.

```
"SmoothScroll"=hex:01,00,00,00
"WheelScrollLines"="3"
"Pattern"=""
"DragWidth"="2"
"DragHeight"="2"
"DoubleClickWidth"="4"
"DoubleClickHeight"="4"
"HungAppTimeout"="inget"
"WaitToKillAppTimeout"="inget"
"CoolSwitchRows"="inget"
"CoolSwitchColumns"="inget"
"MenuShowDelay"="400"
"test"=dword:00000054

[HKEY_CURRENT_USER\Control Panel\Desktop\ResourceLocale]
@="00000409"

[HKEY_CURRENT_USER\Control Panel\Desktop\WindowsMetrics]
"MinAnimate"="1"
```

Table 3.3   **Formats for String, DWORD, and HEX Data**

Type	Example
String	"This is a string value"
DWORD	DWORD:00000001
HEX	HEX:FF 00 FF 00 FF 00 FF 00 FF 00 FF 00

SEE ALSO

➤ Chapter 15, "Script, REG, and INF Files," describes the content of a REG file in greater detail than you'll find in this chapter. Chapter 15 even shows you how to build REG files by hand.

Protecting Yourself from Errant Edits

I can't stress enough how important protecting yourself is while making changes to the Registry. You can restore Registry Checker's most recent backup, but more immediate and less drastic solutions are available. Create a backup copy of a value before changing it, for example, by creating a backup value entry and naming it whatever you like. Then copy the original value to the Clipboard and paste it to the backup value entry.

If you're working with a number of values within a key or even an entire branch, export the branch to a REG file before making changes. If things go wrong, import the REG file to restore the original settings. You can replace the mangled branch by removing it before importing the REG file. If you can't even start Windows 98, import the REG file from the MS-DOS command line as described in the next section.

Using the Real Mode Registry Editor

The Registry Editor provides several command line arguments you can use to automatically import from and export to REG files. To use the command line options, choose **Start**, **Run**, type regedit followed by any of the options you want to use, and press Enter.

The Registry Editor runs as a real mode MS-DOS application too, which means that you can run it when the computer is running in MS-DOS mode. Don't be confused by thinking that there are two different versions of the Registry Editor, one for Windows and one for real mode, because there aren't. It's the same executable file that runs in two different modes. To run the Registry Editor in real mode, start the computer in MS-DOS mode from the boot menu or by choosing **Restart in MS-DOS mode** from the Shut Down Windows dialog box. Then type regedit at the command prompt, followed by any command line arguments, and press Enter.

You can use the real mode Registry Editor to recover from problems when Windows 98 doesn't start properly. The command line arguments allow you to remove keys and import REG files. You can even use the real mode Registry Editor to replace the entire Registry using a REG file you created as a backup. Chapter 2, "Backing Up and Restoring the Registry," contains more information about backing up the Registry with REG files.

The Registry Editor's command line has four different forms, each of which you will learn more about in the following sections. This list describes the command line and each of its arguments as reported by the Registry Editor:

```
REGEDIT [/L:system] [/R:user] filename1

REGEDIT [/L:system] [/R:user] /C filename2

REGEDIT [/L:system] [/R:user] /E filename3 [regpath1]

REGEDIT [/L:system] [/R:user] /D regpath2
```

/L:system	Specifies the location of the System.dat file.
/R:user	Specifies the location of the User.dat file.
filename1	Specifies the file to import into the Registry.
/C filename2	Specifies the file to create the Registry from.
/E filename3	Specifies the file to export the Registry to.
regpath1	Specifies the starting Registry key to export from. (Defaults to exporting the entire Registry.)
/D regpath2	Specifies the Registry key to delete.

REGEDIT [/L:*system*] [/R:*user*] *filename1*

Use this form of the Registry Editor's command line to import one or more REG files into the Registry. /L specifies the location of System.dat, and /R specifies the location of User.dat. Both of these arguments are optional, allowing you to specify locations other than the default. You must use the /R argument if you enable user profiles on the computer, for example, to specify the actual location of the user's User.dat file. The Registry Editor imports each of the files it finds on the remainder of the command line.

REGEDIT [/L:*system*] [/R:*user*] /C *filename2*

This is the scariest form of the Registry Editor's command line. /C replaces the entire contents of the Registry with the contents of *filename2*. This is handy, however, if you've exported the entire Registry as a backup and you need to restore it using the real mode Registry Editor. (See Chapter 2, "Backing Up and Restoring the Registry.")

REGEDIT [/L:*system*] [/R:*user*] /E *filename3* [*regpath1*]

Use this form of the Registry Editor's command line to export the entire Registry or just a specific branch of the Registry to a REG file. /L and /R work as you read in the previous sections. /E specifies the name of the file into which you want to export the Registry. *regpath1* is the fully qualified name of the key that you want to export, including all its subkeys. If you want to export the entire Registry, leave out *regpath1*.

NOTE: The Emergency Startup Disk contains Regedit.exe, which is the same file you run when you launch the Registry Editor in Windows. When you boot the startup disk and run this program, you're running the Registry Editor in real mode.

Troubleshooting

The Registry Editor reports an error that says **Error accessing the Registry: The file may not be complete or Unable to open Registry (14) - System.dat** when you try to import the Registry using the /c argument. Due to a known problem in the real mode Registry Editor, you might get this error message when you try to import very large REG files using the /c switch. Microsoft acknowledges this problem but hasn't provided a solution yet. If you can start the Registry Editor in Windows, that's the best alternative. Otherwise, consider splitting the REG file into multiple sections, editing as necessary, and importing each one into the Registry.

TIP: Create a shortcut that contains the preceding command line so that you can back up a portion of the Registry by double-clicking the shortcut. You'll want to change the name of the REG file and branch to something useful, though. You can then restore this file in MS-DOS mode or within the Windows GUI using the Registry Editor command lines you learn about in this chapter.

```
REGEDIT [/L:system] [/R:user] /D regpath2
```

This form of the Registry Editor's command line removes a key from the Registry files indicated by /L and /R. *regpath2* is the fully qualified name of the key you want to remove, including all its subkeys. This command line can be destructive if you don't use it carefully. Consider exporting the branch you're removing to create a backup before actually removing it.

Using the Norton Registry Editor

Chapter 1, "Inside the Windows 98 Registry," gave you an overview of the different Registry tools you can use. One of those tools comes with Symantec's Norton Utilities and is called the Norton Registry Editor, a much more powerful editor than what comes with Windows 98. Take a look at Figure 3.7. The Key and Contents panes are similar to Windows 98's Registry Editor. The primary differences are that the Norton Registry Editor uses different icons to represent string, binary, and DWORD value entries in the Contents pane.

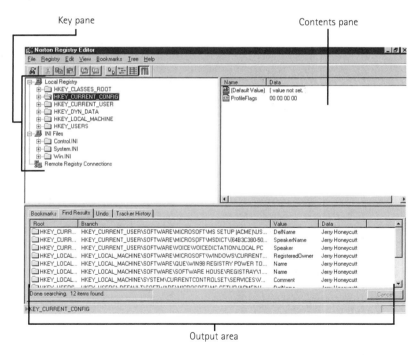

Figure 3.7 Click one of the tabs in the output area to see the results of Norton Registry Editor's unique features.

In the Key pane, you'll notice some new entries at the top of the outline. `Local Registry` is the same as `My Computer` in Windows 98's Registry Editor. `INI Files` contains an entry for each INI file that the Norton Registry Editor is tracking. In this manner, the Norton Registry Editor allows you to work with INI files as if they were part of the Registry. The last entry at the top of the outline is `Remote Registry Connections`, which contains an entry for each remote Registry to which you connect.

The bottom pane is unique to the Norton Registry Editor. It provides output from a number of different features. Click each tab to work with Bookmarks, Find Results, and Undo, for instance. You'll learn more about each of these features in the following sections, which describe what makes the Norton Registry Editor different from Windows 98's Registry Editor.

Find

The Find feature that the Norton Registry Editor provides is far more powerful than Windows 98's Registry Editor—and quicker, too. Press Ctrl+F to open the Find dialog box, and type the text for which you're searching in the space provided. If you click the Advanced tab, you can limit the search to specific branches in the Registry or specific portions such as key names, value names, or value data.

The best part of this feature is that it lists in the Find Results tab all the matches it finds, all at once (see Figure 3.7). Double-click any line in the Find Results tab to open it in the editor's Key pane. This allows you to move randomly through all the matches without having to start the search over again if you missed the value you're looking for.

NOTE: To use the Norton Registry Editor, you must first install Norton Utilities as described in Chapter 1, "Inside the Windows 98 Registry." An evaluation version of Norton Utilities is available from Symantec's Web site, `http://www.symantec.com`, or you can purchase the retail version at your local computer store. Once you've installed Norton Utilities, start the Norton Registry Editor by choosing **Start**, **Programs, Norton Utilities, Norton Registry Editor**.

NOTE: The Norton Registry Editor has a search-and-replace feature that you can use to scan the Registry for specific strings and replace them with other text. Press Ctrl+R, type the text you want to replace in the **Find What** box, and type the text you want to replace it with in the **Replace Where** box. As with the Norton Registry Editor's Find feature, you can limit the search-and-replace to specific root keys in the Registry, as well as specific portions of its anatomy, by clicking the Advanced tab and filling in the information.

Bookmarks

In the Norton Registry Editor, bookmarks work much like they work in a Web browser. They allow you to bookmark a certain Registry key, move to another portion of the Registry hierarchy, and return to the bookmarked key with just a few mouse clicks.

Right-click any key in the Key pane of the Norton Registry Editor, and choose **Bookmark This**. You see the bookmarked key on the Bookmarks tab of the output area, as shown in Figure 3.8. Explore other portions of the Registry. When you're ready to return to the bookmarked key, double-click its name on the Bookmarks tab of the output area. Note that you can bookmark as many keys as you like, because navigating the Bookmarks tab is easy.

Safety Features

The Undo tab of the output area contains a list of all the changes you've made using the Norton Registry Editor. You can undo any change by right-clicking it in the Undo tab and choosing **Undo**. Alternatively, press Ctrl+Z to undo changes in reverse order. That is, pressing Ctrl+Z undoes the most recent change, pressing Ctrl+Z again undoes the change before that, and so on.

One safety feature is the Read Only feature. It allows you to explore the Registry all you like without fear of messing things up. If you choose **Registry**, **Read Only**, you won't be able to change anything in the Registry. To enable changes, choose **Registry**, **Read Only** again to remove the checkmark next to the command.

SEE ALSO

➤ CHAPTER 1, "INSIDE THE WINDOWS 98 REGISTRY," DESCRIBES WHERE TO GET A COPY OF NORTON UTILITIES AND PROVIDES AN OVERVIEW OF ITS FEATURES.

➤ CHAPTER 4, "TROUBLESHOOTING THE REGISTRY," SHOWS YOU HOW TO USE NORTON WINDOCTOR TO MAKE REPAIRS TO THE REGISTRY, INCLUDING REMOVING ORPHANS FROM THE REGISTRY.

➤ CHAPTER 11, "TWEAK UI AND OTHER REGISTRY PROGRAMS," DESCRIBES AN ALTERNATIVE REGISTRY EDITOR CALLED SHELLWIZARD REGISTRY EDITOR. IT HAS FEATURES SIMILAR TO NORTON'S REGISTRY EDITOR AND A WHOLE LOT MORE.

Figure 3.8 The Bookmarks tab organizes bookmarks by root key.

➤ CHAPTER 12, "TRACKING DOWN REGISTRY SETTINGS," INTRODUCES YOU TO ANOTHER UNIQUE REGISTRY FEATURE IN NORTON UTILITIES CALLED REGISTRY TRACKER. THIS FEATURE ALLOWS YOU TO MONITOR CHANGES TO THE REGISTRY OVER A LONG PERIOD OF TIME.

TIP: The Norton Registry Editor supports shortcuts. It treats shortcuts like aliases. In other words, when you create a shortcut for a key, the Norton Registry Editor creates a root key for it that allows you to navigate to that particular branch from the top of the hierarchy. Create a shortcut to the key called HKEY_LOCAL_MACHINE\Software\Microsoft\Windows, for example, and you'll see a new root key by that name that gives you quick access to the entire branch. To create a shortcut, right-click any key and choose **Make Shortcut**.

NOTE: Probably the nicest feature of the Norton Registry Editor is its online help, which is more extensive than the help that comes with Windows 98's Registry Editor. Use this resource to learn more about the unique features found in the Norton Registry Editor and as a refresher when you forget the purpose of certain portions of the Registry.

4

Troubleshooting the Registry

In this chapter:

- Reviewing the Troubleshooting Tools
- Scanning the Registry for Errors: Registry Checker
- Cleaning Up the Registry with REGCLEAN
- Making Sense of Registry Error Messages
- Removing Restrictions That Prevent Registry Editing
- Optimizing the Registry for Performance and Space

Reviewing the Troubleshooting Tools

Microsoft produced a number of utilities for the Windows 95 Registry, none of which were built into the operating system; they were provided separately. CFGBACK made backup copies of the Registry, for example. REGCLEAN fixed a variety of common problems that mostly related to HKEY_CLASSES_ROOT. ERU made backup copies of the most important configuration files, including the Registry. You could even combine other tasks using the Registry Editor. For instance, it was common practice to compress the Registry by removing the Registry files and importing a REG file that you previously exported. You could back up the Registry, too, by exporting all or portions of it to a REG file.

With the exception of REGCLEAN, these utilities aren't necessary in Windows 98—nor are they even desirable—because Windows 98 provides the Registry Checker instead. This utility handles a variety of the tasks that you had to look elsewhere to perform in Windows 95. It automatically makes multiple backup copies of the Registry, providing a sort of version control for your configuration. It can also compress the Registry on demand, or you can let it compress the Registry automatically whenever it includes more than 500 KB of unused space. Last, and most important, Registry Checker scans the Registry for errors and can fix most errors that prevent Windows 98 from starting properly.

Registry Checker does have its limitations, however. It's not as robust as Norton WinDoctor, nor does it go as far as Norton Optimization Wizard does when optimizing the Registry for performance. For example, WinDoctor scans the Registry for orphaned values, which are values that refer to nonexistent files and Registry keys. Other programs that complement or replace the features of the Registry Checker include Tweak UI and the other shareware programs you'll learn about in Chapter 11, "Tweak UI and Other Registry Programs."

SEE ALSO

➤ Chapter 12, "Tracking Down Registry Settings," describes Norton Registry Tracker. You use this utility to monitor changes to the Registry.

➤ Chapter 3, "Using the Windows 98 Registry Editor," describes the Norton Registry Editor. It provides all the features of Windows 98's Registry Editor, but it adds variety of other features.

Using Registry Checker to Scan the Registry for Errors

Windows 98 provides two different versions of Registry Checker: a Windows version and a DOS-based version. The Windows version, whose filename is Scanregw.exe, scans the Registry for errors but doesn't fix them. It also determines whether the Registry requires optimization but again doesn't perform the optimization itself. Last, it backs up the Registry files, System.dat and User.dat, as well as System.ini and Win.ini to CAB files you find in \Windows\Sysbckup. The first backup is named Rb000.cab; the second is Rb001.cab, and so on. The file with the highest number is the most recent backup file; thus, Rb004.cab is a more recent backup than Rb002.cab.

> **TIP:** The *Microsoft Windows 98 Resource Kit* includes additional Registry tools that you might find useful when troubleshooting. These utilities allow you to edit the Registry from the MS-DOS command line.

If SCANREGW detects an error or detects that the Registry must be optimized, it prompts you to restart the computer. The DOS-based version, whose filename is Scanreg.exe (without the w), attempts to fix the Registry. It tries to restore the previous backup first, repairing the Registry only if it can't find a good backup. If SCAN-REGW determines that the Registry requires optimization, SCANREG optimizes the Registry the next time you start Windows 98. This is a bit much to remember, so look at Table 4.1. It summarizes all this so that you can remember the differences between SCANREGW and SCANREG.

Table 4.1 **SCANREGW Versus SCANREG**

Feature	SCANREGW	SCANREG
Runs automatically	Yes	Yes, if a problem is detected
Backs up the Registry	Yes	Yes
Compresses backups	Yes	No
Operating environment	Windows	MS-DOS
Repairs the Registry	No	Yes
Restores the Registry	No	Yes
Runs in Safe Mode	Yes	No
Scans the Registry	Yes	Yes

Both SCANREGW and SCANREG support similar command line options, all of which are listed in Table 4.2. /backup and /comment work in both versions of Registry Checker. /opt, /restore and /fix are available only with SCANREG, and /autorun and /scanonly are available only with SCANREGW.

Table 4.2 **SCANREGW and SCANREG Command Lines**

Switch	Description
/autorun	Automatically scans the Registry, but backs it up only once a day. You see this switch used in the Run key of HKEY_LOCAL_MACHINE.
/backup	Backs up the Registry without prompting the user. Backups are stored in CAB files that you find in \Windows\Sysbckup.
"/comment=x"	Associates a comment with the backup. Use this switch with /backup and be sure to enclose the entire switch in quotation marks.
/fix	Repairs the Registry.
/opt	Stands for "optimize." Compresses unused space.
/restore	Allows you to choose from a list of backup configurations that you can restore.
/scanonly	Scans the Registry and returns an error code. It doesn't back up or repair the Registry.

SEE ALSO

➤ Chapter 2, "Backing Up and Restoring the Registry," describes how to back up the Registry using SCANREGW. Remember that Registry Checker automatically makes one backup each day, but you can force it to make additional backups.

Scanning the Registry for Errors

The Windows-based Registry Checker scans for errors but doesn't fix them. You can launch it anytime by running Scanregw.exe. After scanning the Registry for errors, it asks you if you want to make an additional backup copy of the Registry. Click **Yes** if you want to. Otherwise, click **No**.

The DOS-based Registry Checker scans for and fixes errors. It reports its progress as it goes along. First, it tells you that it's looking for valid system Registry keys. Then it reports that it's checking the system Registry structure. Last, it reports that it's rebuilding the system Registry. To use SCANREG to fix errors in the Registry, follow these steps:

1. Start the computer in MS-DOS mode.

2. Type scanreg /fix at the command prompt. SCANREG runs, reporting its progress as just described.

3. Press Enter when SCANREG reports that Windows successfully fixed your Registry.

If SCANREG finishes without indicating that it successfully fixed the Registry, your problems are more serious than you thought. The only solution is to restore a backup copy of the Registry as described in Chapter 1, "Inside the Windows 98 Registry."

NOTE Each time you start Windows 98, it automatically launches Registry Checker to back up the Registry. This happens because HKEY_LOCAL_MACHINE\Software\Microsoft\Windows\ ➥CurrentVersion\Run contains C:\WINDOWS\scanregw.exe /autorun.

NOTE: SCANREG is the best utility you can use for fixing physical problems in the Registry. It's also the best utility you can use for backing up and restoring the Registry. It doesn't fix organizational problems such as orphans in the Registry, though. The best solution for this problem is a utility such as Norton WinDoctor.

Compressing the Registry

Registry Checker has an undocumented feature that allows you to optimize the Registry. Registry Checker compresses the Registry whenever it detects that it has over 500 KB of dead space, making the file smaller and slightly faster to access. To get an idea of the amount of space you can save, take a look at the following table, which shows you how much space you can save by compressing the Registry. Doing so compressed over 100 KB out of System.dat but didn't save any space in User.dat. Your results will vary, depending on the amount of unused space in each file.

File	Before	After
System.dat	1,740,832	1,630,240
User.dat	221,216	221,216

You can force Registry Checker to optimize the Registry using the /opt command line option. This works only with the DOS-based version of Registry Checker, SCANREG. Remember also that you can't run the DOS-based version in Windows, so you must boot the computer to MS-DOS mode. Thus, use the following steps to optimize the Registry:

1. Start the computer in MS-DOS mode. To do so, choose **Command Prompt Only** from the boot menu, or choose **Start, Sh<u>u</u>t Down**. Then select **Restart in <u>M</u>S-DOS mode** and click **OK**.

2. Type scanreg /opt at the command prompt. SCANREG runs but doesn't report its progress. It just exits to the command prompt.

Refining Registry Checker's Configuration

Both versions of Registry Checker, SCANREGW and SCANREG, load settings from Scanreg.ini. Table 4.3 describes the settings you can change in this file. The most interesting settings include MaxBackupCopies and Files. The first controls the number of backups that the Registry keeps. The first backup is the first one to be deleted. The default value for this setting is 5, which is a bit small if you want to make sure you can always recover from configuration problems. Sometimes you can go several days before noticing that Windows 98 has a problem. By then, Registry Checker has already replaced the last good backup copy of your configuration with a broken copy.

Troubleshooting

I received an error from Registry Checker that reports: Windows found an error in your system files and was unable to fix the problem. You will need to install Windows to a new directory. Don't panic. Although this error message can indicate a serious problem, make sure you have enough disk space for Registry Checker to store a backup copy of your configuration. Registry Checker erroneously displays this message if it doesn't have enough disk space to create the CAB file containing your configuration backup, which is usually less than 5 MB.

Table 4.3   **Settings in Scanreg.ini**

Setting	Description
Backup=[0¦1]	Specifies whether to run SCANREGW each time Windows 98 starts, backing up the Registry. The default value is 1, meaning that the Registry Checker backs up the Registry once each day. 0 = Don't run SCANREGW at startup 1 = Run SCANREGW at startup
Optimize=[0¦1]	Specifies whether to automatically optimize the Registry. The default value is 1, meaning that Registry Checker optimizes the Registry as required. 0 = Don't automatically optimize 1 = Automatically optimize
MaxBackupCopes=x	Specifies the maximum number of backup copies to make of the Registry each time Windows 98 starts. The default value is 5, meaning that Registry Checker keeps only five backup copies. Possible values are 0 to 99.
BackupDirectory=x	Specifies the location in which to store the CAB files containing the configuration backup. The default value is \Windows\Sysbckup. If you use this setting, you must provide a full path starting from the root folder.
Files=[code,]f1,f2	Specifies additional files to include in the configuration backup. You can include this setting as many times as required. Table 4.4 describes the directory codes you can use for *code*.

Files allows you to specify additional configuration files you want to include in each backup. By default, Registry Checker backs up System.ini and Win.ini, but what if you want to include Protocol.ini or your Autoexec.bat file? The syntax looks like this:

```
Files=[dir code,]file1,file2,file3
```

dir code is one of the codes listed in Table 4.4. These codes indicate the location of the configuration file. Note that code 31 is useful only if you're using Registry Checker on a computer with compressed volumes. To back up Protocol.ini from \Windows, for example, you'd write a line like this:

```
Files=10,protocol.ini
```

You can include more than one file in each statement, each separated by a comma.

Table 4.4   **Values for** dir code

Code	Directory	Example
10	Windows installation folder	\Windows
11	Windows system folder	\Windows\System
30	Boot drive	C:\
31	Boot host folder	H:\

Cleaning Up the Registry with REGCLEAN

Microsoft provides a free utility called REGCLEAN that you can use to clean up the contents of the Registry. Although Microsoft provided this utility for Windows 95, it should work equally well with Windows 98. You can download REGCLEAN from Microsoft's Web site or from any of the shareware software sites described in Chapter 11, Once you've downloaded the file, sometimes called Regcln41.exe, launch it to extract its contents into C:\Program Files\RegClean. You can copy a shortcut for Regclean.exe to the Start button.

REGCLEAN works only with Registry keys about which it has previous knowledge. This includes keys common to all versions of Windows and Microsoft Office. It looks for orphans, for example, which you'll learn about later in this chapter. Most of the work that REGCLEAN does is in HKEY_CLASSES_ROOT, HKEY_CLASSES_ROOT\Classes, and HKEY_CLASSES_ROOT\Classes\TypeLib. REGCLEAN has some very important limitations that might cause you to use a different utility for this purpose:

- It doesn't fix orphans. It just removes any Registry keys or values that contain orphans.

- REGCLEAN works only on Registry keys that belong to Windows 98 or Microsoft Office. It doesn't help with Registry keys belonging to other products.

With those caveats out of the way, here's how to use REGCLEAN to clean up the Registry:

1. Start REGCLEAN. REGCLEAN scans the disk for errors, which can take quite a long time. You see the window shown in Figure 4.1.

2. Click **Fix Errors** to make the changes that REGCLEAN recommends. If you aren't sure, click **Cancel**.

3. Open the REG file that REGCLEAN created in the same folder it's installed in. The filename begins with the word Undo. This REG file indicates any Registry keys that REGCLEAN removed from the Registry. If the file is empty, you're finished. If the file contains keys, start over again with step 1. Microsoft states that you might have to run REGCLEAN numerous times before it completely cleans the Registry.

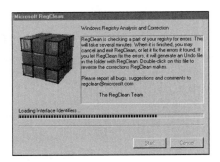

Figure 4.1 REGCLEAN was written for Windows 95, but it works equally well in Windows 98 since the Registry's organization hasn't changed much.

If you find that you want to undo the changes that REGCLEAN makes, you can merge the REG files it created back into the Registry. Each filename has the format Undo *computername date time*.reg and is in the same folder that contains Regclean.exe. Double-click each file, or right-click each file and choose **Merge**.

Making Sense of Registry Error Messages

This section describes a variety of error messages that are related to the Windows 98 Registry. For your convenience, I've separated them into the following six categories:

- **Starting Windows 98**   Errors that occur while the operating system is booting.
- **Editing the Registry**   Errors that occur while you're editing the Registry using the Windows 98 Registry Editor. If you're using a different editor, you might see different but similar messages.

CAUTION: Don't use REGCLEAN if the Registry is corrupted. Use Registry Checker to fix the Registry first, because REGCLEAN only cleans up the Registry's contents and relies on a working Registry.

Check Out the Author's Registry

My Web site, http://www.honeycutt.com, contains the Registry from one of my computers. After installing a fresh copy of Windows 98, I exported the entire Registry to a file called Registry.reg.

Borrow what you need from these files. You can use them in cases where the tools described in this chapter aren't helping you fix the Registry and you need a reference to see what a particular branch of the Registry contains. In some cases, you can copy a key or value from the Registry.reg file on my Web site, build a new REG file that contains it, and import the file into your Registry. Use a bit of common sense when doing this, however. You wouldn't want to import the hardware settings from Registry.reg unless you knew for sure those settings matched your own configuration.

- **Importing and exporting REG files** Errors that occur while you're importing a REG file or exporting the Registry to a REG file.

- **Using the real mode Registry Editor** Errors that occur when you're using the real mode Registry Editor in MS-DOS mode. These errors typically occur when you're importing or exporting the Registry.

- **Working with remote registries** Errors that occur when you're editing a remote Registry. These errors typically occur because you haven't configured remote administration correctly, as described in Chapter 13, "Security and Remote Administration."

- **Using Registry Checker** Errors that occur when you're using the Registry Checker to back up, scan, or fix problems in the Registry. These errors overlap errors starting Windows 98 just a bit, since many of the Registry errors you see while starting Windows 98 are actually reported by SCANREGW.

The following sections contain a number of paragraphs that have an error message followed by a description of the error and a solution for it. In many cases, an error message can end several different ways. In these cases, you see a bulleted list describing each of the possible endings.

Starting Windows 98

Use the following general troubleshooting tips to fix Registry errors that occur as Windows 98 starts:

- Make sure you have a valid Msdos.sys file. If this file becomes corrupt or is missing, Windows 98 can sometimes report Registry errors, even though such messages are erroneous. My Web site, http://www.honeycutt.com, contains an Msdos.sys file that you can copy to the root folder of your boot drive. I named the file Msdos-sys so it wouldn't be hidden in Explorer. Rename it Msdos.sys and copy it to the root folder of your computer's boot disk.

- Scan the Registry for errors using the DOS-based Registry Checker, SCAN-REG. You learned how to use this utility earlier in this chapter. In short, start the computer in MS-DOS mode and type `scanreg /fix` at the command prompt. After running SCANREG, restart the computer.

- Use one of the third-party tools available for fixing a corrupt Registry. A good choice is Norton WinDoctor, a utility that can fix a variety of Registry problems. You'll learn about WinDoctor later in this chapter.

> **TIP:** How did I figure out all the possible error messages? I didn't create errors to see what would happen; I'd never discover all the possible messages. Instead, I used a nifty program called Programmer's Assistant to display a list of all the text messages contained in EXE and DLL files such as Regedit.exe and Kernel32.dll. You can download a copy of Programmer's Assistant from http://www.hotfiles.com.

Error Accessing the System Registry. You should restore the Registry now and restart your computer. My experience suggests that·you can sometimes get past this error message, eventually, if you keep restarting the computer when you see it. I have no explanation for this, but it's worth rebooting the computer a few times to make sure you don't lose any settings. Otherwise, click the **Restore** button to restore the Registry and restart the computer. You'll lose any settings you've changed between backups.

Warning: Windows has detected a registry/configuration error. Choose Command prompt only, and run SCANREG. You might see an additional message similar to the preceding one. If so, click the **Restore** button; otherwise, restore your previous Registry using the DOS-based Registry Checker as described earlier in this chapter. **Registry file was not found. Registry services may not be operative for this session.** Where are your Registry files? If you didn't intentionally hide them from Windows, you must restore the most recent backup using the DOS-based Registry Checker.

Windows was unable to process the registry. This may be fixed by rebooting to Command Prompt Only and running SCANREG /FIX. Otherwise there may not be enough free conventional memory to properly load the registry. In most cases, you should look for other error messages, because low memory is not the problem. If you really are running low on memory, consider freeing conventional memory by removing device drivers from Config.sys and Autoexec.bat or by relocating them into upper memory. Otherwise, do as the message says and type scanreg /fix at the command prompt after starting in MS-DOS mode.

The windows registry or SYSTEM.INI file refers to this device file, but the device file no longer exists. This occurs for a variety of reasons, the most common of which is an errant uninstall program or the manual removal of a program from the computer. The later section "Removing Orphans from the Registry" contains more information about locating and removing from the Registry references to files that no longer exist.

Registry File was replaced with backup copy. Changes made in last session may be missing. Windows 98 didn't give you much choice. The operating system took it upon itself to restore the backup copy of the Registry, causing you to lose any, configuration changes made between backups.

> **TIP:** Some errors you see when Windows 98 starts are misleading—particularly if you see numerous messages, one after another. Address the most logical problem first, and the rest of the errors will most likely go away.

Editing the Registry

Most of the error messages you see while editing the Registry have two causes. The most likely cause is that you're trying to do something with a key or value that another process has open or has already removed. If you're viewing a particular branch in the Registry, for instance, and another program removes a key in that branch, you'll still see the key in the Registry Editor window even though it doesn't exist anymore. When you try to do something with that key, the Registry Editor displays an error message. To make sure the key still exists, press F5 to update the Registry Editor's display. Another likely cause is that you're trying to do something with a dynamic key or value, such as those in HKEY_DYN_DATA. The only thing I can tell you about editing dynamic keys and values is this: *don't*.

Cannot create key: *error message*. The cause of this error depends on the rest of the message:

- **Error while opening the key *name*** Either you don't have permission to edit this particular key, or you're trying to add a subkey to a key that another program deleted in the background. Refresh the Registry Editor by pressing F5 so that you can tell if a program did indeed remove the key.

- **Error writing to the registry** If you try to create a new key underneath one of the dynamic keys in HKEY_DYN_DATA, you'll get this error message. Remember that you can't edit dynamic keys.

- **Unable to generate a unique name** I would be surprised if you ever see this message. It means that the Registry Editor wasn't able to create a unique name for the key, such as New Key #1.

Cannot create value: *error message*. This error message is similar to the one you get when creating a new key. *Error message* is Error writing to the registry if you're trying to create a value in a key that no longer exists or that is dynamic. If you're not trying to create a value in a dynamic key, refresh the Registry by pressing F5 to make sure the key still exists. As far as Unable to generate a unique name, the same goes for values as it does keys: The Registry Editor wasn't able to create a unique name for the value, such as New Value #1.

> NOTE: I found the text for the error messages in this section within two files: Io.sys and Vmm32.vxd. Both files are critical components that Windows 98 loads as it starts. Both are also in MS-DOS executable format, so the only way to extract error messages from these files is to open them in a text editor such as Notepad, ignore the binary garbage, and browse the file, looking for bits of text. Alternatively, you can view both these files in Quick View or any other text editor.

> NOTE: The Registry Editor will allow you to remove an entire key containing dynamic data. Windows 98 will rebuild this information after you restart your computer, however.

Cannot edit *name*: *error message*. The meaning of this error depends on the rest of the message:

- **Error reading the value's contents**   This error message indicates that a Registry key is in use by another process. To avoid this message, close the process that's using the key. Another likely possibility is that another process has removed the key, in which case you can refresh the Registry by pressing F5.

- **Error writing the value's new contents**   This message implies that you're trying to write to one of many dynamic values. Don't do that.

Cannot open *name*: **Error while opening key.** The most likely cause is that you're trying to open a key that another process removed. Remember that just because you see a key in the Registry Editor doesn't mean that another process might not have removed it. To make sure, press F5 to refresh the Registry Editor's display. Another possibility is that the key you're trying to open is corrupted. The only plausible solution to this problem, if indeed the key is corrupt, is to use the Registry Checker to repair the Registry, as described earlier in this chapter.

Cannot rename *name*: *error message*. The reason behind this message depends on the rest of the message:

- **Error while renaming key. or Error while renaming value**   These generally mean that you're trying to rename a dynamic key or value. Don't do that.

- **The specified key name already exists. Type another name and try again**   This message means you're using a name that already exists. Each subkey name within a key must be unique. Likewise, the message The specified value name already exists. Type another name and try again. means you're using a value name that already exists within that same key.

- **The specified key name contains illegal character**   This message implies that you're using a backslash (\) somewhere in the key's name. Don't do that.

- **The specified key name is too long. Type a shorter name and try again**   This error means you're trying to use a name longer than 255 characters. Use a shorter key name. Remember also that creating a key with no certainty that a program will use it is as senseless as it is useless.

Cannot delete *name*: **Error while deleting key.** Remember that you can't remove dynamic keys from the Registry. Thus, don't try to remove keys from HKEY_DYN_DATA. You also see this error message if you try to remove a key after another process has already beaten you to it. Press F5 to refresh the display, verifying that the key does or doesn't exist. Unable to delete all specified values. is a reminder that you can't delete the default value entry for any Registry key. You can delete the default value entry's contents or, if the default value entry is the only item remaining for the key, remove the key itself. You can't delete dynamic values either, so you'll see this error whenever you try to remove a key from HKEY_DYN_DATA.

Cannot print: *error message.* The reason behind this message depends on the rest of the message. In either of the following cases, follow the instructions that the error message gives you in order to solve the problem:

- **Insufficient memory to begin job. Try closing down some applications, and try again. If you still see this message, try restarting Windows.**

- **An error occurred during printing. Check your printer and your printer's settings for problems, and try again.**

Registry Editor: Registry editing has been disabled by your administrator. The system administrator has disabled the Registry Editor using system policies. Chapter 13, tells you more about using the **Disable Registry Editing Tools** policy. If you must unlock this policy so that you can edit the Registry, see the later section "Removing Restrictions That Prevent Registry Editing."

SEE ALSO
➤ Chapter 13, tells you more about preventing users from using the Registry tools.

Importing and Exporting REG Files

Most of the problems you encounter when importing and exporting the Registry come from two sources. First, the path and filename might be invalid. Second (and most likely), the REG file might be invalid, especially if you create it by hand. Look for these two problems when you get any error message during an import or export operation.

Cannot import *filename***:** *error message.* The meaning behind this error depends on the rest of the message:

- **Error accessing the Registry**   For some reason, the Registry Editor is unable to access the Registry. Make sure that if you're editing a remote Registry, you have permission to do so, and make sure that the Registry files are in place if you're working with a local Registry. Otherwise, open the Registry Editor and inspect the Registry to make sure it is indeed okay. If you suspect corruption, run SCANREG with the /fix option to repair the Registry.

- **Error writing to the Registry**   This means that you're trying to import data into a corrupt or dynamic Registry key. If you suspect the Registry key is corrupt, run SCANREG with the /fix options. Remember that you can't import values into HKEY_DYN_DATA.

- **Error opening the file. There may be a disk or file system error**   First, double-check the filename. If you're importing a filename that contains spaces from an MS-DOS command line or the Run dialog box, you'll see this error message when you forget to surround the filename with spaces. If the filename isn't the problem, try opening the file in Notepad. Also run ScanDisk to check the file system for errors. You might have to use a stronger utility such as Norton Disk Doctor to fix this problem, particularly if ScanDisk doesn't fix it.

- **Error reading the file. There may be a disk error or the file may be corrupt** This error is similar to the preceding one, except that the Registry Editor can open the file; it just can't read it. Try reading the REG file in Notepad. Can you see its entire contents in the editor window? Also run ScanDisk to check the file system for errors. If you can read the file using Notepad, but you can't import the file into the Registry, you have a more serious problem, and a utility such as Norton Disk Doctor might be able to fix it.

- **The specified file is not a Registry script. You can import only Registry files** This means you're trying to import a REG file that's invalid. If you're definitely importing a REG file, make sure it's not damaged. Double-check Chapter 15, "Script, REG, and INF Files," to make sure you're using the correct format for REG files. Also make sure that you have REGEDIT4 on the very first line of the file and that the second line is blank.

Cannot export *filename*: Error writing the file. There may be a disk or file system error. Again, double-check the path and filename that you're specifying. Also make sure that you have enough space on the disk to create the file. Other than that, this error usually indicates a more serious problem that involves the file system. Run ScanDisk or Norton Disk Doctor to look for errors in the file system.

Using the Real Mode Registry Editor

Chapter 3, "Using the Windows 98 Registry Editor," describes the difference between the Windows-based Registry Editor and the DOS-based real mode Registry Editor. In short, you can run the real mode Registry only in MS-DOS mode. The only real use for the real mode Registry Editor is to import REG files into the Registry or to export portions of the Registry to a REG file.

Cannot open *filename*. The REG file you're trying to import doesn't exist or doesn't contain valid information. Make sure the format of the REG file is correct, starting with REGEDIT4 followed by a blank line. Also make sure that you're not missing any brackets ([]). Last, make sure you double-check the filename. If the path contains spaces, enclose it in quotation marks.

> **TIP:** If you suspect that a particular Registry branch is corrupt, try removing that branch from the Registry. Back up the Registry first. If you can export that branch to a REG file before removing it, that's even better. That way, you can restore the REG file after removing the branch. You might also consider optimizing the Registry using Registry Checker's /opt switch to recover any dead space before importing the REG file you created as a backup. This and other creative techniques can usually help you salvage a damaged Registry, but in most cases you're better off restoring a recent backup copy.

Cannot import *filename*: *error message*. The meaning of this error depends on the rest of the message. The messages you see when importing a REG file using the real mode Registry Editor are the same as when you're using the Windows-based Registry Editor. The preceding section describes these messages and tells you what to do about them.

Cannot export *filename*: *error message*. The meaning of this error depends on the rest of the error message. The following two messages are unique to the real mode Registry Editor (the preceding section describes any remaining error messages you might see):

- **Error creating the file**   This error message means that you should double-check the filename, making sure that you enclose paths that have spaces in quotation marks. Also, make sure you have enough disk space for the REG file.

- **The specified key name does not exist**   This message means that you're trying to export or delete a key that doesn't exist. Double-check the command line.

Error accessing the Registry: The file may not be complete. The real mode Registry Editor reports this message if you try to import a REG file that's too big. There might not be enough memory available to import the file. Try freeing additional conventional memory by starting the computer with a minimal configuration. Optionally, split the REG file into multiple REG files using a text editor, and then import each REG file separately.

The real mode Registry Editor reports a variety of error messages if you don't get the command line just right:

- Invalid switch

- Parameter format not correct

- Required parameter missing

- Too many parameters

In all of these cases, check Chapter 3, or type `regedit /?` at the command prompt to make sure you're using the correct command line.

Data Is Missing from the Registry

It's a common complaint: "I imported a REG file, but the data is missing from the Registry." The leading cause of this problem is a REG file that isn't using the correct format or has syntax errors. Refer to Chapter 15, to make sure you're using the correct format.

Here are some other notes to help you locate problems in a REG file. Make sure you're not missing any brackets around key names: [HKEY_LOCAL_MACHINE\SOFTWARE]. Make sure you enclose each value name in quotation marks. Use @ to indicate the default value entry. Check the format used for string, binary, and DWORD values. Enclose string values in quotation marks, and prefix DWORD values with DWORD:.

Working with Remote Registries

You cannot connect to your own computer. This error message is self-explanatory. If you want to edit the local Registry, you don't need to try connecting to it by choosing **Registry**, **Connect**.

Error Connecting Network Registry. The Registry Editor reports this error message when it can't connect to the remote computer's Registry. This error is vague and applies to situations in which the other error messages don't apply. In general, double-check the same old things. Make sure you have permission to connect to the remote computer's Registry. Double-check that remote administration is enabled on the remote computer. Also make sure that both computers are running the Microsoft Remote Registry Service.

Unable to connect to _name_. Make sure that this computer is on the network, has remote administration enabled, and that both computers are running the remote registry service. Follow the instructions in this error message to fix the problem. Beyond that, make sure that your own network connection is working properly.

Unable to connect to all of the roots of the computer's registry. Disconnect from the remote registry and then reconnect before trying again. I've never seen this error message when connecting to another Windows 98 Registry. I _have_ seen it when connecting to a Windows NT Registry, however. This is just an indication that you don't have permission to connect to one or more of the root keys in that Registry.

Unable to connect to _name_. Make sure you have permission to administer this computer. As this message states, you probably don't have permission to connect to the remote computer's Registry. Double-check the remote administration settings on the remote computer. You might also double-check that you're a member of the appropriate administrative groups on the server.

Using Registry Checker

Invalid command line parameter. Take another look at the earlier section "Using the Registry Checker to Scan the Registry for Errors" to make sure you understand each of Registry Checker's command line options.

The registry file _filename_ is damaged. This doesn't necessarily mean that you should abandon hope. Registry Checker reports this error when it detects a problem. It then restores the most recent backup copy of the Registry or tries to repair the Registry.

Windows encountered an error accessing the system registry. Windows will restart and repair the system registry for you. Each time you start Windows 98, it runs Registry Checker, which scans the Registry for errors. If Registry Checker finds any errors, it returns this error message. Then it restarts the computer and runs the MS-DOS version of Registry Checker in order to repair the Registry.

`Unable to scan the system registry.` If you see this error message or `Unable to scan the registry file` *filename.*, repairing the Registry is probably beyond hope. Your best bet is to restore the most recent backup copy and move on.

Removing Restrictions That Prevent Registry Editing

If you've been playing with the System Policy Editor, shown in Figure 4.2, you might have set a policy that locked you out of the Registry Editor: **Disable Registry editing tools**. That, or the system administrator might have intentionally locked you out of the Registry Editor. The problem is that you must have access to the Registry in order to remove this restriction, but you don't have access to the Registry because of it. Microsoft's documentation indicates that there isn't an alternative to this problem other than reinstalling Windows 98 or restoring a backup copy of the Registry.

Not so fast.

Windows 98 lets you change the Registry even though this restriction is in place. You can import REG files even when this policy is active. Thus, you can add or change any value in the Registry by creating a REG file and importing it, even though you can't use the Registry Editor to change the Registry. This behavior is by design, in case you're wondering. Many applications use REG files to import their settings into the Registry, and locking out REG files would prevent you from installing those programs. Note that you'll find this listing on my Web site at `http://www.honey-cutt.com`.

Listing 4.1 shows the REG file you must create in order to remove the restrictions that prevent you from editing the Registry with Registry Editor. Type it in exactly as shown, and save it to a file called Unlock.reg. Then double-click Unlock.reg, or right-click it and choose **Merge**.

Figure 4.2 Some rather draconian policies in the System Policy Editor can prevent you from doing anything but a single task.

Listing 4.1 **Removing Restrictions from the Registry**

```
REGEDIT4

[HKEY_CURRENT_USER]\Software\Microsoft\Windows\
➥CurrentVersion\Policies\Explorer]
"RestrictRun"=dword:00000000

[HKEY_CURRENT_USER]\Software\Microsoft\Windows\
➥CurrentVersion\Policies\System]
"DisableRegistryTools"=dword:00000000
```

Optimizing the Registry for Performance and Space

Prior to Windows 98, compressing the Registry was a formidable task that involved the following steps:

1. Exporting the Registry to a REG file.

2. Importing the Registry using the /c switch, which caused the Registry Editor to replace the entire contents of the Registry with the contents of the REG file you exported in step 1.

Windows 98 provides a number of alternatives, however, including Registry Checker. You learned how to compress the Registry using the Registry Checker earlier in this chapter. You can also use Norton Optimization Wizard, which does a better job of compressing the Registry than the Registry Checker does. The following instructions pertain to Norton Utilities 3.0.

1. Launch Norton Optimization Wizard. Choose **Start**, **Programs**, **Norton Utilities**, **Norton Optimization Wizard**.

2. Skip to the Optimize Your Registry page of the wizard. Select **Optimize my Registry** and click **Next**.

3. Click **Reboot**. Norton Optimization Wizard will optimize the Registry and restart Windows 98. Make sure you don't have any applications open on the desktop when you click **Reboot**.

SEE ALSO

➤ Chapter 11, describes how you can download an evaluation version of Norton Utilities. You can also purchase Norton Utilities from most computer retailers and online retailers such as http://www.software.net.

Defragmenting the Disk

In an ideal world, every portion of every file would be stored on the hard disk contiguously. *Fragmentation* occurs when the file system can't find a contiguous area on the disk in which to store the entire file, so it puts a portion of the file in one location, another portion in another location, and so on. The *file allocation table* (FAT) helps the file system put the file back together again by indicating the series of *clusters,* in order, that contain all of the file's pieces.

Fragmentation adversely affects the Registry. The Registry is big and one of the most-used files on the hard disk. Given that the operating system relies on it so much, you'll notice a performance penalty if the Registry becomes severely fragmented.

Windows 98 includes a utility called Disk Defragmenter to defragment files on the hard disk. It doesn't defragment system files, however, so it skips the Registry. Windows 98 doesn't let you remove the system attribute from these files, either, or you could do so before running Disk Defragmenter. Norton Speed Disk (see Figure 4.3) does optimize the Registry, though, as well as the Windows 98 swap file. You launch it by choosing **Start**, **Programs**, **Norton Utilities**, **Speed Disk**. You can customize Speed Disk by clicking **Properties** and then choosing **Options**.

Removing File Types You Don't Use

Removing unused file types won't save a lot of space in the Registry, but it *will* tidy things up a bit and help make navigating HKEY_CLASSES_ROOT a bit easier. The best way to remove unused file types from the Registry is to use the Folder Options dialog box in Windows Explorer:

1. Choose **View**, **Folder Options**. You see the Folder Options dialog box.

2. Click the File Types tab to see a list of registered file types.

3. Remove each file type that you no longer require. Do so by highlighting the file type in the list and clicking **Remove**. The **File type details** area describes the file type so that you can figure out what program opens it.

If you have a number of file types that refer to programs you removed from the computer, you have orphans in the Registry. The next section describes how to remove orphaned Registry keys in a more-or-less automatic manner.

NOTE: Size Doesn't Matter. Compressing the Registry so that the files are smaller doesn't improve Windows 98's performance appreciably. The only real benefit of compressing the Registry is that backing up the Registry is quicker, requiring less space.

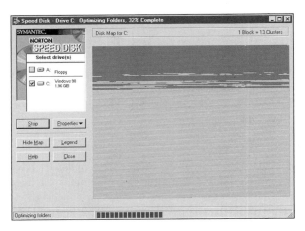

Figure 4.3 Norton Speed Disk defragments the space occupied by the Registry; Windows 98's Disk Defragmenter does not.

Removing Orphans from the Registry

Orphans are Registry keys that point to nonexistent files or other nonexistent Registry keys. They occur when programs don't clean up after themselves or when you manually remove a program from the computer. Uninstall programs don't always remove all of the application's Registry settings, for instance, leaving values that frequently point to missing files. Vendors such as Microsoft think they're doing you a favor by leaving these orphans, so that when you reinstall the program, it can use your previous configuration.

In most cases, nothing bad happens as a result of orphans; they just clutter up the Registry and waste a small bit of space. In other cases, orphans wreak havoc with your computer system:

- If a program leaves a key in `PropertySheetHandlers` that points to a missing DLL, the property sheet for that object might not work correctly.
- If a program leaves a reference to a device driver after removing the device driver from the disk, Windows 98 will report an error when it starts.

REGCLEAN, which you learned about earlier in this chapter, can fix a small number of orphans related specifically to Windows 98 and Microsoft Office, but it doesn't go as far as Norton WinDoctor. WinDoctor checks for orphans in all portions of the Registry, including `HKEY_CLASSES_ROOT`, `Application Paths`, `Run`, `VxD`, and much more. The best part is that Norton WinDoctor detects when an orphan points to a file or folder that you moved and fixes the value accordingly. Don't confuse WinDoctor with System Doctor. System Doctor monitors your computer in real time, while WinDoctor proactively probes your computer, looking for and fixing problems. Here's how to use it to repair orphans in the Registry:

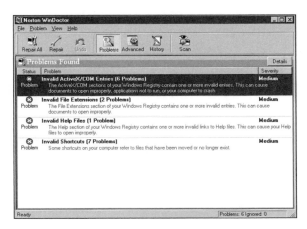

Figure 4.4 Norton WinDoctor is the best utility for repairing the contents of the Registry and finding orphans.

1. Start Norton WinDoctor. Choose **Start**, **Programs**, **Norton Utilities**, **Norton WinDoctor**.

2. Choose **Perform All Norton WinDoctor Tests (Recommended)** and click **Next**.

3. Click **Next** after Norton WinDoctor finishes scanning for errors, and then click **Finish**. Norton WinDoctor displays a list of the errors it found, as shown in Figure 4.4.

4. Double-click each item in the list to repair it.

SEE ALSO

➤ See Chapter 10, "Fixing Common Problems Via the Registry," to remove a VXD from the Registry when Windows 98 displays an error at startup.

CAUTION: Norton WinDoctor doesn't remove orphans that point to removable drives or network volumes. It assumes that these files are temporarily unavailable but that they might be available again at a later time. If you want to remove these orphans, you must replace step 2 in the preceding instructions with the following: Choose **Let me choose which tests to run**, click **Analysis Agents** in the following window, and deselect **Ignore missing files on removable drives and UNC paths**.

B

Exploring the Registry

HKEY_CLASSES_ROOT

The Bigger Picture

Remember *aliases* from Chapter 1? HKEY_CLASSES_ROOT is an alias for
HKEY_LOCAL_MACHINE\Software\Classes. That means that any change you make to
HKEY_CLASSES_ROOT is actually made in \CLASSES. Likewise, HKEY_CLASSES_ROOT reflects
any changes you make in \CLASSES. The pragmatic reason that this alias exists is for
backward compatibility with Windows 3.1. Yes, Windows 3.1 did have a Registry,
which it used for OLE, DDE, and related settings. As far as you're concerned, though,
HKEY_CLASSES_ROOT just makes getting to this information quicker since you don't have
to click your way to \CLASSES.

HKEY_CLASSES_ROOT is the single largest branch in the Registry. On a test computer,
I found that this branch contained over 50 percent of the Registry's data. You can

verify this fact yourself by exporting HKEY_CLASSES_ROOT to a REG file called Classes.reg and exporting the entire Registry to another REG file called All.reg. Divide the file size of Classes.reg by the file size of All.reg to figure out how much of the Registry is HKEY_CLASSES_ROOT. In my case, Classes.reg was 2.69 MB and All.reg was 5.23 MB.

HKEY_CLASSES_ROOT contains thousands upon thousands of keys and values that associate file extensions with programs, define COM (*Component Object Model*) classes, and much more. If you look closely at this branch, you'll notice two different types of subkeys. The subkeys toward the top, with the exception of the * subkey, are called *filename extension subkeys,* and they all begin with a period. They look like normal MS-DOS file extensions: .*ext*. They can contain any number of characters. Examples are .bat, .doc, and .html. * and the subkeys toward the bottom of HKEY_CLASSES_ROOT are *class definition subkeys,* and they include program identifiers and class identifiers:

- **Program identifiers** are subkeys in HKEY_CLASSES_ROOT that define the actions a program can perform on a file. Examples are batfile, docfile, and inifile. Some program identifiers also associate a program with a COM class. These are like aliases that make accessing a class easier. Examples are Word.Document.8 and Excel.Sheet.8.

- **Class identifiers** uniquely identify a COM class such as an ActiveX control. HKEY_CLASSES_ROOT\CLSID contains all the class identifiers. Each class identifier is a globally unique 16-byte number. An example is {3B7C8860-D78F-101B-B9B5-04021C009402}. Windows 98 uses class identifiers extensively.

You'll learn much more about filename extension subkeys and class definitions in the following sections. "Miscellaneous Subkeys in HKEY_CLASSES_ROOT" describes a number of subkeys that you frequently find under both types of keys.

SEE ALSO
➤ Chapter 1, "Inside the Windows 98 Registry," describes other aliases in the Registry.

➤ Chapter 3, "Using the Windows 98 Registry Editor," shows you how to export all or part of the Registry to a REG file so that you can compare the size of HKEY_CLASSES_ROOT to the entire Registry, as described in this section.

NOTE: When you install Windows 98, it registers a large number of filename extension and class definition subkeys. Also, most applications register filename extensions and class definitions during installation.

NOTE: Some programs store user preferences in HKEY_CLASSES_ROOT. It might seem odd to see \Software\Progressive Networks\RealAudio Player in this branch, for instance, but its presence is not necessarily an error. Some vendors, such as Progressive Networks, must create programs that work in both Windows 3.1 and Windows 98. In order to do that, the vendor writes its configuration data to HKEY_CLASSES_ROOT, the only root key that Windows 3.1 provides. In other words, *just live with it.*

Filename Extension Subkeys

Anytime Windows 98 accesses a file, whether it's to open the file or display information about it in Windows Explorer, the operating system looks up the file's extension under HKEY_CLASSES_ROOT. If you open a DOC file, for example, Windows 98 looks up .doc. The filename extension subkey doesn't contain enough information to tell the operating system much about the file, however, so the operating system looks in the filename extension's default value entry for the name of a program identifier, a class definition subkey, that does contain more information. Look up the default value in .dll and you'll see that DLL files are associated with dllfile. You find the program identifier's subkey in the same place as the file extension: under HKEY_CLASSES_ROOT. Figure 5.1 illustrates the relationship by showing how AVI files are associated with the avifile program identifier via the .avi file extension subkey.

Figure 5.1   AVI files are associated with the avifile file type via the
.avi file extension subkey.

> **TIP:** All you need to remember about filename extension subkeys is that they are under HKEY_CLASSES_ROOT, they look like .*ext* (where *ext* is a valid file extension), and their default value points to one of the program identifiers that are also defined in HKEY_CLASSES_ROOT.

Microsoft really cleaned up the filename extension subkeys for Windows 98. In a fresh installation of Windows 98, the only subkeys you find under a filename extension are `shellex` and `ShellNew`. `shellex` describes shell extensions for that particular filename extension. An example is a context menu handler that adds additional items to a file's shortcut menu, which you display by right-clicking the file in Windows Explorer. In Windows 95, filename extension subkeys contained a strange mix of various `DefaultIcon`, `shell`, `shellex`, and `ShellNew` subkeys, most of which are more appropriate under class definition subkeys. If you upgrade to Windows 98, you're left with all this clutter in the Registry. Don't forget, too, that many Windows 98 applications will add these subkeys to the filename extension key when you install them. Even though these subkeys might be misplaced under a file extension rather than in a class definition, they still work for that particular file extension.

Content Type

Typically, the only value you see in a filename extension subkey is `Content Type`. This value associates the file extension with a MIME type (*Multipurpose Internet Mail Extensions*), a standard for specifying data types on the Internet.

A MIME type specifies the type of content embedded in a Web page or contained in a mail message's attachments. Sometimes the server provides the MIME type of the data it's transmitting, and other times the MIME type is embedded in the document itself. You'd think that the server and document could just specify a file extension, but recall that the Internet is platform-neutral. This means that the Internet must support a wide variety of platforms, each of which might have different conventions for naming files.

MIME types look like *type/subtype*. *Type* is usually something like `application`, `audio`, `image`, or `text`. `application` specifies that the data is raw and doesn't fit into one of the other MIME types. `audio`, `image`, and `text` speak for themselves. *subtype* can vary, but there are standards. A subtype for `text` might be `plain` or `rich`, for example, which specifies that the content is either plain text or richly formatted text. A type or subtype that begins with `x-` means that it's a private MIME type that isn't standardized. Just because a MIME type isn't standardized doesn't mean it's not in popular use.

The later section "MIME Types" contains more information about how Windows 98 uses `Content Type`. You'll also learn how the operating system cross-references MIME types so that looking them up is quicker than searching each individual filename extension subkey.

Class Definition Subkeys

Class definition subkeys define a particular type of document or object. It might be a file type, which a program can open for editing, printing, and so on. It might be a COM class such as a compound document or ActiveX control.

Class definition subkeys come in two flavors. Program identifiers, which are associated with a filename extension subkey via the extension's default value entry, describe a program and the actions it can perform on a file. You'll learn about program identifiers in the following section. A class identifier uniquely identifies a COM class, which can generate objects such as a system folder. Familiar terms associated with COM classes are *object, module,* and *component.* ActiveX and OLE are related technologies that are actually part of COM.

You'll learn about each type of class definition in the following sections. You'll also learn about HKEY_CLASSES_ROOT\MIME, a database that makes cross-referencing a MIME type with a file extension quicker, in "MIME Types." You'll learn about a variety of subkeys that you might find under class definition keys in "Miscellaneous Subkeys in HKEY_CLASSES_ROOT."

Program Identifiers

Flexibility—that's the reason Windows 98 splits information between filename extensions and program identifiers. The operating system *could* store all the information it needs in a filename extension, but doing so would leave the operating system incapable of handling anything but a one-to-one relationship between a file extension and a program. Some documents can have more than one file extension, for instance, as is the case with HTM and HTML files and JPG and JPEG files. Some programs can open more than one file extension, too. For example, Microsoft Word can open DOC, DOT, RTF, and other files. The organization of filename extensions and program identifiers allows the operating system to handle all these cases.

Recall that each filename extension's default value entry refers to a program identifier under HKEY_CLASSES_ROOT. The default value entry for .bat is batfile, for example. Look in HKEY_CLASSES_ROOT\batfile and you see the information that the operating system requires to open, edit, and print BAT files. Given the way in which the Registry organizes this information, you can associate many different filename extension with a single program, but you can't associate many different programs with a single file extension. The following table shows you several examples of how a filename extension subkey's default value relates it to a program identifier:

> NOTE: If the word *COM* throws you, you might know it better as ActiveX or OLE (Object Linking and Embedding). Let's straighten these terms out for you. COM (*Component Object Model*) is Microsoft's technology for allowing application's to interoperate. COM technologies include ActiveX Controls and much more. ActiveX controls are COM objects designed for distribution via Web pages. OLE, on the other hand, strictly refers to Windows 98's *Object Linking and Embedding* capabilities, and you'll only see this term used when referring to *OLE drag and drop* or *embedded OLE objects.*

Filename Extension Subkey	File Type/Default Value
.avi	avifile
.dll	dllfile
.exe	exefile
.htm	htmlfile
.lnk	lnkfile
.reg	regfile
.txt	txtfile

Each program identifier can have a number of different values. The default value entry usually contains a plain-English description of the program and the files it can open. You see this description when you view a file's details in Windows Explorer. The mere presence of AlwaysShowExt, a string value, indicates whether Windows Explorer will always display the file's extension in a folder, regardless of **Hide file extensions for known file types** on the View tab of Windows Explorer's Folder Options dialog box. NeverShowExt, another string value, does the opposite. The presence of IsShortcut indicates whether the file is a shortcut and whether the operating system should display the shortcut overlay on top of the file's icon. Table 5.1 summarizes these values, as well as EditFlags, another common value in most program identifiers. This is a 4-byte binary value that indicates how much editing you're allowed to do in the File Types tab of Windows Explorer's Folder Options dialog box, shown in Figure 5.2. The following table describes the bits that are used in this 32-bit value; just remember to count the bits from right to left, starting from 0:

Bit	Hex	Description
8	00 00 01 00	Clear **Confirm open after download**
16	00 01 00 00	Disable **Description of type**
17	00 02 00 00	Disable **Change Icon button**
18	00 04 00 00	Disable the **Set Default** button
20	00 10 00 00	Disable **Application used to…**
21	00 20 00 00	Disable **Use DDE** checkbox
23	00 80 00 00	Disable **Content Type (MIME)**
24	01 00 00 00	Don't display in **Registered file types**
25	02 00 00 00	Do display in **Registered file types**
27	08 00 00 00	Disable the **Edit** on File Types tab

28	10 00 00 00	Disable the **Remove** on File Types tab
29	20 00 00 00	Disable the **New** button
30	40 00 00 00	Disable the **Edit** button
31	80 00 00 00	Disable the **Remove** button

Table 5.1 **Common Values for File Types**

Value	Type	Description
AlwaysShowExt	String	The presence of this value indicates that Windows Explorer should always display the filename extension in a folder.
NeverShowExt	String	The presence of this value indicates that Windows Explorer should never display the filename extension in a folder.
IsShortcut	String	The presence of this value indicates that the file represents a shortcut, and the operating system displays the shortcut overlay on top of the file's icon.
EditFlags	Binary	Contains flags that determine how much editing the user can do in the File Types tab of Windows Explorer's Folder Options dialog box.

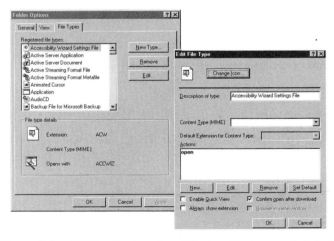

Figure 5.2 Choose **View**, **Folder Options** from Windows Explorer, and click the File Types tab to view these dialogs.

Program identifiers are also an alternative method for identifying COM classes. You'll learn about COM classes in the later section "COM Class Identifiers." Sometimes known as a *progid,* program identifiers allow a program to refer to a class without using the nasty class identifiers. Contrast looking up a class under CLSID using {00020906-0000-0000-C000-000000000046} versus looking up the same class under HKEY_CLASSES_ROOT using Word.Document.8. The latter makes more sense. In this manner, you can think of program identifiers as aliases.

Program identifiers that represent COM classes are specified using a standard notation: *vendor.component.version.* An example would be Microsoft.Word.8. You'll notice that in the Registry they look more like Word.Document.8, which deviates a bit from the standard notation. Regardless, you can also recognize this type of program identifier in one of two ways:

■ The name is separated into parts by periods (.).

■ Program identifiers that represent a COM class always have a subkey called CLSID, which refers to a class identifier in HKEY_CLASSES_ROOT\CLSID.

CLSID

Since a program identifier can refer to a COM class, it must have a way to link itself to a class identifier. It does. Each program identifier can have a subkey called CLSID whose default value entry is the class identifier of a COM class.

CurVer

Imagine the following scenario: An application depends on a class labeled Word.Document.8. Later, the user installs an upgrade that changes the program identifier to Word.Document.9. The application can no longer find the class it needs since the program identifier to which it refers is missing. The solution is *version-independent program identifiers.*

Some program identifiers leave out the version number on the end of their name: *vendor.component.* Examples are Excel.Sheet and Word.Document. These are called version-independent program identifiers. They allow an application to refer to a class without explicitly specifying a version number in the program identifier. A version-independent program identifier always has a subkey called CurVer. The default value of CurVer is the complete program identifier, including the current version.

> NOTE: Program identifiers prevent the programmer from having to know a class' identifier. The programmer can instead use one of the operating system's functions that translate a program identifier into a class identifier, and vice versa. Note that since the program identifier uses some combination of the vendor or application name, component name, and version, there is little chance that two different applications will try to create the same program identifier.

> NOTE: You'll notice that the primary perpetrator of program identifiers is Microsoft. Just about every Microsoft Office product that you install creates several program identifiers.

Now change the scenario so that it uses version-independent program identifiers. An application refers to `Word.Document`, whose `CurVer` subkey's default value is set to `Word.Document.8`. When the user installs the upgrade, the application changes the default value entry of `CurVer` in `Word.Document` so that it refers to the new program identifier called `Word.Document.9`. The user got his upgrade, and the application can still find its object.

COM Class Identifiers

COM class identifiers are like Social Security numbers that uniquely identify people. They identify a COM class using a unique number called a *globally unique identifier* (GUID). A program called Guidgen.exe, which comes with Visual C++ and the WIN32 SDK, generates this number. Don't let `HKEY_CLASSES_ROOT\CLSID`, the location of all the class identifiers in the Registry, daunt you. Each GUID is really nothing more than a class' Social Security number. Notice that all of these class identifiers have the same peculiar format. They're 16-byte hexadecimal numbers separated into 8-, 4-, 4-, 4-, and 12-digit sections by a hyphen, with braces surrounding the whole mess:

`{XXXXXXXX-XXXX-XXXX-XXXX-XXXXXXXXXXXX}`

The default value entry for a class identifier describes the class. In most cases, you see a plain-English description of the class. `Microsoft Excel Chart`, `HTML Thumbnail Extractor`, and `Desktop Task` are examples. In other cases, you see nothing, which leaves you wondering what the class represents. In those cases, you can search the Registry for references to the class identifier. The reference to the class is usually enough to tell you what it does. If you find a class identifier with no name, here are some techniques for uncovering its purpose:

- Search the Registry for the class identifier. The location in which the class identifier is used might tell you the class' purpose.

- Look for a subkey called `ProgID`, which is a link to a related program identifier in `HKEY_CLASSES_ROOT`. The program identifier might provide additional information about the class.

- Look in each of the class identifier's subkeys for a reference to a DLL or other file. View the file's properties by right-clicking it and choosing **Properties**. Frequently, the Version tab will give you a brief description of the file, indicating its purpose.

> NOTE: Two subkeys are common in both program and class identifiers: `Insertable` and `NotInsertable`. The mere presence of a subkey called `Insertable` indicates that the class will appear on the Object dialog box of any application that supports it. You open the Object dialog box by choosing **Insert, Object** from the application. The presence of `NotInsertable` indicates that the class will not appear in the Object dialog box.

Class identifiers don't usually contain values. They are defined by their subkeys, as you'll learn in the following sections. One exception is a value called InfoTip. You commonly find this value entry in classes that create user interface objects, special system folders, and so on. Windows Explorer displays the contents of InfoTip in a small yellow box, also known as a ToolTip, when the user hovers the mouse pointer over the object. This is an additional way that the operating system provides help to the user. When you hover the mouse pointer over My Computer on the desktop, for example, you see a tip that reads Displays the contents of your computer. Adding InfoTip to classes that don't already define this value doesn't seem to do much good. You can customize InfoTip for classes that do include it, though.

NOTE: Anytime you see a GUID elsewhere in the Registry, you can almost always find a matching class identifier in CLSID. Exceptions do exist, however. Sometimes programs use a GUID to uniquely name subkeys or values in other parts of the Registry. These don't lead to class identifiers, but they look like them.

Generating Class Identifiers: Guidgen.exe

Programmers use a program called Guidgen.exe, which comes with Visual C++ and the WIN32 SDK, to generate GUIDs. Microsoft guarantees that each GUID that Guidgen.exe generates will be globally unique. That is, the program will generate a new 16-byte integer GUID every time it runs—no matter how many times it runs.

It does so using a complex algorithm that uses a combination of data. The current date and time are in the GUID. The clock sequence on the computer is in there. An IEEE machine identifier, which Guidgen.exe gets from the network card if available, is in there. If the computer doesn't have a network card, Guidgen.exe generates a machine identifier from extremely variable machine data. This quote from the Microsoft Developer Network Library explains it all: "The chance of [Guidgen.exe] generating duplicate GUIDs...is about the same as two random atoms in the universe colliding to form a small California avocado mated to a New York City sewer rat."

ShellFolder

If you see `ShellFolder` underneath a class identifier, it will have a single value called `attributes`. `attributes` indicates the built-in commands that Windows Explorer displays on the object's shortcut menu. `attributes` is a 4-byte binary value with each bit representing a flag that enables or disables a specific command. Table 5.2 describes the bits used by Windows 98. Setting a particular bit to 0 disables the command, while setting it to 1 enables the command. Remember that you count bits right to left in a binary value, so bit 0 is the first bit on the right, bit 1 is the second bit on the right, and so on. Since the Registry shows `attributes` as a hexadecimal value, you must convert it to binary to figure out which commands are enabled. Work with this value in binary until you're ready to change `attributes`, and then convert it to hexadecimal.

Here's a real-world example. The `attributes` value for the Internet Explorer icon is `72000000` in hexadecimal, which is `01110010000000000000000000000000` in binary. Counting from right to left, bits 25, 28, 29, and 30 are 1s. Thus, Windows 98 displays the **Cut**, **Rename**, **Delete**, and **Properties** commands on the Internet Explorer icon's shortcut menu. You can remove the **Cut** command from the shortcut menu by turning off bit 25, which leaves you with a hexadecimal value of `70000000`.

Table 5.2 **Bits in the `attributes` Value**

Bit Number	Command
30	**Properties**
29	**Delete**
28	**Rename**
25	**Cut**
24	**Copy**
16	**Paste**
5	**Open** and **Explore** for the Recycle Bin

SEE ALSO
➤ Chapter 9, "Customizing the Windows 98 Desktop," describes how to use `ShellFolder` to make shortcut menus look the way you want.

LocalServer and LocalServer32

The default values of the subkeys called `LocalServer` and `LocalServer32` specify the path of an EXE that implements the server application. `LocalServer` specifies a 16-bit server application, while `LocalServer32` specifies a 32-bit server application. Local servers run in their own address space.

InprocServer and InprocServer32

The default values of the subkeys called `InprocServer` and `InprocServer32` specify the path of a DLL file that implements the server. `InprocServer` specifies a 16-bit server, while `LocalServer32` specifies a 32-bit server. In-process servers run in the client process's address space.

If an in-process server is multithreaded, you see an additional value entry called ThreadingModel. This value can be one of the following:

Apartment	This represents the *apartment threading model*. Each object exists in only a single thread.
Both	An object can exist in a single thread, as with apartment threading, or it can exist in multiple threads of a single process—*free threading*.

InprocHandler and InprocHandler32

The default values of the subkeys called `InprocHandler` and `InprocHandler32` specify the path of a DLL file that handles objects defined by the class identifier. `InprocHandler` specifies a 16-bit handler, while `InprocHandler32` specifies a 32-bit handler. In-process handlers work in conjunction with local or in-process servers. You'll notice that this value almost always contains Ole32.dll, which provides COM functionality to the operating system and other applications.

ProgID

Earlier in this chapter, you learned that a program identifier can be an alias for a class. Each program identifier can contain a subkey called `CLSID` whose default value contains the class identifier of the associated class. Each class identifier also contains a reference to its matching program identifier, if it exists, in a subkey called `ProgID`. The default value entry of `ProgID` is the program identifier or the version-independent program identifier.

MIME Types

In the earlier section called "Filename Extension Subkeys," you learned how the operating system associates a MIME type with a variety of file extensions. These file extensions contain a value called `Content Type`, which defines the MIME type associated with that extension. When a client program such as Internet Explorer or Outlook Express Mail needs to associate a program with a bit of data, it searches for the MIME type in the Registry. The search yields a file extension that in turn yields information about the program used to display and edit the data.

> **NOTE:** The difference between in-process and local servers is the address space in which they run. In-process servers run in the host application's address space. Local servers run in their own address space. In-process servers perform better but can crash the client application. Local servers perform worse than in-process servers do, but they don't affect the host application if they crash.

Windows 98 doesn't examine each and every filename extension subkey for a matching Content Type value, however, because doing so would make the whole process pathetically slow. It looks up the MIME type in HKEY_CLASSES_ROOT\MIME\Database\Content Type instead. This key contains a subkey for each MIME type registered in the Registry. Content Type*MimeType* contains a value called Extension that associates the MIME type with a file extension. Content Type\Text/Plain contains information about the Text/Plain MIME type, for example, and Extension contains .txt, which associates the Text/Plain MIME type with the TXT file extension. The Extension value entry for Content Type\image/gif contains .gif, which associates the image/gif MIME type with the GIF file extension.

Underneath some MIME types you see a subkey called Bits. This subkey contains terrific information about the header that begins each type of file. Each value entry—the first being 0, the second being 1, and so on—in Bits defines a possible file header that identifies a file matching the MIME type. The first 32-bit DWORD specifies the length of the file header. The next *n* bytes, where *n* is the length of the file header, appear to be a mask that determines which bits of the header to check. This portion is almost always FF FF FF FF ..., indicating that the operating system should check every bit of the file header. The next *n* bytes, up to the end of the binary value entry, are the actual file header. If the operating system encounters a file with an unknown MIME type or file extension, it can sometimes identify the file's MIME type by comparing its header to the values in Bits. Likewise, the operating system can test a file's header against the values in Bits to make sure that the file is valid. You see 02 00 00 00 FF FF 42 4D in the value entry called 0 found under MIME\Database\Content Type\image/bmp\Bits, a subkey of HKEY_CLASSES_ROOT. This indicates that a BMP file's header has two bytes, 42 4D, and every bit in each of those bytes is significant. Sure enough, if you view a BMP file in a hex editor, the file starts with 42 4D.

Miscellaneous Subkeys in HKEY_CLASSES_ROOT

Filename extensions and class definitions can contain a number of subkeys that define how they look and behave. It's more common for class definitions to contain such subkeys as shell and DefaultIcon, but these subkeys are still valid under filename extensions. shellex and ShellNew subkeys are common under filename extensions, however.

The following sections describe the most common subkeys. Here's an overview of each:

shell	Defines commands that appear on the shortcut menu of the file or object.
shellex	Defines shell extensions for the file or object, such as extensions to the property sheet or shortcut menu.

`ShellNew`	Defines a template for a new empty file with a particular file extension that the user creates by right-clicking a folder and choosing **New**.
`DefaultIcon`	Defines an icon for the file or object.

shell

When you right-click a file or object in Windows Explorer, it displays a shortcut menu. Some of the items on the shortcut menu are built into the operating system (Shell32.dll); these appear at the bottom of the menu. You learned how to control these options in the earlier section "`ShellFolder`." Other items come from class definitions such as Unknown or *, both of which you'll learn about later in this chapter. The remaining items are at the top of the shortcut menu and come from the `shell` subkey of the class definition. `HKEY_CLASSES_ROOT\txtfile\shell` defines items you see at the top of a TXT file's shortcut menu, for example. In some unlikely cases, a filename extension key might have a `shell` subkey too, which adds items to the file's shortcut menu only if the filename extension subkey is not connected to a program identifier by the subkey's default value entry. All this is a bit much to swallow, so look at the following generalization about how Windows Explorer builds the shortcut menu after the user right-clicks a file:

1. Windows 98 notes the file's extension and looks up that extension in `HKEY_CLASSES_ROOT`.

2. Windows 98 notes the default value entry of the filename extension subkey, which is the associated program identifier. If this value is empty, the operating system looks for a `shell` subkey in the filename extension key and adds those commands to the top of the shortcut menu. Otherwise, the operating system adds any commands it finds in the program identifier's `shell` subkey to the top of the shortcut menu.

3. Windows 98 adds any commands it finds in the * and `AllFilessystemObjects` keys' `shell` subkey to the middle of the shortcut menu. These are commands that apply to all files and all file system objects on the computer.

4. Windows 98 adds any built-in commands to the bottom of the shortcut menu. These are defined in Shell32.dll.

Verbs

Each subkey under `shell` is a verb. A verb shows action in the user interface, just as it does in the English language. "Open Readme.txt," "Edit Budget.xls," and "Print Picture.bmp" all represent examples of verb phrases that contain an action and a direct object. The actions are open, edit, and print. The direct objects are Readme.txt, Budget.xls, and Picture.bmp. The user completes one of these verb phrases by right-clicking a file, which supplies the direct object, and choosing one of the commands on the menu, which supplies the verb. In the Registry, verbs have simple, arbitrary names such as open, edit, and print. The default value of shell indicates which verb defines the default command on the menu. Thus, if a shell key has two subkeys, open and edit, and the shell key's default value is open, the shortcut menu starts with the commands **Open** and **Edit**, and **Open** is the default choice. If the user clicks the file in the single-click user interface or double-clicks the file in the double-click interface, Windows 98 opens the file using the command defined in shell\open.

The default value of each verb contains the text that Windows 98 displays on the shortcut menu. If the default value is blank, the operating system takes the text for the menu item from Shell32.dll, if the verb is canonical, or from the verb's name. **Find, Open**, **Open With**, and **Print** are canonical, so the operating system will look to Shell32.dll for the shortcut menu's text if the default value of the verb is empty. If the operating system uses the verb's name, it uses it verbatim, without capitalizing it or adding a hot key to it. The operating system does maintain the capitalization you use in the verb's default value, and you can indicate a hot key by prefixing the letter with an ampersand (&). Here are examples of what different values look like on a shortcut menu:

In the Registry	On the Shortcut menu
open	open
&Open	Open
open in Wordpad	open in Wordpad
open in &Wordpad	open in Wordpad

Commands

Underneath each verb, you see a single subkey called command whose default value defines the command line that Windows 98 executes when you choose that command from the shortcut menu. The command line for different verbs varies. In some cases, you see only the path and filename of the program, allowing the operating system to affix the file or object's name to the end of the command.

> **NOTE:** Microsoft documentation refers to some verbs as *canonical verbs*. If you look in the dictionary, you'll discover that *canonical* means official, sanctioned, or approved. open, openas, print, find, and explore are recognized by and built into the operating system and are therefore canonical verbs. Canonical verbs are localized by Windows 98, so the operating system always uses the appropriate language when displaying them on a menu.

In most cases, however, you see commands that explicitly include the file or object's name in the command line using the %1 placeholder. Windows 98 substitutes the file or object for %1 when it executes the command. Using %1 becomes particularly important when the command line contains switches and you must include the filename in a specific location: `myprog /p /k "%1" /s`, for example. In cases where the program has trouble with long filenames that include spaces, probably because the program is expecting multiple filenames or options on the command line, you see %1 surrounded by quotes, like this: `"%1"`. This ensures that the program sees the entire filename as a single unit, such as `filename with spaces.txt`, rather than individual chunks of text, such as `filename`, `with`, and `spaces.txt`.

> **TIP:** Some command lines contain nothing but %1. Recall that Windows 98 replaces %1 with the filename when the operating system executes the command. A command line that contains nothing but %1 treats the file as a program, launching it as a new process. You see this in `scrfile` and `exefile`, for example.

The Least You Need to Know

All you need to remember about `shell` subkeys is described here:

```
HKEY_CLASSES_ROOT\Name
    shell
        (default) = default
        verb
            (default) = name
            command
                (default) = command
```

Name is a filename extension subkey or program identifier. *default* is the name of one the subkeys under `shell`, the verbs, and it identifies the default command on the shortcut menu. *verb* is an arbitrary name, and *name* is the text that the operating system displays on the shortcut menu for that command. The operating system maintains the text's capitalization, and an ampersand (&) precedes a hot key. *command* is the command line that the operating system executes when you choose the command from the shortcut menu.

Some command lines launch Rundll.exe or Rundll32.exe. This might seem kind of odd when you look at the command line for `cplfile\open`, which opens a dialog box in the Control Panel. Some programs aren't EXE files, though; they're DLL files, and the operating system provides Rundll.exe and Rundll32.exe to launch a specific function within a DLL file. The command line looks like this: `rundll.exe` *filename,function options*. *filename* is the name of the DLL file, and *function* is the name of the function within the DLL to execute. The remainder of the command line contains options that Rundll.exe passes to the function.

SEE ALSO

➤ Chapter 9 shows you how to put the information you learned in this section to practical use. You learn how to add, change, and remove items on the shortcut menu.

shellex

The term *shell extension* is almost but not quite self-explanatory. A shell extension enhances the user interface beyond its normal capabilities. A shell extension can add a tab to a property sheet, add commands to a shortcut menu, or provide an alternative means for a user to browse the contents of a folder. Other shell extensions provide icons for a file or object, add features to Windows 98's Drag and Drop functionality, and more. You know you're dealing with a shell extension when you see something called a *handler,* which is a 32-bit in-process server. A *property sheet handler* is a shell extension that adds tabs to a property sheet, for example, and an *icon handler* is a shell extension that supplies icons for an object. Windows 98 supports a variety of shell extensions:

- **Context menu handlers** add items to a shortcut menu, which the user opens by right-clicking a file or object.
- **Drag handlers** provide Drag and Drop support to file or object.
- **Drop handlers** provide support for additional commands when the user drops a file or object.
- **Icon handlers** supply icons for a file or object.
- **Property sheet handlers** add new tabs to a file or object's property sheet, which you display by right-clicking it and choosing **P**roperties.
- **Copy-hook handlers** extend the copy, move, delete, or rename operations for a file or object.

Windows 98 defines shell extensions for a filename extension or class definition in its `shellex` subkey. `shellex` is usually devoid of values, deriving its meaning from its subkeys instead. A handful of filename extension subkeys contain `shellex`, extending the shell just for that particular file extension. `shellex` is more common under class definitions, however, extending the shell for all file extensions belonging to an application or for a particular class. `shellex` will have different subkeys, depending on the types of shell extension registered in it:

- `ContextMenuHandlers`
- `CopyHookHandlers`
- `DataHandler`
- `DragDropHandlers`
- `DropHandler`
- `ExtShellFolderViews`
- `IconHandler`
- `PropertySheetHandlers`

The format of each subkey, `shellex\`*handler*, can differ a bit. First, the default value of *handler* might contain a class identifier that implements that particular handler. A typical example is `shellex\IconHandler` with its default value entry set to the class identifier of a COM class that can supply icons for that particular file or object. Second, *handler* might contain a subkey whose name is the class identifier of a COM class, and its default value entry is the plain-English name of the handler. Last, *handler* might contain a subkey whose name is a plain-English name, and its default value entry is the class identifier of a COM class. You'll find all of these formats in the Registry. They all work equally well.

Some subkeys under `shellex` have unintelligible names that look like GUIDs. They are in fact GUIDs, but you won't find them defined in HKEY_CLASSES_ROOT\CLSID. That is, they aren't class identifiers. These unknown GUIDs just represent another type of shell extension, or handler, that extends a filename extension or class definition. Most of these oddities are due to Internet Explorer 4.0, and they represent the first wrinkle in an otherwise flawless design. In a typical installation of Windows 98, I found the following subkeys under `shellex`, whose default value entries don't refer to an actual class definition under `CLSID`:

- `{BB2E617C-0920-11d1-9A0B-00C04FC2D6C1}` contains the GUID of a thumbnail extractor. It's common in the `shellex` subkeys of images, since Windows Explorer can display a thumbnail of images when you view a folder as a Web page.
- `{00021500-0000-0000-C000-000000000046}` contains the GUID of an InfoTip handler. An InfoTip handler displays help text in a yellow box when the user hovers the mouse pointer over the object.
- `{000214EE-0000-0000-C000-000000000046}` contains the GUID of a shortcut handler for Internet shortcuts. Four other `shellex` subkeys also refer to shortcut handlers: `{000214F9-0000-0000-C000-000000000046}`, `{00021500-0000-0000-`

C000-000000000046}, {CABB0DA0-DA57-11CF-9974-0020AFD79762}, and {FBF23B80-E3F0-101B-8488-00AA003E56F8}.

■ {D4029EC0-0920-11d1-9A0B-00C04FC2D6C1} contains the GUID of a channel handler.

SEE ALSO

➤ Chapter 4, "Troubleshooting the Registry," shows you how to diagnose and fix problems that relate to orphaned shell extensions in shellex keys.

➤ Chapter 10, "Fixing Common Problems Via the Registry," describes how to fix a number of problems that result from incorrect keys and values in shellex.

ExtShellFolderView **is an Odd Bird**

ExtShellFolderView is a subkey you frequently see under the shellex subkey of folders and classes that act as folders. It's an odd key that contains handlers for displaying a folder as a Web page. In every case, ExtShellFolderView contains a single subkey called {5984FFE0-28D4-11CF-AE66-08002B2E1262}. You don't find this GUID in HKEY_CLASSES_ROOT\CLSID, though, meaning that this GUID isn't a class identifier.

Discovering how the operating system uses ExtShellFolderView took a bit more digging than just looking in CLSID. I used Registry Monitor, a utility you'll learn about in Chapter 12, "Tracking Down Registry Settings," to see what happens when I display a folder as a Web page:

1. Windows Explorer opens shellex\ExtShellFolderView in the class definition subkey. If you're viewing a folder, for example, Explorer opens shellex\ExtShellFolderView underneath HKEY_CLASSES_ROOT\folder.

2. Windows Explorer enumerates each subkey of ExtShellFolderView and makes a note of its name. It also looks for a value called PersistMoniker in each subkey, which contains the path to the HTML file that Windows Explorer uses to draw the folder.

3. Windows Explorer displays the folder using the HTML file it found in PersistMoniker.

{5984FFE0-28D4-11CF-AE66-08002B2E1262}, which is the subkey that Windows Explorer finds in step 2, is an arbitrary GUID. You can rename this subkey to any valid GUID, and the operating system still finds PersistMoniker. The only special significance that this GUID might have is that Windows 98 creates an identical subkey under HKEY_LOCAL_MACHINE\Software\Microsoft\ Windows\CurrentVersion\ExtShellViews, which describes the view's menu command, as Web Page, on Windows Explorer's View menu.

ShellNew

Right-click any folder and choose **New** to display a menu of new documents you can create in the folder. This is a quick way to create a new document. You can then open the new document to edit its contents. If the associated program identifier has a verb called new, Windows 98 automatically opens the file using the command line specified in new\command.

Windows 98 builds this menu of templates by examining each filename extension subkey in the Registry to see if it has a ShellNew subkey. This process is why the **New** menu sometimes takes so long to display. ShellNew defines a template for the file extension. If Windows 98 finds a ShellNew subkey, the operating system looks up the program identifier associated with it and displays a description of the file type on the **New** menu. Four different methods are available for specifying a template within ShellNew. Each method involves adding a different value entry to the filename extension's ShellNew subkey:

- **Command**   This string value entry indicates the command line to execute to create the new file.

- **NullFile**   This empty string value entry indicates that the new file will be completely empty.

- **FileName**   This string value indicates the filename of a particular template file that the operating system looks for in \Windows\Shellnew.

- **Data**   This is a binary value whose contents Windows 98 uses to create the new file when the user chooses it from the **New** menu. Windows 98 just copies the bytes from this value entry directly into the file.

SEE ALSO

➤ Chapter 9 provides step-by-step instructions for customizing the <u>N</u>ew menu using ShellNew.

DefaultIcon

All filename extension and class definition keys support the DefaultIcon subkey, which defines the icon for a file or object. You also see this icon used in folders, on an application's title bar, on the Start menu, and so on.

> NOTE: These three terms are similar, but they mean different things in the Registry. Shell defines commands that you can perform on a file or object. ShellEx defines shell extensions that enhance how you interact with the object. ShellNew defines a template so that you can easily create a new file of a particular type in a folder.

The default value entry of DefaultIcon specifies the location of the icon that Windows Explorer displays for the file. Icons come from EXE, DLL, RES, ICO, and other files. ICO, BMP, and similar files contain a single icon; you specify them by giving the path and filename of the image file. EXE, DLL, and RES files can contain any number of icons. You reference a particular icon in such files using the icon's index, starting from 0. The first icon is 0, the second is 1, and so on. You specify an icon in an EXE, DLL, or RES file by giving the file's path and filename, followed by the icon's index, like this: *path,index. path* is the full path and filename of the file, and *index* is the index of the icon in the file.

There is one more convention you should be aware of. Windows 98 allows a programmer to assign a fixed identifier to each icon. This identifier is usually called a *resource ID*. The resource ID is any arbitrary integer value, such as 1037. It provides an easier way for the programmer to reference an exact icon without having to figure out the icon's index. The programmer can assign the integer value to a symbol and then use that symbol in the code. You can also specify an icon using its resource ID, assuming that you know it, by writing a line like this: *path,-resource. path* is the full path and filename of the file, and *resource* is the icon's resource ID. The following list shows you an example of both methods for specifying the location of an icon:

Index   C:\Windows\System\Shell32.dll,9

Resource ID   C:\Windows\System\Shell32.dll,-37

If you see %1 in DefaultIcon, this means that the icon handler will provide the icon. Look for a subkey under shellex called iconhandler, which you learned about earlier in this chapter. This shell extension will supply the icon specified by the %1 in DefaultIcon. If you don't find an icon handler for the class, the file is probably an image, so Windows Explorer uses a scaled-down copy of the file's contents as the icon.

SEE ALSO

➤ Chapter 9 describes how to change the icon that the operating system uses for a file or object.

NOTE: Windows 98 doesn't even look at DefaultIcon if it finds the item's icon in the icon cache, Shelliconcache. You'll learn how to work with this file in Chapter 9.

Significant Class Definitions

Many class definitions look like `txtfile`, `docfile`, and `regfile`. These define programs such as a text editor, word processor, or Registry Editor. Other class definitions have names like `*` and `folder`. These don't define a particular program; they define special-purpose classes and classes for special types of objects. These aren't usually associated with a file extension or COM class. Windows 98 just knows to look for them by name.

The following sections describe the most interesting of these special class definitions. If you don't find an explanation in this chapter for a class definition that appears to have a special purpose, you can almost always figure out its purpose by examining its contents. If that doesn't help, use a program such as Registry Monitor to see what types of files and objects access that class definition.

SEE ALSO

➤ Chapter 12 describes how to observe Registry access in real time using a program called Registry Monitor.

*

Windows 98 applies the contents of `HKEY_CLASSES_ROOT\*` to every file on the computer. Usually the first subkey of `HKEY_CLASSES_ROOT`, `*` is a wildcard. Keep in mind that this is not a filename extension, contrary to what you might have read elsewhere. It's a class definition with all the features of any other class definition subkey.

`*` usually has a single subkey called `shellex` that leads to two other subkeys. `ContextMenuHandlers` adds additional items to every file's shortcut menu. An example is a handler that adds **Update** to a file's shortcut menu when the file is in a briefcase. `PropertySheetHandlers` adds additional tabs to every file's property sheet, which you open by right-clicking the file and choosing **P**roperties.

Unknown

When you right-click a file for which Windows Explorer doesn't find a matching filename extension, the operating system uses the `Unknown` class definition to build the file's shortcut menu. `Unknown\shell` typically contains a single verb called `openas`, which adds the **Op**en **With** option to the file's shortcut menu. You can add additional verbs to `Unknown` to provide additional commands for unknown files. Consider adding a verb that opens an unknown file in Notepad, for instance, which allows you to easily open any unregistered file in Notepad. This is a handy feature considering the variety of file extensions that vendors use to name Readme files: Read.me, Readme.txt, Readme.doc, Readme.1st, etc.

AllFilesystemObjects

`AllFilesystemObjects` is a special class that applies to every object in the file system, including removable drives, folders, and files. By default, the only thing this class does is add the **Send _To_** menu to each removable drive, folder, and file's shortcut menu.

Directory, Drive, and Folder

`Directory`, `Drive`, and `Folder` are similar class definitions. They extend the user interface for directories, drives, and folders. The distinction lies in which class the operating system uses when you work with different types of folders:

Folder Type	Example	Class Definitions
System folders	Control Panel	Folder
Drives	C:\	Drive and Folder
Normal folders	C:\Windows	Directory and Folder

AudioCD

Windows 98 uses this class definition for audio CDs. It adds the **_Play_** option to an audio CD's shortcut menu.

AutoRun

When you insert a data CD into the CD-ROM drive, Windows 98 copies several values from the Autorun.inf file in the disk's root folder, if it exists, to `AutoRun`. Listing 5.1 shows an example of a typical Autorun.inf file. Windows 98 puts the value assigned to `icon` in the default value of the `DefaultIcon` subkey. It puts the value assigned to `open` in the default value `AutoRun\`_num_`\Shell\AutoRun\command`, where _num_ is 0 if the disk is in drive A, 1 if it's in drive B, 2 if it's in drive C, and so on. Windows 98 automatically executes the program indicated in the disk's `AutoRun\Command` subkey after the user inserts the disk. The user can also right-click the disk in Windows Explorer and choose **Auto_Play_**, defined by the verb `Shell\AutoRun`.

> **NOTE:** A folder is any container that you can open and browse. This includes normal file system folders and special system folders. Windows 98 provides a number of system folders. Examples include the Control Panel, Dial-Up Networking, Microsoft Network, My Computer, Network Neighborhood, Printers, and Recycle Bin folders.

Listing 5.1   **A Typical Autorun.inf File**

```
[autorun]
open=autorun.exe
icon=autorun.ico
```

regfile

regfile is a plain old program identifier. So what's it doing here? I mention it because the Registry Editor has an annoying habit of automatically importing REG files when you double-click them.

The default command for a REG file is to merge the file's contents into the Registry. If you accidentally double-click the file thinking that you're going to edit it, you'll make a mistake. You can avoid this mistake by changing the default command for a REG file. To do so, change the default value of regfile\shell to edit, which then makes regfile\shell\edit the default command on the shortcut menu.

Significant COM Class Identifiers

Some classes have special significance. These are primarily classes that Windows 98 adds to the namespaces of the desktop and the My Computer folder. The following table provides the names and class identifiers of these significant classes:

Folder	Class Identifier
ActiveX Cache Folder	{88C6C381-2E85-11D0-94DE-444553540000}
Briefcase	{85BBD920-42A0-1069-A2E4-08002B30309D}
Control Panel	{21EC2020-3AEA-1069-A2DD-08002B30309D}
Dial-Up Networking	{992CFFA0-F557-101A-88EC-00DD010CCC48}
Infrared Recipient	{00435AE0-BBFB-11CF-A9D8-00AA00423596}
Internet Cache...	{7BD29E00-76C1-11CF-9DD0-00A0C9034933}
Internet Explorer	{FBF23B42-E3F0-101B-8488-00AA003E56F8}

TIP: In order for AutoRun to work properly, A̲uto insert notification must be enabled on the Settings tab of the CD-ROM drive's property sheet. Open the Device Manger from the Control Panel, double-click the CD-ROM drive to open its property sheet, and click the Settings tab. Enable A̲uto insert notification, and close the drive's property sheet and the Device Manager to save your changes.

My Computer	{20D04FE0-3AEA-1069-A2D8-08002B30309D}
My Documents	{450D8FBA-AD25-11D0-98A8-0800361B1103}
Network Neighborhood	{208D2C60-3AEA-1069-A2D7-08002B30309D}
Printers	{2227A280-3AEA-1069-A2DE-08002B30309D}
Recycle Bin	{645FF040-5081-101B-9F08-00AA002F954E}
Scheduled Tasks	{D6277990-4C6A-11CF-8D87-00AA0060F5BF}
Shell Favorite...	{1A9BA3A0-143A-11CF-8350-444553540000}
Subscription Folder	{F5175861-2688-11d0-9C5E-00AA00A45957}
The Internet	{3DC7A020-0ACD-11CF-A9BB-00AA004AE837}
URL History Folder	{FF393560-C2A7-11CF-BFF4-444553540000}

TIP: The best way to search for special class identifiers (those that you can insert into the desktop's namespace) is to search CLSID for any keys that contain a subkey called ExtShellFoldersView. Doing so uncovers only those shell folders that can actually display content in a folder.

GUIDs in Memory

The binary representation of a GUID in memory is a bit different than the string definition you see in the Registry. The first four bytes are stored as a DWORD, so the bytes are reversed. (See Chapter 15, "Script, REG, and INF Files," to learn how the computer stores DWORD values in memory.) The next four bytes are stored as two words, again with their bytes reversed. The remaining bytes are stored as single bytes, so the order is not reversed. Thus, when you're looking for {5984FFE0-28D4-11CF-AE66-08002B2E1262} in memory, you're actually looking for a binary string like e0,ff,84,59,d4,28,cf,11,ae,66,08,00,2b,2e,12,62.

This is good information to know if you're trying to track down how Windows 98 is using a particular class identifier. You find class identifiers referenced in a surprisingly large number of binary value entries. These aren't obvious until you export the entire Registry to a REG file and start examining each binary value. After doing so, you start to see patterns emerge. Therefore, if you're trying to figure out how the operating system uses a particular class identifier, search a complete REG file for the binary representation of it. A REG file might split a large binary value across multiple lines, by the way, so search for a portion of the GUID. In the preceding example, searching for D4,28 (remember that the fifth and sixth bytes are stored as a single word with the bytes reversed) yields the desired result.

SEE ALSO

➤ Chapter 9 shows you how to use the special class identifiers you learned about in this section to customize the operating system in a variety of ways.

HKEY_LOCAL_MACHINE

6

In this chapter:

- Config
- Driver
- Enum
- Hardware
- Network
- Security
- Software
- System\CurrentControlSet

Config

Within Config, look for one or more subkeys called 0001, 0002, and so on, each of which represents a single hardware profile. Remember that you create hardware profiles on the Hardware Profiles tab of the System Properties dialog box. Windows 98 automatically manages hardware profiles in most cases, such as when it detects a portable computer with docked and undocked configurations. On such a configuration, 0001 might represent the docked configuration, while 0002 might represent the undocked configuration. Multiple profiles are highly unlikely on desktop computers and equally useless—unless you have situations in which a prominent device is available only part-time.

The subkeys under `Config`, `Display`, `Enum`, `Infrared`, `Software`, and `System` describe the hardware profile. Except for `Display`, these subkeys contain minimal amounts of information. If you're interested in learning more about this branch, though, take a look at Chapter 8, "`HKEY_CURRENT_CONFIG` and `HKEY_DYN_DATA`."

SEE ALSO

➤ Chapter 8 describes `Config` in much more detail. You learn how to determine which sub-key of `Config` HKEY_CURRENT_CONFIG represents, for example.

Enum

`Enum` contains configuration data for every device installed on the computer. Even if a device isn't present at the moment, you still see it listed in this branch. Needless to say, the contents of `Enum` are different from computer to computer, because each computer's configuration is different. Not only that, but each hardware vendor has certain twists to how it stores configuration data in the Registry. If you want to get a glimpse of how a vendor configures the Registry for a certain device, take a look at the INF files you used to install the device's drivers. You'll find them in \Windows\Inf.

`Enum` leads to a number of subkeys, one for each type of enumerator. (See the sidebar called "The Windows 98 Configuration Manager" for more information about enumerators.) Following each enumerator is a subkey—whose name represents a *device ID*—for each specific device installed on the computer. Thus, the Registry path `Enum\`*Enumerator*`\`*Device* represents a device that is or once was present. The name used for *Device* is different within different types of enumerators. Under `BIOS`, for example, *Device* looks like **PNPXXXX*. This is called the EISA format. It starts with an asterisk (*) and is followed by a three-letter manufacturer code, a three-digit identification number, and a one-digit revision number. If the device is generic, you'll typically see `PNP` used for the manufacturer code. In other enumerators, *Device* looks like *VENDOR&DEVICE&SUBSYS&REV*, which contains vendor and device codes as well a revision number.

NOTE: Understanding how Windows 98 stores hardware configuration data in the Registry is helpful. Trying to configure hardware via the Registry is not. Stick with the Device Manager and Add New Hardware Wizard when configuring hardware.

Enum*enumerator**Device**Instance* represents an actual instance of the device and
is therefore called an *instance ID*. You might see two or more instances under a device)
ID if there are two or more devices of that type on the computer. For instance, if you
have two communications ports, you'll see two instances under the device ID. The
name used for *Instance* is typically one of three types: a sequence number, a device
number as assigned on the bus, or a combination of the bus, device, and function
numbers that looks like *BUS&DEVICE&FUNCTION*. In cases where a device has a parent
device (a serial mouse's parent device is the serial port), an instance ID might look like
BUS&DEVICE&INSTANCE, allowing you to find the parent device by opening
Enum*BUS**DEVICE**INSTANCE*. This gets a bit complicated when the parent device and
instance IDs are *VENDOR&DEVICE&SUBSYS&REV* and *BUS&DEVICE&FUNCTION*, since you end
up with instance IDs that look like *BUS&VENDOR&DEVICE&SUBSYS&REV&BUS&DEVICE&FUNC-
TION*.

Enum*Enumerator* and Enum*Enumerator**Device* are usually devoid of any values.
Windows 98 frequently infers meaning from the name of *Device*, however, particularly
in the case of devices listed under Enum\PCI or when a device has a parent listed elsewhere within Enum. The instance subkey, Enum*Enumerator**Device**Instance*, contains
the actual configuration data for each device, and it usually contains all of the following values and then some):

- Capabilities
- CompatibleIDs
- ClassGUID
- Class
- ConfigFlags
- Driver
- DeviceDesc
- FriendlyName
- HardwareID
- Mfg

Some of these values are interesting, but none of them are useful for configuring
the Registry. Class contains a name that describes the device's hardware class. The
string value in Class refers you to a branch under
HKEY_LOCAL_MACHINE\System\CurrentControlSet\Services\Class for the class's plain-
English description. The string value in Driver refers you to a branch under the same
key that contains information about the device's driver, including its filename, date,
INF file and section, provider, and so on. DeviceDesc is the device's description as you
see it in the Device Manager. To make things a bit clearer, Figure 6.1 shows how these
values relate to what you see in the Device Manager.

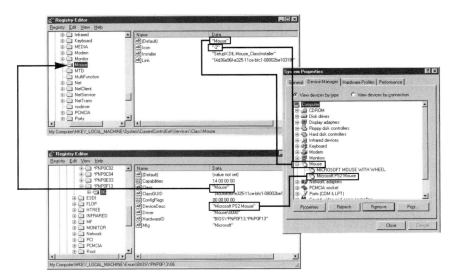

Figure 6.1 This diagram shows the relationship between the Device Manager and the settings in Enum and Class.

Table 6.1 lists a variety of examples of how Windows 98 stores device information in Enum. I've divided this table into categories that are similar to what the Device Manager uses. The first column contains the device's description as you see it in the Device Manager. The second column indicates the branch under Enum in which Windows 98 stores the device's configuration).

Table 6.1   **Devices Under HKEY_LOCAL_MACHINE\Enum**

Device Description	**Enumerator and Device**
CD-ROM	
Sanyo CRD-S372B	SCSI\SANYO___CR
DISK DRIVES	
Generic NEC floppy disk	FLOP\GENERIC_NEC__FLOP...
Generic IDE disk type<7	ESDI\GENERIC_IDE__DISK...
FLOPPY DISK CONTROLLERS	
Standard Floppy Disk Controller	BIOS*PNP0700\08
HARD DISK CONTROLLERS	
Intel 82371AB/EB PCI Bus Mas...	PCI\VEN_8086&DEV_7111&...
Primary IDE controller (dual...	MF\CHILD0000\PCI&VEN_8...
Secondary IDE controller (du...	MF\CHILD0001\PCI&VEN_8...

Device Description	Enumerator and Device
INFRARED DEVICES	
Infrared Communication Device	Root\Infrared\0000
KEYBOARD	
Standard 101/102-Key or Mi...	BIOS*PNP0303\05
MODEM	
Standard PCMCIA Card Modem	PCMCIA\IBM-56K_PC_CARD...
MONITORS	
Laptop Display Panel (800×600)	MONITOR\DEFAULT_MONITO...
MOUSE	
PS/2 Compatible Mouse Port	BIOS*PNP0F13\06
Microsoft mouse with wheel	SERENUM\MSH0001\BIOS&*...
NETWORK ADAPTERS	
Dial-Up Adapter	Root\Net\0000
IBM ThinkPad Fast Infrared Port	BIOS*IBM0071\13
Xircom CreditCard Ethernet	PCMCIA\XIRCOM-...[sr]
Adapter 10/100	
PCMCIA SOCKET	
PCMCIA Card Services	PCMCIA\PCCARD\HTREE&ROOT&0
Texas Instruments PCI-1131...	PCI\VEN_104C&DEV_AC15&...
Texas Instruments PCI-1250 ...	PCI\VEN_104C&DEV_AC16&...
Texas Instruments PCI-1250 ...	PCI\VEN_104C&DEV_AC16&...
PORTS (COM AND LPT)	
Infrared Serial (COM) Port	INFRARED\COM\ROOT&INF...
Infrared Printing (LPT) Port	INFRARED\LPT\ROOT&INF...
Printer Port (LPT1)	BIOS*PNP0400\0B
Communications Port (COM1)	BIOS*PNP0501\0D

continues

Table 6.1 **Continued**

Device Description	Enumerator and Device
SOUND, VIDEO, AND GAME CONTROLLERS	
Crystal PnP Audio System CODEC	BIOS*CSC0000\0E
Crystal PnP Audio System Con…	BIOS*CSC0010\0F
Gameport Joystick	BIOS*CSC0001\10
Crystal PnP Audio System MPU…	BIOS*CSC0003\11
SYSTEM DEVICES	
Plug and Play Software Device…	Root\SwEnum\0000
Plug and Play BIOS	Root*PNP0C00\0000
System board	Root*PNP0C01\0000
Advanced Power Management support	Root*PNP0C05\0000
Programmable interrupt controller	BIOS*PNP0000\00
Direct memory access controller	BIOS*PNP0200\01
System timer	BIOS*PNP0100\02
System CMOS/real-time clock	BIOS*PNP0B00\03
System speaker	BIOS*PNP0800\04
Numeric data processor	BIOS*PNP0C04\07
PCI bus	BIOS*PNP0A03\09
Motherboard resources	BIOS*PNP0C02\0A
Motherboard resources	BIOS*PNP0C02\1B
IRQ Holder for PCI Steering	PCI\IRQHOLDER\60
IRQ Holder for PCI Steering	PCI\IRQHOLDER\61
IRQ Holder for PCI Steering	PCI\IRQHOLDER\63
Intel 82439TX Pentium Pro…	PCI\VEN_8086&DEV_7100&…
Intel 82371AB Power Manageme…	PCI\VEN_8086&DEV_7113&…
Composite Power Source	ACPI\COMPBATT\0
APM Battery Slot	VPOWERD\BATTERY\0
TapeDetection	TAPECONTROLLER\TAPEDET…
TapeDetection	TAPECONTROLLER\TAPEDET…
TapeDetection)	TAPECONTROLLER\TAPEDET…

NOTE: Within each device's subkey, you see a value called Driver. This string value indicates the path to the device's driver, starting from HKEY_LOCAL_MACHINE\System\CurrentControlSet\ ➥Services\Class. Thus, if you see MODEM\0001 in a device's Driver value, look up Class\MODEM\0001 to find more information about that device's driver and INF file).

ACPI

ACPI standards for *Advanced Configuration and Power Interface*. Windows 98 stores power-management devices in this enumerator subkey. In my experience, the device ID is a plain-English name, and the instance number is just a sequence number.

BIOS

You see this enumerator subkey on computers that have a Plug and Play–compliant BIOS. It contains a variety of devices that are embedded in the computer's motherboard. The BIOS reports them to the operating system. Each device ID is in the EISA format (for example, `*PNP0001`), and each instance ID is a hexadecimal sequence number. Microsoft assigns certain ranges of device IDs to certain types of devices, as described in the following table:

The Windows 98 Configuration Manager

Plug and Play. It is responsible for managing the computer's configuration process. It identifies each bus on your computer (PCI, SCSI, ISA) and all of the devices on each bus. It notes the configuration of each device, making sure that each device is using unique resources (IRQ, I/O address).

The Configuration Manager uses three key components to make all of this happen: bus enumerators, arbitrators, and device drivers. Here's a summary of the purpose of each component:

Bus enumerators	Bus enumerators are responsible for building the *hardware tree*. They query each device or device driver for configuration information.
Arbitrators	Arbitrators assign resources to each device in the hardware tree. That is, they dole out IRQs, I/O addresses, and such to each device, resolving conflicts as they arise.
Device drivers	The Configuration Manager loads a device driver for each device in the hardware tree and communicates the device's configuration to the driver.

Range	Description
PNP0000-PNP0004	Interrupt controllers
PNP0100-PNP0102	System timers
PNP0200-PNP0202	DMA controllers
PNP0300-PNP0313	Keyboard controllers
PNP0400-PNP0401	Printer ports
PNP0500-PNP0501	Communication ports
PNP0600-PNP0602	Hard disk controllers
PNP0700	Standard floppy disk controller
PNP0800	System speaker
PNP0900-PNP0915	Display adapters
PNP0930-PNP0931	Expansion buses
PNP0940-PNP0941	Expansion buses
PNP0A00-PNP0A04	Expansion buses
PNP0B00	CMOS real-time clock
PNP0C01	System board extension
PNP0C02	Reserved
PNP0C04	Numeric data processor
PNP0E00-PNP0E02	PCMCIA controllers
PNP0F01	Microsoft Serial Mouse
PNP0F00-PNP0F13	Mouse ports

Range	Description
PNP8000-PNP8FFF	Network adapters
PNPA030	Mitsumi CD-ROM controller
PNPB000-PNPB0FF	Other adapters

EISA

You see this enumerator subkey on computers that have an EISA bus. Each subkey represents a device installed on that bus. You will see at least one subkey called *PNP0A00 under EISA that represents the ISA Plug and Play bus. Note that this subkey isn't common on newer computers that don't use this bus. And, of course, the device IDs are in the EISA format.

ESDI

You see this enumerator subkey on computers that have an ESDI device installed—notably hard disks. The device IDs are plain-English names that usually indicate the type of disk, and the instance IDs look like *BUS&DEVICE&INSTANCE*, allowing you to find the parent device by following the path to Enum*BUS**DEVICE**INSTANCE*. Each instance's subkey contains additional values not found for other devices, such as CurrentDriveLetter, which indicates the drive letter assigned to the device. If you partitioned the drive, this string value entry will contain a letter for each drive, such as "CD".

FLOP

Most computers contain this enumerator subkey because it describes the floppy drives installed on the computer. Each device and instance ID is named similarly to those in ESDI. As with the subkeys of ESDI, you see additional values, such as CurrentDriveLetter, which indicates the drive letter assigned to the floppy drive.

HTREE

This subkey doesn't contain any devices. HTREE\RESERVED maintains a list of resources that you reserve via the Device Manager.

TIP: A good way to search the Registry for disk information is to search for value entries named CurrentDriveLetter.

ISAPNP

You see this enumerator subkey on computers with ISA or EISA buses when the computer doesn't have a Plug and Play BIOS. Each subkey describes a device installed on that bus and uses the EISA name format without the asterisk (*).

INFRARED

Some computers, particularly newer portable computers, have infrared ports. You see a subkey under INFRARED for each virtual device attached to this port. In particular, you'll see COM and LPT.

LPTENUM

LPTENUM exists only if you install a Plug and Play printer on the parallel port.

MF

MF contains a subkey for each multifunction device installed on the computer. Since most modern computers have a primary and secondary IDE controller, you'll see two device IDs: CHILD0000 and CHILD0001. The devices in MF have parent devices that are listed elsewhere in Enum. Like devices in ESDI, the instance IDs look like *BUS&DEVICE&INSTANCE*, allowing you to find the parent device by opening Enum*BUS**DEVICE**INSTANCE*.

MONITOR

MONITOR usually contains a single subkey: DEFAULT_MONITOR. If you're using two monitors, a new feature for Windows 98, you might see additional subkeys. Below the monitor's subkey, you see additional subkeys called 0001, 0002, and so on, one for each hardware profile. The only time you'll see more than one key is in cases where you might be using different monitors at different times, such as docked and undocked configurations. While a portable is docked, the computer might use a regular monitor, but while it's undocked, the computer might use the LCD panel. To see which monitor Windows 98 is using, you must look in HKEY_DYN_DATA\\Config Manager\\Enum.

SEE ALSO

➤ Chapter 8 contains more information about determining the current monitor.

NOTE: When you see an instance ID that begins with the name of an enumerator in Enum, that's a good indication that the ID refers to a parent device. Follow the path given in the instance ID, beginning with Enum. Thus, if you see the instance ID BIOS&*PNP0700&0800, open BIOS under Enum, followed by *PNP0700 and 08.

Network

Unlike the other subkeys in Enum, this subkey doesn't describe hardware; it describes the network protocols, clients, and services installed in Windows 98. On a Microsoft Network, you typically see the following subkeys:

FASTIR	Fast Infrared Protocol
MSTCP	TCP/IP
VREDIR	Client for Microsoft Networks
VSERVER	File and Printer Sharing

PCI

On computers that have a PCI bus, you see a subkey under PCI for each device on it. Each device ID looks something like VEN_*XXXX*&DEV_*YYYY*&SUBSYS_*ZZZZZZZZ*&REV_*NN*. *XXXX* is a vendor code, and *YYYY* is a device code. Each instance looks like BUS_*XX*&DEV_*YY*&FUNC_*ZZ*, where *XX* is a bus code, *YY* is a device code, and *ZZ* is a function code.

PCMCIA

PCMCIA contains a single subkey for each PC Card device installed in the computer. When you remove a PC Card from the computer, Windows 98 retains its settings under PCMCIA. The device IDs used in PCMCIA seem to be plain-English values queried from each PC Card device. The instance ID can be a simple device number, or it can be in the form *BUS&DEVICE&INSTANCE*, which refers to the parent device within Enum.

Root

This enumerator subkey contains a subkey for each legacy ISA and VLB device installed on the computer. These devices include those detected via the Add New Hardware Wizard. You find a combination of names used for device IDs in this key. Device IDs that use the EISA format are actual legacy devices. Device IDs that have names such as SwEnum and Net are virtual Windows devices. Net represents the Dial-Up Networking adapter, for example.

SCSI

This enumerator subkey contains a single subkey for each SCSI device installed on the computer. Note that the host adapter is installed under the PCI key, not SCSI. SCSI uses naming conventions similar to ESDI and FLOP.

SERENUM

SERENUM contains a single subkey for each device attached to a serial port. For example, if you plug a mouse into a serial port, you see a subkey for that mouse under SERENUM. The instance ID is *BUS&DEVICE&INSTANCE*, allowing you to find the serial port to which the device is attached by opening Enum*BUS**DEVICE**INSTANCE*.

USB

You see a single subkey for each device connected to the Universal Serial Bus. You also see a subkey that represents the USB hub called ROOT_HUB. The instance ID is *BUS&DEVICE&INSTANCE*, allowing you to find the root hub by opening Enum*BUS**DEVICE**INSTANCE*.

VPOWERD

This enumerator subkey leads to additional subkeys that contain configuration data for Windows 98's power management devices. One such example includes the APM Battery Slot. The device IDs in this enumerator use plain-English names.

Hardware

Hardware is an itty-bitty branch that contains dubious information about the computer's hardware configuration. The Description\System subkey leads to three additional subkeys called CentralProcessor, FloatingPointProcessor, and MultifunctionAdapter. Each subkey provides identification and configuration data for that particular component.

The Devicemap subkey is empty but leads to a key called SerialComm, which seems to map port names to actual communication ports. The *Microsoft Windows 98 Resource Kit*, published by Microsoft Press, states that this information is used by HyperTerminal, and apparently it has no other useful purpose.

NOTE: Hardware seems to be borrowed from Windows NT, providing compatibility between the two operating systems' Registries. The same branch in Windows NT contains much more extensive information about the hardware installed in the computer, including information about keyboards, pointers, video adapters, SCSI adapters, and much more.

Network

Network\Logon is present on computers connected to a network. It contains information about the security provider and the current username. Logonvalidated indicates that the security provider validated the user's logon credentials. Note that if you install support for group policies using the Add/Remove Programs Properties dialog box, you see an additional value called PolicyHandler. This subkey indicates the name of the DLL file that handles group policies. Last, username always contains the username of the current user, assuming that the user logged onto the computer properly.

Security

Admin\Remote contains a value entry for each user or group that has administrative privileges on the user's computer. A computer using user-level security that's connected to a Microsoft Network will usually have a single value entry called *DOMAIN*\Domain Admins, indicating that anyone in the Domain Admins group has administrative rights on the computer.

Provider describes the security provider on the network as indicated by the primary network logon. Container indicates the domain name on an NT network. Platform_Type indicates the type of server providing security: 00 00 00 00 for share-level, 01 00 00 00 for a domain, or 02 00 00 00 for a regular server.

Software

Software contains a variety of computer-specific software settings. That is, the settings you find in this branch apply to every user who logs onto the computer. HKEY_CURRENT_USER has a similar key, which you'll learn about in Chapter 7, "HKEY_USERS and HKEY_CURRENT_USER," but those settings apply to the individual user. Applications such as text editors and graphics programs tend to store settings in the Software subkey in HKEY_CURRENT_USER, while hardware and utility vendors tend to store settings in HKEY_LOCAL_MACHINE\Software. Seagate and Symantec are examples of vendors that store settings in HKEY_LOCAL_MACHINE.

Within Software, applications use an organization similar to *Company**Product**Version*. *Company* is the name of the company that produces the application, *Product* is the name of the application, and *Version* is the version of the application whose settings you find in that branch. Thus, Honeycutt\Power Tools\1.0 contains preferences for version 1.0 of a program called Power Tools developed by a company called Honeycutt. Some companies use the name CurrentVersion instead of an actual version number, as Microsoft does for Windows.

> NOTE: HKEY_LOCAL_MACHINE\Software\CLASSES is also known as HKEY_CLASSES_ROOT. Chapter 5, "HKEY_CLASSES_ROOT," is dedicated to this branch, so you won't find it covered in this chapter.

Microsoft, immediately under HKEY_LOCAL_MACHINE\Software, contains computer-specific settings for Microsoft products such as Office and, more importantly, Windows 98. The settings in this portion of the Registry are very useful for troubleshooting and customizing the operating system. The following sections describe these in more detail.

SEE ALSO

➤ Chapter 5 tells you more about the organization of this Registry branch.

➤ Chapter 7 shows you how the Software branch looks for user-specific data.

Clients

Clients is an oddball; it doesn't conform to these rules. Within Clients, you find a single subkey for each type of client you can configure on the Programs tab of Internet Explorer's Internet Options dialog box. In other words, you can associate mail, news, conferencing, calendar, and contact list clients with Internet Explorer. When you choose **Go**, **Mail** or **Go**, **News** from Internet Explorer, the browser will open the correct program.

Clients contains five subkeys: Calendar, Contacts, Internet Call, Mail, and News. The default value for each key names the application currently chosen and points to one of the subkeys one level below. Thus, the default value for Clients\Mail is *Client*, and Clients\Mail*Client* describes that application. The organization of each client's subkey is virtually the same as for programs in HKEY_CLASSES_ROOT. For example, under Outlook, Express\shell\open\command contains the command line that starts the program. Outlook Express\Protocols\mailto\shell\open\command contains the command line that Internet Explorer launches when you click a mailto: link on a Web page. Other types of clients have the same two subkeys, shell and Protocols.

Microsoft\Active Setup

Microsoft first introduced Active Setup with Internet Explorer 4.0. Active Setup is different from other setup programs in that you download an installer from the Internet, which in turn downloads and installs the program to your computer.

Active Setup stores most of its settings in Active Setup. The most interesting thing you'll find in this subkey is a list of installed components. When you go to the Windows Update site, it takes an inventory of the components you've installed and their version numbers. The information in Active Setup is how the setup program makes recommendations for components you should upgrade or install.

Microsoft\Internet Explorer

`Internet Explorer` contains browser settings that apply to every user who logs onto the computer. For example, `AboutURLs` has a number of values that point to HTML files for certain errors. `Advanced Options` contains templates that Internet Explorer uses to display the options on the Advanced tab of the Internet Options dialog box. `Main` is the most interesting subkey of `Internet Explorer`. It contains settings such as the default search URL, the amount of disk space used for the cache, and the size of placeholders used for images on a Web page.

Microsoft\Windows\CurrentVersion

`Windows\CurrentVersion` contains a plethora of values, most of which the Setup program created when you installed Windows 98. Of interest are `RegisteredOrganization` and `RegisteredOwner`, which you can change if you don't like the values you supplied when you installed the operating system.

You find some of the most interesting configuration data under `Microsoft\Windows\CurrentVersion`. This is where the operating system stores its machine-specific settings, such as application paths and setup parameters. The following sections describe the most interesting of these subkeys and values.

Applets

`Applets` contains a single subkey for each Windows 98 accessory that you've used. The actual data that each accessory stores is different, but in most cases you'll see things such as most recently used lists, paths, and anything else the applet requires to run.

App Paths

Immediately under `CurrentVersion` is a subkey called `App Paths`. This is how you can run a program from the Run dialog box or MS-DOS command prompt just by typing its name, even though the program isn't in the path.

The default value entry for `App Paths\`*filename*, where *filename* is the name of the executable file including the EXE file extension, contains the command line that executes the program. An optional value called `Path` might contain a path that describes where to find other files, perhaps DLLs, that the program might require. Here's an example: If you want to be able to run a program called Myprog.exe without putting the program in the path, add a subkey to `App Paths` called `Myprog.exe` and set the default value entry to the program's path and filename.

> NOTE: Right after `Active Setup`, you'll see a key called `ActiveSetup`. This is an example of where Microsoft got sloppy with where it put configuration data. Thanks to a simple typo, the programmer left out a space, so there are two different keys for the same thing. Not only that, but Active Setup will never look in `ActiveSetup`, so the information stored there is just wasting space.

explorer

`explorer` contains settings that mostly affect Windows Explorer but sometimes affect the desktop. In reality, the similar key you find in `HKEY_CURRENT_USER` is more customizable than this one, but there are other options.

`explorer\Desktop\Namespace` contains subkeys whose names reflect class identifiers. For each subkey under `Namespace`, Explorer puts the corresponding object on the desktop. The default value entry for the key contains the name of the object, which you'll see under its desktop icon. Chapter 9, "Customizing the Windows 98 Desktop," contains more information about using `Namespace` to customize the desktop. `MyComputer\Namespace`, `Internet\Namespace`, `RemoteComputer\Namespace`, and `NetworkNeighborhood\Namespace` are similar to `Desktop\Namespace`, but each subkey in these represents objects that Windows Explorer will add to the My Computer, Internet, Remote Computer, and Network Neighborhood folders, respectively.

When you choose **Start**, **Find**, you find that the submenu contains a number of commands that let you search in various places. Explorer gets these from `explorer\FindExtensions`. If you see an extension on the **Find** menu that you want to remove, remove its corresponding subkey from `FindExtensions`.

`explorer\Shell Folders` and `explorer\User Shell Folders` work similar to the same branches in `HKEY_CURRENT_USER`. The `HKEY_LOCAL_MACHINE` key's versions of these two subkeys are limited, though, usually just containing values for two folders: `Common Desktop` and `Common Startup`.

`explorer\Shell Icons` allows you to redefine a variety of icons that Windows 98 uses in places such as the Start menu or in Windows Explorer. Add the icon's value to this subkey and set its value to the icon's path and index. Chapter 9 gives you explicit instructions for customizing this subkey and even has a table that describes all the icons available in Shell32.dll.

SEE ALSO

➤ Chapter 9 shows you how to use `Namespace`, `Shell Folders`, and `Shell Icons` to fully customize the desktop.

FS Templates

`FS Templates` contains a subkey for each file system role that you can choose by clicking the **File System** button on the Performance tab of the System Properties dialog box. (You'll see this dialog box in Figure 6.2, later in this chapter.) The default value entry in each subkey contains the name of the template. `NameCache` indicates the number of filenames that Windows 98 will store in the cache, and `PathCache` indicates the number of paths. After you choose a template, the operating system copies the values to `HKEY_LOCAL_MACHINE\System\CurrentControlSet\FileSystem`.

Run, RunOnce, RunOnceEx, and So On

A popular question on the Internet is "Why does such-and-such a program automatically start when I boot Windows 98?" If you don't see the program in the Start menu's Startup group, the answer must be one of the `Run` keys.

Each time you start the operating system and possibly before the user closes the login dialog box, Windows 98 starts any application it finds in Run. This subkey contains a value, whose name is arbitrary, for each application the operating system runs at startup. The string data in each value is the command line that the operating system uses to launch the program. Windows 98 starts the programs it finds in Run Once and then removes the value for it. That way, the program runs only once. An example of such a program that you would run only one time is one that completes a program's installation after you restart the computer.

RunServices and RunServicesOnce are similar to Run and Run Once. The difference is that they are used for network and system services, as opposed to regular old programs, which load at a different point in the boot process. You'll frequently find programs in Run that really should be in RunServices, given this distinction between the two.

SEE ALSO

➤ Chapter 11, "Tweak UI and Other Registry Programs," describes a few programs that simplify editing Run.

➤ Chapter 14, "Profiles, System Policies, and the Registry," describes how to use the System Policy Editor to change the Run key.

Setup

Setup contains values that describe how you installed Windows 98. In it, you find the following values (among many, many others):

BackupDir	The folder that contains uninstall information. Used only if you're upgrading.
CommandLine	The command line used to start the Setup program.
SourcePath	The path from which you installed Windows 98. Change this path if you've relocated the setup files.

Setup\OptionalComponents contains a subkey for each Windows 98 component you see on the Windows Setup tab of the Add/Remove Programs Properties dialog box. Each subkey has three values: INF, Installed, and Section. INF and Section indicate the INF file and section that describe how to install the component. Installed indicates whether the component is installed on the computer.

TIP: It's sometimes easier to edit the Run keys using the System Policy Editor than it is to use the Registry Editor.

SharedDLLs

Immediately under `CurrentVersion` is a subkey called `SharedDLLs`. This key contains a value for each DLL installed on the computer. The name of the value is the path and filename of the DLL. The value assigned to this DWORD is the number of applications using it. If you see a DLL in this subkey that's assigned a value of 2, that means two different applications are using it.

`SharedDLLs` is how uninstall programs know when it's safe to remove a DLL from the computer and when it's not. When a DLL's value under `SharedDLLs` is 0, removing the DLL is safe. That's the theory, but here's the rule: Since some programs don't use this subkey properly, you can't really rely on this method.

Uninstall

`Uninstall` is another interesting subkey of `CurrentVersion`. Each subkey, `Uninstall\Application`, contains information about an application's uninstall program. The Add/Remove Program Properties dialog box uses the value of the string `DisplayName` to fill its list, and `UninstallString` contains the command line that starts the application's uninstall program.

If you manually remove a program from your computer as described in Chapter 10, "Fixing Common Problems Via the Registry," make sure you remove the program's entry in `Uninstall`. That way, you won't see an entry for the program in the Add/Remove Programs Properties dialog box when the program no longer exists.

SEE ALSO

➤ Chapter 10 shows you how to manually remove a program from your computer.

System\CurrentControlSet

`System` leads to two subkeys, `Control` and `Services`, that describe how Windows 98 starts. You'll learn about each of these subkeys in the following sections.

Control

`CurrentControlSet\Control` contains a single value entry called `Current User` that indicates the name of the current user if he successfully logged onto Windows 98.

ASD

The Automatic Skip Driver agent stores its settings in `ASD`. `List` contains a number of subkeys whose names resemble a GUID. `List\Class` contains a single value called `Problem` that contains a message. You'll find matching subkeys under `Prob` that are named after a device ID and whose values indicate whether there was a problem.

TIP: Removing an application's uninstall program from `Uninstall` is a good way to prevent users from accidentally removing a program.

Figure 6.2 ASD lets you disable a device when it detects a problem related to that device.

Change any of the values in `Prob` to `01`, and then run the Automatic Skip Driver Agent by typing `ASD` in the Run dialog box and pressing Enter. You'll see the dialog box shown in Figure 6.2. The message to the left of `=>` comes from `List`, and the device name on the right side comes from the device's name, as you will see if you look up the device ID `Prob` within `\HKEY_LOCAL_MACHINE\Enum`.

ComputerName

`ComputerName` in `ComputerName\ComputerName` contains the name of the computer as provided on the Identification tab of the Network dialog box, which you open from the Control Panel. If you change its name here, you must also change it in `Services\VxD\VNETSUP`.

> NOTE: If the name `CurrentControlSet` caught your attention, it's probably because unlike other similarly named keys where `CurrentSomething` implies an alias, `CurrentControlSet` isn't an alias for anything. This key represents the one and only control set in Windows 98. Windows NT does allow multiple control sets, so the operating system uses `CurrentControlSet` as an alias for the one in use at the time.

FileSystem

FileSystem contains a number of settings that control how the Windows 98 file system works. You can disable long filenames, for example, by changing Win31FileSystem from 00 to 01. You can change how Windows 98 creates 8.3 aliases for long filenames by adding a binary value called NameNumericTail and setting it to 00. This means that the operating system will try to create filenames that use eight full characters of the long filename (if doing so doesn't create a duplicate filename) instead of adding a tilde (~) followed by a number. The following table describes a variety of other settings you can change in FileSystem, most of which you can gain access to by clicking the **File System** button on the Performance tab of the System Properties dialog box (see Figure 6.3):

Value	Description
AsyncFileCommit	00 = enable synchronous buffer commits 01 = enable asynchronous file commits
LastBootPMDrvs	Contains the number of the last boot driver
ReadAheadThreshold	Read-ahead optimization
DriveWriteBehind	00 00 00 00 = disable write-behind caching FF FF FF FF = enable write-behind caching
PreserveLongFilenames	00 00 00 00 = disable preservation FF FF FF FF = enable preservation
ForceRMIO	00 = use protected mode disk I/O 01 = force real mode disk I/O
VirtualHDIRQ	0 = disable protected mode HD interrupts 1 = enable protected mode HD interrupts
SoftCompatMode	00 = disable file-sharing semantics 01 = enable file-sharing semantics

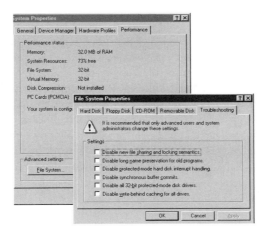

Figure 6.3 Windows 98 describes each of these options in more detail.

If you configured the computer as a desktop computer on the Hard Disk tab of the File System Properties dialog box, you won't see NameCache or PathCache in FileSystem. If you configured the computer for the remaining two roles, mobile or network server, you do see these values. NameCache specifies the number of filenames that Windows 98 will store in the cache. PathCache specifies how many paths to store in the cache. The larger these two caches are, the better the computer's performance, and the more risk there is that a sudden failure will cause data loss. That's why the mobile computer role has a smaller cache than the network server role.

Immediately under FileSystem, you see two subkeys. CDFS describes characteristics that control the CD-ROM file system's cache size. The operating system uses a combination of CacheSize, Prefetch, and PrefetchTail to calculate the total size of the cache. NoVolTrack disables volume tracking for certain disks. Normally, Windows 98 writes a volume ID to a disk in a region called the OEM field. This causes some disks to fail, however. Windows 98 looks at each value entry in NoVolTrack and notes the offset given in the first two bytes. Then it compares the value it finds on the disk at that offset to the remaining 8 bytes given in the value entry. If the values match, Windows 98 doesn't write a volume ID to the disk.

IDConfigDB

IDConfigDB indicates the current hardware profile. As you will learn in Chapter 8, HKEY_CURRENT_CONFIG is an alias for one of the hardware profiles in HKEY_LOCAL_MACHINE\Config, which are numbered 0001, 0002, and so on. CurrentConfig, under IDConfigDB, indicates which of those profiles is in HKEY_CURRENT_CONFIG. FriendlyName*XXXX* indicates the name of each configuration.

SessionManager

SessionManager leads to a series of subkeys that don't really relate to the name of this key. In fact, most of the subkeys in SessionManager help Windows 98 keep track of various DLL files or help it determine if an application can run in Windows and what it would take in order for it to do so. Here's a description of each subkey:

AppPatches	This subkey leads to additional subkeys, each of which leads to the name of a program. Windows 98 can make these programs work by patching them after it loads them into memory. The subkeys under each application describe each patch.
CheckBadApps	This subkey leads to additional subkeys, each of which describes a program that won't run in Windows 98. The value entries in each subkey indicate a message that Windows 98 will display. The message explains why the application won't run properly.
CheckBadApps400	This subkey fulfills the same purpose as CheckBadApps, but it's new to Windows 98.
CheckVerDLLs	You find a value under this key for each DLL installed in Windows 98. Each value contains version information that an installation program should check to make sure it doesn't overwrite a newer version of the DLL.
HackIniFiles	Each value entry under this subkey indicates a change that Windows 98 will make to the INI file when it loads the file into memory.

Known16DLLs

This subkey contains a value entry for each 16-bit DLL that Windows 98 knows about. When searching for DLLs in this list, Windows 98 changes the search order so that it looks in \Windows\System first instead of \Windows.

KnownDLLs

This subkey contains a value entry for each 32-bit DLL that Windows 98 knows about.

Shutdown

Shutdown contains a single string value entry called FastReboot that indicates whether Windows 98 shuts down quickly. If you're having a problem with Windows 98 failing when you shut it down, change this value to 0.

Services

Services leads to a series of subkeys that define what happens when Windows 98 loads. The most interesting of these include Arbitrators, Class, and VxD. You'll learn about all three in the following sections.

Arbitrators

AddrArb, DMAArb, IOArb, and IRQArb indicate the resources that Windows 98 has allocated thus far. AddrArb keeps track of memory ranges, DMAArb keeps track of DMA channels, IOArb keeps track of I/O ports, and IRQArb keeps track of interrupt request numbers. The format of these values is irrelevant, because changing them is senseless.

Class

There are two kinds of subkeys under Class: those that look like COM class identifiers ({4D36E964-E325-11CE-BFC1-08002BE10318}), and those that have regular names, such as Mouse. You find one of each for every device class. The IDs are new to Windows 98 and provide a method for accessing devices that's similar to how Windows 98 accesses other objects. Each ID has two value entries: Class and Link. In almost all cases, they both contain the same value, which is a reference to another subkey under Class that contains more information about the device class.

The subkeys with regular device class names such as Mouse and CDROM describe the device class. The default value contains the class's name as you see it in the Device

Manager. You usually see the following three values and possibly more, depending on the device class:

Icon	Indicates the icon that Windows 98 displays in the Device Manager. This is an index or resource ID. The icon comes from the DLL file given by `Installer`.
Installer	Indicates the program file that's responsible for installing the device. This is also where the Device Manager gets the icon you see in the list.
Link	Links the device class to its class definition, which is `Class\`*`ClassName`*.

Each instance ID under `HKEY_LOCAL_MACHINE\Enum` contains a value entry called `Driver` that points to one of the branches under `Class`. For example, `Enum\BIOS\*PNP0501\0D` contains a value called `Driver` whose string value is `Ports\0001`. Look up `Class\Ports\0001` to find more information about the device's driver, INF file, and so on. If you don't see any numbered subkeys under a device class, a device of that class is not installed on the computer. Otherwise, you see those familiar subkeys numbered `0000`, `0001`, and so on. Each subkey under a device class typically has the same types of values. You might find values and subkeys unique to a particular device, though, particularly in the case of more-complex devices such as modems and network adapters. Here's a description of the typical values you find for `\Class\`*`ClassName`*`\Device`:

DevLoader	Describes the device driver responsible for the device. Drivers that begin with an asterisk (★) are part of the monolithic Vmm32.vxd or are loaded from \Windows\System\Vmm32.
DriverDate	Contains the date that the device driver was released from the vendor.
DriverDesc	Contains a brief description of the device driver. You see this description in the Device Manager.
InfPath	Contains the filename of the INF file used to install the device. You find this INF file in \Windows\Inf.

InfSection	Contains the section name within the INF file that was used to install the device.
MatchingDeviceId	Contains the device ID of the device as you find it in HKEY_LOCAL_MACHINE\Enum.
ProviderName	The name of the device driver vendor.

VxD

Within VxD, you find a subkey for each virtual device driver installed in Windows 98. Many of these keys contain additional configuration data specific to each driver; thus, any subkeys you see under each subkey are unique to that driver.

7

HKEY_USERS and HKEY_CURRENT_USER

In this chapter:

- HKEY_USERS
- HKEY_CURRENT_USER
- HKEY_CURRENT_USER\Software\Microsoft

HKEY_USERS

HKEY_USERS contains subkeys that define user-specific preferences. What you see under HKEY_USERS depends on whether or not you enable user profiles on your computer. If user profiles are not enabled on your computer, you see a single subkey called .DEFAULT. This subkey contains settings that apply to all users, and it corresponds to the User.dat file in \Windows. Note that .DEFAULT is frequently called the *default profile* or the *default user*. That's because all you see under HKEY_USERS is .DEFAULT if the user logs onto Windows 98 without providing credentials by pressing Esc at the logon dialog box.

If user profiles are enabled and the user logs onto Windows 98 properly, you see the same .DEFAULT subkey, as well as a subkey called *Username*, which is the name that the current user used to log onto Windows 98. Windows 98 still loads .DEFAULT from the User.dat file in \Windows, contrary to what other publications state. *Username* corresponds to the User.dat file you find in \Windows\Profiles*Username*, though. If the administrator enables roving profiles, Windows 98 loads the user's profile, which includes User.dat, from the user's home folder on the network as long as it's newer than the local profile.

Windows 98 creates new user profiles based on the existing default profile. That is, after creating a folder under \Windows\Profiles, Windows 98 copies User.dat from \Windows to \Windows\Profiles*Username*. The operating system also fixes any references to the default profile so that they now point to the user's profile. It replaces any reference to .DEFAULT with a reference to *Username* and replaces any reference to the profile folders in \Windows with references to the new profile folders in \Windows\Profiles*Username*.

SEE ALSO

➤ Chapter 13, "Security and Remote Administration," shows you how to improve Windows 98 security by applying significant restrictions as to what the default user can do on the computer.

➤ Chapter 14, "Profiles, System Policies, and the Registry," shows you how to enable user profiles and how to apply policies to individual users as well as groups. More importantly, this chapter describes how user profiles affect the Registry.

HKEY_CURRENT_USER

HKEY_CURRENT_USER is an alias for HKEY_USERS*Subkey*. *Subkey* depends on whether user profiles are enabled and whether the user logs onto the computer properly. It's an alias for HKEY_USERS\.DEFAULT if profiles aren't enabled or the user bypasses the login dialog box by pressing Esc. Otherwise, it's an alias for HKEY_USERS*Username*. To better understand which subkey HKEY_CURRENT_USER refers to, look at the whole matter from a different perspective:

■ If the only subkey under HKEY_USERS is .DEFAULT, that means either profiles are not enabled on the computer or the user started Windows 98 without providing logon credentials. HKEY_CURRENT_USER is an alias for .DEFAULT in either case.

■ If you see .DEFAULT and *Username* under HKEY_USERS, that means profiles are enabled and the user logged onto Windows 98 properly. In either case, HKEY_CURRENT_USER is an alias for *Username*.

CAUTION: Windows 98 allows anyone to gain access to a computer by bypassing the logon dialog box. Since this causes Windows 98 to use the default profile, you can protect the computer by enabling user profiles and using the System Policy Editor to set draconian restrictions as to what the default user can do on the computer.

NOTE: Recall from Chapter 1, "Inside the Windows 98 Registry," that an alias is a shortcut to another branch. When you change a value in the alias, the Registry reflects that change in the original branch. Thus, the Registry reflects any change you make to HKEY_CURRENT_USER in HKEY_USERS*Subkey*, and vice versa.

Below HKEY_CURRENT_USER, you normally see seven subkeys that define the user's preferences. You'll learn about each subkey in the following sections, starting with AppEvents.

AppEvents

In Windows 98, an application event is any event to which you can assign a sound. The operating system plays the sound when that event occurs. Maximizing a window is an event for which Windows 98 will play a sound, for instance. So is a critical error. You assign sounds to events using the Sounds Properties dialog box, which you open from the Control Panel.

Windows 98 and each application you install define the events that you can associate sounds with, so inventing events out of thin air does you little good. Windows 98 and applications only recognize events that they register. They register events by listing them in the following two subkeys of AppEvents, a subkey of HKEY_CURRENT_USER:

EventLabels	Defines the label for each event.
Schemes	Associates sounds with each event.

EventLabels

Figure 7.1 shows the relationship between the Sounds Properties dialog box and the two subkeys you see under AppEvents: EventLabels and Schemes. EventLabels defines the name of each event. The name of each subkey under EventLabels is the internal name of the event, and the default value entry of each is the label for the event as you see it in the Sounds Properties dialog box. Thus, the subkey called Close describes an event whose label is Close program. Table 7.1 describes the event labels you typically find in EventLabels.

> **NOTE:** Although you can certainly customize sound events in the Registry, doing so is senseless. First, trying to register new events for an application is useless, because each application only looks for events that it registers. Second, the Sounds Properties dialog box makes choosing Sound Themes or associating sound files with particular events much easier than doing the same task in the Registry.

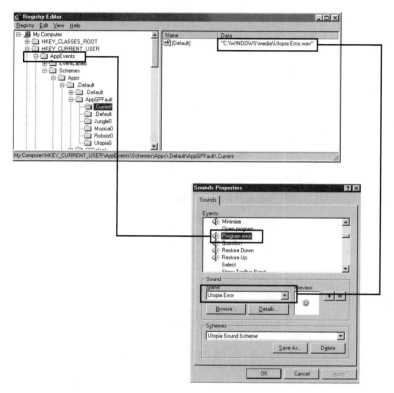

Figure 7.1 The Sounds Properties dialog box retrieves its information from the subkeys under AppEvents.

Table 7.1 **Sound Events Defined in Windows 98**

Subkey	Event Label
WINDOWS	
.Default	Default sound
AppGPFault	Program error
CCSelect	Select
Close	Close program
InfraredBeginCommunication	Infrared: Begin Communication
InfraredBeginDeviceInRange	Infrared: Begin Device(s) In Range
InfraredEndCommunication	Infrared: End Communication
InfraredEndDeviceInRange	Infrared: End Device(s) In Range
InfraredInterrupted	Infrared: Interrupted
InfraredNewFiles	Infrared: New Files Notification

Subkey	Event Label
Maximize	Maximize
MenuCommand	Menu command
MenuPopup	Menu popup
Minimize	Minimize
Open	Open program
RestoreDown	Restore Down
RestoreUp	Restore Up
ShowBand	Show Toolbar Band
SystemAsterisk	Asterisk
SystemExclamation	Exclamation
SystemExit	Exit Windows
SystemHand	Critical Stop
SystemQuestion	Question
SystemStart	Start Windows
WINDOWS EXPLORER	
ActivatingDocument	Complete Navigation
EmptyRecycleBin	Empty Recycle Bin
MoveMenuItem	Move Menu Item
Navigating	Start Navigation
MEDIA PLAYER	
Close	Close program
Open	Open program
POWER MANAGEMENT	
CriticalBatteryAlarm	Critical Battery Alarm
LowBatteryAlarm	Low Battery Alarm
SOUND RECORDER	
Close	Close program
Open	Open program
MICROSOFT OFFICE	
Office97-AddItemtoView	Add Item to View
Office97-Alert	Alert
Office97-AutoCorrect	AutoCorrect
Office97-BestFit	Best Fit
Office97-Clear	Clear
Office97-Cut&Clear	Cut & Clear
Office97-Delete	Delete
Office97-DeleteRow	Delete Row
Office97-DialogCancel	Dialog Cancel
Office97-DialogOk	Dialog Ok

continues

Table 7.1 **Continued**

Subkey	Event Label
MICROSOFT OFFICE	
Office97-Drag	Drag
Office97-Drop	Drop
Office97-Expand/Collapse	Expand/Collapse
Office97-FolderSwitch	Folder Switch
Office97-GroupScopeSwitch	Group Scope Switch
Office97-GroupSwitch	Group Switch
Office97-InsertRow	Insert Row
Office97-ModeSwitch	Mode Switch
Office97-NewItem	New Item
Office97-PlyScroll	Ply Scroll
Office97-PlySelect	Ply Select
Office97-ProcessComplete	Process Complete
Office97-Redo	Redo
Office97-ScrollArrow	Scroll Arrow
Office97-ScrollBar	Scroll Bar
Office97-ScrollThumb	Scroll Thumb
Office97-Send	Send
Office97-Sort	Sort
Office97-ToolbarClick	Toolbar Click
Office97-ToolbarClose	Toolbar Close
Office97-ToolbarDock	Toolbar Dock
Office97-ToolbarDrop	Toolbar Drop
Office97-ToolbarFocus	Toolbar Focus
Office97-ToolbarUndock	Toolbar Undock
Office97-Undo	Undo
Office97-ViewSwitch	View Switch
Office97-ZoomIn	Zoom In
Office97-ZoomOut	Zoom Out

Schemes

Schemes\Apps associates sounds with the events registered by Windows 98 and each application. Underneath this key, you see a single subkey for each application. .Default contains events that Windows 98 registered, for example, and MPlayer contains the events that the Media Player registered. Look to the default value entry for each Schemes\Apps*AppName* key to see the actual name of the application that registered the events. In a typical installation that includes Microsoft Office, *AppName* would be the following subkeys:

AppName	Application Name
.Default	Windows
Explorer	Windows Explorer
MPlayer	Media Player
Office97	Microsoft Office
PowerCfg	Power Management
SndRec32	Sound Recorder

Each subkey under Schemes\Apps*AppName*, which we'll call *Event*, is one of the events you learned about in the preceding section. In other words, each is a registered event whose label can be found in EventLabels*AppName**Event*. Underneath each event, you see a subkey called .Current whose default value entry contains the path and filename of the sound file associated with the event. You might see several other subkeys that associate sound files with sound themes, too, such as Jungle0 and Utopia0. The default value entry of Schemes indicates the current sound theme, and Windows 98 looks up that name in Schemes\Names. For instance, if the current sound theme is Utopia0, Windows 98 looks in Schemes\Names\Utopia0 to find that the name of this sound theme is Utopia Sound Theme.

To help you sort out all this, take a look at what happens when an event occurs. The application looks up HKEY_CURRENT_USER\AppEvents\Schemes\Apps*AppName*, where *AppName* is the name under which the application registered the event. Underneath that subkey, the application looks up *Event*\.Current, where *Event* is the name of the registered event, and plays the sound file indicated by the default value entry of .Current. Also, look what happens when the Sounds Properties dialog box displays information about the events registered in AppEvents:

- In the **Events** list, you see one category for each subkey of AppEvents\Schemes\Apps. The label you see comes from the subkey's default value entry.

- Underneath each category, you see an event for each subkey of AppEvents\Schemes\Apps*AppName*. The label you see comes from AppEvents\EventLabels*Event*, where *Event* is the same under both branches.

- The sound file you see in **Name** comes from the default value entry of AppEvents\Schemes\Apps*AppName**Event*\.Current.

NOTE: Some applications don't register sounds events in their own category. They add events to the Windows category, Apps\.Default.

Control Panel

Table 7.2 describes each subkey of `Control Panel` and indicates the Control Panel icon that sets the configuration data in it. I've divided the table into sections, each of which describes a single Control Panel icon. The third column indicates the tab on which you configure the options found in each subkey. Keep in mind that only a handful of the icons in the Control Panel store configuration data in this branch of the Registry. Other Control Panel icons store configuration data in `HKEY_LOCAL_MACHINE`, especially machine-specific data, or in other branches within `HKEY_CURRENT_USER`.

While Table 7.2 helps you determine which Control Panel icon sets configuration data in each subkey of `Control Panel`, the following sections help you make sense of the data you find in each of these subkeys. Some are completely uninteresting, so their descriptions are brief, but others contain very useful information.

Table 7.2 **Control Panel Subkeys**

Key	Subkey	Tab
ACCESSIBILITY OPTIONS		
Accessibility		Keyboard
Accessibility	\HighContrast	Display
Accessibility	\KeyboardResponse	Keyboard
Accessibility	\MouseKeys	Mouse
Accessibility	\SerialKeys	General
Accessibility	\ShowSounds	Sound
Accessibility	\SoundSentry	Sound
Accessibility	\Stickykeys	Keyboard
Accessibility	\TimeOut	General
Accessibility	\ToggleKeys	Keyboard
DISPLAY		
Appearance		Appearance
Appearance	\Schemes	Appearance
Colors		Appearance
Desktop	\WindowMetrics	Appearance
Desktop		Screen Saver
Desktop		Background
Desktop		Effects
MOUSE		
Cursor		Pointers
Cursor	\Schemes	Pointers
Infrared		
Infrared		Options
Infrared	\Monitor	Preferences

Key	Subkey	Tab
REGIONAL SETTINGS		
International		Regional Settings
POWER MANAGEMENT		
PowerCfg		Power Schemes
PowerCfg	\GlobalPowerPolicy	Power Schemes
PowerCfg	\PowerPolicies	Power Schemes

Accessibility

This subkey defines the accessibility settings you set in the Accessibility Options dialog box, which you open from the Control Panel. Table 7.2 shows you how each subkey matches up to each tab on this dialog box. Each value entry you find in these subkeys is self-explanatory. Although you can configure the accessibility options using the Registry Editor, stick with the Accessibility Options dialog box, because it makes the task much easier.

The most interesting value entry in each of these subkeys is called HotKeyActive. Recall that a disabled user can activate accessibility options using one of the shortcuts. Pressing the Shift key five times turns on StickyKeys, for example. The problem is you must enable StickyKeys before using it, and some users can't use the computer without StickyKeys being turned on in advance. Get the paradox? If you support a user who is in this situation, you can enable the hot keys for him by opening his Registry in the Registry Editor and setting the appropriate value, as described in Table 7.3. Listing 7.1 is an INF file that you can distribute to users via their login script. Note that these changes don't take effect until the user logs onto the computer again.

Table 7.3 **Accessibility Emergency Hot Keys**

Feature	Hot Key	Subkey of Accessibility
StickyKeys	Press Shift five times	StickyKeys
FilterKeys	Hold down Right Shift for eight seconds	KeyboardResponse
ToggleKeys	Hold down Num Lock for five seconds	ToggleKeys
High Contrast	Press Left Alt+Left Shift+Print Screen	HighContrast
MouseKeys	Press Left Alt+Left Shift+Num Lock	MouseKeys

NOTE: Of all the subkeys in Control Panel, the most interesting is Desktop. This subkey contains a variety of settings that determine how Windows 98 looks and feels. You'll learn more about these settings in Chapter 9, "Customizing the Windows 98 Desktop."

Listing 7.1 **Enabling Accessibility Emergency Hot Keys**

```
[Version]
signature="$CHICAGO$"

[DefaultInstall]
AddReg=Enable.Hotkeys

[Enable.Hotkeys]
HKCU,"Control Panel\Accessibility\Stickykeys",HotKeyActive,
➡0,"1"
HKCU,"Control Panel\Accessibility\KeyboardResponse",
➡HotKeyActive,0,"1"
HKCU,"Control Panel\Accessibility\ToggleKeys",HotKeyActive,
➡0,"1"
HKCU,"Control Panel\Accessibility\HighContrast",HotKeyActive,
➡0,"1"
HKCU,"Control Panel\Accessibility\MouseKeys",HotKeyActive,
➡0,"1"
```

SEE ALSO

➤ Chapter 13, "Security and Remote Administration," shows you how to enable remote administration and how to open a remote Registry in the Registry Editor.

➤ Chapter 15, "Script, REG, and INF Files," describes how to write scripts that make these types of changes and distribute them via email messages or login scripts.

Appearance

HKEY_CURRENT_USER\Control Panel\Appearance\Schemes contains a value entry for each scheme you see in the **Scheme** list of the Display Properties dialog box's Appearance tab. Each entry in this list corresponds to each value entry name under this key. The format of each value's binary data is almost indecipherable, so you're better off defining themes using the Display Properties dialog box.

Appearance does contain one interesting value, however. When you define custom colors by clicking the **Color** button on the Appearance tab, you have to define those colors in decimal notation or use the color wheel. Both are difficult to use because most people are accustomed to defining RGB values in hexadecimal notation, as is common in HTML. The binary value entry, CustomColors, defines these custom colors; they're in hexadecimal notation. The first 4 bytes define the first color in RGB notation followed by 0x00, the second 4 bytes define the second color, and so on. Thus, if you want to set the first color to the khaki color that Microsoft is fond of on their Web pages, type CC CC 99 00 in the first 4 bytes of CustomColors. Figure 7.2 shows the relationship between these values and the Color dialog box.

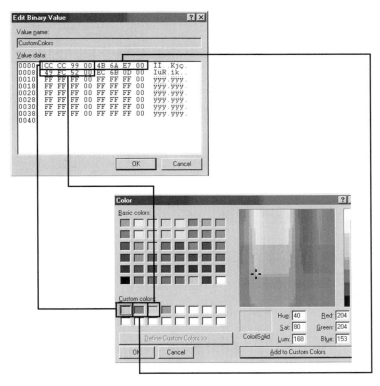

Figure 7.2 Defining custom colors in the Registry is frequently easier than doing so via the Color dialog box.

Colors

The values in `Colors` define the color for each element in the user interface. `ActiveTitle` defines the color of each window's active title bar, for example, and `Window` defines the background color for each window. Each value entry uses the RGB notation, but it does so in decimal, not hexadecimal. This is one of those cases in which changing these values on the Appearance tab of the Display Properties dialog box is easier than changing them in the Registry. If you like to use the same odd colors every time you install Windows 98, you might consider saving this branch to a REG file so that you can import your colors the next time you install the operating system.

Cursors

Each value under `Cursors` indicates the path and filename of a CUR file for that particular pointer. The value's name indicates the name of the pointer, which isn't necessarily what you see in the Pointers tab of the Mouse Properties dialog box. Note that this key's default value entry contains the name of the current scheme.

`Cursors\Schemes` defines the pointer schemes you see in the **Schemes** list of the Mouse Properties dialog box. Each value entry is named after a particular theme, and its string contents contain a comma-separated list of CUR files for each pointer in the theme. The order of this comma-separated list is as follows:

- Arrow
- Help
- AppStarting
- Wait
- Crosshair
- IBeam
- NWPen
- No
- SizeNS
- SizeWE
- SizeNWSE
- SizeNESW
- SizeAll
- UpArrow

Desktop

`Desktop` is one of the most useful subkeys in `Control Panel`. It contains a variety of settings that control how Windows 98 looks and feels. You define most of these settings using the Display Properties dialog box. Also note that you can define any settings you don't find in a traditional Windows 98 dialog box via Tweak UI. With the exception of `SmoothScroll` and `UserPreferenceMask`, which are DWORDs represented as binary values, all of the settings described here are string values. The following table describes the most useful settings for customizing the operating system:

Value	Description
DoubleClickHeight	Describes the maximum distance between two clicks for Windows 98 to consider them a double-click. This value is in half-pixels (8 equals 4 pixels, for example).
DoubleClickWidth	See DoubleClickHeight.
DragFullWindows	Determines whether you see the full window or its outline as you move it around the desktop: 0 = drag window outline 1 = drag full window contents

Value	Description
DragHeight	Describes the distance that the mouse pointer must move with the button held down before Windows 98 recognizes that you're dragging an object. This value is in pixels.
DragWidth	See DragHeight.
FontSmoothing	Determines whether Windows 98 smoothes fonts when it displays them onscreen: 0 = don't smooth screen fonts 1 = smooth screen fonts
MenuShowDelay	Time in milliseconds that the user must hover the mouse pointer over a submenu's name before Windows 98 opens the menu (500ms equals 171 seconds).
PaintDesktopVersion	Determines whether Windows 98 displays the operating system version in the lower-right corner of the desktop: 0 = don't display version 1 = display version number
SmoothScroll	Determines whether windows scroll smoothly when you scroll them. This affects Windows Explorer and Internet Explorer. For example: 0 = don't scroll smoothly 1 = scroll window contents smoothly
UserPreferenceMask	See the following discussion.

UserPreferenceMask is the most interesting value in Desktop and is in fact one of the most useful values in the Registry for customizing the look and feel of Windows 98. UserPreferenceMask is a 32-bit DWORD represented in binary. You only care about the first two bytes of this value, though, which are a bit mask. Each bit is a flag that enables or disables an option. Table 7.4 describes what each bit represents. If you want to prevent menus, combo boxes, and list boxes from animating when you open them, turn off bits 1, 2, and 3 of the first word in UserPreferenceMask. Turn off bit 5 if you don't want Windows 98 to underline hot keys in menus. Bit 6 controls whether

> **TIP:** Is the checkmark gray in **Animate menus, windows, and lists** on the Effects tab of the Display Properties dialog box? If so, it means that either SmoothScroll is set and animation is disabled in UserPreferenceMask, or vice versa. **Animate menus, windows, and lists** is linked to both values in the Registry.

windows come to the foreground when you hover the mouse over them, and bit 7 controls whether you see those annoying tips in yellow boxes when you hover the mouse over the minimize, maximize, and close buttons in a program's title bar. Here are some examples:

Old Value	Old Binary	To Do This	New Binary	New Value
0x2e	00101110	Disable menu hot keys	00001110	0x0e
0x2e	00101110	Enable X-mouse effects	01101110	0x6e
0x20	00100000	Enable mouse tracking	10100000	0xa0
0x20	0010000	Enable animations	00101110	0x2e

Table 7.4 **UserPreferenceMask**

Bit	Mask	Hex	Description
0	00000001	0x01	Unused
1	00000010	0x02	Menu animation
2	00000100	0x04	Combo box animation
3	00001000	0x08	List box animation
4	00010000	0x10	Unused
5	00100000	0x20	Menu hot keys
6	01000000	0x40	X-mouse effects
7	10000000	0x80	Mouse tracking effects

The two subkeys of `Desktop` are `ResourceLocale` and `WindowMetrics`. The default value entry in `ResourceLocale` contains the locale for the version of Windows 98 that you purchased. This value is set when you install Windows 98, and you can't change it. You see a definition of this value in the Locale.inf file that you find in `\Windows\Inf`. Note that the value used for the United States is `409`, which is defined as `English (United States)`. Versions of Windows 98 sold in other regions might have a different value. The remaining subkey, `WindowMetrics`, defines various characteristics of icons, menus, and so on. Most of these values are uninteresting, except for `MinAnimate`, which controls whether Windows 98 animates windows as they minimize to the taskbar and restore to the desktop. You'll learn more about this setting in Chapter 9, "Customizing the Windows 98 Desktop."

SEE ALSO

➤ Chapter 9 describes more ways you can customize your Windows 98 desktop.

➤ Chapter 15 shows you how to convert DWORD values to binary strings and vice versa. In short, you reverse the bytes of a binary string to get the DWORD value.

Bit Masks for the Binary-Illiterate

If you don't understand binary or hexadecimal notation, you'll have difficulty working with bit masks in the Registry. I won't teach you everything you need to know about these notations. I'll teach you just enough so that you can work with masks.

First, understand that each digit in a hexadecimal byte (there are two digits) has a 4-bit binary equivalent. Thus, the hexadecimal numbers 0xAC, 0x01, and 0xF3 are bytes that have two *nibbles* that are 4 bits each. To translate a hexadecimal byte into an 8-bit binary number, look up each nibble in the following table and combine (concatenate) them. If you were to translate 0xFA to binary, you'd find that F is 1111 and A is 1010, so 0xFA must be 11111010. Likewise, 0x93 is 10010011. Refer to Table 7.4 to translate bit numbers into masks.

Digit	Nibble	Digit	Nibble
0	0000	8	1000
1	0001	9	1001
2	0010	A	1010
3	0011	B	1011
4	0100	C	1100
5	0101	D	1101
6	0110	E	1110
7	0111	F	1111

Now that you know the binary representation for the byte, you need to figure out which bit you want to enable or disable. If you're working with bit 6, counting from 0, 1, 2, 3, 4, 5, 6 from the right, your mask is 01000000. Working with bit 3, your mask is 00001000. This mask helps you determine which bit you need to tweak in your 8-bit binary number. Line up your mask with the binary number so that you can identify the bit. Then turn that bit off in the number to disable the option, or turn that bit on to enable the option. After you've tweaked the bit in the mask, translate the number back to hexadecimal by reversing the procedure. For example, if you're left with 01111110, the first four digits represent a 7, and the second four represent an E. Thus, the hexadecimal number is 0x7E.

Here are some examples:

Hex	To Binary	Mask	Leaves Binary	To Hex
0x7E	01111110	Disable bit 3	01110110	0x76
0x2D	00101101	Enable bit 7	10101101	0xAD
0xFF	11111111	Disable bit 0	11111110	0xFE
0xB2	10110010	Enable bit 3	10111010	0xBA
0x25	00100101	Enable bit 4	00110101	0x35

Infrared

This subkey defines configuration data set by the Infrared Monitor dialog box in the Control Panel. Most of these settings are uninteresting, because they're easier to configure in the dialog box rather than via the Registry.

International

In most cases, International contains a single value entry called Locale, which is similar to the ResourceLocale defined in the Desktop subkey. Locale.inf in \Windows\Inf defines each of the possible settings. You control this setting in the Regional Settings tab of the Regional Settings dialog box. If you further customize the computer's international settings, you'll see several other values. These define things such as the currency symbol, date format, list separator, and so on. I don't recommend that you change this value in the Registry, because you'll miss a variety of related settings in the Registry that the Regional Settings dialog box changes.

PowerCfg

PowerCfg defines the schemes you see in the **Power Schemes** list in the Power Schemes tab of the Power Management Properties dialog box. CurrentPowerPolicy is a string value entry that contains the name of the current scheme. PowerCfg\PowerPolicies contains a subkey for each default scheme: 0, 1, or 3. Thus, if CurrentPowerPolicy is 1, PowerCfg\PowerPolicies\1 contains the current power management settings. Each subkey contains the following value entries to describe the power scheme:

```
Description

Name

Policies
```

Sound

The Sound subkey has a single value called Beep. This string value indicates whether Windows 98 beeps on errors. Yes means it will beep. No means it won't.

> NOTE: So far in this chapter, you've seen three different cases in which Windows 98 stores schemes in the Registry: colors, pointers, and power. You might have noticed that Windows 98 doesn't use the same organization for any of these. That's the usual case for data stored in the Registry: The same type of data is seldom stored using the same organization or data types.

InstallLocationsMRU

`Control Panel\InstallLocationsMRU` contains a value entry for each location from which you've installed components into Windows 98. This includes times when you've added components using the Add/Remove Programs Properties dialog box or when you've clicked the **Have Disk** button in the Add New Hardware Wizard. The first value name is a, the second is b, and so on. Since the order of these values changes over time, Windows 98 stores the order in `MRUList`, which is a string value entry that indicates the order in which Windows 98 displays these paths in history lists. For instance, if `MRUList` contains ebcad, the value in e is first in the list, the value in b is the second, and so on.

Keyboard layout

`Keyboard layout\preload` contains a numbered subkey for each keyboard language you install via the Language tab of the Keyboard Properties dialog box. The default value entry of each subkey contains the locale ID of the keyboard language as defined in Local.inf and Multilng.inf, which you find in `\Windows\Inf`.

`Keyboard layout\substitutes` contains a value entry that defines substitutes for many of the keyboard layouts defined in `preload`. The default value entry for a subkey called `00000809` might be `00010409`, indicating that the keyboard language defined by `00010409` is a viable substitute for `00000809`.

The last subkey, `toggle`, indicates whether the user can toggle between each keyboard layout using the shortcut keys Ctrl+Shift and Alt+Shift. You set this and the other options in the Languages tab of the Keyboard Properties dialog box.

Most Recently Used Lists

Windows 98 stores MRU lists in a consistent manner throughout the Registry. The key with the MRU list contains a number of value entries, all named a through z. The data for each value depends on how the operating system uses the list.

You also find a value called `MRUList`, or something similar. This value indicates the order of the items in the MRU list. It's a string value that contains a single character for each item a through z, and the order of the characters determines the order of the list. If `MRUList` contains feabcd, f is first, e is second, a is third, and so on. You'll also notice that `MRUList` contains as many characters as the key contains entries.

NOTE: As with similar locale-type settings, changing `Keyboard layout` in the Registry is senseless. You're better off changing these values using the appropriate Control Panel icon, since you're likely to miss related values or mess things up completely.

Network

Network contains two different subkeys: Persistent and Recent. You see these keys on networked computers when you map a network share to a drive letter using the Map Network Drive dialog box.

If you permanently map a drive by checking **Reconnect at logon**, you see a subkey under Persistent for the drive to which you mapped the network share. Persistent*Drive* contains three value entries that define the network provider, path, and username used to connect to the share. If you disconnect from the mapped drive, Windows 98 removes its subkey under Persistent.

Recent contains subkeys for recent network shares that the user has accessed but may or may not have permanently mapped, contrary to what other sources have to say on this topic. The name of each subkey is the path to the network share. Notice, however, that Windows 98 stores the path using ./ instead of a backslash since you can't use a backslash in a key's name (./.SERVER./BOOKS). The value entries under each connection describe the type of connection, the network provider, and the username used to connect to the share.

RemoteAccess

RemoteAccess describes the Dial-Up Networking connections you've configured in the Dial-Up Networking folder. You see a binary value entry under RemoteAccess\Addresses for each connection you create. The content of this value is indecipherable.

RemoteAccess\Profile*Connection* contains additional information about each connection if necessary. If you configure a connection to use a script, for example, you see information about that script in *Connection*. Likewise, if you configure a connection to use Multilink, you see information about the additional devices to use for that connection. The format of the values in RemoteAccess is indecipherable, so don't try creating Dial-Up Networking connections using the Registry.

> **TIP:** Dial-Up Networking connections aren't files. You can't copy them from computer to computer like you can files. Almost. You can export HKEY_CURRENT_USER\RemoteAccess to a REG file and then copy the file to another computer and import it into the Registry. This has the same effect as copying the connection between both computers. This is also a great way to back up your connections so that you can re-create them after reinstalling a fresh copy of Windows 98.

Software

Most applications store user-specific configuration data in HKEY_CURRENT_USER\
Software. They do so using organization similar to *Company\Product\Version. Company*
is the name of the company that produces the application, *Product* is the name of the
application, and *Version* is the version of the application whose settings you find in
that branch. Thus, Honeycutt\Power Tools\1.0 contains preferences for version 1.0 of
a program called Power Tools developed by a company called Honeycutt. Some companies use the name CurrentVersion instead of an actual version number, as Microsoft
does for Windows.

Microsoft is generally the most interesting subkey of HKEY_CURRENT_USER. Aside
from containing the user-specific settings for Windows 98 in \Windows\
CurrentVersion, it also contains a plethora of settings that govern Internet Explorer.
This branch is so interesting that it is covered all by itself in the following sections.

SEE ALSO

➤ Chapter 6, "HKEY_LOCAL_MACHINE," describes a similar branch that contains machine-
  specific configuration data for applications.

➤ Microsoft's logo requirements, which a program must meet in order for the vendor to
  slap the "Designed for Windows" logo on the product's box, define how programs must
  store settings in this branch. You can learn more about the logo program by visiting
  http://www.microsoft.com.

HKEY_CURRENT_USER\Software\Microsoft

This branch contains thousands of settings that control just about every user-specific
aspect of Windows 98 and Internet Explorer. Many of this key's subkeys are uninteresting; you can't really use them to troubleshoot, repair, or customize Windows 98.
Internet Connection Wizard contains a value that indicates whether the user has completed the wizard, for example. SystemCertificates contains information about the
certificates installed in Internet Explorer. These aren't very useful.

NOTE: If you find a key or value that seems out of place, it probably is. Windows 98, more than any
previous version of Windows, stores data in the Registry where it shouldn't be located. This problem is
most likely due to human error—probably too many programmers with their hands in the cookie jar.

NOTE: Other sources of information about the Windows Registry make a distinction between the
Software key under HKEY_CURRENT_USER and HKEY_LOCAL_MACHINE. You can't count on the case
difference between the Software keys under each root, because key names are not case-sensitive and
because Windows 98 capitalizes both subkeys the same.

Most of the immediate subkeys in this branch are new and are related to the Internet enhancements that Microsoft built into Windows 98. Conferencing, FrontPage Express, IEAK, and Internet Explorer are all examples of new Internet-related subkeys. Internet Explorer contains a number of settings that control aspects of the Web browser. Of particular interest is a subkey called Main, which contains values that reflect the settings in the Advanced tab of the Internet Options dialog box. The settings in this subkey are mostly self-explanatory, so I won't waste much space on them.

Windows\CurrentVersion contains settings that directly affect the operating system. Look and feel, shell folders, and menu settings are examples of what you find here. The remaining sections describe the various parts of this branch—at least those that are useful for customizing the operating system. In particular, you'll find discussions of Explorer and Policies.

Windows\CurrentVersion\Explorer

HKEY_CURRENT_USER\Software\Microsoft\Windows\CurrentVersion\Explorer is one of the most important Registry branches for customizing Windows 98. You can add objects to the desktop's name space via this branch. You can clear the MRU lists via this branch. You can relocate shell folders via this branch.

Advanced contains settings that you change in the Advanced tab of the Folder Options dialog box. In Windows Explorer, choose **View**, **Folder Options** and click the Advanced tab. Each setting in this tab reflects a value entry in Advanced. The names are—you guessed it—self-explanatory. AutoComplete, BrowseNewProcess, and SmallIcons come from the Advanced tab of the Internet Options dialog box, not Folder Options.

Some of the subkeys under Windows\CurrentVersion\Explorer are indecipherable, but you can make an educated guess as to their functions. CabinetState, DeskView, ExpView, StreamMRU, Streams, and StuckRects are among that elite group of subkeys. They mostly contain settings that reflect the current state of the desktop and Windows Explorer. These are mostly bit masks. Uncovering what each bit means is difficult, however.

> NOTE: Each Windows 98 accessory stores settings in the Windows\CurrentVersion\Applets branch of HKEY_CURRENT_USER\Software\Microsoft. Look for the following subkeys: Briefcase, Paint, PolEdit, Regedit, System File Checker, System Monitor, Volume Control, Wordpad, and more.

MenuOrder

MenuOrder*Menu*, where *Menu* can be Favorites or Start Menu, indicates the sort order for the specified menu. Underneath *Menu*, you find a subkey for each submenu. Thus, under Start Menu, you'll find &Documents, &Programs, and so on. You'll also find a subkey called Menu, which contains a value called Order that indicates the sort order of each command on the menu. Go one level down, and you'll notice that this whole structure repeats itself. Look under the key for one of the submenus, and you'll notice more subkeys, one for each command on the submenu. Again, you'll find another subkey called Menu with a value called Order.

The best way to sort all this out is to take a look at Figure 7.3. It shows the MenuOrder key with Favorites and Start Menu directly under it. Under Start Menu, you see several subkeys, one for each of the Start menu's submenus. I've expanded &Programs so that you can see the structure under it, which also has a subkey for each of the **Program** menu's submenus. This organization goes on until it arrives at a menu that doesn't have any more submenus. Also notice that each level has a Menu subkey with an Order value that indicates the menu's sort order.

SEE ALSO

➤ Chapter 9 shows you how to restore the Start menu's sort order by removing this branch.

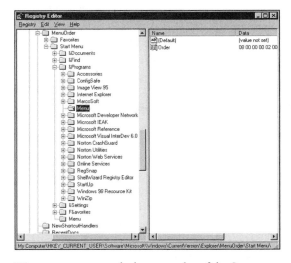

Figure 7.3   MenuOrder controls the sort order of the Start menu.

Doc Find Spec MRU, Recent Docs, and RunMRU

These three subkeys contain MRU lists:

Doc Find Spec MRU	Contains the list of recent file specs used in the Find: All Files dialog box.
Recent Docs	Contains the list of recently opened documents that you see on the Start menu's **Documents** submenu.
RunMRU	Contains the list of recently run documents that you see in the Run dialog box.

Editing these MRU lists is senseless. `Recent Docs` stores each entry as a binary value that contains the document's name and the filename of the shortcut in `\Windows\Recent`, for example. The only reason you should really care about these lists is if you want to clear them, in which case you can simply remove the entire subkey that contains the list you want to delete. The earlier sidenote called "Most Recently Used Lists" described how Windows 98 stores MRU lists in the Registry. In this case, all three MRU lists use this format.

SEE ALSO

➤ Chapter 11 shows you how to configure Tweak UI so that it automatically clears these MRU lists every time you start the operating system.

➤ Chapter 9 shows you how to write an INF file that automatically clears these MRU lists each time you start the operating system.

Shell Folders and User Shell Folders

These two subkeys contain paths for Windows 98's shell folders. When the operating system or some other program wants to know the location of the Favorites folder, for instance, the operating system looks in these keys to find it.

`Shell Folders` contains string values for every shell folder Windows 98 supports. Each value contains the fully qualified path to the folder. `User Shell Folders` contains similar values for each folder you customize. Note that in most cases, the operating system recognizes when you move a shell folder to a new location and updates these values automatically.

➤ Chapter 9 contains more information about these two subkeys and shows you how to customize them.

Windows\CurrentVersion\Policies

Many of the best customizations are actually policies that you can set with the System Policy Editor. If you don't want to install the System Policy Editor, or you want to create an INF file that you can use to import the same policies repeatedly, you should know how each policy translates to values in the Registry.

Table 7.5 describes the majority of user-specific policies you can set in Windows 98. I've divided the table into sections. The title of each section indicates the subkey under Windows\CurrentVersion\Policies in which you create the DWORD value named in the first column. To enable a particular policy, set the DWORD value to 0x00000001. To disable the policy, remove the value or set it to 0x00000000. For example, if you want to remove the Network Neighborhood icon from the desktop, create a new DWORD value called NoNetHood under HKEY_CURRENT_USER\Software\ Microsoft\Windows\CurrentVersion\Policies\Explorer and set its value to 0x00000001. If you want to disable all items on the desktop, create a new DWORD value called NoComponents under \ActiveDesktop and set its value to 0x00000001.

Table 7.5 **System Policies and Values**

Value	Policy
\Explorer	
NoSaveSettings	Don't save settings at exit
NoActiveDesktop	Disable Active Desktop
NoActiveDesktopChanges	Do not allow changes to Active Desktop
NoInternetIcon	Hide Internet Explorer icon
NoNetHood	Hide Network Neighborhood icon
NoDesktop	Hide all desktop items
NoFavoritesMenu	Remove the Favorites submenu from the Start menu
NoFind	Remove the Find submenu from the Start menu
NoRun	Remove the Run submenu from the Start menu
NoSetActiveDesktop	Remove the Active Desktop item from the Settings submenu
NoChangeStartMenu	Disable drag-and-drop context menus on the Start menu
NoFolderOptions	Remove the Folder Options menu item from the Settings submenu
NoRecentDocsMenu	Remove the Documents submenu from the Start menu
NoRecentDocsHistory	Do not keep a history of recently opened documents
ClearRecentDocsOnExit	Clear history of recently opened documents
NoLogoff	Disable logoff

continues

Table 7.5 **Continued**

Value	Policy
NoClose	Disable the Shut Down command
NoSetFolders	Disable changes to Printers and Control Panel Settings
NoSetTaskbar	Disable changes to the Taskbar and Start menu settings
NoTrayContextMenu	Disable the context menu for the Taskbar
NoStartMenuSubFolders	Hide custom Programs folders
ClassicShell	Enable the Classic Shell
NoFileMenu	Disable the File menu in Shell folders
NoViewContextMenu	Disable the context menu in Shell folders
EnforceShellExtensionSecurity	Only allow approved Shell extensions
LinkResolveIgnoreLinkInfo	Do not track Shell shortcuts during roaming
NoDrives	Hide Floppy Drives in My Computer
NoNetConnectDisconnect	Disable network connections and disconnections
NoPrinterTabs	Hide the General and Details tabs in Printer Properties
NoDeletePrinter	Disable Deletion of Printers
NoAddPrinter	Disable Addition of Printers
RestrictRun	Run only specified Windows applications
\ACTIVEDESKTOP	
NoComponents	Disable *all* desktop items
NoAddingComponents	Disable adding *any* desktop items
NoDeletingComponents	Disable deleting *any* desktop items
NoEditingComponents	Disable editing *any* desktop items
NoClosingComponents	Disable closing *any* desktop items
NoHTMLWallPaper	No HTML wallpaper
NoChangingWallPaper	Disable changing wallpaper
NoCloseDragDropBands	Disable dragging, dropping, and closing *all* toolbars
NoMovingBands	Disable resizing *all* toolbars
\WINOLDAPP	
NoRealMode	Do not allow the computer to restart in MS-DOS mode
Disabled	Disable the MS-DOS prompt
\SYSTEM	
DisableRegistryTools	Disable Registry editing tools
NoDispCPL	Disable the Display Control Panel
NoDispBackgroundPage	Hide the Background page
NoDispScrSavPage	Hide the Screen Saver page
NoDispAppearancePage	Hide the Appearance page
NoDispSettingsPage	Hide the Settings page
NoSecCPL	Disable the Passwords Control Panel
NoPwdPage	Hide the Change Passwords page

Value	Policy
NoAdminPage	Hide the Remote Administration page
NoProfilePage	Hide the User Profiles page
NoDevMgrPage	Hide the Device Manager page
NoConfigPage	Hide the Hardware Profiles page
NoFileSysPage	Hide the File System button
NoVirtMemPage	Hide the Virtual Memory button
\NETWORK	
NoNetSetup	Disable the Network Control Panel
NoNetSetupIDPage	Hide the Identification Page
NoNetSetupSecurityPage	Hide the Access Page
NoEntireNetwork	No "Entire Network" in Network Neighborhood
NoWorkgroupContents	No workgroup contents in Network Neighborhood

SEE ALSO

➤ Chapter 14 describes how to install and use the System Policy Editor.

➤ Chapter 15 shows you how to create INF files that you can use to update system policies without using the editor.

NOTE: In general, setting policies is easier using the System Policy Editor. You can think of this program as another customization tool rather than an administrative tool.

HKEY_CURRENT_CONFIG and HKEY_DYN_DATA

In this chapter:

- HKEY_CURRENT_CONFIG
- HKEY_DYN_DATA

HKEY_CURRENT_CONFIG

Each subkey under HKEY_LOCAL_MACHINE\Config defines the settings for the hardware profiles that the user defines in the System Properties dialog box. The first hardware profile is called 0001, the second is 0002, and so on. If you have only one hardware profile, 0001 is the only subkey under Config. To display the hardware profiles on your computer, open the System Properties dialog box and click the Hardware Profiles tab, shown in Figure 8.1.

Windows 98 stores the friendly name of each hardware profile in HKEY_LOCAL_ MACHINE\System\CurrentControlSet\Control\IDConfigDB\ as value entries FriendlyName*Number*, where *Number* is the profile number under Config. The most important value entry in this key is called CurrentConfig, which tells you which hardware profile Windows 98 is using. This is also the hardware profile contained in HKEY_CURRENT_CONFIG.

Figure 8.1   Hardware profiles are common for portable computers, where you have separate docked and undocked configurations.

HKEY_CURRENT_CONFIG is an alias for the current hardware profile under HKEY_LOCAL_MACHINE\Config. If IDConfigDB indicates that 0002 is the current hardware profile, HKEY_CURRENT_CONFIG reflects the entire contents of HKEY_LOCAL_MACHINE\Config\0002. HKEY_CURRENT_CONFIG contains three subkeys that are interesting and another that is erroneous. You see all of them in Figure 8.2. The following sections describe the first two. The Software subkey is an error on Microsoft's part. Instead of storing these few settings under HKEY_LOCAL_MACHINE, they store them here, under HKEY_CURRENT_CONFIG.

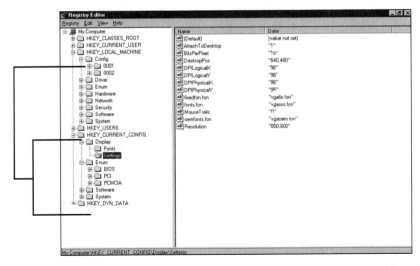

Figure 8.2   HKEY_CURRENT_CONFIG is an alias for the current hardware profile under HKEY_LOCAL_MACHINE\Config.

Display

Display contains two subkeys that contain different display settings. The first is Fonts, which maps screen fonts to font names. Windows 3.1 defined the same information in Win.ini. There just aren't many things you can do to this subkey to customize Windows 98.

The second subkey is Settings, which contains metric information for the current display adapter. The value entries in this subkey define the color depth of the display, the logical and physical dot pitch of the display, and the system fonts that were originally set in the [boot] section of System.ini. Since this subkey just reflects the computer's current configuration, changing them has no effect. It is an interesting place to check up on your display adapter's settings, however.

Enum

This subkey contains additional subkeys that indicate the devices included in the current hardware profile. Subkeys to look for include BIOS, PCMCIA, and SCSI. Each of these subkeys is typically empty, but each branch just below HKEY_CURRENT_CONFIG\ Enum reflects the same organization as HKEY_LOCAL_MACHINE\Enum, allowing you to look up each device in HKEY_LOCAL_MACHINE so that you can identify it. Figure 8.3 illustrates this relationship.

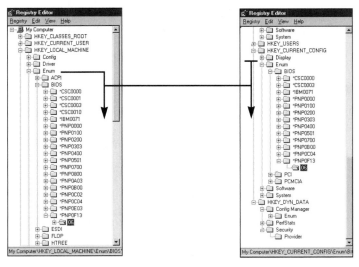

Figure 8.3   The organization of Enum is the same under HKEY_LOCAL_MACHINE and HKEY_CURRENT_CONFIG.

SEE ALSO

➤ See Chapter 6, "HKEY_LOCAL_MACHINE," to learn more about Config and Enum under HKEY_LOCAL_MACHINE.

System

HKEY_CURRENT_CONFIG\System leads to a number of subkeys that indicate the printers that are available. Similar to Enum, this subkey reflects the organization of another portion of the Registry, HKEY_LOCAL_MACHINE\System, so that you can easily find additional information about the printer in the hardware profile. Thus, if you see System\CurrentControlSet\Control\Print\Printers\HP LaserJet 5 under HKEY_CURRENT_CONFIG, look up the same branch under HKEY_LOCAL_MACHINE to see more configuration data for the printer, such as port, name, printer driver, and so on.

HKEY_DYN_DATA

HKEY_DYN_DATA is a dynamic root key that Windows 98 rebuilds and stores in memory each time it starts. It never writes this key to disk, as it does with HKEY_LOCAL_MACHINE and HKEY_USERS\Name.

You see two subkeys under HKEY_DYN_DATA, Config Manager and PerfStatus. They contain data that has the following two characteristics:

- The data is dynamically updated during the session.

- Quick access to the data is necessary due to the data's purpose (performance data, for example).

Config Manager

Windows 98's Configuration Manager is the component responsible for making Plug and Play work. It recognizes and configures the devices that it finds on the computer. The Configuration Manager stores the hardware tree in Config Manager.

In turn, Config Manager contains a single subkey called Enum, which leads to a large number of subkeys that define the configuration of each device that the Configuration Manager recognizes. Each of these subkeys has an eight-digit hexadecimal name such as C29A2530, C29A4070, and so on. The HardwareKey value entry in each subkey defines the device's corresponding branch under HKEY_LOCAL_MACHINE\Enum. Thus, if a HardwareKey value entry contains BIOS*PNP0501\0D, look up HKEY_LOCAL_MACHINE\Enum\BIOS*PNP0501\0D to discover that this device is COM1. Figure 8.4 shows this relationship.

> **TIP:** Most users don't need to worry about hardware profiles. If Windows 98 detects that you need to use them, as in docked versus undocked configurations, it handles hardware profiles automatically.

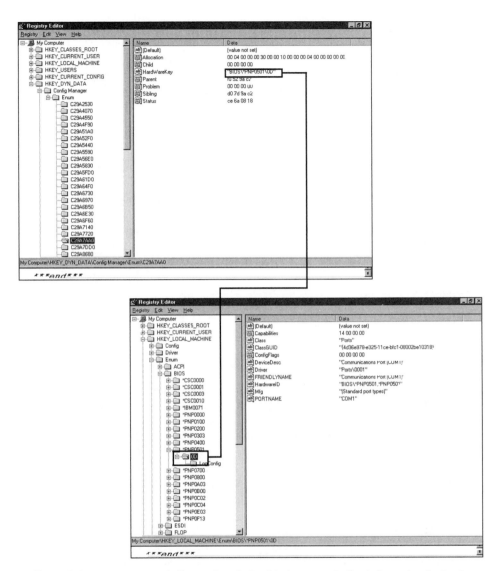

Figure 8.4   HardwareKey indicates the relationship between similar information in Config Manager and HKEY_LOCAL_MACHINE\Enum.

The `Allocation` value entry under each subkey indicates the computer resources allocated to the device, including IRQs, I/O ports, and DMA channels. The format of this binary value entry isn't decipherable, but if you compare what you see in it to the resources that the Device Manager indicates are allocated to the device, you can easily pick out the appropriate portions of the value. An interesting relationship to note is that each entry under `HKEY_LOCAL_MACHINE\Enum` has a subkey further down called `LogConfig`. This subkey contains a binary value entry for each *basic configuration* you see in on the Resources tab of the device's property sheet: `0000`, `0001`, `0002`, and so on. `Allocation` contains one of these values.

`HKEY_DYN_DATA` is dynamic and updated continuously throughout the session. As such, it's always up-to-date, and it always reflects the hardware currently recognized by the Configuration Manager. Being dynamic, however, the names of each subkey under `Config Manager` will be different from machine to machine, and the hardware that each subkey refers to in `HKEY_LOCAL_MACHINE\Enum` will be different depending on which hardware Windows 98 finds in the computer. Still, Table 8.1 gives you a sample of what I found in `Config Manager` on my computer. The first column contains the subkey under `Config Manager`. The second column lists the contents of `HardwareKey`, which identifies a branch under `HKEY_LOCAL_MACHINE\Enum`. The third column lists the name of the device as indicated by the `DeviceDesc` value entry.

Table 8.1   **Subkeys in** `HKEY_DYN_DATA\Config Manager`

Subkey	Branch	Device Description
C29A2530	HTREE\ROOT\0	N/A
C29A4070	BIOS*PNP0700\08	Standard floppy disk controller
C29A4550	BIOS*PNP0F13\06	Standard PS/2 port mouse
C29A4F90	HTREE\RESERVED\0	N/A
C29A51A0	ROOT\SWENUM\0000	Plug and Play software device enumerator
C29A52F0	ROOT*PNP0C00\0000	Plug and Play BIOS
C29A5440	ROOT*PNP0C01\0000	System board
C29A5590	ROOT*PNP0C05\0000	Advanced power management support
C29A56E0	ROOT\INFRARED\0000	Infrared communication device
C29A5830	ROOT\PRINTER\0000	HP LaserJet 5
C29A5FD0	BIOS*PNP0000\00	Programmable interrupt controller
C29A61D0	BIOS*PNP0200\01	Direct memory access controller
C29A64F0	BIOS*PNP0100\02	System timer
C29A6730	BIOS*PNP0B00\03	System CMOS/real-time clock
C29A6970	BIOS*PNP0800\04	System speaker
C29A6B50	BIOS*PNP0303\05	Standard 101/102-key or Microsoft Natural Keyboard
C29A6E30	BIOS*PNP0C04\07	Numeric data processor
C29A6F60	BIOS*PNP0A03\09	PCI bus

Subkey	Branch	Device Description
C29A7140	BIOS*PNP0C02\0A	Motherboard resources
C29A7720	BIOS*PNP0400\0B	Printer port (LPT1)
C29A7AA0	BIOS*PNP0501\0D	Communications port (COM1)
C29A7DD0	BIOS*CSC0000\0E	Crystal PnP audio system CODEC
C29A8680	BIOS*CSC0010\0F	Crystal PnP audio system control registers
C29A8920	BIOS*CSC0001\10	Gameport joystick
C29A8AD0	BIOS*CSC0003\11	Crystal PnP audio system MPU–401 compatible
C29A8CB0	BIOS*IBM0071\13	IBM ThinkPad fast infrared port
C29A92E0	BIOS*PNP0C02\1B	Motherboard resources
C29AE7D0	PCI\IRQHOLDER\60	IRQ holder for PCI steering
C29AE960	PCI\IRQHOLDER\61	IRQ holder for PCI steering
C29AEB20	PCI\IRQHOLDER\63	IRQ holder for PCI steering
C29B31D0	ACPI\COMPBATT\0	Composite power source
C29B32F0	VPOWERD\BATTERY\0	APM battery slot
C29B6BB0	PCMCIA\PCCARD\...	PCMCIA card services
C29B6E30	PCMCIA\IBM-56K...	Standard PCMCIA card modem
C29B80D0	MONITOR\DEFAUL...	Laptop display panel (800×600)
C29B8330	MF\CHILD0000\P...	Primary IDE controller (dual fifo)
C29B84E0	MF\CHILD0001\P...	Secondary IDE controller (dual fifo)
C29B8B70	NETWORK\FASTIR...	Fast infrared protocol
C29BFA00	USB\ROOT_HUB\P...	USB root hub
C29C0EB0	FLOP\GENERIC_N...	Generic NEC floppy disk
C29C1140	ESDI\GENERIC_I...	Generic IDE disk type <7
C29C1510	SCSI\SANYO___CR	Sanyo CRD-S372B

PerfStats

Windows 98 stores dynamic performance data in PerfStats, which you can view using the System Monitor. You see the five subkeys described here:

- StartSrv
- StartStat
- StatData
- StopSrv
- StopStat

NOTE: The Parent, Child, and Sibling value entries indicate the relationships between each device in the hardware tree. Deciphering these values to graph the hardware tree is next to impossible, however.

The best way to see the relationship between the data in `PerfStats` and System Monitor is to start with the program itself. Open System Monitor and add the `Threads` item. You see a window similar to the one shown in Figure 8.5. It shows the `Processor Usage (%)` and `Threads` items for the `Kernel` category. Notice the last value shown for the `Threads` graph in the status bar: 48. Now, look in `PerfStats\StatData` for the value entry called `Kernel\Threads`, which corresponds to this graph. This is a 4-byte binary value that contains the last value for this performance measurement. Since this is a DWORD value represented as a 4-byte binary value, you must reverse the order of the bytes before converting to decimal. The hexadecimal value 30 corresponds to the decimal value 48 reported by System Monitor.

System Monitor gets the descriptions of each performance measurement from a source other than `HKEY_DYN_DATA`. Look in `HKEY_LOCAL_MACHINE\System\CurrentControlSet\Control\PerfStats\Enum\`, as shown in Figure 8.6. You see a subkey for each category, and the default value entry of each subkey provides the name of the category. Each subkey under the category represents a performance measurement, and it contains the item's name and description. Thus, under the `Enum` key, you see branches such as `KERNEL\CPUUsage` and `KERNEL\Threads`. Look familiar? The structure beneath the Enum key corresponds to the value entry names you learned about earlier. The Kernel\Threads value that indicates the number of running threads has a matching subkey at `HKEY_LOCAL_MACHINE\System\CurrentControlSet\Control\PerfStatus\Enum\KERNEL\Threads`. Here, you find the name of the performance measurement and a brief description of it. System Monitor displays the item's name in a variety of places, including at the top of the graph. It displays the description when you click the **Explain** button in the Add Item dialog box.

Taking the opposite approach, which is what System Monitor actually does, you'd start with `HKEY_LOCAL_MACHINE` and end up in `HKEY_DYN_DATA`. Look up the performance measurement in `HKEY_LOCAL_MACHINE\System\CurrentControlSet\Control\PerfStats\Enum`. Note its branch, perhaps `VMM\cPageFaults`, and note its name and description. Then look up the corresponding value entry under `HKEY_DYN_DATA\PerfStats\StatData` to see the latest value measured for this item.

> **TIP:** If the values you see in `PerfStats` don't agree with the information that System Monitor reports, try refreshing the Registry by pressing F5 in the Registry Editor. Also keep in mind that performance statistics can change in milliseconds due to simple actions such as switching between windows or moving the mouse.

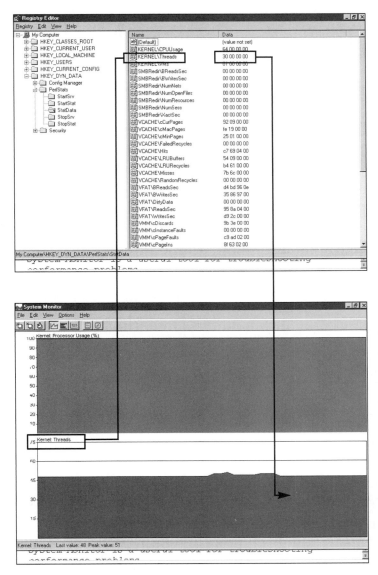

Figure 8.5   System Monitor is a useful tool for checking the health of Windows 98 and your computer.

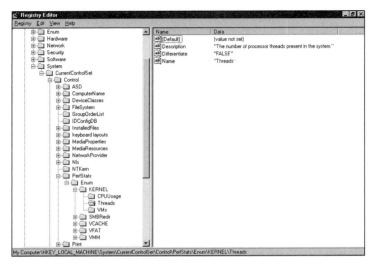

Figure 8.6 Each branch under `PerfStats\Enum` matches a value entry name under `HKEY_DYN_DATA\PerfStats\StatData`.

Security

`HKEY_DYN_DATA\Security` is an alias for `HKEY_LOCAL_MACHINE\Security`. It contains a single subkey called `Provider` that describes the primary security provider as you configured it in the Network dialog box. You'll typically see the following four value entries in this subkey, assuming that you're logging onto a network:

Value Entry	Example	Description
Address_Book	Msab32.dll	The network address book
Address_Server	MyServer	The server providing security
Container	MyDomain	The domain providing security
Platform_Type	02 00 00 00	The authenticator platform

`Platform_Type` deserves special mention. This value indicates the type of authenticator you chose in the Network dialog box, as shown in Figure 8.7. If you choose share-level security, `Platform_Type` is 00 00 00 00 and you don't see the `Security` subkey under `HKEY_DYN_DATA`, but you do see it under `HKEY_LOCAL_MACHINE\Security`. You do see `Security` under `HKEY_DYN_DATA` with the remaining two choices, however, which correspond to the following options in the list of authenticators:

01 00 00 00   Windows NT Server

02 00 00 00   Windows NT Domain

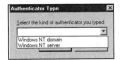

Figure 8.7 The Authenticator Type determines whether credentials are validated by a stand-alone server or an NT domain.

Changing Values in HKEY_DYN_DATA

If you try to change a value in HKEY_DYN_DATA, you'll see an error that says `Error writing the value's new contents`. Remember that you can't change dynamic values in the Registry, so there is little value in this branch for configuration or customization.

C

Customizing and Troubleshooting

9

Customizing the Windows 98 Desktop

Karanjit S. Siyan, Ph.D

In this chapter:

- Relocating Shell Folders
- Working with Shell Folders
- Customizing Icons for Files and Other Objects
- Mastering Shortcut Menus for Objects and Files
- Customizing the Start Menu and Its Contents
- Fixing Menu and Window Behavior Problems
- Removing the Overlay from Shortcut Icons
- Personalizing Internet Explorer 4.0
- Clearing the Most Recently Used Lists
- Locating Programs that Open When Windows 98 Starts
- Logging onto the Network Automatically
- Changing Installation Information

Relocating Shell Folders

Folders that Windows 98 uses for special purposes are called *shell folders*. The Favorites folder is a shell folder, for instance, as are the Start Menu and My Documents folders.

Table 9.1 describes the shell folders that Windows 98 defines and includes the default path for each (the default path will be different if you've enabled profiles). The actual location of each folder isn't important, though. That's because Windows 98 uses the internal name of the folder to look up its path in the Registry. You're free to change a shell folder's location by pointing the operating system to the new location.

You might want to change a shell folder's location for a variety of reasons. You can share a single Favorites folder among several users, for example, by pointing Windows 98 to a folder on a network share. Maybe you prefer to put the My Documents folder on your desktop or move the Startup folder to a different location.

Table 9.1 **Windows 98 Shell Folders**

Name	Default Location
AppData	\Windows\Application Data
Cache	\Windows\Temporary Internet Files
Cookies	\Windows\Cookies
Desktop	\Windows\Desktop
Fonts	\Windows\Fonts
Favorites	\Windows\Favorites
History	\Windows\History
NetHood	\Windows\NetHood
Programs	\Windows\Start Menu\Programs
Personal	\My Documents
PrintHood	\Windows\PrintHood
Recent	\Windows\Recent
Start menu	\Windows\Start Menu
Startup	\Windows\Start Menu\Programs\StartUp
SendTo	\Windows\SendTo
Templates	\Windows\ShellNew

Windows 98 retrieves the location of each shell folder from `HKEY_CURRENT_USER\Software\Microsoft\Windows\CurrentVersion\Explorer\Shell Folders`. Within this key, you find a value entry for each shell folder, each of which has one of the names shown in Table 9.1. The string value of the value entry is the fully qualified path of the folder's location. You'll notice another subkey at the same level called `User Shell Folder`, which contains value entries for any shell folders that you've customized. Get this straight—`Shell Folders` contains value entries for all the shell folders, including the ones you've customized, and `User Shell Folders` contains value entries only for the ones you've customized. Armed with this information, here's how to change the location of a shell folder:

NOTE: The actual location of each shell folder will be different if user profiles are enabled on the computer. In that case, look in \Windows\Profiles*username* for the folders you see in Table 9.1.

1. Add a string value entry for the shell folder to `HKEY_CURRENT_USER\SOFTWARE\ Microsoft\Windows\CurrentVersion\explorer\User Shell Folder`. Get the name for the new value from Table 9.1. Set its value to the fully qualified path of the folder.

2. Change the value of the corresponding value entry in `HKEY_CURRENT_USER\ SOFTWARE\Microsoft\Windows\CurrentVersion\explorer\Shell Folder`. The path in this value should match the path you specified in step 1.

3. Restart the computer, because this change won't take effect until you do so. Alternatively, you can log off and back on again.

Changing Machine-Specific Shell Folders

You find similar branches under `HKEY_LOCAL_MACHINE`. The shell folders in `HKEY_ CURRENT_USER` are user-specific, while the shell folders in `HKEY_LOCAL_MACHINE` apply to every user who logs onto the computer. The values have different names, too, including `Common Desktop` and `Common Startup`. By default, these are the only two common shell folders that Windows 98 defines. You can customize the location of each common shell folder using the same steps you learned for customizing user-specific shell folders.

> **CAUTION:** Be careful about overlapping shell folders. For instance, don't use the same path for the Favorites and My Documents folders. Windows 98 writes special information to Desktop.ini, which is a hidden file in these folders, and the information for one shell folder will wipe out information for the other.

Sharing the Favorites Folder

I can think of two reasons for sharing a common Favorites folder. First, you can share a single Favorites folder among all the users on a network. Second, you can share a Favorites folder between your portable and desktop computers so that you can take your favorite Internet shortcuts with you on the road.

In either case, the instructions for sharing a Favorites folder are roughly the same:

1. Determine where you want to put the Favorites folder. If you're sharing it on the network, create a share for it. If you're sharing it between networked portable and desktop computers, create a share on the portable computer.

2. Copy the contents of the original folder to the new Favorites folder that you shared in step 1. Make sure you copy all the hidden files you find in the original Favorites folder, so that you'll pick up the various Desktop.ini files in it.

3. Change the location of the Favorites folder on each user's computer. You might want to use an INF or REG file to distribute this file to multiple users. Or you can use the System Policy Editor, as described in Chapter 14, "Profiles, System Policies, and the Registry."

Working with Shell Folders

Some folders you see in My Computer or on the desktop don't actually exist on the hard disk. They look just like folders in Windows Explorer, but they're actually objects that display the contents of the folder in a window. Table 9.2 shows you the unique class identifier for many of these objects, which Windows 98 defines in the Registry under HKEY_CLASSES_ROOT\CLSID. Thus, you find the Control Panel at {21EC2020-3AEA-1069-A2DD-08002B30309D} and the Recycle Bin at {645FF040-5081-101B-9F08-00AA002F954E} under HKEY_CLASSES_ROOT\CLSID.

As you've learned, these folders don't exist in this location on the hard disk; they exist in Windows Explorer's or the desktop's name space. *Name space* is an abstract term that describes all the objects within that folder; real or imaginary. Notice that I've consistently referred to Windows Explorer's name space separately from the desktop's name space. That's because Windows 98 defines two different name spaces, one for each of these objects, as shown in Figure 9.1. Windows 98 defines each in the Registry at HKEY_LOCAL_MACHINE\Software\Microsoft\Windows\CurrentVersion\explorer. The subkey Desktop\NameSpace contains the name space for the desktop, and MyComputer\NameSpace contains the name space for My Computer.

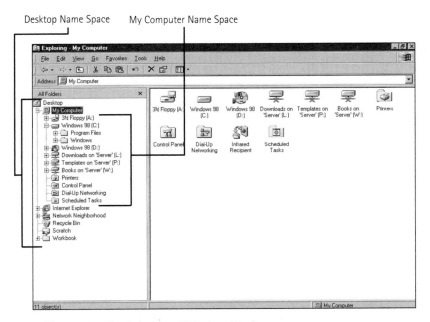

Figure 9.1 The desktop and Windows Explorer use separate name spaces.

Windows 98 adds each subkey it finds in `Desktop\NameSpace` to the desktop's name space and each subkey it finds in `MyComputer\NameSpace` to My Computer's name space. You usually see the class identifiers for the Recycle Bin and My Documents folders in the desktop's name space and the class identifiers for the Dial-Up Networking and Scheduled Tasks folders in My Computer's name space. What you don't see in either `NameSpace` key are subkeys for the Control Panel, Printers, Network Neighborhood, and Internet Explorer folders. These are built into the operating system. You can't remove the Control Panel or Printers folders from My Computer, but you can remove the Internet Explorer and Network Neighborhood icons from the desktop, as you will learn in the next section.

Table 9.2   **Class Identifierss for Windows 98 Shell Folders**

Folder	Class Identifiers
Control Panel	{21EC2020-3AEA-1069-A2DD-08002B30309D}
Dial-Up Networking	{992CFFA0-F557-101A-88EC-00DD010CCC48}
Internet Explorer	{FBF23842-E3F0-101B-8488-00AA003E56F8}
My Computer	{20D04FE0-3AEA-1069-A2D8-08002B30309D}
Network Neighborhood	{208D2C60-3AEA-1069-A2D7-08002B30309D}
Printers	{2227A280-3AEA-1069-A2DE-08002B30309D}
Recycle Bin	{645FF040-5081-101B-9F08-00AA002F954E}
Scheduled Tasks	{D6277990-4C6A-11CF-8D87-00AA0060F5BF}

SEE ALSO

➤ See Chapter 5, "HKEY_CLASSES_ROOT," to learn more about the organization of class definitions.

Removing a Shell Folder from the Desktop

How you remove a shell folder from the desktop depends on the folder. If you're removing the Recycle Bin or My Documents folders, for example, delete the folder's class identifier subkey from `HKEY_LOCAL_MACHINE\Software\Microsoft\Windows\CurrentVersion\explorer\Desktop\NameSpace`. Easy enough. You don't see a subkey for Internet Explorer or Network Neighborhood in the desktop's namespace, but you can remove them from the desktop by setting the following values under `HKEY_CURRENT_USER\Software\Microsoft\Windows\CurrentVersion\Policies\Explorer`:

TIP: Table 9.2 listed the folders that you can put on the desktop or on the Start menu after installing Windows 98, but other applications might provide special folders you can use as well. How do you find them? Search the Registry for any class identifiers that have a `ShellFolder` subkey with an `attributes` value entry. The default value entry of the class identifier describes the folder.

Icon	Value Entry	Enabled	Disabled
Internet Explorer	NoInternetIcon	00 00 00 00	01 00 00 00
Network Neighborhood	NoNetHood	00 00 00 00	01 00 00 00

SEE ALSO

➤ See Chapter 11, "Tweak UI and Other Registry Programs," to learn an easier way to remove icons from the desktop.

➤ See Chapter 6, "HKEY_LOCAL_MACHINE," to learn more about the contents of HKEY_LOCAL_MACHINE\Software\Microsoft\Windows\CurrentVersion\explorer.

Renaming Desktop Folders Such as Recycle Bin

You can rename the My Computer, Network Neighborhood, and Internet Explorer icons on the desktop. Right-click any of them, choose **Rename**, type the new name of the icon, and press Enter. Renaming the Recycle Bin and some other icons is a bit harder, however, because they don't have a similar command on their shortcut menu. Note that none of the icons in Desktop\NameSpace or MyComputer\NameSpace have **Rename** on their shortcut menus.

Regardless, you can rename the icons you see in Table 9.2 by changing the default value entry of the icon's class identifier in HKEY_CLASSES_ROOT\CLSID. To rename the Recycle Bin, change the default value entry of HKEY_CLASSES_ROOT\CLSID\{645FF040-5081-101B-9F08-00AA002F954E} to the name that you want Windows 98 to display on the desktop and in Windows Explorer. To rename the Control Panel icon, change the default value entry of HKEY_CLASSES_ROOT\CLSID\{21EC2020-3AEA-1069-A2DD-08002B30309D}.

Customizing Icons for Files and Other Objects

Icons come from EXE, DLL, RES, BMP, and ICO files. ICO, BMP, and similar files contain a single icon, and you specify them by giving the path and filename of the ICO file. EXE, DLL, and RES files can contain any number of icons, however. You reference a particular icon in such files using the icon's index, starting from 0. The first icon is 0, the second is 1, and so on. You specify an icon in an EXE, DLL, or RES file by giving the path and filename of the file, followed by the index of the icon, like this: *path\filename,index*.

> NOTE: The default value entry of each class identifier under Desktop\NameSpace and MyComputer\NameSpace also contains the name of the icon. Changing it doesn't change the name of the icon on the desktop or in My Computer, however.

There is one more convention of which you should be aware. Windows 98 allows a programmer to assign a fixed identifier to each icon. This identifier is usually called a *resource ID*. The resource ID is any arbitrary integer value, such as 1037, that provides an easier way for the programmer to reference an exact icon without having to figure out the icon's index. The programmer can assign the integer value to a symbol and then use that symbol in the code. You can also specify an icon using its resource ID, assuming you know it, by writing a line such as this: `path\filename,-resource`. The following list shows you an example of both methods for specifying the location of an icon:

Index	`C:\Windows\System\Shell32.dll,9`
Resource ID	`C:\Windows\System\Shell32.dll,-37`

Shell Folders

Windows 98 retrieves the icon to use for shell folders from the `DefaultIcon` subkey of the class identifier in `HKEY_CLASSES_ROOT\CLSID`. The default value entry of this subkey contains the icon specification you just learned about. Thus, to change the icon that Windows 98 uses for a shell folder, follow these steps:

1. Remove a file called ShellIconCache from \Windows. See the sidenote called "Icon Cache" to learn more about this file.

2. Change the default value entry of `HKEY_CLASSES_ROOT\CLSID\`*clsid*`\DefaultIcon` to the location of the icon. *clsid* is the class identifier of the object you're changing. See Table 9.2 for a list of possibilities.

3. Refresh the desktop and Windows Explorer so that you can see your changes. To refresh the desktop, right-click it and choose **Refresh**. To refresh Windows Explorer, choose **View**, **Refresh**.

NOTE: Windows 98 caches icons in a file called ShellIconCache, which you find in \Windows. It does this so that it doesn't have to reload the icons from their original locations, making displaying icons on the desktop and in Windows Explorer much faster. You can adjust the size of this cache by changing the value entry called Max Cached Icons in HKEY_LOCAL_MACHINE\Software\Microsoft\Windows\CurrentVersion\explorer to any number greater than 512, which is the default value. Create this DWORD value if it doesn't exist.

Files

Changing the icons for files is similar to changing the icon for a shell folder. Instead of changing the default value entry of HKEY_CLASSES_ROOT\CLSID*clsid*\DefaultIcon to the location of the icon, change the default value entry of HKEY_CLASSES_ROOT\ *progid*\DefaultIcon. The trick is to find the program identifier associated with a file extension. Look up the file extension in the Registry under HKEY_CLASSES_ROOT. For example, the subkey for the DOC file extension is HKEY_CLASSES_ROOT\.doc. The default value entry of each file extension's subkey is the name of the program identifier it's associated with. Thus, to change the icon displayed for a file using a particular extension, follow these steps:

1. Note the default value entry of HKEY_CLASSES_ROOT\.*ext*, where *ext* is the file extension. The default value entry is the program identifier that the extension is associated with.

2. Open HKEY_CLASSES_ROOT*progid*\DefaultIcon, where *progid* is the program identifier you looked up in step 1.

3. Change the default value entry of DefaultIcon to indicate the location of the icon you want to use for files associated with that program.

If after changing the icon for a program identifier and refreshing the display you don't notice a change, you'll have to do a bit of tracking to find any overriding DefaultIcon keys. Check to see if a class identifier is associated with the program identifier (look in the program identifier's CLSID subkey), and look up that class under HKEY_CLASSES_ROOT\CLSID. If you see a DefaultIcon subkey under the class identifier's subkey, it might be overriding the icon specified in the program identifier. Note also that some icons are specified via the ShellIcons key, as you'll learn in the next section.

Shell Icons

The icons you see on the Start menu don't come from HKEY_CLASSES_ROOT, as do the icons for shell folders and files. They come from Shell32.dll. Ditto for the icons that Windows 98 displays for different types of disk drives. Table 9.3 shows you the index number for each icon in Shell32.dll. It also shows you the index for comparable icons in Cool.dll, which is an alternative collection of icons that Windows 98 provides.

You can replace any shell icon by adding a string value entry to HKEY_LOCAL_MACHINE\Software\Microsoft\Windows\CurrentVersion\explorer\ Shell Icons. If you don't see this subkey, add it. The name of the value entry is the index of the icon in Shell32. Refer to Table 9.3 to determine the index of each icon. The value is the location of the icon: a path if you're using an ICO file, or a path and index if you're using a DLL, EXE, or RES file. Windows 98 substitutes your icon for each entry it finds in Shell Icons. Thus, to use icon 28 in Cool.dll instead of the default icon for My Computer, create a new value entry called 15 in Shell Icons and set its value to C:\Windows\System\Cool.dll,28. If you don't see the change you made after refreshing the desktop, follow these steps to force Windows 98 to notice the new icon:

1. Restart the Computer in Safe Mode. To do so, hold down the Ctrl key while you start the computer, and then choose Safe Mode from the boot menu.

2. Delete the ShellIconCache file from \Windows. You might have to show hidden files in Windows Explorer in order to see this file.

3. Change the icon in Shell Icons as described in the preceding paragraph.

4. Restart the computer normally.

Specifying certain icons in Shell Icons has no effect. Windows 98 uses the icon specified in the DefaultIcon subkey of a class identifier instead of the icon listed in Shell Icons. Thus, adding entries for the Recycle Bin, Dial-Up Networking, Control Panel, and Printers icons to Shell Icons doesn't do anything. To change these icons, change their DefaultIcon subkey as described the earlier section "Shell Folders." Windows 98 defines the icons for various DefaultIcon keys, too, so changing that icon in Shell Icons doesn't change what you see in Windows Explorer.

Table 9.3 **Sample Icons in Shell32.dll**

Icon	Name	Index in Shell32.dll	Index in Cool.dll
	Generic document	0	37
	MSN and other documents	1	
	Applications	2	
	Closed folders	3	11
	Open folders	4	18
	5 1/4-inch disk drives	5	9
	3 1/2-inch disk drives	6	8
	Removable drives	7	
	Hard drive	8	0
	Network drive	9	1
	Offline network drive	10	29
	CD-ROM drive	11	10
	RAM drive	12	
	Entire Network	13	13
	Network	14	
	My Computer	15	16
	Printer	16	22

continues

Table 9.3 **Continued**

Icon	Name	Index in Shell32.dll	Index in Cool.d
	Network Neighborhood	17	17
	Workgroup Network	18	
	Programs on Start menu	19	4
	Documents on Start menu	20	2
	Settings on Start menu	21	6
	Find on Start menu	22	3
	Help on Start menu	23	15
	Run on Start menu	24	5
	Suspend on Start menu	25	33
	Eject PC on Start menu	26	32
	Shut Down on Start menu	27	7
	Share overlay	28	34
	Shortcut overlay	29	
	Other overlay	30	
	Empty Recycle Bin	31	20
	Full Recycle Bin	32	21
	Dial-up Networking folder	33	27
	Desktop folder in Explorer	34	
	Control Panel on **Settings** menu	35	12
	Program Group folder	36	24
	Printers on **Settings** menu	37	19
	Fonts folder	38	14
	Taskbar on **Settings** menu	39	
	Audio CD	40	26
	Tree	41	
	Saved Find icon	42	
	Favorites on Start menu	43	
	Log Off on Start menu	44	
	Windows Explorer icon	45	23

Icon	Name	Index in Shell32.dll	Index in Cool.d
	Windows Update on **Settings** menu	46	
	Generic documents	47	
	Files or Folders on **Find** menu	48	
	Computer on **Find** menu	49	
	Computer	50	28
	Control Panel	51	
	Printers on **Settings** menu	52	
	Add Printer in Printers folder	53	
	Network Printer	54	
	File Printer	55	
	Full Recycle Bin	56	
	Full Recycle Bin	57	
	Full Recycle Bin	58	
	Delete icon	59	
	Copy icon	60	
	Rename icon	61	38
	TXT file	64	
	Move icon	62	
	INI file	63	43
	BAT file	65	
	DLL file	66	36
	FON icon	67	
	TTF icon	68	
	Font icon	69	
	Run dialog	70	
	Confirm delete icon	71	
	Backup device icon	72	
	ScanDisk icon	73	
	Disk Defragmenter icon	74	

continues

Table 9.3   **Continued**

Icon	Name	Index in Shell32.dll	Index in Cool.d
	Online local printer	75	
	Online network printer	76	
	Online file printer	77	
	Folder icon	78	
	Favorites icon	79	

Individual Disks and Network Volumes

Adding value entries 5 through 12 to Shell Icons affects every drive of that type. Specifying a new icon for removable drives by adding a value entry of 7 to Shell Icons changes the icon for every removable drive on the computer, for example.

You can use a different icon for each disk individually, though, including individual hard disks, floppy disks, and network volumes. Have you ever noticed that when you insert a certain CD-ROM into the drive, Windows 98 automatically starts it and changes the icon that it displays in Windows Explorer? This works because the disk has an Autorun.inf file in its root folder. This file contains a line that looks like icon= *location*, which causes Windows 98 to display the icon specified by *location* in Windows Explorer as long as that disk is mounted. *location* can be the path to an ICO file, or it can be the path to a DLL, EXE, or RES file and an index.

The first trick to make this work for devices other than CD-ROMs is to enable Autorun.inf for those devices. Open HKEY_USERS\.DEFAULT\Software\Microsoft\ Windows\CurrentVersion\Policies\Explorer. You see a value entry called NoDriveTypeAutoRun. This value entry indicates the drives for which Autorun.inf is disabled. It's a four-byte binary value entry, and each bit corresponds to a different type of drive, as described in Table 9.4. Setting the bit corresponding to a drive type to 1 disables Autorun.inf for that type. Setting the bit to 0 enables Autorun.inf. The default value for this entry is 95 00 00 00, or 1001 0101 binary, which means that hard drives, CD-ROMs, and RAM drives are enabled while other drive types are not. Change this value to 91 00 00 00, or 1001 0001 binary, if you want to include removable disks such as floppies and ZIP disks in the list of drives for which Autorun.inf is enabled.

> TIP: Shell32.dll contains more icons than shown in Table 9.3. Windows 98 contains other files that have icons, too. The easiest way to view the icons in a file is to download an icon viewer from your favorite shareware site. My personal favorite is IconRipper, which you can download from http:// www.hotfiles.com.

Table 9.4 `NoDriveTypeAutoRun`

Bit	Drive Type
0	Unknown Drives
2	Removable Drives
3	Hard Drives
4	Remote Drives
5	CD-ROM Drives
6	RAM Drives

Now that you've enabled Autorun.inf for the appropriate devices, you're ready to change the icon that Windows Explorer displays for each disk. Create an Autorun.inf and place it in the root folder of each disk. The Autorun.inf file should look similar to Listing 9.1. Replace everything to the right of `icon=` with the location of the icon, whether it's an ICO file or an indexed icon within an EXE, DLL, or RES file. Remember that you can create a unique Autorun.inf file for each disk. Every one of your floppies can use a distinct icon, for example, and you can store the icon file on the disk itself.

Listing 9.1 **A Sample Autorun.inf File**

```
[autorun]
icon=c:\windows\system32\cool.dll,8
```

Specific Drive Letters

Windows Explorer examines an undocumented and seldom-used branch of `HKEY_LOCAL_MACHINE` called `Software\Microsoft\Windows\CurrentVersion\explorer\DriveIcons` to find drive icons. It looks for a subkey matching each possible drive letter and a subkey under those called `DefaultIcon`. The default value entry of `DefaultIcon` should be the specification of an icon. As you learned a moment ago, you can specify the path and filename of an ICO or other image file. You can also use the path and filename of a DLL, EXE, or RES file in combination with an index number, or the path and filename of a DLL, EXE, or RES file in combination with a resource ID.

If you want to display a custom icon for drive D, for example, add `D\DefaultIcon` to `DriveIcons` and change the default value entry of `DefaultIcon` to the location of the icon. If you want to display a custom icon for drive X, add `X\DefaultIcon` to `DriveIcons`, and change the default value entry of `DefaultIcon`.

NOTE: Changing a drive's icon by creating a Autorun.inf file will not work in all drive types in all computers. It depends largely on the hardware and the device driver provided by the manufacturer. Experiment with this file to see what you can customize. Note that you might have to press F5 in Windows Explorer in order to see the disk's new icon.

Specific Folders in Explorer

The ability to display unique icons for specific folders is a feature that Internet Explorer 4.0 added to Windows 95. Windows 98 includes it by default. Windows Explorer takes special notice any time it finds a hidden file called Desktop.ini within a system folder. The attribute of the folder in conjunction with this file indicates that the folder is special and usually points to an object that handles the folder's contents.

You can use this file to indicate an icon for any folder, as well as a tip that Windows Explorer displays when you hover over it with the mouse pointer. Create a Desktop.ini file and place it in the folder, setting the hidden attribute using the MS-DOS `Attrib` command or the General tab of the file's property sheet. You should also turn on the folder's system attribute, which you can only do by typing `attrib +s` *foldername* at the command prompt. The file should look similar to Listing 9.2. Set *IconFile* to the path of the ICO file or to the path of an EXE, DLL, or RES file and the icon's index. You can also set *InfoTip* to any text you want Windows Explorer to display in a popup window when you hover the mouse pointer over the folder.

Listing 9.2 **A Sample Desktop.ini**

```
[.ShellClassInfo]
IconFile=C:\Windows\Winupd.ico
InfoTip=This is the tip Windows displays when you hover over
➡the folder.
```

Mastering Shortcut Menus for Objects and Files

Figure 9.2 shows a typical shortcut menu, which you open by right-clicking a file or folder. Windows Explorer builds a shortcut menu from a variety of sources, all of which are under `HKEY_CLASSES_ROOT` in the following order:

- ***class*\\shell** You see these at the top of the shortcut menu, as shown in the figure.

- ***class*\\shellex\\ContextMenuHandlers** Each subkey under this key defines an object that adds commands to the shortcut menu. The name of the subkey is the class identifier of the object, and its default value entry is its name; or the subkey is the name of the object, and the default value entry contains its class identifier.

- ***\\shell** This key adds commands that are common to all types of files. You see these just below the class's own commands and just above the first divider.

- ***\\shellex\\ContextMenuHandlers** Each subkey under this key defines an object that adds commands to every file's shortcut menu. See *class*\\shellex\\ContextMenuHandlers, earlier in this list.

- **\AllFilesystemObjects\shellex\ContextMenuHandlers**   Each subkey under this defines an object that adds commands to every file system object's shortcut menu. In most cases, this just adds the **Send To** submenu.

- **Shell32.dll**   Windows 98 adds a number of commands that are built into the operating system. These are also known as *canonical verbs*, which means that they're officially supported commands defined by the operating system. Windows Explorer places these at the bottom of each file's shortcut menu, including commands such as **Cut**, **Copy**, and so on.

When you right-click a file for which Windows Explorer doesn't find an associated program, you see the **Open With** command, which opens the Open With dialog box so that you can choose a program in which you want to open the file. This is also the default command, so if you double-click a file with no association, you also see the Open With dialog box. The commands for files with no associations come from HKEY_CLASSES_ROOT\unknown\shell. unknown\shell typically contains a single subkey, a verb, for the **Open With** command, but you can add additional commands to it, just as you can for any other file or class. You can add a command to unknown\shell that opens an unassociated file in Notepad, for instance.

Windows Explorer handles the shortcut menu for objects similarly, except that it looks in HKEY_CLASSES_ROOT\CLSID*clsid*\shell for commands instead, as well as in HKEY_CLASSES_ROOT\CLSID*clsid*\shellex\ContextMenuHandlers, which you learned about earlier in this section. One addition, however, is that it looks in HKEY_CLASSES_ROOT\CLSID*clsid*\shellfolder for an attributes value entry that enables or disables built-in or canonical verbs defined in Shell32.dll. You'll learn more about attributes a bit later in this chapter.

Documenting Changes to the Registry

Keeping track of each change you make is difficult. You can keep a separate log file, but you're not likely to keep it updated, and the information isn't handy when you really need it.

The best way to document each change you make to the Registry is to add a bogus value entry containing a description of the change you made. You might include the date you made the change, too, so that you can relate changes you make to changes in the operating system's behavior. The best name to use for this bogus value entry is a combination of the changed value entry's name and the word "Note." Thus, if you change a value entry called maxMTU, add a new string value entry called maxMTUNote and set its value to a brief description of the change you made and the date you made it.

When you name the notes this way and put them within the subkey containing the changed value entry, they appear next to the original value. For instance, to continue the example, the two value entries maxMTU and maxMTUNote would appear next to each other in the Registry key that contains them both.

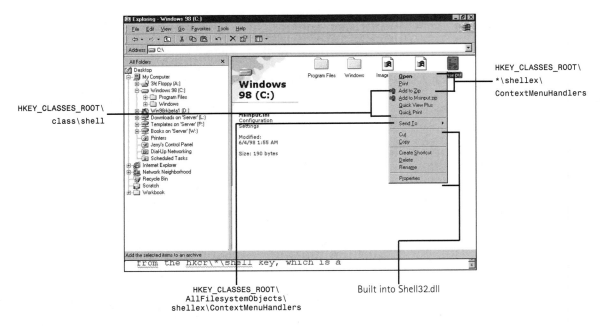

HKEY_CLASSES_ROOT\
class\shell

HKEY_CLASSES_ROOT\
*\shellex\
ContextMenuHandlers

HKEY_CLASSES_ROOT\
AllFilesystemObjects\
shellex\ContextMenuHandlers

Built into Shell32.dll

Figure 9.2 Windows 98 defines menu items such as **Properties** that you see below the first divider.

The organization of each `shell` subkey is the same. The default value entry of the `shell` subkey contains the name of the verb that defines the default command on the shortcut menu. You see a subkey for each verb, each of which has a `command` subkey whose default value entry contains the command line to execute. The default value entry for the verb optionally contains the text that Windows Explorer will display on the shortcut menu for the command. For example, the **Open** command on a text file's shortcut menu is due to the Registry entries shown in Figure 9.3. What you don't see in the figure is that the default value entry of `shell` can contain the name of the default verb, and the default value entry of `open` can contain the text that Windows Explorer displays on the shortcut menu.

> NOTE: The easiest way to find a subkey for a file type or object is to search the Registry for its name. To find the class identifier for the Recycle Bin in the Registry, for instance, search the Registry for the string "Recycle Bin." To quickly find a file type in the Registry, note the description that Windows Explorer displays for it in the file's property sheet, and search for that string in the Registry.

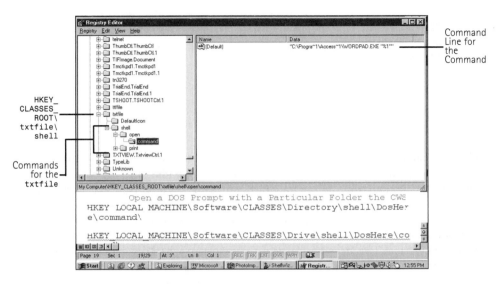

Figure 9.3 This figure shows two commands: **Open** and **Print**.

Adding Commands

Adding commands to a shortcut menu requires you to duplicate the structure under the class's shell key, which you learned about in the preceding section. This structure looks like *verb*\command. *verb* is the name of the verb, and the default value entry of command contains the command line you want to execute when the user chooses that verb. Thus, to add a command to a TXT file's shortcut menu that opens it in Wordpad, follow steps similar to these (see Listing 9.3 for an outline of the subkeys and value entries added using these steps):

1. Look up the program identifier associated with a TXT file by looking at the default value entry of .txt under HKEY_CLASSES_ROOT.

2. Open HKEY_CLASSES_ROOT*progid*\shell, where *progid* is the program identifier you looked up in step 1. If you don't see the shell subkey, add it.

3. Add a subkey under shell called wordpad. Change the default value entry of wordpad to Open in Wordpad so that you'll see this text on the shortcut menu.

4. Add a subkey under shell\wordpad called command, and set its default value entry to C:\Program Files\Accessories\Wordpad.exe "%1", which causes Windows 98 to open the target file in WordPad when you choose this command from the shortcut menu.

Listing 9.3 **Adding a Command to a Text File's Shortcut Menu**

```
HKEY_CLASSES_ROOT
    txtfile
        shell
            wordpad
                default = "Open in Wordpad"
                command
                    default = "C:\Program Files\Accessories\
                    ➥Wordpad.exe "%1"
```

The command line for commands varies. In cases where you want to open the file in a specific program, you can sometimes get away with providing just the path and file-name of the program. You can use long or 8.3 filenames. Windows 98 will automatically pass the name of the target file as a command line argument to the program. In other cases, you must explicitly specify the location of the filename by using the %1 placeholder, which Windows 98 substitutes with the target filename when it launches the command line. This becomes particularly important when the command line contains switches and you must include the filename in a specific place within it: myprog /p /k "%1" /s, for example. If you think the program might have trouble with long filenames that include spaces, be sure to put %1 in quotes, as shown in Listing 9.3. This ensures that the program won't assume that everything up to the first space is the file-name and that everything after the first space is additional filenames or garbage.

Changing the Default Command

The default command of any shortcut menu is the command that Windows Explorer executes whenever you double-click the file. You'll also notice that the default command is bolded in the shortcut menu. Here's how to change the default for any shortcut menu:

1. Locate the class's shell subkey under HKEY_CLASSES_ROOT in the Registry. For instance, text files are in HKEY_CLASSES_ROOT\txtfile\shell.

2. Note the names of the verbs under shell, open, and print for text files, choosing the one you want to be the default command on the shortcut menu.

3. Change the default value entry of the shell key so that it contains the name of the verb representing the default command. Set it to print if you want the default command for text files to be printing them.

Here's a real-world example for changing the default command of a shortcut menu. When you open a folder on the desktop, Windows 98 opens it in a single-pane window instead of a double-pane Explorer window. If you change the default command of HKEY_CLASSES_ROOT\folder from open to explore, Windows 98 will open it in a double-pane Explorer window instead of a single-pane window.

Changing the Menu's Appearance

You can change the text that Windows Explorer displays on any shortcut menu command that comes from a `shell` key. It doesn't matter whether the key comes from a program identifier, defined as `HKEY_CLASSES_ROOT\`*`progid`*, or from an object, defined as `HKEY_CLASSES_ROOT\CLSID\`*`clsid`*. However, you can't change the text that a context menu handler, defined in a `ContextMenuHandler` subkey of a class, puts on a shortcut menu. Nor can you change the text that Windows 98 displays for the built-in commands you see at the bottom of a shortcut menu.

To change the text you see on a shortcut menu, find the class's `shell` key in the Registry. As you'll recall, each command is a verb in `shell`. Change the default value entry of each verb to the text you want to see on the shortcut menu. To change the text you see for the **Open** command of a text file's shortcut menu to **Edit**, for instance, change the default value entry of `\txtfile\shell\open` to `&Edit` under `HKEY_CLASSES_ROOT`. Windows Explorer maintains the capitalization you use in the default entry, and you can indicate a hot key by putting an ampersand in front of the letter. Here are a few examples of what various default value entries look like on a shortcut menu:

> NOTE: Put "%1" in the command line at the exact location where you want Windows 98 to expand the path and name of the target file when it launches the command line.

Useful Things to Add to a Context Menu

Here are some useful commands to add to a folder or file's shortcut menu:

- To open a command prompt with a particular folder as the current working directory, add a new verb to the `Directory` and `Drive` classes, whose command line is `c:\windows\command.com /k cd "%1"`. Then, right-click any folder or disk, and choose the new command you added to the shortcut menu.

- To open Windows Explorer with a particular folder at the root, add the following command to the `Folder` class: `explorer.exe /e,/root,/idlist,%I`. Then, right-click any folder and choose the new command you added to the shortcut menu.

- To open a Control Panel icon by typing its filename in the Run dialog box, rename the `cplopenkey` subkey of the `cplfile` file type to `open`. Then, type the filename, perhaps Powercfg.cpl, of the Control Panel icon in the Run dialog box and press Enter.

- To open Tweak UI from My Computer, add the following command line to `{20D04FE0-3AEA-1069-A2D8-08002B30309D}`: `C:\WINDOWS\rundll32.exe shell32.dll,Control_RunDLL Tweakui.cpl`. Then, right-click My Computer, and choose the new command you added to the shortcut menu. You can add any other Control Panel application to My Computer's shortcut menu by replacing Tweakui.cpl with the application's filename.

In the Registry	On the Shortcut Menu
open	**open**
&Open	**Open**
open in Wordpad	**open in Wordpad**
open in &Wordpad	**open in Wordpad**

Things get a bit more complicated if the default value entry for a verb is empty. Windows Explorer gets the name from one of two places if a name is not explicitly defined in the Registry:

- **Shell32.dll**   Windows 98 retrieves the string to display on the shortcut menu from Shell32.dll. It does this for the canonical verbs **Find, Open, Open With,** and **Print**.

- **Subkey name**   Windows 98 uses the name of the verb as the text it displays on the shortcut menu. For instance, if `HKEY_CLASSES_ROOT\txtfile\shell\edit`'s default value entry is empty, Windows 98 puts **edit** on the shortcut menu.

Removing Commands

To remove a command from a shortcut menu, identify where in the Registry the command is defined. Then remove the command as described in the following list:

- **`shell`**   If the command comes from a `shell` key, remove the command's verb. This is true for *, unknown, and any other place where you see a `shell` subkey.

- **`shellex\ContextMenuHandler`**   If the command comes from a `ContextMenuHandler` subkey of a file type or object, remove the handler's subkey. This might remove multiple commands from the shortcut menu, however, depending on how many commands it adds.

- **Shell32.dll**   If the command is on an object's shortcut menu and is one of the canonical verbs defined by Shell32.dll, change the object's `attributes` value. You'll learn more about this value following this list.

> **TIP:** Changing the default value entry of `folder\shell` to `explore` also changes the default command for the My Computer icon's shortcut menu. After making this change, double-click the My Computer icon on the desktop to open it in the double-pane Explorer window rather than the single-pane window.

Many objects have an `attributes` value in `HKEY_CLASSES_ROOT\CLSID\` *clsid*`\ShellFolder`, where *clsid* is the class identifier of the object. This value indicates the canonical verbs, or built-in commands, that Windows 98 displays on the object's shortcut menu. `attributes` is a 4-byte binary value, with each bit representing a flag that enables or disables a specific command. Table 9.5 describes the bits currently used by Windows 98. Setting a particular bit to 0 disables the command, while setting it to 1 enables the command. Remember that you count bits right-to-left in a binary value, so bit 0 is the first bit on the right, bit 1 is the second bit on the right, and so on. Since the Registry shows `attributes` as a hexadecimal value, you must convert it to binary to figure out which commands are enabled. Work with this value in binary until you're ready to change `attributes`, and then convert it to hexadecimal.

Here's a real-world example. The `attributes` value for the Internet Explorer icon is `72000000` in hexadecimal, which is 11100100000000000000000000000000 in binary. Counting from right to left, bits 25, 28, 29, and 30 are 1s. Thus, Windows 98 displays the **Cut**, **Rename**, **Delete**, and **Properties** commands on Internet Explorer's shortcut menu. You can remove the **Cut** command from the shortcut menu by turning off bit 25, which leaves you with a hexadecimal value of `70000000`.

Table 9.5 **Bits in the** `attributes` **Value**

Bit Number	Command
30	**P**roperties
29	**D**elete
28	**Rena**me
25	**Cut**
24	**C**opy
16	**P**aste
5	**O**pen and **E**xplore for the Recycle Bin

Adding Templates to the New Menu

Right-click any folder and choose **New** to display a menu of new documents you can create in the folder, as shown in Figure 9.4. This is a quick way to create a new document. Then open the document to edit its contents.

`HKEY_CLASSES_ROOT\`*.ext*`\ShellNew`, where *.ext* is a file extension such as `.doc` or `.txt`, defines a template for the New menu. You can put only one template on the New menu for each file extension. You add one of three value entries to this subkey to add the extension to the New menu:

- **`NullFile`**   Make sure this string value entry is empty, causing Windows 98 to create an empty file in the folder when the user chooses this file type.

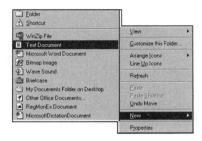

Figure 9.4 The Folder and Shortcut items are hard-coded by the operating system; you can't change or remove them.

- **FileName**   Copy a template file with the same file extension to \Windows\ShellNew, and then set this value entry to the name of the file, excluding the path. When the user chooses this file type from the New menu, Windows 98 creates a new file using the template in \Windows\ShellNew.

- **Data**   This is a binary value whose contents Windows 98 uses to create the new file when the user chooses it from the New menu. Windows 98 just copies the bytes from this value entry directly into the file.

SEE ALSO

➤ See Chapter 11, "Tweak UI and Other Registry Programs," to learn how Tweak UI makes adding templates to the New menu much easier. You drag a file onto the New tab of Tweak UI in order to create a new template or change an existing one.

Customizing the Start Menu and Its Contents

The following sections describe various ways you can customize the Start menu:

- How to restore a sorted Start menu
- How to disable any submenu on the Start menu
- How to customize a submenu's icon
- How to add shell folders as cascading menus
- How to point Find to a better location

Restoring a Sorted Start Menu

With the introduction of Internet Explorer 4.0 into Windows 95 and subsequently Windows 98, the Start and Favorites menus are customizable. The user can sort the menu using drag and drop or even edit both menus in place by right-clicking the objects on it.

Windows 98 stores the sort order of the Start menu in `HKEY_CURRENT_USER\`
`Software\Microsoft\Windows\CurrentVersion\Explorer\MenuOrder`. You find two
subkeys here: `Favorites` and `Start Menu`. Within each, you find a subkey for each submenu and a subkey called `Menu` that indicates the sort order of all the items on the
menu. Each of the subkeys for submenus contains a `Menu` subkey as well. Take a look at
Figure 9.5 if this description confuses you. You can't really change the sort order by
editing the `Menu` subkey, because editing it is almost impossible. You can use the following two tricks to make working with the Start menu's sort order easier, however:

- Export the entire `MenuOrder` branch to a REG file that you can later import to
  restore the sort order of the Start menu if it goes awry.

- Remove the `Favorites` and `Start Menu` subkeys of `MenuOrder` to restore the sort
  order for both menus to their Windows 98 defaults.

Disabling Commands: Documents, Run, and So On

One of the biggest questions I hear from administrators is how to remove commands
such as **Run** and **Find** from the Start menu. This wasn't easy to accomplish in
Windows 95 prior to Internet Explorer 4.0 and Windows 98.

Each of the policies you see in Table 9.6 is under `HKEY_CURRENT_USER\Software\`
`Microsoft\Windows\CurrentVersion\Policies\Explorer`. If you don't find this branch
in the Registry, create it. Then add the DWORD value entry corresponding to the
submenu or command you want to disable, as shown in the table. To disable the menu
command, set the policy value to 1; to enable the menu command, set the policy value
to 0. Note that Windows 98 doesn't provide policies for removing **Programs**,
Settings, or **Shut Down** from the Start menu.

Table 9.6   **Policies for Disabling Icons on the Start Menu**

Value Entry	Description
NoFavoritesMenu	Enables or disables the **Favorites** menu
NoFind	Enables or disables the **Find** menu
NoRecentDocsMenu	Enables or disables the **Documents** menu
NoRun	Enables or disables the **Run** command
NoLogOff	Enables or disables the **Log Off** command

SEE ALSO

➤ See Chapter 11, "Tweak UI and Other Registry Programs," to learn about other programs
   that make changing these settings easier.

➤ See Chapter 14, "Profiles, System Policies, and the Registry," to learn how you can use
   the System Policy Editor to change these settings.

TIP: Many times, you'll need to convert hexadecimal to binary and vice versa as you edit the Registry.
Use the Windows Calculator in Scientific mode to do so quickly.

Menu subkeys
indicate sort order

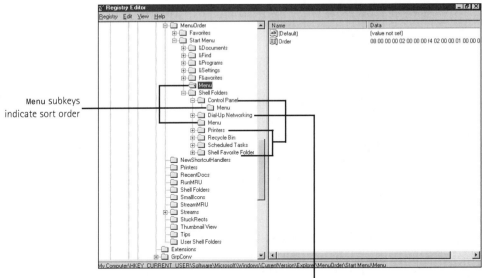

Other subkeys represent submenus

Figure 9.5 Each level within this branch contains a `Menu` subkey that
describes how the folders and shortcuts are sorted.

Customizing Each Command's Icon

The earlier section "Shell folders" showed you how to customize the icons that
Windows 98 displays in various locations. These icons include the images you see on
the Start menu. Specifically, you add a string value entry to `HKEY_LOCAL_MACHINE\`
`Software\Microsoft\Windows\CurrentVersion\explorer\Shell Icons` that corresponds to the command you want to change, as described in Table 9.7. If you want to
change the icon that the Start menu displays for the **<u>Settings</u>** command, for example,
create a string value entry called `21` to this key. Assign to the default value entry of the
new key the location of the icon you want to use. The location can be the path and
filename of an ICO file, or it can be the path and filename of an EXE, DLL, or RES
file combined with the index of the icon. Here are more-specific instructions for
changing an icon on the Start menu to make sure Windows 98 updates your changes:

1. Restart the Computer in Safe Mode.

2. Delete the ShellIconCache file from \Windows. You might have to show hidden
    files in Windows Explorer in order to see this file.

3. Add the value entry corresponding to one of the value entries in Table 9.7, and
    set its default value entry to the location of the icon.

4. Restart the computer normally.

Table 9.7 **Customizing Icons on the Start Menu**

Value Name	Command
19	**P**rograms
20	**D**ocuments
21	**S**ettings
22	**F**ind
23	**H**elp
24	**R**un
25	**S**uspend
26	**E**ject PC
27	**Sh**ut Down

Adding Shell Folders as Cascading Menus

Some of the objects you saw earlier in Table 9.2 make great additions to the Start menu. In particular, the Control Panel, Dial-Up Networking, Printers, Recycle Bin, and Scheduled Tasks folders work well on the Start menu (but the others don't). When you add them, Windows 98 displays their contents as cascading menus instead of opening a separate folder to display their contents. Figure 9.6 shows you an example of what the Control Panel looks like when you add it to the Start menu as a cascading menu.

To add one of the objects from Table 9.2 to the Start menu, create a new folder anywhere within the Start Menu folder and name it *name.clsid*. *name* is the name of the folder as shown in the table, and *clsid* is the class identifier of the folder as shown in the table. By the way, make sure you include the braces in the class identifier. The following list shows you the names to use for the five folders just mentioned and shown in Figure 9.6:

Control Panel	{21EC2020-3AEA-1069-A2DD-08002B30309D}
Dial-Up Networking	{992CFFA0-F557-101A-88EC-00DD010CCC48}
Printers	{2227A280-3AEA-1069-A2DE-08002B30309D}
Recycle Bin	{645FF040-5081-101B-9F08-00AA002F954E}
Scheduled Tasks	{D6277990-4C6A-11CF-8D87-00AA0060F5BF}

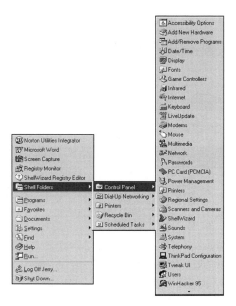

Figure 9.6 The Control Panel is much easier to access if you add
it to the Start menu as a cascading menu.

Fixing Menu and Window Behavior Problems

Windows have a habit of zooming when you minimize or restore them. That is, you
see the outline of the window grow as a minimized window restores onto the desktop. You also see the outline of a window shrink as a normal window minimizes to the
taskbar. Microsoft designed this behavior so that users can more easily see where the
window lands. However, this feature isn't necessary for most users and actually robs the
user of that crisp feeling when a window pops open on the desktop or instantly minimizes to the taskbar. You can prevent windows from zooming by setting `MinAnimate` to
`0` in `HKEY_CURRENT_USER\Control Panel\Desktop\WindowMetrics`. If this string value
entry doesn't exist, add it.

Another annoying behavior is that menus tend to follow the mouse like a stray dog
looking for kibble. This behavior is noticeable on the Start menu. Hover the mouse
pointer over any submenu, and Windows 98 automatically opens the submenu after
half a second (500ms). Hover the mouse pointer over any other submenu, and
Windows 98 automatically closes the previous menu and opens the submenu. Some
people like the delay to be a bit shorter so that the menus follow the mouse more
quickly. Other people like the delay to be longer so that menus work more like they
did in Windows 95 prior to this feature. To adjust this setting, change the
`MenuShowDelay` value entry you find under `HKEY_CURRENT_USER\Control Panel\`
`Desktop`. `MenuShowDelay` is a string value entry that you can add if you don't see it in
the key. It represents the delay in milliseconds before a menu follows the mouse. The

default value is `500`. Set it to a lower number to make the menus snappier, or set it to an extremely large number such as 65535 to keep menus from following the mouse.

You can cause Windows 98 to align menu commands to the left or the right. Set the `MenuDropAlignment` value entry under `HKEY_CURRENT_USER\Control Panel\Desktop` to 1 if you want to align menus to the right, or set it to 0 to align menus to the left. Each time you shut down Windows, it remembers the position of all the desktop icons, taskbar, and any open Explorer windows. If you put Explorer in your StartUp program folder and forget to close Explorer before shutting down Windows, for example, you'll have two copies of Explorer on your desktop when you restart Windows. These are the copy you loaded in the StartUp program menu and the copy that you left on your desktop when you shut down Windows. If you'd like Windows's memory to be a bit less permanent, set the binary value entry `NoSaveSettings` under `HKEY_CURRENT_USER\Software\Microsoft\Windows\CurrentVersion\Policies\Explorer\` to 1. If you don't see this value entry, add it.

Removing the Overlay from Shortcut Icons

Windows displays a small arrow on the bottom-left corner of shortcut icons. Microsoft calls this an *overlay*. Remove this arrow by removing the `IsShortcut` value entry from `HKEY_CLASSES_ROOT\lnkfile`. Remove the same value entry from `HKEY_CLASSES_ROOT\piffile` so that you don't see arrows on the bottom-left corner of PIF files.

Personalizing Internet Explorer 4.0

Internet Explorer 4.0 provides a number of methods you can use to customize it. The Internet Explorer Administration Kit (IEAK) allows you to completely customize Internet Explorer. You can even change the text that appears on the browser's title bar. You can't change most of the settings via the Registry; you can only change them by creating INS files via the administration kit. The *Microsoft Windows 98 Resource Kit,* published by Microsoft Press, includes a copy of the Internet Explorer Administration Kit.

The remainder of this section describes three ways you can customize Internet Explorer 4.0 via the Registry. You can extend its shortcut menus, for one. You can also change the bitmap displayed on the background of toolbars and you can change the default protocol that the browser uses when you type a URL with the protocol.

SEE ALSO
➤ Chapter 10, "Fixing Common Problems via the Registry," describes how to disable Internet Explorer 4.0's desktop integration.

NOTE: Tweak UI contains a number of other ways that you can change how windows and menus behave in Windows. See Chapter 11, "Tweak UI and Other Registry Programs," for more information.

Extending the Shortcut Menus

Internet Explorer 4.0 displays a shortcut menu when you right-click anywhere within a Web page. You can add items to this shortcut menu, each of which are linked to scripts you create and place in an HTML file. You can customize the shortcut menu to open a frame in a new window, for example, or you can customize it to resize the font in a block of text.

To add a command to Internet Explorer 4.0's shortcut menu, create a new subkey under HKEY_CURRENT_USER\Software\Microsoft\Internet Explorer\MenuExt. If you don't see MenuExt, add it. Internet Explorer uses this name for the command's text on the shortcut menu. You can put an ampersand in front of any character to indicate it as a hotkey. Then, set the default value to the path and filename of the HTML file containing the script that executes the command. If you want to add a command called **Test** to the shortcut menu that launches an HTML file called Test.htm in C:\Windows, you'd add a subkey called &Test to MenuExt and set its default value entry to C:\Windows\Test.htm.

When you click the command in the shortcut menu, Internet Explorer opens the HTML file and executes any inline scripts it finds there. The scripting property external.menuArguments contains the window object on which you executed the command. Thus, if you right-click a Web page and choose **Test**, external. menuArguments contains the window object on which you right-clicked. With access to the window object, you can pretty much do anything you want to the current Web page, including changing its contents, format, etc. With all that said, the following listing is an example of an HTML file that changes the font size of a text selection so that you can read it easier. To try it out, type the listing in an HTML file, and add a subkey to MenuExt and set its default value entry to the path and filename of the HTML file. Then, open a Web page in Internet Explorer, select some text, right-click the selected text, and choose the new command you added.

```
<HTML>
<SCRIPT LANGUAGE="JavaScript" defer>
var objWin = external.menuArguments;
var objDoc = objWin.document;
var objSel = objDoc.selection;
var objRange = objSel.createRange();
objRange.execCommand( "FontSize", 0, "+2" );
</SCRIPT>
</HTML>
```

CAUTION: Removing the overlay from shortcuts by removing the IsShortcut value entry might cause Windows 98 to behave erratically.

There is an additional value you can add to the command's subkey that controls which context menus display the command. It's called `Contexts`. Add this one byte binary value to the command's subkey and set its value according to the masks described in the following table. If you wanted to limit the previous example so that it only appears on the shortcut menu displayed for text selections, add the binary value called `Contexts` to the new subkey under `MenuExt` and set its value to `0x10`. Note that you might have to restart Internet Explorer 4.0 in order to see your changes to this subkey.

Value	Menu
0x01	Default Menu
0x02	Image Menu
0x04	Control Menu
0x08	Table Menu
0x10	Text Selection Menu
0x11	Anchor Menu
0x12	Unknown Menu

Changing the Toolbar's Background

The background you see on Internet Explorer's toolbar is nothing more than a bitmap. To change the background, create a new string value entry called `BackBitmap` under `HKEY_CURRENT_USER\Software\Microsoft\Internet Explorer\Toolbar`. Change the value to the path of the bitmap you want to display on the background of Internet Explorer's toolbar. If the bitmap doesn't fill the entire toolbar, Internet Explorer tiles it horizontally and vertically.

Changing the Default Protocol

If you type a URL in Internet Explorer's toolbar or in the Run dialog box, Internet Explorer automatically prefixes it with the appropriate protocol. If you type `www.microsoft.com`, for example, Internet Explorer changes it to `http://www.microsoft.com`. If you type `ftp.microsoft.com`, Internet Explorer changes it to `ftp://ftp.microsoft.com`. Notice that it chooses the protocol based on how the URL begins. But what happens when you type `rampages.onramp.net/~jerry`? By default, Internet Explorer is going to assume it's a Web page and add **http://** to the beginning of it. If this isn't the behavior you want, you can specify a different prefix by changing the default value entry of `HKEY_LOCAL_MACHINE\Software\Microsoft\Windows\CurrentVersion\URL\DefaultPrefix` to the protocol you want Internet Explorer to use by default—for example, **ftp://**.

> NOTE: This section assumes some familiarity with how to write scripts for Web pages, whether they be in VBScript or JavaScript. If you don't know how to write scripts, check out Macmillan Publishing's *Special Edition Using HTML* or one of Macmillan's other books on the topic. You can also find more information about extending Internet Explorer 4.0's shortcut menus at Microsoft's Web site. Here's the URL: `http://www.microsoft.com/ie/ie40/powertoys/Contextm.htm`.

Clearing the Most Recently Used Lists

Windows 98 keeps various history lists, also called MRU or most recently used lists. It keeps histories of the documents you've opened recently, programs you've run, file specifications you've searched for, and computers you've searched for on the network. You might consider this a personal security risk if you're concerned about other people knowing what you've been up to recently. You can clear all these history lists by removing the keys listed in Table 9.8 from `HKEY_CURRENT_USER\Software\Microsoft\Windows\CurrentVersion\explorer`.

Table 9.8 **History Lists**

Location	Location in Registry
Documents menu	`RecentDocs`
Run dialog	`RunMru`
Find Files dialog	`Doc Find Spec MRU`
Find Computer dialog	`FindComputerMRU`

After removing these keys from the Registry, you have to erase the contents of \Windows\Recent to finish clearing the contents of the **Documents** menu. If user profiles are enabled on the computer, erase the contents of \Windows\Profiles*username*\Recent, where *username* is your logon name.

Clearing Automatically

You can clear these history lists automatically by creating an INF file to remove them. Right-click the INF file and choose **Install**. Listing 9.4 shows the INF file, which you might want to call Cleanup.inf or something similar. To automatically launch the INF file and simultaneously erase the contents of \Windows\Recent, create a BAT file that looks like Listing 9.5 called Cleanup.bat.

Listing 9.4 **An INF File to Clear the MRU Lists**

```
[version]
signature=$Chicago$

[DefaultInstall]
DelReg=DelRegKey

[DelRegKey]
HKCU,"Software\Microsoft\Windows\CurrentVersion\Explorer\
➥Doc Find Spec MRU",
HKCU,Software\Microsoft\Windows\CurrentVersion\Explorer\
➥FindComputerMRU,
HKCU,Software\Microsoft\Windows\CurrentVersion\Explorer\
➥RecentDocs,
HKCU,Software\Microsoft\Windows\CurrentVersion\Explorer\RunMRU
```

Listing 9.5 **Cleaning Out the MRU Lists and \Windows\Recent**

```
@Echo Off
C:\Windows\rundll.exe setupx.dll,InstallHinfSection
➥DefaultInstall 132 Cleanup.inf
Echo Y ¦ Erase C:\Windows\Recent
```

Clearing When Windows 98 Starts

Launching the BAT file every time you want to clean up the MRU lists isn't convenient, particularly if you want to do it every time you start Windows 98. You can add
the BAT file to your StartUp folder. Alternatively, add the BAT file to `HKEY_LOCAL_`
`MACHINE\Software\Microsoft\Windows\CurrentVersion\Run\`. You'll learn more about
this key in the following section.

> SEE ALSO

> ➤ Chapter 11, "Tweak UI and Other Registry Programs," describes a variety of customiza-
> tion tools that launch automatically when Windows 98 starts in order to clear the history
> lists.

> ➤ See Chapter 15, "Script, REG, and INF Files," to learn more about writing INF files.

Locating Programs that Open When Windows 98 Starts

Windows 98 launches any shortcuts it finds in the StartUp folder after the user logs
onto the computer. These are obvious. What's not obvious is why certain programs run
automatically even though they don't appear in the StartUp group. Programs that start
automatically *before* a user logs onto the computer do so because of entries in the `Run`
and `RunOnce` subkeys under `HKEY_LOCAL_MACHINE\Software\Microsoft\Windows\`
`CurrentVersion`. Windows 98 launches the command line specified in every value
entry it finds there. It does so every time the operating system starts. `RunOnce` is a special case containing value entries for commands that Windows 98 will launch once
and then remove. The name of each value entry isn't important, but it should be
descriptive.

`HKEY_CURRENT_USER\Software\Microsoft\Windows\CurrentVersion` also contains
`Run` and `RunOnce` subkeys. Windows 98 launches the commands in these subkeys *after*
the user logs onto the computer. Again, the name of each value entry doesn't matter,
but its value contains the command line to execute. Windows 98 executes commands
in `Run` every time the operating system starts and executes commands in `RunOnce` a
single time before removing them from the Registry.

NOTE: The quotation marks around the first key in Listing 9.4 are a must. That's because the key name
contains spaces, which would confuse Windows 98 if you didn't use the quotes.

Logging onto the Network Automatically

Windows 98 requires a username and password if you configure it to connect to the network. It also asks for a username and password even if you don't connect to a network. Change the following value entries under `HKEY_LOCAL_MACHINE\Software\Microsoft\Windows\CurrentVersion\Winlogon` so that you can log onto Windows 98 automatically without retyping your credentials:

Value	Description
DefaultUserName	Set this string value entry to the username you use to log onto Windows.
DefaultPassword	Set this string value entry to the password you use to log onto Windows.
AutoAdminLogon	Set this string value entry to 1 to enable automatic logon, or set it to 0 to disable automatic logon.

Changing Installation Information

Windows 98 stores the path of its installation folder in the Registry at `HKEY_LOCAL_MACHINE\Software\Microsoft\Windows\CurrentVersion\Setup`. If you change the location of the source files, you might want to change the `SourcePath` value entry in this key so that the next time you add components to Windows 98 it automatically finds the files without having to prompt you for their location.

Windows 98 prompts you for a user name and organization when you install it. Windows 98 doesn't provide a means to change this information after installation, but you can change it in the Registry. It stores the organization, owner, and product ID in the following value entries found in `HKEY_LOCAL_MACHINE\SOFTWARE\Microsoft\Windows\CurrentVersion`:

    RegisteredOrganization

    RegisteredOwner

    ProductID

> CAUTION: Don't use this customization if you're logging onto a network on which security is a concern. This allows anyone to walk up to your computer and access the network without providing credentials.

Finding More Registry Hints and Tips

Many of the customization tips in this chapter were found on the Internet. Several Web pages on the Internet are dedicated to Windows 98 hints and tips. My Web site, `http://www.honeycutt.com`, contains links to some of the best. If you're not content with the list in my Web site, you can use one of the search tools in the following mini-table to find your own:

Search Tool	Web Address
AltaVista	`http://www.altavista.digital.com`
Deja News	`http://www.dejanews.com`
Excite	`http://www.excite.com`
Lycos	`http://www.lycos.com`
WebCrawler	`http://www.webcrawler.com`
Yahoo	`http://www.yahoo.com`

If you type the word `registry` in these search tools, you'll find everything from bridal registries to a registry that documents speed traps across the nation (`http://www.nashville.net/speedtrap`). Limit your search a bit more by including the word `Windows`. Also, I suggest that you not limit your search to Windows NT if you're a Windows NT user. Most of the Windows 98 hints-and-tips-type of Web pages contain information that's equally useful to Windows NT. The following list shows you some of the keyword phrases that I've found to be useful for finding Windows Registry tips:

```
windows registry
windows registry tip
windows hint
windows custom
windows q&a
windows registry faq
windows secret
```

If you're using a search tool that supports advanced searches with boolean logic (Alta Vista), you'll have even better luck by combining search terms. Try this:

```
(windows and registry) and (hint or tip or secret)
```

This searches for all Web pages that contain the words *windows* and *registry* (it must find both) and that contain at least one of *hint, tip,* or *secret.* So a Web page that contains *windows, registry,* and *tip* will match your search. A Web page that contains *windows* and *tip,* without the word *registry,* won't match your search.

Many Web pages containing Registry tips also provide REG files that you can use to automatically make the changes for you. Before merging the REG file with your Registry, open it in Notepad. Make sure that you fully understand and agree to the changes it will make. Well-meaning authors sometimes provide REG files that might break Windows 98.

10

Fixing Common Problems via the Registry

Karanjit S. Siyan, Ph.D

In this chapter:

- Starting in Safe Mode
- Allowing Windows 98 to Fix the Registry
- Removing a Program from the Registry Manually
- Extracting Files from CAB Files
- Diagnosing Common Registry-Related Error Messages
- Fixing Other Common Problems in Windows 98

Starting in Safe Mode

If you can't start Windows 98, and you suspect the culprit is configuration data in the Registry, start Windows 98 in Safe Mode, which is a special mode that forces Windows 98 to load without most of its device driver support. It loads the standard VGA, mouse, and keyboard drivers only. It skips everything in the Registry, Config.sys, Autoexec.bat, and the [Boot] and [386Enh] sections of System.ini. Networking support is not available in Windows 98 Safe Mode, whereas it was available in Windows 95. Note that most of your other devices won't work properly in Safe Mode since Windows 98 loaded their device drivers or configuration from the Registry. Here's how to start Windows 98 in Safe Mode:

1. Hold down the left Ctrl key or press F8 as Windows 98 starts to display the boot menu.

2. Choose **Safe Mode** from the boot menu. The boot menu contains other useful options, such as **Safe Mode Command Prompt Only**, which is guaranteed to work even when regular Safe Mode doesn't, and **Command Prompt Only**, which starts directly to the MS-DOS command prompt. Here's what a typical boot menu looks like:

   1. Normal
   2. Logged (\BOOTLOG.TXT)
   3. Safe mode
   4. Step-by-step confirmation
   5. Command prompt only
   6. Safe mode command prompt only

Safe Mode is useful for recovering from serious problems. Your video configuration might cause Windows 98 to crash as it starts, for instance, but you can change the configuration in Safe Mode and boot normally into a working operating system.

There are a few caveats with Safe Mode, however. The CD-ROM is unavailable, for example—even if you load the real mode driver in Config.sys. To avoid this problem, add the real mode driver to Config.sys and Mscdex.exe to Autoexec.bat, and then start the computer to the command prompt by choosing **Command Prompt Only** from the boot menu. Once you've recovered your configuration and started Windows 98 normally, you'll notice that your desktop might be messed up. Safe Mode operates at a video resolution of 640×480, so Windows 98 moves things around on the desktop to make sure everything fits. The last annoying issue I have with Safe Mode is that it changes the Start menu to large icons even though you might have configured it to use small icons.

You might be surprised when Windows 98 occasionally starts the computer in Safe Mode without your consent. It does so in the following situations:

■ The previous attempt at starting failed.

■ The signature file Wnbbotng.sts exists in \Windows.

■ An application requested Safe Mode.

■ The Registry file is corrupted.

> TIP: Windows 98 introduces a new way to display the boot menu. After restarting the computer, hold down the Ctrl key until you see the boot menu. The Ctrl key makes more sense than F8, because the Ctrl key doesn't automatically repeat like F8 does.

Allowing Windows 98 to Fix the Registry

Avoid editing the Registry whenever possible. It's a good rule to live by, since human error doesn't affect the result nearly as much as when you're editing the Registry. Simple changes that you make via the Windows 98 user interface ripple throughout the Registry. The simple act of enabling the Active Desktop by right-clicking the desktop and choosing **Active Desktop**, **View as Web Page** causes Windows 98 to write data to over 30 value entries that are scattered across three areas of the Registry. Which way do you prefer to perform the task?

Windows will fix some errors before you even know they exist, and you can fix the remaining problems using the variety of tools that Windows 98 provides. Let the Device Manager and Add/Remove Hardware Wizard deal with hardware problems, and let the Folder Options dialog box in Explorer handle problems with file associations. Instead of trying to fix an application's corrupted Registry entries, run the application's setup program and allow it to restore its Registry entries. You'll learn about these solutions in the remainder of this section.

> NOTE: Before problems strike, create one or more emergency disks that contain all the files you think you'll need if things go awry. You can also copy the most important bits of the Windows 98 CD-ROM to your computer's hard disk, assuming that you have enough space. Copying the \Tools and \Win98 folders requires approximately 200MB of free disk space.

> TIP: You can change most of the configuration data in the Registry via the **Settings** submenu on the Start menu, which provides access to the Control Panel.

Don't Reinstall Windows 98

After a support technician ventures beyond his level of competence, he'll usually tell you to reinstall Windows in order to fix the problem. This is a favorite line of support technicians around the globe, even at Microsoft.

What happens when you reinstall Windows 98 depends on how you do it. In either case, the setup program treats your actions as an upgrade, so the same rules apply. If you start the setup program from within Windows, it migrates your settings from the existing Registry, redetecting all the Plug and Play devices. If you start the setup program from MS-DOS mode, it redetects all the devices on the computer, including legacy and Plug and Play. In either case, Windows 98 keeps most of your personal preferences, other than a handful relating to Internet Explorer and the desktop. All your applications work the same as before.

Reinstalling Windows 98 just isn't necessary, as you can see from the preceding explanation. The only benefit you might receive by doing so is that the setup program will redetect your hardware, possibly rebuilding that portion of the Registry. Even that is questionable, however, because you can do the same thing yourself, as described in the next section.

Redetect Your Hardware

If your hardware configuration is behaving strangely, you won't be able to fix it using the Registry Editor. Figure 10.1 shows a portion of the Registry that contains configuration data for the display adapter. This branch isn't the only portion of the Registry connected to the display, and sorting it all out is a real nightmare. The bottom line is that the hardware entries in the Registry are far too complicated to do anything other than delete hardware profiles.

I suggest that you rely on the Add New Hardware wizard or the Device Manager tab of the System Properties dialog box to work with your hardware configuration. If you're changing the resources allocated to a device, use the Device Manager. If you're trying to fix a configuration problem, use a combination of both. The following list describes a few different approaches:

- **Reconfiguring a device** Use the Device Manager tab of the System Properties dialog box to change a device's resources. Double-click the device to open its property sheet, and click the Resources tab, shown in Figure 10.2. The Device Manager warns you when you're setting up a device conflict and automatically programs Plug and Play devices to use the resources you assign.

- **Troubleshooting a device** Run the Add New Hardware Wizard from the Control Panel. It will present a list of devices that aren't working properly. If you see the device you're troubleshooting, select it so that the Add New Hardware wizard can help you figure out what's wrong with it.

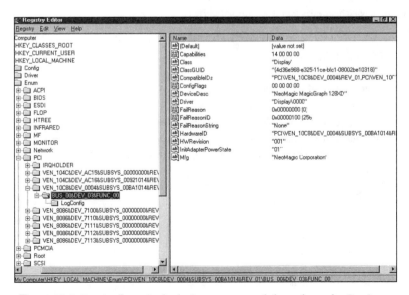

Figure 10.1 Entries for a single device are scattered throughout the Registry.

Figure 10.2 Deselect **Use automatic settings** if you want to override Windows 98's default settings.

- **Reloading a device** Open the Device Manager, and remove the device you're having trouble with. Restart the computer to see if Windows 98 automatically detects the device. If it doesn't, run the Add New Hardware wizard. When it asks you if you want to automatically detect the hardware in your computer, click **Yes**.

Don't assume that the Device Manager represents the extent to which you can configure the hardware on your computer. The Device Manager allows you to shuffle resources and set some very low-level settings, but it doesn't allow you to specify preferences or higher-level settings. For that, turn to the variety of icons in the Control Panel. Allocate memory regions to a display adapter in the Device Manager, for example, but set its scan rate and resolution using the Display Properties dialog box. Bind your network adapter to particular protocols using the Network dialog box. The same goes for multimedia devices, input devices, power management, and so on.

SEE ALSO

➤ See Chapter 6, "HKEY_LOCAL_MACHINE," to learn more about how Windows 98 stores your hardware configuration in the Registry.

NOTE: Windows 98 provides a number of troubleshooters in online help that help you diagnose and fix common hardware problems. These troubleshooters aren't just for novices, however. They include help for modems, display adapters, hardware conflicts, and more.

Reinstall an Offending Program

If a program's settings are messed up, it's often easier to reinstall the program. You don't have to remove the program first—just install right over it. You'll replace the program's files on the hard drive and the program's settings in the Registry. This is a particularly good way to fix problems with property sheet handlers and other shell extensions that an application installs. Be sure to install over the same folder, or you'll end up with two copies of the application on your computer, and only one will be usable.

Smarter programs know enough to leave your preferences alone while they correctly fix other Registry settings. If you reinstall Netscape Navigator, for example, it preserves all your server settings while it resets all the program's settings in HKEY_CLASSES_ROOT. Internet Explorer 4.0 isn't as smart, because it trashes many of your personal preferences each time you install the latest service pack.

There are other ways to restore a program's Registry settings. Many setup programs use one or more REG files to create their initial settings in the Registry. You might be able to use the REG file again to restore damaged settings without reinstalling the program. Look in the program's installation folder and carefully inspect the REG file. If it looks like it will fix the problem, merge it into the Registry. If you want to merge only a portion of the REG file, make a copy of it, remove the extraneous content, and merge it into the Registry. REG files aren't nearly as common as INF files, though. They're a bit harder to understand but contain similar information for adding, removing, and changing values in the Registry. Again, look in the program's installation folder for its INF file and examine it carefully to determine what portions you want to merge with your configuration.

SEE ALSO

➤ See Chapter 15, "Script, REG, and INF Files," to learn more about the format of REG and INF files.

Reassociate a File Extension

The portion of the Registry that loses its wits most often is HKEY_CLASSES_ROOT. Not surprisingly, this is also the single largest branch in the Registry. The order in which you install programs affects file associations. Shockingly, some programs disregard your preferences altogether and change associations that have extremely loose ties to it. Internet Explorer is one of the worst culprits, taking associations for most image files for itself. One other scenario exists in which a particular file extension remains unassociated with any program. You'll notice one of the following two symptoms:

- You double-click a document, and Windows 98 opens it in the wrong program.
- You double-click a document, and Windows 98 opens the Open With dialog box, which prompts you for the program in which you want to open the document.

Figure 10.3 This list shows the programs with which you can open files.

Some programs are good about detecting that they're no longer associated with a particular file extension. Internet Explorer and WinZip are examples. In these cases, you can let the program fix the problem automatically. In other cases, you'll have to manually associate the program with a particular program:

1. Open Windows Explorer, and select a file that has the extension that you want to associate with a program.

2. Hold down the Shift key, right-click the file, and choose **Open With**. You see the Open With dialog box, shown in Figure 10.3.

3. Choose the program you want to associate with the file extension, select **Always use this program to open this type of file**, and click **OK**. Alternatively, click **Other** to locate an unregistered program.

SEE ALSO

➤ See Chapter 9, "Customizing the Windows 98 Desktop," to learn about using the File Types tab in Windows Explorer's Folder Options dialog box to customize each file's shortcut menu.

➤ Chapter 5, "HKEY_CLASSES_ROOT," describes how Windows 98 stores file associations in the Registry. It's quite clever and a big improvement over Windows 3.1.

Remember that program identifiers and file extensions are separate entities. Program identifiers include information about a program such as actions that you can perform on a file. In the Registry, file extensions subkeys associate a file's extension with a program's identifier. Windows 98 can associate more than one file extension with each program.

Borrow a Key from Another Computer

If you've tried everything you can think of and nothing fixes your configuration, try borrowing the offending Registry key from another computer. Take some precautions before doing so, however. First, make sure you're not overreaching your capabilities and that you're comfortable doing this. Also, don't try borrowing hardware information from another computer, even if it's the same make and model. This technique is fine for repairing file associations but not for repairing your hardware configuration. Last, make sure you back up your own Registry before importing a portion of another computer's Registry into your own.

Here's how to borrow a key from another computer, importing it into your computer's Registry:

1. On the source computer, export the key you're borrowing to a REG file.

2. Trim the REG file so that it contains only the information you need and no more. Remember that the Registry Editor exports the entire branch below the key. If that's your intention, fine, but inspect the contents of the REG file to make sure you know what you're getting.

3. Back up your Registry using Registry Checker or a comparable utility. Don't skip this step, no matter how unnecessary you think it is.

4. Copy the REG file to your computer, and merge it into the Registry by double-clicking it.

If you don't have a computer from which you can borrow a key, use the Registry.reg file you find on my Web site: `http://www.honeycutt.com`. This REG file contains an exported copy of my Registry, which I created after a fresh installation of Windows 98 using a somewhat typical setup. I removed the `ProductKey` subkey so as not to upset Microsoft, and I have removed any other keys that I wouldn't want the public to see. Other than that, the REG file is complete.

Removing a Program from the Registry Manually

Most programs are rather predictable, storing the same types of information in the same types of places. They store program files in C:\Program Files and file associations in `HKEY_CLASSES_ROOT`. They put user-specific and machine-specific configuration data in `HKEY_CURRENT_USER\SOFTWARE` and `HKEY_LOCAL_MACHINE\SOFTWARE`, respectively. Last, they sprinkle some settings in places such as the uninstall list and the installed components list.

Take advantage of this information to remove an application that doesn't provide an uninstall program. Back up your computer, including the Registry. Then make a list of the DLL and EXE files you find in the program's installation folder, and delete it. You'll probably find them in a folder under C:\Program Files. After removing the program's folder, open the Registry Editor to search for any entries belonging to the program, and remove them. Here are some suggestions for the types of things you should search for:

- Search the Registry for each of the program's installation paths. If the program has two paths, C:\Program Files*Company* and C:\Program Files*Company**Program,* search for both paths in the Registry. Delete any keys or value entries that contain this path. Use a bit of common sense here, and don't remove a key that another application obviously uses.

- Search the Registry for the program's name. If you're removing a program called "Elvis Lives for Windows 98," search the Registry for any key or value entry that contains "Elvis" or "Elvis Lives." Search for the program's executables, too. Within reason, delete any keys or value entries that contain the name of the program or the filename of the executable.

- Search the Registry for the EXE and DLL files that you recorded earlier. Delete the key or value entry containing the reference to the file. Again, use common sense and don't remove keys that other programs obviously use.

- Use a utility such as REGCLEAN or Norton WinDoctor to scan the Registry for errors. In particular, these programs remove orphaned value entries from the Registry. After removing a program by hand, you're likely to leave several value entries in the Registry, and these programs can help fix them.

Extracting Files from CAB Files

At one point or another, you'll have to restore system files from the Windows 98 CD-ROM. The problem is that Microsoft stores these files in CAB files that you find in \Win98, making finding the exact location of the system file a challenge. Use the Find dialog box to locate the CAB file. Choose **Start**, **Find, Files or Folders** and fill in the Find dialog box so that it searches the \Win98 folder of the Windows 98 CD-ROM for all CAB files that contains the filename. Figure 10.4 shows you an example.

> **Troubleshooting**
>
> **You can't start Windows 98 after installing a new program.** The program is most likely loading shell extensions, device drivers, or other files when Windows 98 tries to start, and these files are preventing Windows 98 from starting properly. You have two choices. Start Windows 98 in Safe Mode, and then remove the program using the Add/Remove Programs Properties dialog box from the Control Panel. Otherwise, you can remove the program using more drastic measures. Restart the computer to the command prompt, and completely remove the program's installation folder from C:\Program Files. Restart the computer. Windows 98 will start, complaining all the while about missing files. Using the steps in this section, remove the program's Registry entries. After doing so, restart the computer. Windows 98 will no longer complain about the missing files.

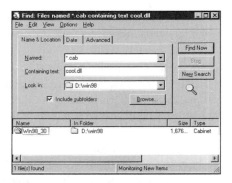

Figure 10.4 Each CAB file contains a list of its contents, so Find can locate the CAB file with the system file you need.

After locating the CAB file in the Find dialog box, right-click it and choose **View**. Windows 98 opens the CAB file in an Explorer window so that you can view its contents. Locate the file in the list, and extract it by dragging it from the list to another folder on your computer, such as the desktop. In most cases, you can replace the system file by copying the new file over the old one and confirming that you want to replace it when Windows 98 asks. If the file you're trying to replace is in use, however, you won't be able to replace it. If that's the case, restart the computer in MS-DOS mode, copy the new file over the old, and restart the computer.

Diagnosing Common Registry-Related Error Messages

This section helps you figure out a variety of Windows 98 error messages whose solutions lie in the Registry.

Cannot find a device file that may be needed to run Windows. The Windows Registry or SYSTEM.INI refers to this device file, but the device no longer exists. You get this error as Windows 98 starts. All it's saying is that the Registry or System.ini is telling the operating system to load a device driver that it can't find. First, check the [386Enh] section for any entry that looks like device=*filename*.vxd, where *filename*.vxd is the name of the missing device driver. Either erase that line from System.ini, or, if you believe the file is necessary to run Windows 98, replace it from the CD-ROM, as you learned how to do in the preceding section. If you don't find the file in System.ini, search the Registry for the root filename, or look in HKEY_LOCAL_MACHINE\System\CurrentControlset\Services\VxD for it. Remove the key if the VxD is no longer required; otherwise, replace the file from the Windows 98 CD-ROM. One other note: If Windows 98 doesn't provide a filename in the error message, look for values named StaticVxD that don't contain valid data, and remove them.

Your display adapter is not configured properly. To correct the problem, click OK to start the Hardware Installation Wizard. Windows might have restore System.1st because it thinks the Registry was corrupted and it couldn't find a suitable backup copy to restore. Restore one of your own backup copies of the Registry, or click OK to reconfigure the display adapter.

Error occurred while trying to remove *name*. **Uninstallation has been canceled.** You've already removed the program from your computer, but it still has an uninstall entry in the Add/Remove Programs Properties dialog box, and you tried to remove it. Remove it from the list as described in Chapter 9, "Customizing the Windows 98 Desktop," or using Tweak UI as described in Chapter 11, "Tweak UI and Other Registry Programs."

Properties for this item are not available. The cause of this problem is usually a bad `PropertySheetHandlers` subkey for a class or program identifier in `HKEY_CLASSES_ROOT`. See the later section, "Property Sheets Don't Work Properly." In addition, the attribute flag for this particular object might erroneously enable the **Properties** command even though a property sheet isn't available for it. Chapter 9, "Customizing the Windows 98 Desktop," shows you how to adjust this value entry. A better solution to this problem is to reinstall the offending application, allowing it to make the appropriate repairs.

Fixing Other Common Problems in Windows 98

The following sections show you how to fix a variety of common problems in Windows 98. Some of these problems occur when an errant program messes up your system. Other problems are peculiar to Windows 98:

- Restrictions are too restrictive
- The wrong program runs when you open a file
- Fonts don't work properly
- Property sheets don't work properly
- Special folders won't open
- Duplicate or bad options on shortcut menus
- Shortcuts don't work properly
- Your password doesn't work after you upgrade
- The logitech mouse doesn't work properly
- Internet security settings aren't accessible
- Program won't install because of Window's version

Restrictions Are Too Restrictive

Here's the rub: You can't edit the Registry because of policy restrictions, but you can't change the policy restrictions because you can't edit the Registry. There are a couple of different solutions to this problem that your administrator probably doesn't want you to know about. First, create the INF file shown in Listing 10.1. Right-click the INF file and choose **Install**. This works because Windows 98 allows an application to change the Registry via an INF file even though policies prevent the user from editing the Registry. Note also that you can use the System Policy Editor to remove this restriction as long as you have access to the program.

Listing 10.1 **The INF File to Remove Restrictions**

```
[version]
signature="$CHICAGO$"

[DefaultInstall]
DelReg=Restrictions

[Restrictions]
HKCU,SOFTWARE\Microsoft\Windows\CurrentVersion\Policies
```

The second solution is even more straightforward. Start the computer in MS-DOS mode by choosing **Command Prompt Only** from the boot menu. Then type the following command line at the prompt, and press Enter:

```
regedit /d HKEY_CURRENT_USER\SOFTWARE\Microsoft\Windows\
➥CurrentVersion\Policies
```

This command removes the entire policies branch from the Registry, and Windows 98 doesn't balk a bit.

SEE ALSO

➤ See Chapter 13, "Security and Remote Administration," to learn how administrators can use policies to prevent users from editing the Registry.

➤ See Chapter 14, "Profiles, System Policies, and the Registry," to learn more about how system policies work, particularly on a network.

NOTE: The steps you learn in this section work when policies are defined in the Registry. If restrictions are coming from a Config.pol on your computer, disable the POL file by renaming or removing it to remove the restrictions. If the restrictions are coming from a Config.pol that Windows 98 automatically downloads from the network, you're out of luck as long as you log onto the network.

The Wrong Program Runs When You Open a File

This problem is self-explanatory. You double-click a document's filename and Windows 98 doesn't open it in the program you expect. The solution is to reassociate the file extension with the program in which you want to open the file. You learned how to do this in the earlier section, "Reassociate a File Extension."

Fonts Don't Work Properly

The most common cause of fonts not working correctly is that `HKLM\SOFTWARE\Microsoft\Windows\CurrentVersion\Fonts` is corrupted or missing from the Registry. Windows 98 provides a small utility to fix these Registry settings called Fontreg.exe. Execute this program to fix the font information in the Registry. Note that this program doesn't open a window, display progress information, or let you know if it succeeds or fails.

If you run Fontreg.exe but the Fonts folder still doesn't work properly, rebuild \Windows\Fonts:

1. Move the contents of \Windows\Fonts to a scratch folder on your desktop.

2. Delete the contents of \Windows\Fonts and remove `HKLM\SOFTWARE\Microsoft\Windows\CurrentVersion\Fonts` from the Registry.

3. Drag each font file from the scratch folder to \Windows\Fonts. This task might be easier using file cut-and-paste or if you open two different Explorer windows.

Property Sheets Don't Work Properly

Property sheets don't get messed up very often, but when they do, they wreak havoc. A Registry entry that refers to a missing property sheet handler causes Windows 98 to not open the property sheet at all. A corrupted property sheet handler might cause Explorer to crash when it tries to display the property sheet.

Your first step to fix this problem is to identify the program or class identifier causing it. If you know that the Recycle Bin's property sheet causes Explorer to crash, for example, locate the Recycle Bin's key in `HKEY_CLASSES_ROOT\CLSID`. If Explorer won't open the property sheet for a particular file, locate the extension for that file in `HKEY_CLASSES_ROOT`. Then use that key's default value entry to locate the program identifier with which it's associated, and open the program identifier in `HKEY_CLASSES_ROOT`. Then again, if the problem affects virtually every document in Windows Explorer, start with `HKEY_CLASSES_ROOT\*`, which adds features to every file's shortcut menu and property sheet.

After locating the problem key, which is either a program or class identifier, examine the `shellex\PropertySheetHandlers` subkey underneath it. This key contains an additional subkey for each handler that adds tabs to the object's property sheet. Take a look at Figure 10.5 to better understand this organization. Identify the application that owns each subkey in `PropertySheetHandlers` by looking up each class identifier in `HKEY_CLASSES_ROOT\CLSID`. Given the example in Figure 10.5, I would open `HKEY_CLASSES_ROOT\CLSID\{ABBE31D0-6DAE-11D0-BECA-00C04FD940BE}` to find that Internet Explorer's subscription manager owned this property sheet and that it's implemented via a DLL called Webcheck.dll. I would also learn that `{FBF23B40-E3F0-101B-8488-00AA003E56F8}` is implemented via Shdocvw.dll, implementing the Internet shortcut tab. After gathering this information, the action you take depends on the problem you're having:

- **The property sheet displays tabs it shouldn't**   The property sheet displays duplicate tabs or includes a tab that just doesn't make sense. Either way, the solution is the same. You've already made the connection between each subkey and the application that owns it. Using that information, remove the subkey belonging to that subkey.

- **A tab is missing from the property sheet**   This is a bit more difficult to fix, since the problem is likely that the subkey for that tab is missing from the `PropertySheetHandlers` key. You must somehow identify the class identifier of the property sheet handler, which you can do by looking at another computer's Registry or by looking through the application's REG and INF files to see what value it used when you installed the program.

- **Explorer crashes when opening the property sheet**   First, try removing the subkey for each property sheet handler from `PropertySheetHandlers` and test the change in Windows Explorer. If it works, one of the DLL files might be corrupted. Restore each DLL file from the Windows 98 CD-ROM as described in "Extracting Files from CAB Files" earlier in this chapter. If you're still out of luck, trying reinstalling the application.

NOTE: If you can pinpoint an application that is causing problems with a property sheet, reinstall it. The application's setup program will restore health to the property sheet while maintaining most of your preferences.

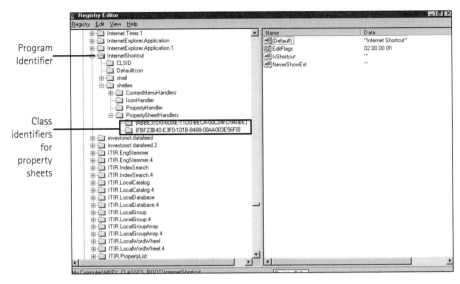

Figure 10.5 Property sheet handlers are much more common for program identifiers than for class identifiers.

SEE ALSO

➤ See Chapter 5, "HKEY_CLASSES_ROOT," to make sure you understand how Windows 98 stores property sheet handles in the Registry.

Special Folders Won't Open

This problem isn't too common, but it's frustrating nonetheless. You double-click the Control Panel icon and nothing happens. You can't access the Recycle Bin to recover files you deleted. This is easily fixed.

Make sure each shell folder's class identifier's subkey is correctly configured in the Registry. Table 10.1 shows the class identifier for Windows 98's shell folders, as well as the name of the DLL file that implements it. You should find a subkey under HKEY_CLASSES_ROOT\CLSID for each class identifier. Each class identifier's subkey should also contain an InprocServer32 subkey whose default value entry indicates the correct DLL file, as described in Table 10.1. Remember to type the complete path of the DLL file in InprocServer32 so that Windows can find the file.

If fixing the shell folder's subkey in the Registry doesn't help, restore the DLL file from the Windows 98 CD-ROM. You can also run the System File Checker to verify that the system has been corrupted. Choose **Start**, **Programs**, **Accessories**, **System Tools**, **System File Checker**. Follow the instructions you see onscreen.

Table 10.1 **Replacing a Shell Folder's Class Identifier**

Name	Class Identifier/DLL File
Control Panel	{21EC2020-3AEA-1069-A2DD-08002B30309D} C:\Windows\System\Shell32.dll
Dial-Up Networking	{992CFFA0-F557-101A-88EC-00DD010CCC48} C:\Windows\System\Rnaui.dll
Printers	{2227A280-3AEA-1069-A2DE-08002B30309D} C:\Windows\System\Shell32.dll
Recycle Bin	{645FF040-5081-101B-9F08-00AA002F954E} C:\Winodw\System\Shell32.dll
Scheduled Tasks	{D6277990-4C6A-11CF-8D87-00AA0060F5BF} C:\Windows\Shell\Mstask.dll
Briefcase	{85BBD920-42A0-1069-A2E4-08002B3039D} C:\Windows\System\Syncui.dll
My Computer	{20D04FE0-3AEA-1069-A2D8-08002B30309D} C:\Windows\System\Shell32.dll
The Internet	{3DC7A020-OACD-11CF-A9BB-00AA004AE837} C:\Windows\System\Shdocvw.dll
Network Neighborhood	{208D2C60-3AEA-1069-A2D7-08002B30309D} C:\Windows\System\Shell32.dll

Duplicate or Bad Commands on Shortcut Menus

Chapter 9, "Customizing the Windows 98 Desktop," describes how to customize a shortcut menu two different ways. First, you can add or remove built-in menu commands, which include menu commands such as **Cut** and **Properties**, to or from a shortcut menu using the `Attributes` subkey. Second, you can add additional commands to a file's shortcut menu by adding them to the appropriate `shell` subkey. Use the information you learned in that chapter to help you remove bogus commands on the shortcut menu, add missing commands, or change how it works.

Shortcuts Don't Work Properly

When shortcuts stop working, the problem is usually with `HKEY_CLASSES_ROOT\piffile` or `HKEY_CLASSES_ROOT\lnkfile`. If DOS shortcuts no longer work, import the REG file shown in Listing 10.2, or repair the Registry so that it matches the listing. If Windows 98 shortcuts don't work, import the REG file shown in Listing 10.3.

Listing 10.2   **The REG File for DOS Links**

```
REGEDIT4

[HKEY_CLASSES_ROOT\piffile]
@="Shortcut to MS-DOS Program"
"EditFlags"=hex:01,00,00,00
"IsShortcut"=" "
"NeverShowExt"=""

[HKEY_CLASSES_ROOT\piffile\shell]

[HKEY_CLASSES_ROOT\piffile\shell\open]
@=" "

[HKEY_CLASSES_ROOT\piffile\shell\open\command]
@="\"%1\" %*"

[HKEY_CLASSES_ROOT\piffile\shellex]

[HKEY_CLASSES_ROOT\piffile\shellex\PropertySheetHandlers]

[HKEY_CLASSES_ROOT\piffile\shellex\PropertySheetHandlers\
➥{86F19A00-42A0-1069-A2E9-08002B30309D}]
@=" "

[HKEY_CLASSES_ROOT\piffile\shellex\IconHandler]
@="{00021401-0000-0000-C000-000000000046}"
```

Listing 10.3   **The REG File for Windows Links**

```
REGEDIT4

[HKEY_CLASSES_ROOT\CLSID\
➥{00021401-0000-0000-C000-000000000046}]
@="Shortcut"

[HKEY_CLASSES_ROOT\CLSID\
➥{00021401-0000-0000-C000-000000000046}\InProcServer32]
@="shell32.dll"
"ThreadingModel"="Apartment"

[HKEY_CLASSES_ROOT\CLSID\
➥{00021401-0000-0000-C000-000000000046}\shellex]

[HKEY_CLASSES_ROOT\CLSID\
➥{00021401-0000-0000-C000-000000000046}\shellex\
```

continues

Listing 10.3 **Continued**

```
➥MayChangeDefaultMenu]
@=""

[HKEY_CLASSES_ROOT\CLSID\
➥{00021401-0000-0000-C000-000000000046}\ProgID]
@="lnkfile"

[HKEY_CLASSES_ROOT\lnkfile]
@="Shortcut"
"EditFlags"=hex:01,00,00,00
"IsShortcut"=" "
"NeverShowExt"=""

[HKEY_CLASSES_ROOT\lnkfile\CLSID]
@="{00021401-0000-0000-C000-000000000046}"

[HKEY_CLASSES_ROOT\lnkfile\shellex]

[HKEY_CLASSES_ROOT\lnkfile\shellex\IconHandler]
@="{00021401-0000-0000-C000-000000000046}"

[HKEY_CLASSES_ROOT\lnkfile\shellex\DropHandler]
@="{00021401-0000-0000-C000-000000000046}"

[HKEY_CLASSES_ROOT\lnkfile\shellex\ContextMenuHandlers]

[HKEY_CLASSES_ROOT\lnkfile\shellex\ContextMenuHandlers\
➥{00021401-0000-0000-C000-000000000046}]
@=""
```

Your Password Doesn't Work After You Upgrade

Upgrading to Windows 98 isn't always as seamless as Microsoft would have liked. One example is that in some cases, after you upgrade to Windows 98, you see an error message that says Invalid Password, even though you're absolutely sure you typed the correct password and it worked properly before you upgraded. This is true if you're connecting to an older server that doesn't support encrypted passwords and you enabled the use of plain-text passwords. The upgrade process disables this feature. To fix this problem, re-enable plain-text passwords by creating a DWORD value called EnablePlainTextPassword under HKEY_LOCAL_MACHINE\System\CurrentControlSet\ Services\Vxd\Vnetsup.

The Logitech Mouse Doesn't Work Properly

It doesn't happen all the time, but sometimes Windows 98 doesn't recognize Logitech mice correctly. I don't want to speculate on the reason for this, but I can offer you a solution if you're stuck without a working mouse. By default, Windows 98 uses the standard mouse drivers when it detects a Logitech mouse, and these don't always work properly. To fix the problem, install Logitech's version 8.0 or greater mouse drivers, which come with Windows 98, using the Device Manager:

1. Open the System Properties dialog box from the Control Panel, and click Device Manager.

2. Open the property sheet for the mouse by double-clicking its icon underneath the Mouse icon, and click the Driver tab.

3. Click **Update Driver**, and use the Update Device Driver Wizard to choose the appropriate driver. The manufacturer is Logitech, and the actual device depends on the model you purchased. Look on the bottom of the device if you're not sure.

If you're using a C-series Logitech mouse, which you can verify by checking the model number on the bottom of the mouse, you also need to change a value in the Registry in order for it to work properly. Change the `SearchCSeries` value entry under `HKEY_LOCAL_MACHINE\Software\Logitech\MouseWare\CurrentVersion\Technical` Registry key so that it says `Off`.

Internet Security Settings Aren't Accessible

`HKEY_CURRENT_USER\Software\Microsoft\Windows\CurrentVersion\Internet Settings\Zones` contains Internet Explorer's security settings. If it becomes damaged, Windows 98 can't display the Security tab in the Internet Properties dialog box. The solution to this problem is to completely remove the key from the Registry and allow Internet Explorer to rebuild it.

> **TIP:** You can learn about other mouse features that you can enable via the Registry by visiting Logitech's Web site: `http://www.logitech.com`. Examples include enabling DragLock and Double-click.

> **NOTE:** You can force Windows 98 to redetect your mouse by removing a handful of subkeys from `HKEY_LOCAL_MACHINE`. Remove `0000` and so on from `System\CurrentControlSet\Services\Class\Mouse`. Remove the same subkeys from `Enum\Root\Mouse`. Then, if they exist, remove `Enum\Serenum` and `Software\Logitech\Mouseware`. After removing these keys, use the Add New Hardware Wizard to redetect your mouse.

A Program Won't Install Because of Windows's Version

Some programs look for a specific version of Windows and won't install if they don't find what they expect. However, you can fool this kind of setup program into thinking that you're installing it in Windows 95 by changing the version in the Registry. Here's how:

1. Record the value you find for `VersionNumber` in `HKEY_LOCAL_MACHINE\Software\Microsoft\Windows\Current_Version`. Do the same for `Version`. `VersionNumber` is normally something like `4.10.1998`, and `Version` is normally `Windows 98`.

2. Change `VersionNumber` to `4.00.1111`, and change `Version` to `Windows 95`. Both values are string value entries.

3. Install the program as normal. It shouldn't complain about the version of Windows you're using anymore.

4. Change `VersionNumber` and `Version` back to their original values.

Disabling Internet Explorer 4.0 Integration

Many folks, including me, think Internet Explorer's integration into Windows 98 is a good thing. It doesn't quite blend the Internet into my desktop, as Microsoft claims, because the separation between the two realms is still very distinguishable. It *does* add new features. Terrific features. It brings Web-style navigation to the desktop, for instance. It provides powerful scripting capabilities. It lets me customize the look and feel of the desktop and individual folders. Thus, boiling it down to two simple reasons that Internet Explorer integration is good, it makes Windows more customizable and easier to use.

That's just one side of the story, however. Here's the other side. Microsoft has forced end-users to accept and use software that they don't want. They'd rather use a different browser. They don't want to be forced to use Internet Explorer to view the contents of their computers or to browse the Internet. The don't like the new features. (Animated menus and flying-paper animations, I'll concede, are very annoying.) And, most importantly, they're afraid that Internet Explorer's integration into the Windows operating system gives Microsoft a shot at monopolizing the Internet.

If you're in the first camp, you can skip the rest of this section. If you're in the second camp, you'll be interested to note that you can minimize the integration of Internet Explorer into the operating system. You can't remove Internet Explorer, because Microsoft makes Windows 98 almost totally dependent on its code. You *can*

CAUTION: Don't try fooling disk utility programs into running under Windows 98 when they only support Windows 95. Some disk utilities don't work correctly with FAT32 and using them under Windows 98 can result in data loss.

return Windows 98 to a look and feel that's closer to Windows 95, however. Doing so is quite easy, too; you change only a few Registry settings. You can pick and choose which of the settings in Table 10.2 you want to change. All of the values you see in the table are in `HKEY_CURRENT_USER\Software\Microsoft\Windows\CurrentVersion\Policies\Explorer` and are therefore policies. The first column indicates the name of the DWORD value entry to add to this key, and the second column describes what it does. In each case, set the value to `1` to enable that policy or to `0` to disable it. Alternatively, you can use the Registry Power Tools program that you find on my Web site, `http://www.honeycutt.com`, or the INF file in Listing 10.4 to change these settings. The INF file in Listing 10.5 reverses them, allowing you to switch back and forth.

Table 10.2 **Disabling Internet Explorer 4.0 Integration**

Value	Description
ClassicShell	Enables the classic shell, which has the old double-click user interface.
NoActiveDesktop	Disables the Active Desktop, reverting to the classic desktop.
NoActiveDesktopChanges	Removes the Web tab from the Display Properties dialog box.
NoChangeStartMenu	Disables drag and drop on the Start menu, reverting to the old version.
NoFavoritesMenu	Removes the Favorites command from the Start menu.
NoInternetIcon	Removes the Internet icon from the desktop.
NoSetActiveDesktop	Removes the **Active Desktop** command from the Start menu's **Settings** submenu.

The `ClassicShell` value has side effects. Setting `ClassicShell` disables the taskbar's toolbar features and removes the **as Web Page** command from Windows Explorer's **View** menu. It also disables the **Windows Desktop Update** section of Explorer's Folder Options dialog box so that the user can't re-enable the new shell. Likewise, `NoActiveDesktop` prevents the user from using the Active Desktop by removing the **Active Desktop** command from the desktop's shortcut menu.

Even though you disable the Active Desktop, you might still see Internet Explorer's channel bar on the classic desktop. You can easily remove it by closing it. When Windows 98 asks if you want to open it again when you restart the operating system, click **No**. Alternatively, you can disable it in the Registry. Set the string value entry `Show_ChannelBand` to `No` in `HKEY_CURRENT_USER\Software\Microsoft\Internet Explorer\Main`.

> CAUTION: You can change the settings listed in Table 10.2 using the System Policy Editor. Well, almost. The policy template uses the wrong Registry key for some of the values, including `NoChangeStartMenu`. Thus, you're better off relying on the INF files shown in this section or the Registry Power Tools.

Listing 10.4 **Disabling Internet Explorer 4.0 Integration**

```
[version]
signature="$CHICAGO$"

[DefaultInstall]
AddReg=Integration

[Integration]
HKCU,Software\Microsoft\Windows\CurrentVersion\Policies\
➥Explorer, ClassicShell,0x10001,01,00,00,00
HKCU,Software\Microsoft\Windows\CurrentVersion\Policies\
➥Explorer, NoActiveDesktop,0x10001,01,00,00,00
HKCU,Software\Microsoft\Windows\CurrentVersion\Policies\
➥Explorer, NoActiveDesktopChanges,0x10001,01,00,00,00
HKCU,Software\Microsoft\Windows\CurrentVersion\Policies\
➥Explorer, NoChangeStartMenu,0x10001,01,00,00,00
HKCU,Software\Microsoft\Windows\CurrentVersion\Policies\
➥Explorer, NoFavoritesMenu,0x10001,01,00,00,00
HKCU,Software\Microsoft\Windows\CurrentVersion\Policies\
➥Explorer, NoInternetIcon,0x10001,01,00,00,00
HKCU,Software\Microsoft\Windows\CurrentVersion\Policies\
➥Explorer, NoSetActiveDesktop,0x10001,01,00,00,00
HKCU,"Software\Microsoft\Internet Explorer\Main",
➥Show_ChannelBand,0,"No"
```

Listing 10.5 **Enabling Internet Explorer 4.0 Integration**

```
[version]
signature="$CHICAGO$"

[DefaultInstall]
DelReg=Integration
AddReg=ChannelBand

[Integration]
HKCU,Software\Microsoft\Windows\CurrentVersion\Policies\
➥Explorer, ClassicShell
HKCU,Software\Microsoft\Windows\CurrentVersion\Policies\
➥Explorer, NoActiveDesktop
HKCU,Software\Microsoft\Windows\CurrentVersion\Policies\
➥Explorer, NoActiveDesktopChanges
HKCU,Software\Microsoft\Windows\CurrentVersion\Policies\
➥Explorer, NoChangeStartMenu
HKCU,Software\Microsoft\Windows\CurrentVersion\Policies\
➥Explorer, NoFavoritesMenu
HKCU,Software\Microsoft\Windows\CurrentVersion\Policies\
```

```
➥Explorer, NoInternetIcon
HKCU,Software\Microsoft\Windows\CurrentVersion\Policies\
➥Explorer, NoSetActiveDesktop

[ChannelBand]
HKCU,"Software\Microsoft\Internet Explorer\Main",
➥Show_ChannelBand,0,"Yes"
```

11

Tweak UI and Other Registry Programs

Karanjit S. Siyan, Ph.D

In this chapter:

- Installing Tweak UI
- Checking for Newer Versions of Tweak UI
- Using Tweak UI to Customize Windows 98
- Other Shareware Registry Programs

Installing Tweak UI

According to Brian Livingston in the November 6, 1995 issue of *InfoWorld* magazine, "Tweak UI gives you control over a fistful of Win95 user-interface options that previously required messy editing of your Registry database." Likewise, Edward Mendelson said in the May 14, 1996 issue of *PC Magazine*, "Microsoft Corp.'s Power Toys make Windows 95 more convenient, customizable, and powerful than you ever imagined—and won't cost you anything except for the connect time to download them from the company's Web site."

Prior to Windows 98, Tweak UI was a free, unsupported utility from Microsoft that was part of Power Toys, a collection of must-have utilities for power users. You had to download it from Microsoft's Web site, because it didn't come with Windows 95. Microsoft updated Tweak UI for Windows 98, though, and included it on the CD-ROM. To install Tweak UI, right-click Tweakui.inf in the \Tools\Reskit\Powertoy folder of the CD-ROM, and choose **Install**. Windows 98 copies the required files to the computer and displays online help with an overview of how to use Tweak UI. Close the help document to finish installing Tweak UI.

Tweakui.inf describes the values that Windows 98 writes to the Registry. These values include uninstall information so that you can easily remove Tweak UI using the Add/Remove Programs Properties dialog box. This INF file also describes the files that Windows 98 copies to the computer:

- Tweakui.cpl is a Control Panel extension that Windows 98 copies to \Windows\System.
- Tweakui.hlp and Tweakui.cnt are help files that Windows 98 copies to \Windows\Help.

Checking for Newer Versions of Tweak UI

The current version of Tweak UI is 1.25, but Microsoft occasionally updates it. To find out what version of Tweak UI you're using, right-click Tweakui.cpl in \Windows\System, choose **Properties**, and click the Version tab; the file version number is at the top of the dialog box. Although you might find updates to Tweak UI using Windows Update, Microsoft's download site is always a sure thing: http://www.microsoft.com/windows/downloads. Select **Windows 98** from the first drop-down list, select **Power Toys & Kernel Toys** from the second, and click **Go**. If the version available at the Web site is a later version than the one you're using, download and install it. You can also compare the modification date given at the Web site with the modification date of Tweakui.cpl in \Windows\System.

You can download Tweak UI by itself, or you can download it as part of Microsoft Power Toys. Power Toys is a must-have collection of utilities for Windows 95 that should be available for Windows 98 by the time you read this book. Here are some of the tools available in it:

- **CabView** lets you view and extract the contents of CAB files. This utility is no longer required, however, since Windows 98 includes this feature. Open a CAB file in Windows Explorer by right-clicking it and choosing **View**.
- **CD AutoPlay Extender** lets you control Windows 98's AutoPlay feature. It allows you to configure a CD-ROM to start automatically even though the disk doesn't have an INF file.
- **FlexiCD** lets you control musical CD-ROMs from the Windows 98 status area, located on the right side of the taskbar.
- **QuickRes** lets you change screen resolution and color depth via an icon on the status area. This utility isn't useful in Windows 98, however, because Windows 98 includes this feature. You configure it using the Display Properties dialog box.

- **Round Clock** uses a good old-fashioned round clock that looks similar to the old analog windup clocks.

- **Telephone Location Selector** a must for road warriors, because it lets you choose your dialing location from the status area.

- **Xmouse 1.2** lets you bring a window to the foreground by moving your mouse over it. This utility isn't useful in Windows 98 because Windows 98 includes a Registry setting that allows you to configure the same functionality. See Chapter 9, "Customizing the Windows 98 Desktop," for more information. As well, these settings are now available in Tweak UI.

- **Command Prompt Here 1.1.** When you right-click any folder and choose **DOS Prompt Here**, Windows 98 opens an MS-DOS window with that folder set as the current working directory. You don't have to have Power Toys to set this up, however, as you learned in Chapter 9, "Customizing the Windows 98 Desktop."

- **Contents Menu** displays the entire contents of a folder as a submenu of its shortcut menu.

- **Desktop Menu** displays the entire contents of the desktop as a submenu that you pop up from Windows 98's status area, which is on the taskbar.

- **Explore from Here.** If you right-click any folder and choose **Explore from Here**, Windows 98 opens a new Explorer window with that folder at the top, as described in Chapter 9, "Customizing the Windows 98 Desktop."

- **Find X 1.2** uses a number of extensions to the Start menu's Find submenu.

- **Send to X 1.2.** Right-click any file or folder, choose **Send To**, and choose from a variety of new locations where you can send that object. The two most useful locations include **Any Folder**, which allows you to browse for a folder, and **Clipboard as Name**, which sends the name of the file or folder to the Clipboard.

- **Shortcut Target Menu 1.2** lets you open the shortcut menu of a shortcut's target object without actually locating the target object on the computer. This is particularly useful for shortcuts on the desktop.

Download Power Toys from `http://www.microsoft.com/windows/downloads`. Select Windows 98 from the first drop-down list, select **Power Toys & Kernel Toys** from the second, and click **Go**. Download the file Powertoys.exe into an empty scratch folder. You must do this because it contains a large number of compressed files and you have to clean up the file droppings yourself. Decompress the file by launching it in Windows Explorer, making sure to launch it from within the scratch folder. Install each Power Toy individually by right-clicking its INF file and clicking **Install**.

NOTE: If you're having trouble accessing Microsoft's Web site, you can download Tweak UI from just about any shareware site. For example, try `http://www.hotfiles.com`, which is a Ziff-Davis site, or `http://www.winfiles.com`.

Using Tweak UI to Customize Windows 98

When you double-click the Tweak UI icon in the Control Panel, you see the window shown in Figure 11.1. Click one of the tabs to set options related to its name. Here's a description of what you find on each tab:

Mouse	Contains settings to adjust the mouse's sensitivity.
General	Changes the behavior of individual windows, the location of special folders, and the default search engine used by Internet Explorer 4.0.
Explorer	Changes the overlay displayed on the bottom-left corner of shortcuts, what happens when Windows 98 starts, and various other settings, such as whether Windows 98 remembers open Explorer windows and their positions between sessions.
IE4	Changes a variety of advanced settings for customizing how Internet Explorer 4.0 looks and feels.
Desktop	Adds or removes special icons to or from the desktop. You can also create special icons as a file, which allows you to put them on the Start menu—or anywhere else, for that matter.
My Computer	Enables or disables specific drive letters in the My Computer folder.
Control Panel	Enables or disables specific applets in the Control Panel folder.
Network	Automatically logs onto the network without providing a username and password.
New	Creates new templates that will appear on the New menu when you right-click a folder and choose New.
Add/Remove	Edits the list of programs that appear in the Add/Remove Programs Properties dialog box.
Boot	Changes a variety of boot options that are defined in the Msdos.sys file.
Repair	Fixes various aspects of the operating system, including desktop icons and the Fonts folder.
Paranoia	Clears various history lists each time you log onto the computer, such as the Run MRU list, documents MRU list, and Find Files MRU list. This tab also provides a variety of methods for covering your tracks so that prying eyes can't see what you've been up to.

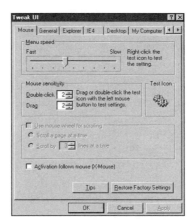

Figure 11.1 Tweak UI uses a tabbed dialog box similar to the other property sheets you find in the Control Panel.

Customizing How the Mouse Works

You can change Windows 98's mouse settings on the Mouse tab of Tweak UI. This tab hasn't changed since the original version of Tweak UI that Microsoft provided for Windows 95. Note that all of the values you find on this tab are in `HKEY_CURRENT_USER\Control Panel\Desktop`; thus, any subkeys you learn about in this section start there.

Menu speed controls the span of time before a menu automatically follows the mouse pointer. Drag the slider to the left to make menus follow faster, or drag it to the right to make them follow slower. Right-click **Test Icon** to test this setting. Tweak UI writes this value to `MenuShowDelay`, a string value containing a delay time in milliseconds (400ms is the default).

Mouse sensitivity has two options. First, **Double-click** determines how close together two mouse clicks must be before Windows 98 considers them a double-click. **Drag** determines how far the mouse pointer must move with the button held down before Windows 98 recognizes that you're dragging an object. Both values are in pixels, but Tweak UI stores the first as half-pixels in the Registry. Tweak UI stores these values in the following string value entries:

NOTE: Click the **Tips** button on the Mouse tab to open Tweak UI's help. Also, you can restore Windows 98's original factory settings for the Mouse, Explorer, and Boot tabs by clicking the **Restore Factory Settings** button on those tabs.

- ▪ DoubleClickWidth
- ▪ DoubleClickHeight
- ▪ DragWidth
- ▪ DragHeight

Activation follows mouse (X-Mouse) prevents you from having to click a background window to bring it forward, since windows automatically come forward as you move the mouse over them. Windows 98 reads this value from UserPreferenceMask, which is a binary value whose bits indicate a variety of user preferences. For more information, see Chapter 7, "HKEY_USERS and HKEY_CURRENT_USER."

SEE ALSO

➤ See Chapter 7, "HKEY_USERS and HKEY_CURRENT_USER," to learn more about the values stored in HKEY_CURRENT_USER\Control Panel\Desktop.

➤ See Chapter 9, "Customizing the Windows 98 Desktop," to learn other ways you can customize how the mouse works in Windows 98.

Controlling the Behavior of Individual Windows

The General tab, shown in Figure 11.2, contains a variety of settings that control how Windows 98 looks and where it locates special shell folders. **Effects** contains a number self-explanatory options that control how Windows 98 looks, all of which are checkboxes that you enable or disable:

- ▪ Window animation
- ▪ Smooth scrolling
- ▪ Beep on errors
- ▪ Menu animation
- ▪ Combo box animation
- ▪ List box animation
- ▪ Menu underlines
- ▪ X-mouse AutoRaise
- ▪ Mouse hot tracking effects
- ▪ Show Windows version on desktop

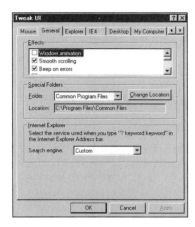

Figure 11.2   The middle portion of this tab allows you to relocate Windows 98's shell folders. You'll learn more about this in the next section.

Look in `HKEY_CURRENT_USER\Control Panel\Desktop` for all of these values, which are set by the options just listed:

- `PaintDesktopVersion`
- `UserPreferenceMask`
- `SmoothScroll`
- `WindowMetrics\MinAnimate`
- `Sound\Beep`

Specifying the Location of Special System Folders

You can change the location of special shell folders in the middle of the General tab. Select the name of the folder whose location you want to change from the **Folder** box. Then click **Change Location**, select a folder on the disk, and click **OK**. Tweak UI allows you to change the location of any shell folder defined in the `Software\Microsoft\Windows\CurrentVersion\Explorer\Shell Folders` branch of either `HKEY_LOCAL_MACHINE` or `HKEY_CURRENT_USER`. Here are some typical examples of the folders you find in this list:

Name	Default Location
Common Program Files	C:\Program Files\Common
Desktop	C:\Windows\Desktop
Document Templates	C:\Windows\ShellNew
Favorites	C:\Windows\Favorites
My Documents	C:\My Documents
Program Files	C:\Program Files
Programs	C:\Windows\Start Menu\Programs
Recent Documents	C:\Windows\Recent
Send To	C:\Windows\SendTo
Start Menu	C:\Windows\Start Menu
Startup	C:\Windows\Start Menu\Programs\Startup

SEE ALSO

➤ See Chapter 9, "Customizing the Windows 98 Desktop," to learn more about how Windows 98 stores the location of shell folders.

Controlling the Appearance and Name of Shortcuts

Windows 98 displays a small square icon in the bottom-left corner of each shortcut you create. This icon is called an *overlay*. When you create a shortcut to a document, for instance, Windows 98 combines the original icon with the overlay so that you can readily identify it as a shortcut to the document rather than the document itself.

You can choose which icon Windows 98 uses for that overlay, or even choose not to use an overlay at all. Open the Explorer tab of Tweak UI, shown in Figure 11.3, and select either **Arrow**, **Light arrow**, **None**, or **Custom**. If you choose **None**, you won't be able to distinguish between shortcuts and documents unless you open the icon's property sheet. If you choose **Custom**, Tweak UI displays a dialog box that you use to browse the computer for an icon you want to use as the overlay. Note that Tweak UI changes the following values to reflect the setting you chose:

```
HKEY_LOCAL_MACHINE\Software\Microsoft\Windows\
➥CurrentVersion\explorer\Shell Icons
```

```
HKEY_CURRENT_USER\Software\Microsoft\Windows\
➥CurrentVersion\explorer\link
```

NOTE: Changing the location of a shell folder using Tweak UI doesn't actually move the current shell folder. It just points Windows 98 to a different folder for that purpose. You must move the contents of the original folder to the new one if you want to keep them.

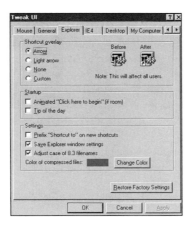

Figure 11.3 The icons on the right side of this tab show you what a shortcut will look like after you change this setting.

Aside from choosing an overlay to use for shortcuts, you can also prevent Windows 98 from prefixing the words "Shortcut to" to each shortcut's filename. Disable **Prefix "Shortcut to" on new shortcuts**. You don't need to worry about duplicate filenames, by the way, because shortcuts use the LNK file extension, and the original document keeps its own file extension.

SEE ALSO

➤ See Chapter 5, "HKEY_CLASSES_ROOT," to learn more about how Windows 98 uses the Registry for shortcuts and shell icons.

Specifying What Happens When Windows 98 Starts

Each time you start Windows 98, it displays the tip of the day. You probably disabled this feature straight away. The Explorer tab, shown earlier in Figure 11.3, allows you to restore this setting if you did. Select **Tip of the day**. Show in HKEY_CURRENT_USER\Software\Microsoft\Windows\CurrentVersion\explorer\Tips contains this setting.

Windows 98 also displays a bouncing message on the taskbar each time it starts that says Click here to begin (if there is enough room on the taskbar). If this message annoys you, deselect **Animated "Click here to begin"** on the Explorer tab. Windows 98 retrieves this setting from NoStartBanner in HKEY_CURRENT_USERS\Software\Microsoft\Windows\CurrentVersion\Policies\Explorer.

CAUTION: Windows 95 was known to misbehave when you disabled the shortcut overlay. While I haven't confirmed this problem in Windows 98, revert this setting to its original value if you start experiencing bizarre problems after changing it.

Saving Open Windows and Locations Between Sessions

Windows 98 remembers certain information about your desktop between sessions. Each time you start Windows 98, for example, it restores any Explorer windows that you left open when you shut it down. This includes single-pane folder windows and Internet Explorer. It also remembers the location of each Explorer window. Since every window has the same name, Windows remembers the position of each window in stacking order. In other words, it remembers the position of the first, second, and third Explorer windows.

To prevent Windows 98 from saving these settings between sessions, disable **Save Explorer window settings** in the Explorer tab of Tweak UI (shown earlier in Figure 11.3). Tweak UI writes this setting to the Registry a value of `HKEY_CURRENT_USER\Software\Microsoft\Windows\CurrentVersion\Policies\Explorer\` called `NoSaveSettings`.

Setting Advanced Options for Internet Explorer 4.0

On the IE4 tab, shown in Figure 11.4, Tweak UI contains a variety of settings that control the look and feel of Internet Explorer 4.0. These settings are self-explanatory:

- Active desktop enabled
- Add new documents to Documents on Start Menu
- Allow changes to Active Desktop
- Allow Logoff
- Clear document, run, typed-URL history on exit
- Detect accidental double-clicks
- IE4 enabled
- Show Documents on Start menu
- Show Favorites on Start menu

TIP: One option is to arrange your Explorer windows just the way you want them, reboot, and then disable **Save Explorer window settings** in Tweak UI. A better option is to use a shareware product called EzDesk, which gives you complete control over your desktop's layout. You can download EzDesk from `http://members.aol.com/EzDesk95/index.html`.

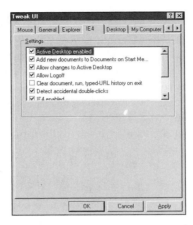

Figure 11.4 You can set all of these values on the IE4 tab of Tweak UI in the System Policy Editor.

What's not self-explanatory is where in the Registry Windows 98 stores these settings. All of the value entries described in the following table are in the Registry under HKEY_CURRENT_USER\Software\Microsoft\Windows\CurrentVersion\Policies\ Explorer:

Setting	Registry Value
Active desktop enabled	NoActiveDesktop
Add new documents to Documents on Start menu	NoRecentDocsHistory
Allow changes to Active Desktop	NoActiveDesktopChanges
Allow Logoff	NoLogoff
Clear document, run, typed-URL history on exit	ClearRecentDocsOnExit
IE4 enabled	ClassicShell
Show Documents on Start menu	NoRecentDocsMenu
Show Favorites on Start menu	NoFavoritesMenu
Show Internet icon on desktop	NoInternetIcon

The one exception is **Detect accidental double-clicks**, which you find in called UseDoubleClickTimer under HKEY_CURRENT_USER\Software\Microsoft\Windows\ CurrentVersion\Explorer\Advanced.

Controlling Which Shell Icons Are on the Desktop

A typical desktop includes the My Computer, Recycle Bin, Network Neighborhood, and Internet Explorer icons—and possibly more. While there is little you can do to remove the My Computer icon from the desktop (it's hard-coded into the operating system), Windows 98 allows you to control the remaining icons.

Tweak UI is the simplest method for adding or removing shell icons to or from the desktop. The Desktop tab, shown in Figure 11.5, contains a list of all the icons you can put on the desktop. Some of the icons you see in this list are absolutely meaningless on the desktop—ActiveX Cache Folder, for example. The following icons *are* useful on the desktop, however. You can remove any of the icons in the list from the desktop:

Name	Class Identifier
Control Panel	{21EC2020-3AEA-1069-A2DD-08002B30309D}
Dial-Up Networking	{992CFFA0-F557-101A-88EC-00DD010CCC48}
Internet Explorer	{871C5380-42A0-1069-A2EA-08002B30309D}
Recycle Bin	{645FF040-5081-101B-9F08-00AA002F954E}
Microsoft Outlook	{00020D75-0000-0000-C000-000000000046}
Network Neighborhood	{208D2C60-3AEA-1069-A2D7-08002B30309D}
Printers	{2227A280-3AEA-1069-A2DE-08002B30309D}
Scheduled Tasks	{D6277990-4C6A-11CF-8D87-00AA0060F5BF}

Attention: Administrators

A frequent question I receive from readers is how to lock down the Start menu as well as the desktop. Windows 95 didn't provide much help in removing some of the menu commands, such as Find and Documents, from the Start menu.

Windows 98 does contain Registry entries that allow you to control this menu, and you can set those values using Tweak UI. Better still, you can change those values for an individual user, a group of users, or a group of machines using the System Policy Editor, as described in Chapter 14, "Profiles, System Policies, and the Registry." In this chapter, you'll learn how to distribute policies via both Microsoft and Novell networks that allow you to remove submenus from the Start menu and special icons from the desktop.

The best part? It's not easy for a user to get around. Since Windows 98 enforces policies as the user logs onto the network, the user must be quite knowledgeable about Windows before he can circumvent these settings.

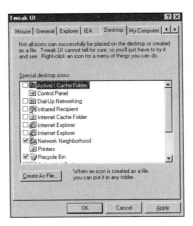

Figure 11.5 You can't add objects that don't have a checkmark next to their names to the desktop as an object.

You can work with shell icons in two different ways:

- **As an object in the desktop's name space**   To add a shell icon to the desktop as an object, select the checkbox next to it. Deselect an icon's checkbox to remove the icon from the desktop. When you add an icon to the desktop's name space, you don't see a file in the \Windows\Desktop folder. Tweak UI adds the icon's class identifier to
  HKEY_LOCAL_MACHINE\Software\Microsoft\Windows\CurrentVersion\explorer\
  Desktop\NameSpace instead.

- **As a file or folder located anywhere**   To add a shell icon to any folder on the computer, select the icon in the list and click **Create As File**. Select the folder in which you want to create the icon, and click **Save**. Note that Tweak UI creates files for some icons and folders for others. In particular, it creates the Control Panel and Printers icons as folders. To remove a shell icon as a file or folder, simply delete it within Windows Explorer.

CAUTION: When you try to remove Network Neighborhood using Tweak UI, you see a message that says Removing the Network Neighborhood from the desktop has additional consequences which are not obvious. In a nutshell, after removing the Network Neighborhood icon from the desktop, you won't be able to use UNC paths, which look like *Server**Resource*, to access resources on the network. You'll have to map directly to those resources instead. Removing this icon also prevents Direct Cable Connection from displaying the contents of the host computer properly.

Enabling and Disabling Specific Drive Letters

Tweak UI allows you to easily disable specific drive letters in My Computer. Although this does prevent drives from showing up in My Computer or Windows Explorer, it doesn't prevent those same drives from showing up in the Save As and Open dialog boxes; thus, don't look at this as a way to prevent users from copying files to a floppy disk. If that's your requirement, disable the disk in the BIOS.

To enable or disable specific drive letters, open Tweak UI's My Computer tab, shown in Figure 11.6. To disable a drive, deselect the checkmark next to it. To enable a drive, select the checkmark.

How Tweak UI stores these settings in the Registry deserves a brief explanation. Windows 98 uses each bit of a 32-bit value to indicate whether a drive is enabled or disabled. The first bit corresponds to drive A, the second bit corresponds to B, and so on. Thus, in the binary value 1010, drives B and D are disabled because the second and fourth bits are 1. Note that Tweak UI stores this DWORD value as a binary value, so when you look at it in the Registry, you must reverse the order of the bytes. If you see 06 00 00 00 in the Registry, reverse the order of the bytes to 00 00 00 06. Then examine each bit to determine which drives are disabled. To find this value, look in `NoDrives` under `HKEY_CURRENT_USER\Software\Microsoft\Windows\CurrentVersion\Policies\Explorer`.

Enabling and Disabling Specific Control Panel Icons

Just as you can disable individual drive letters in My Computer, you can disable individual Control Panel icons. Open the Control Panel tab, shown in Figure 11.7. To enable a Control Panel icon, select the checkmark next to it. To disable an icon, deselect the checkmark next to it.

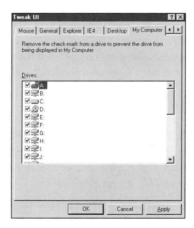

Figure 11.6 The My Computer tab helps reduce clutter in the My Computer folder or in Windows Explorer, but don't rely on it as a security measure.

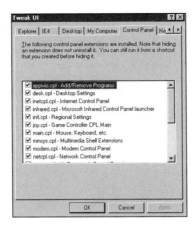

Figure 11.7 Tweak UI shows you the filename and title of each icon.

Do not rely on this as a security measure, however, because the user can easily restore the icon. When you disable a Control Panel icon, Tweak UI adds a line to the [don't load] section of Control.ini that disables the icon. It has the format filename=no: main.cpl=no, for example.

Logging onto Windows 98 Automatically

If you aren't logging onto a network, or you're logging onto a network where security isn't a concern, you can avoid typing your username and password every time you start Windows 98.

Go to the Network tab of Tweak UI, shown in Figure 11.8, and select **Log on automatically at system startup**. Then type your user name and password in the spaces provided. Tweak UI configures automatic logon in the Registry under HKEY_LOCAL_MACHINE\Software\Microsoft\Windows\CurrentVersion\Winlogon:

- ■ AutoAdminLogon contains a logical value that enables or disables this feature.
- ■ DefaultPassword contains the readable text password that you typed in the Network tab.
- ■ DefaultUserName contains the username you provided.

TIP: An alternative method of disabling a specific Control Panel icon is to simply remove its corresponding CPL file from \Windows\System.

CAUTION: Tweak UI doesn't encrypt your password when you use this feature. It's stored in the Registry as plain text that can be read by anyone.

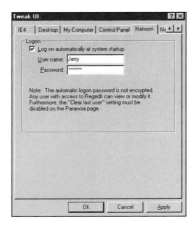

Figure 11.8 Even though Tweak UI doesn't display your password in this dialog box, it doesn't encrypt your password in the Registry.

Adding New Templates to the New Menu

If you right-click any open area in a folder and choose **New**, you see a list of file types you can create from a template. Rename the file, and open it in the associated program to edit it. Windows 98 gets the items on the New menu from the Registry. It looks in HKEY_CLASSES_ROOT for any extension that contains a ShellNew subkey. When it finds one, it adds it to the New menu. Some ShellNew subkeys refer to an additional template file in \Windows\Templates that Windows 98 uses to create the new file.

Tweak UI allows you to define additional templates that you'll see on the New menu. In every case, you create a template from a file that you build and drag it onto the New tab, shown in Figure 11.9. Tweak UI copies the file to \Windows\Templates and adds the ShellNew subkey to the file's extension under HKEY_CLASSES_ROOT. There are two ways to remove a type from the New menu:

- If you deselect the checkbox next to the file type, Tweak UI merely hides the file's ShellNew subkey so that it no longer appears on the menu. You can restore it by reselecting the checkbox.

- Select the file type and click **Remove**. This permanently removes the file type from the New menu and removes the type's ShellNew subkey.

SEE ALSO

➤ See Chapter 5, "HKEY_CLASSES_ROOT," to learn more about how Windows 98 organizes file associations in the Registry. Chapter 5 also shows you more about how templates work.

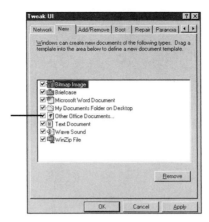

Figure 11.9 Tweak UI allows you to permanently remove or temporarily hide file types from the New menu.

Editing the Add/Remove Programs Properties List

Windows 98 displays a list of programs you can remove automatically in the Add/Remove Programs Properties dialog box. If you manually remove a program, the entry for that program still appears in the list. On the flip side, if an application has an uninstall program but it doesn't appear in the list, you can add it. Just remember that editing this list doesn't actually change the programs on your disk. In other words, removing an item from this list doesn't remove the program, just its uninstall information.

Open Tweak UI's Add/Remove tab, shown in Figure 11.10. Then you can carry out the following tasks:

- **To remove a program from the list**, select the program you want to remove, and click **Remove**. Confirm the operation.

- **To add a program to the list**, click **New**. Provide a description and the path to the uninstall program, and click **OK** to save your changes.

- **To change a program in the list**, click **Edit**. Change the description and path, and click **OK** to save your changes.

TIP: Removing an item from the Add/Remove Programs Properties dialog box is a decent way to keep users from removing programs. While you can edit this list at the user's computer using Tweak UI, you're better off distributing an INF file (as described in Chapter 15, "Script, REG, and INF Files") or editing the user's Registry remotely (as described in Chapter 13, "Security and Remote Administration").

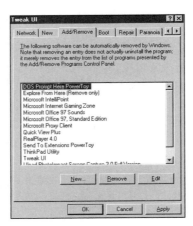

Figure 11.10 Removing an item from this list doesn't remove the program from your computer.

Windows 98 stores uninstall information in the Registry at HKEY_LOCAL_MACHINE\Software\Microsoft\Windows\CurrentVersion\Uninstall. For each application, you'll find two values. DisplayName corresponds to what Tweak UI calls **Description**. UninstallString corresponds to **Command** in Tweak UI.

Setting Windows 98's Boot Options (Msdos.sys)

Msdos.sys, which you find in the root folder of the boot disk, contains a number of options that control how Windows 98 starts. You can boot directly to an MS-DOS command prompt, for example, rather than to the Windows 98 user interface.

The *Microsoft Windows 98 Resource Kit,* published by Microsoft Press, contains a complete description of the options available in Msdos.sys. However, Tweak UI lets you change many of these options on the Boot tab, shown in Figure 11.11, as described here:

- **Function keys available** determines whether or not you can use keys such as F4 and F8 to change how Windows 98 starts.

- **Start GUI automatically** determines whether Windows 98 starts to the MS-DOS command prompt or to the graphical user interface.

- **Display splash screen while booting** determines whether you see the Windows 98 animated splash screen as the operating system boots.

- **Allow F4 to boot previous operating system** enables or disables the dual-boot capability. This must be enabled if you want to start the previous system.

- **Autorun Scandisk** determines whether Windows 98 never runs Scandisk when it starts, runs Scandisk only after prompting the user, or always runs Scandisk when it starts.

- **Always show boot menu** allows you to make sure that Windows 98 always displays the boot menu every time it starts. If you're not quick enough at pressing F8 to display the boot menu, enable this option.

- **Continue booting after *xx* seconds** specifies the amount of time that must pass before Windows 98 continues booting, accepting the default boot menu selection.

This Tweak UI tab doesn't affect the Registry at all. It writes all its changes to Msdos.sys instead. To help you make sense out of the values it writes to this entry, the following table describes the items it changes:

Tweak UI Setting	Msdos.sys Setting
Function keys available	BootKeys=
Start GUI automatically	BootGUI=
Display splash screen while booting	Logo=
Allow F4 to boot previous operating system	BootMulti=
Autorun Scandisk	AutoScan=
Always show boot menu	BootMenu=
Continue booting after *xx* seconds	BootMenuDelay=

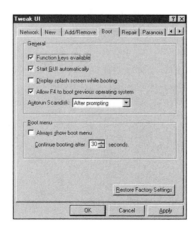

Figure 11.11 If things get out of hand, click **Restore Factory Settings** to return Msdos.sys to its original condition.

Repairing Windows 98 Icons, System Files, and More

Tweak UI's Repair tab, shown in Figure 11.12, provides the capability to fix a variety of common problems in Windows 98. Select the item you want to repair from the drop-down list, and click **Repair Now**. The following options are self explanatory:

- Rebuild Icons
- Repair Associations
- Repair font Folder
- Repair Regedit
- Repair System Files
- Repair Temporary Internet Files
- Repair URL History

Keeping Your Activities Private

If you're uncomfortable with the fact that other people using your computer can come along and see everything you've been doing, you need to check out Tweak UI's Paranoia tab, shown in Figure 11.13. It provides a good measure of privacy by clearing Windows 98's MRU (Most Recently Used) lists each time the operating system starts. The options you see in the **Covering Your Tracks** list are self-explanatory:

- Clear Document history at logon
- Clear Find Computer history at logon
- Clear Find Files history at logon

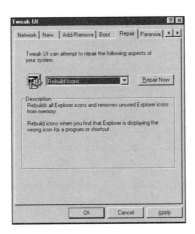

Figure 11.12 In the middle of this tab, Tweak UI provides a description of the repair option you've selected.

- Clear Internet Explorer history at logon
- Clear Last User at logon
- Clear Network Connection history at logon
- Clear Run history at logon
- Clear Telnet history at logon

TweakUI implements these settings through the following three Registry keys:

- `HKEY_LOCAL_MACHINE\Software\Microsoft\Windows\CurrentVersion\`
  `Winlogon\DontDisplayLastUserName`
- `HKEY_LOCAL_MACHINE\Software\Microsoft\Windows\CurrentVersion\`
  `Applets\TweakUI\1`
- `HKEY_CURRENT_USER\Software\Microsoft\Windows\CurrentVersion\`
  `Explorer\RecentDocs`

This tab also keeps you from embarrassing yourself thanks to Windows 98's AutoPlay feature. If you've ever had a game CD-ROM start automatically, blaring loud music to the entire office, you know what I'm talking about. Prevent audio CDs from starting automatically upon insertion by deselecting **Play audio CDs automatically**. Prevent CD-ROMs from starting automatically by deselecting **Play data CDs automatically**. Windows 98 retrieves these settings from `HKEY_CLASSES_ROOT\` `AudioCD\Shell\(default)` and `HKEY_CURRENT_USER\Software\Microsoft\Windows\` `CurrentVersion\Policies\Explorer\NoDriveTypeAutorun`.

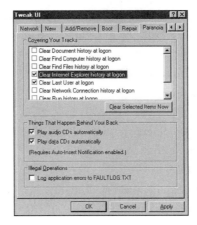

Figure 11.13 Tweak UI's Paranoia tab.

Other Shareware Registry Programs

The remainder of this chapter describes some of the best programs outside of Windows 98 that you can use to both edit the Registry and customize Windows 98. The first few sections describe what I consider best-of-breed. The section "Other Registry Programs" provides an overview of over a dozen additional shareware programs that you might want to evaluate. You can download them from the Web sites given with the descriptions.

Of all the Registry programs you can download, a serious power user needs three types: a good Registry editor, a good customization utility, and a good monitoring program. The best shareware Registry editor I've found is ShellWizard's Registry Editor. It's much better than Windows 98's Registry Editor and goes beyond what the Norton Registry Editor provides. You'll learn more about it soon. The best customization utility is More Properties. It provides similar features to Tweak UI or any other customization utility but does so better. By far the best program for monitoring Registry access is Regmon (Registry Monitor), which you'll also learn about in this chapter.

More Properties

Cost:	Freeware
Vendor:	Imaginary Software
Address:	`http://www.imaginary.co.za/mp20`

More Properties is one of the most popular freeware customization utilities on the Internet. With over 82,000 downloads and a four-star-out-of-five rating, you can't go wrong. This utility lets you perform the following tasks and more:

- Change Explorer's save on exit settings.
- Change the colors used in Windows 98 Help.
- Change the menu delay.
- Change the Recycle Bin.
- Clear the Run and Document histories at startup.
- Customize shell icons, including the Start button.
- Customize tip of the day messages.
- Customize Windows Explorer's shortcut menus.
- Enable AutoRun for drive types other than CD-ROM.

NOTE: The Windows NT and Windows 98 resource kits contain additional Registry utilities that are worthwhile, particularly for the administrator. Many of the Registry programs in the Windows NT resource kit work with Windows 98. The Microsoft Windows 98 Resource Kit wasn't available when I wrote this chapter, so I can't describe the utilities you find in it.

- Enable or disable individual drives.

- Enable or disable smooth scrolling.

- Enable or disable window animation.

- Hide desktop icons, including Network Neighborhood.

- Optimize the Maximum Transmission Unit settings.

- Rename and relocate shell folders.

- Update Windows 98's license information.

Figure 11.14 shows More Properties open on the desktop. It looks more like the System Policy Editor than Tweak UI. It has many of the same features found in Tweak UI, however. Click the tab containing the setting you want to change, and expand the outline to expose the settings. Most settings have a checkbox that you enable or disable. Other settings have a small icon next to them indicating that, if you select the setting, you can edit its value at the bottom of the window.

Follow the instructions you find at the bottom of Imaginary Software's Web page to download and install More Properties. You can download two different installation files: full setup and lite setup. Use the full setup, which is 1.7 MB, if you don't have the Visual Basic runtime libraries installed on your computer. Otherwise, download the 351 KB lite setup, which doesn't include the runtime libraries.

Norton Utilities

Cost:	Free evaluation
Vendor:	Symantec Corporation
Address:	`http://www.symantec.com`

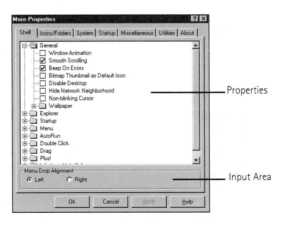

Figure 11.14 More Properties looks a bit like the System Policy Editor.

Norton Utilities comes with two useful Registry programs which, if you already own and use Norton Utilities, make a handy addition to your Registry toolkit.

The two utilities include Norton Registry Editor and Norton Registry Tracker. The Norton Registry Editor provides similar features to ShellWizard's Registry Editor. It provides a bit of navigation. Registry Tracker does similar work to ConfigSafe, which you'll learn about in Chapter 12, "Tracking Down Registry Settings," but it does so in real time. The problem with Registry Tracker is that if you try to use it to its full potential, it grinds your computer to halt, making the simplest tasks painfully time-consuming.

SEE ALSO

➤ To learn more about using Norton Registry Editor to edit the Registry, see Chapter 3, "Using the Windows 98 Registry Editor."

➤ To learn more about using Norton Registry Tracker to track changes to the Registry, see Chapter 12, "Tracking Down Registry Settings."

Registry Search & Replace

Cost:	Shareware, $20
Vendor:	Stephen J. Hoek
Address:	`http://www.hotfiles.com`

Registry Search & Replace is a familiar utility you can use to automatically locate and change entries in the Registry. Windows Notepad has a search-and-replace feature, as do WordPad and Microsoft Word. Registry Search & Replace is a bit more complicated, however, because it works with the Windows Registry. Here's an overview of its features:

■ Search for any string of characters. You can restrict the search to values or data, as well as certain types of data and certain root keys. This utility can't search for both values and data at the same time, however.

Troubleshooting

More Properties does not start or report a missing DLL or other system file? More Properties requires several runtime files from Visual Basic. Windows 98 comes with all the files required to run More Properties. If you do have problems, however, make sure the following files exist on your computer, and double-check to make sure you're using the most recent version: Comctrl32.ocx, Mfc40.dll, Msvcrt40.dll, Olepro32.dll, Vb40032.dll, Ven2232.olb, Stdole2.tlb, Msvbvm50.dll, Msvcirt.dll, Msvcrt.dll, and Regsvr32.exe. You can download these files from Imaginary Software. .

TIP: Because very little has changed between Windows 98 and Windows 95 with regard to the Windows Registry, most Windows 95 Registry programs work just fine in Windows 98. In fact, the lion's share of the programs you'll read about in this chapter were written for Windows 95.

- Use Registry Search & Replace with remote computers. Both computers must be configured to use the Remote Registry Search, as described in Chapter 13, "Security and Remote Administration."

- For each match that Registry Search & Replace finds, have it prompt you for a replacement, automatically replace the matching string with another string, or just display the matching entry.

As far as I can tell, the author no longer maintains this utility. His Web site is no longer available, and the download file hasn't changed since 1996. Regardless, you can still download this utility from ZDNet's Software Library at http://www.hotfiles.com. Even though the author has in all likelihood abandoned this program, it's still useful and worth considering.

Regmon

Cost:	Freeware
Vendor:	Systems Internals
Address:	http://www.sysinternals.com/regmon.htm

Besides being a must-have utility, Regmon is a very popular download on the Ziff-Davis Software Library. It has over 36,000 downloads and a five-star-out-of-five rating. Regmon is an extremely powerful utility that allows you to watch Registry access in real time, as shown in Figure 11.15. This means that you can see every value read from and written to the Registry as the operation happens. Regmon does this with little impact on the computer's performance. Regmon allows you to filter the list by process, Registry path, or type of access. If you're interested in viewing the values that Windows Explorer reads, for instance, limit Regmon to read-only access from Windows Explorer. Here are some additional notes on how to use Regmon:

- **To search the log for specific information**, choose **Search**, **Find**. Type the text for which you're searching, and click **Find Next.**

- **To see a truncated path or value**, right-click it. You'll see a small window displaying the entire item. You'll use this feature frequently, because many Registry branches are too large to fit in the small column provided by Regmon.

- **To filter the information that Regmon displays**, choose **Events**, **Filter**. Then provide the following values:

CAUTION: Registry Search & Replace can make sweeping changes to the Registry, which you might not be prepared to make. Therefore, always perform a search first to make sure you know what it's going to change. After confirming what will change, do a full search-and-replace. Alternatively, you can have Registry Search & Replace confirm each change before it makes the change.

Value	Description
Process	The name of the process you want to watch. You can specify only one. The best way to figure out the name of the process is to observe the entries that Regmon logs. An asterisk is a wildcard that stands for all processes.
Path Include	The Registry path to include in the filter, starting from the top. An asterisk is a wildcard that stands for all Registry paths.
Path Exclude	A Registry path to exclude from the filter, starting from the top.
History Depth	The maximum number of lines that Regmon will display in the History window. The first lines in are the first lines out.
Log Reads	Indicates whether to include read access in the log. Reads include any operation that retrieves data from the Registry, such as iterating a branch or reading a value entry.
Log Writes	Indicates whether to include write access in the log. Writes include any operations that change the Registry, such as creating a new key or writing to a value entry.
Log Success	Indicates whether to include successful read or write accesses.
Log Errors	Indicates whether to include unsuccessful read or write accesses.

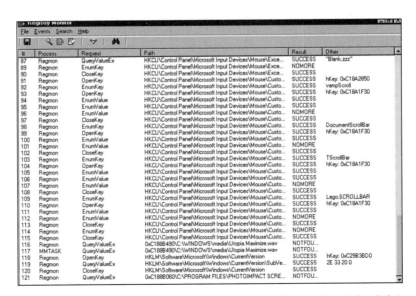

Figure 11.15 If Regmon truncates any key or value in the window, right-click it to see the whole string in a pop-up window.

Regmon is a quick download and is easy to install. Follow the instructions you find at the bottom of the Web page to download the 32 KB installation file. It doesn't include a setup program, so you must unzip Regmon.zip into any folder and drag Regmon.exe to the Start menu if you want a shortcut. If you're interested in seeing how Regmon works, download the source code, too.

SEE ALSO

➤ See Chapter 12, "Tracking Down Registry Settings," to learn more about using Regmon to track down changes to the Registry. This chapter also describes a program called ConfigSafe that monitors changes to the Registry over a longer period of time than Regmon.

ShellWizard Pro

Cost:	Shareware, $20
Vendor:	ShellWizard
Address:	http://www.shellwizard.com

ShellWizard Pro provides features similar to the other Registry customization programs, but it has a different user interface, as shown in Figure 11.16. Instead of a tabbed dialog box, it uses the wizard concept to walk you step-by-step through customizing the computer. Power users will most likely find the user interface annoying, but basic-to-intermediate users will appreciate the extra bit of help. You preview changes before actually making them permanent. ShellWizard Pro contains extensive, well-built online help and Experts that provide guidance as you work.

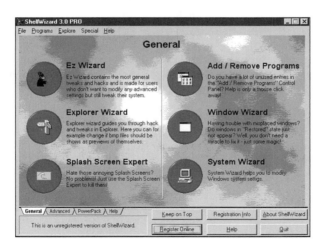

Figure 11.16 ShellWizard Pro follows Microsoft's guidelines for building wizards; thus it meshes well with Windows 98.

As shown in the figure, ShellWizard Pro has four tabs: General, Advanced, PowerPack, and Help. The General tab contains buttons for most of the typical settings found in utilities such as Tweak UI and More Properties. The Advanced tab provides the Startup Wizard to edit the Run and Run Once keys in the Registry, allowing you to control which programs start when you boot Windows 98. The PowerPack tab provides access to ShellWizard Pro's other utilities, including the following:

- **Program Doctor** helps you determine what DLL files a program is missing from the computer. If you've ever seen the message Required DLL file is missing, this utility can save you time.

- **Sfx Explorer** provides access to Microsoft's CAB files. You don't need this utility in Windows 98, however, because it is built into Windows Explorer.

- **Explorer Extension** adds additional features to Windows Explorer. This utility lives on the taskbar's status area, next to the clock. It provides quick access to folders, windows, and the Run dialog box.

- **File Split** allows you to split large files so that you can copy them to a floppy disk and rejoin them later.

ShellWizard Pro is at http://www.shellwizard.com. It's not available via the Ziff-Davis Software Library. Click Download under ShellWizard and follow the onscreen instructions. To install ShellWizard Pro, execute the file you downloaded.

ShellWizard Registry Editor

Cost:	Shareware, $30
Vendor:	ShellWizard
Address:	http://www.shellwizard.com

ShellWizard Registry Editor, shown in Figure 11.17, blows the heck out of the Windows 98 Registry Editor. It offers all the same features but goes much further. It's easier to use, provides more useful information, and makes navigating the Registry easier:

- Supports copy and paste.

- Provides awesome navigation via bookmarks, which work much like bookmarks in a Web browser.

- Offers a very fast search capability.

- SmartTips tell you about each class identifier.

- Provides a description, which you see in the bottom pane of the window, of many Registry keys.

- Includes a powerful macro language for writing complex scripts to add, change, or remove data.

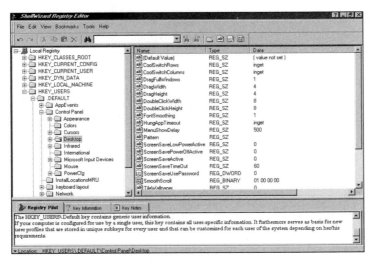

Figure 11.17 Notice the additional menu commands that the Windows 98 doesn't provide, and the bottom pane, which describes the selected Registry key.

Open `http://www.shellwizard.com` and click **Download** under ShellWizard Registry Editor. This program is not available on the Ziff-Davis Software Library. Follow the onscreen instructions to finish downloading it. To install the ShellWizard Registry Editor, execute the file you downloaded.

Other Registry Programs

The following sections describe a number of additional Registry programs that have a following. Each section provides a price, vendor, address, and brief description. These shareware programs are listed in alphabetical order, with no regard given to usefulness, popularity, or any other quality. In some cases, I've noted when a certain program has become hugely popular or when the Ziff-Davis Software Library gives the program an exceptionally high rating.

NOTE: If you already have Norton Utilities, don't pay for ShellWizard Registry Editor. Even though ShellWizard Registry Editor is better in many circumstances, the features of the two are quite similar.

TIP: You can download all the programs you read about in this chapter from Ziff-Davis's Software Library at `http://www.hotfiles.com`. Another good site for downloading system utilities is `http://www.danworld.com`.

Associate File Utility

Cost:	Shareware, $12
Vendor:	CT Software
Address:	`http://members.aol.com/ron2222`

The Associate File Utility makes associating file extensions with applications easier than through Windows Explorer. Simply provide the extension and the path to the application. It also allows you to define specific commands such as editing, printing, and so on. It's hardly worth the $12 registration fee, however.

Config97

Cost:	Shareware, $10
Vendor:	Springer Software
Address:	

`http://members.tripod.com/~SpringerSoftware/Config97.htm`

Config97 displays certain configuration information from the Registry. Although it repeats functionality provided by Windows 98, it offers a single location to access everything. This utility isn't really worth the $10 registration fee, considering that Windows 98 now provides the System Information utilities, which do the same thing.

JumpToRegKey

Cost:	Shareware, $15.95
Vendor:	PACT ONE Software
Address:	`http://www.pact1.com`

This utility doesn't have many downloads, but the Ziff-Davis Software Library gives it five stars out of five. It is definitely useful, creating shortcuts to specific Registry keys that you can put on the desktop. Double-click the shortcut, and JumpToRegKey opens the Registry Editor with that particular key highlighted. You can also choose a Registry key from an icon on the status area, which is on the right side of the taskbar.

Multi-Remote Registry Change

Cost:	Shareware, $25
Vendor:	Greg Eytcheson
Address:	`http://www54.pair.com/eytch`

Multi-Remote Registry Change isn't very popular and is an exceptionally large download file. It should be more popular among administrators, however, since it does something that no other utility does: It allows you to change a Registry value on any number of remote computers, all at the same time. Select the computers to change from the list, and specify the key and value you want to change.

RegChk

Cost:	Freeware
Vendor:	Ron Thompson
Address:	`http://www.sageinst.com/regchk`

RegChk looks in the Registry for references to files that no longer exist. It generates a report, allowing you to clean up the Registry on your own. Nifty.

Regfind

Cost:	Freeware
Vendor:	Intellisoft, Inc.
Address:	`http://www.hotfiles.com`

You use Regfind to search the Registry. It's good for locating problems such as value entries containing data from deleted programs. Because I couldn't find the author's Web site, I'm referring you to the Ziff-Davis Software Library to download this file.

RegisTray

Cost:	Shareware
Vendor:	Software House
Address:	`http://www.hotfiles.com`

RegisTray allows you to customize features in Windows that you can't through the normal interface.

Registry Editor Extensions

Cost:	Freeware
Vendor:	DC Software Design
Address:	`http://www.hotfiles.com`

Registry Editor Extensions adds a number of new features to the Registry Editor. For example, it adds a combo box that acts like the history list you use in a Web browser. If you're using ShellWizard Registry Editor or Norton Registry Editor, you don't need this utility.

RegMonEx

Cost:	Freeware
Vendor:	Jan Sultan
Address:	`http://www.hotfiles.com`

RegMonEx monitors each call to the Registry API. It includes the name of the program making the call, the Registry key, the result, and any values retrieved from the Registry. RegMonEx provides a filter, like Regmon.

RegRepair 2000

Cost:	Shareware, $29.95
Vendor:	Easy Desk Software
Address:	http://members.aol.com/wcguy06

RegRepair 2000 has over 10,000 downloads from the Ziff-Davis Software Library and a five-star-out-of-five rating. It helps you fix pesky IOS errors and repairs files that failed to load, as noted in Bootlog.txt. It automatically scans Bootlog.txt for errors and tries to fix them. Note that this program backs up the Registry, but you don't need this feature, since Windows 98 does an admirable job of that all by itself.

RegTune 98

Cost:	Shareware, $35
Vendor:	Ashish Computer Systems
Address:	http://www.ashishsystems.com

RegTune 98 helps you change security settings in Windows. You can hide drivers, for instance, or manage passwords, Start menu submenus, and more. This program leaves holes that let the user reverse the settings that an administrator might configure, so I wouldn't rely on it if tight security is a must.

RegView for Windows 95

Cost:	Shareware, $39
Vendor:	Vincent Chiu
Address:	http://www.xnet.com/~vchiu

RegView looks and feels similar to the Windows 98 Registry Editor, but it provides a few new features. It has a better search feature and allows you to perform a search and replace. It can compare the current Registry to the latest backup you've made using its backup feature.

> NOTE: If you have to choose between RegMonEx and RegMon, choose RegMon. RegMonEx is an extension to RegMon's original source code that was created by a programmer other than the original authors. RegMonEx is a bit clumsy compared to RegMon, because it adds more complexity and doesn't always get the job done. RegMonEx has more-advanced filtering capabilities, but using them can test your patience.

> TIP: If you're in the market for a new Registry Editor, consider using the ShellWizard Registry Editor, described earlier in this chapter.

SecLOCK

Cost:	Freeware
Vendor:	CMSystems
Address:	http://www.strebersdorf.ac.at/ CMSystems/CMSystems.html

SecLOCK helps you lock down the Windows 98 desktop. It works with user profiles, allows you to set up restrictions similar to the System Policy Editor, hide desktop icons, remove submenus from the Start menu, and more. You can use it in lieu of the System Policy Editor. (Note that Tweak UI provides many of these features.) This is a German program that's roughly translated into English, but you should have no problems understanding the prompts.

Set Me Up 98

Cost:	Shareware
Vendor:	Omniquad
Address:	http://www.omniquad.com

Omniquad's Set Me Up 98 is clunky compared to the other Registry and customization tools (it suffers from diseases common to Visual Basic programs), but it offers features not found anywhere else. You can change how individual folders look by creating custom Desktop.ini files, for instance. Use your own splash screens for when Windows 98 starts or shuts down. You can even customize Internet Explorer 4.0 options not available through the traditional user interface.

StartEd

Cost:	Shareware, $15
Vendor:	Thomas Reimann
Address:	http://www.alberts.com/authorpages/ 00014860/prod_687.htm

With a five-star-out-of-five rating and a whopping 21,000 downloads, this program must have something going for it. It allows you to control what programs Windows 98 starts using the Run, Run Once, and RunServices keys in the Registry. The primary purpose of this utility is to avoid editing these keys using the Registry Editor. You can even add your own programs to the Run key instead of adding them to the Startup group of the Start menu. You must be the judge as to whether this simple program is worth the cost, considering that the StartUp Manager, described next, is free.

StartUp Manager

Cost:	Freeware
Vendor:	Daniel Hofman
Address:	`http://www.hotfiles.com`

The StartUp Manager allows you to edit the `Run`, `Run Once`, `Run Services`, and `Run Services Once` Registry keys, as well as Win.ini's `Run` and `Load` entries. It helps you understand why a program might start when Windows 98 starts and you don't see it in the Startup group. It's also a good alternative to adding programs to the startup group.

Tip Editor

Cost:	Freeware
Vendor:	Jelsoft Enterprises
Address:	`http://www.hotfiles.com`

Use Tip Editor to edit the tips displayed when Windows 98 starts without doing so through the Registry Editor. It's a great way to add tips, export them to a REG file, and distribute them to a larger user base.

SEE ALSO

➤ See Chapter 15, "Script, REG, and INF Files," to learn more about scripting changes to the Registry using INF files.

TweakDUN

Cost:	Shareware, $15
Vendor:	Patterson Design Systems
Address:	`http://pattersondesigns.com/tweakdun/`

TweakDUN gets five stars out of five and has over 25,000 downloads from the Ziff-Davis Software Library. You use it to tune up your TCP/IP settings to improve the performance of your Internet connection. In particular, TweakDUN adjusts the size of certain packets and buffers to limit fragmenting. It can optimize these settings so that they work better with your ISP, too. You can easily change these settings yourself using the Registry Editor, but no other program provides the convenient user interface that TweakDUN provides, and no other program can detect the appropriate settings to use.

> TIP: You find the `Run` and `Run Once` keys in both the `HKEY_LOCAL_MACHINE` and `HKEY_CURRENT_USER` branches of the Registry. The difference is that items in the former start *before* the user logs onto Windows 98, and items in the latter start *after* the user logs onto Windows 98.

Win-eXpose-Registry

Cost:	Shareware, $29
Vendor:	Shetef Solutions Ltd.
Address:	`http://www.shetef.com`

Use Win-eXpose-Registry to trace and monitor access to the Windows 98 Registry.

WinHacker95

Cost:	Shareware, $17.95
Vendor:	Wedge Software
Address:	`http://www.wedgesoftware.com`

WinHacker 95 is the granddaddy of shareware Registry customization tools, but it hasn't improved much since the original version, and it certainly doesn't meet the bar set by Tweak UI and More Properties, both described earlier in this chapter. It offers all the basic settings, most of which are described in Chapter 9, "Customizing the Windows 98 Desktop." If you're looking for an alternative to Tweak UI and More Properties, however, download WinHacker95 from Wedge Software's Web site.

WinRescue 98

Cost:	Shareware, $19.95
Vendor:	Super Win Software
Address:	`http://members.aol.com/evanetten`

The Ziff-Davis Software Library gives this popular program a five-star-out-of-five rating. It allows for preventative maintenance to recover from the inevitable crashes. It backs up important configuration files, as well as the Startup menu, desktop, Favorites folder, Recent folder, and many others. It compresses these backups into zip files.

WinTweak

Cost:	Shareware, $8
Vendor:	Gooch Computer Services
Address:	`http://www.hotfiles.com`

WinTweak allows you to customize Internet Explorer 4.0. You can change default mail and news folders; remove **Documents**, **Favorites**, **Find**, and **Run** from the Start menu; change search pages; and more.

12

Tracking Down Registry Settings

Karanjit S. Siyan, Ph.D

In this chapter:

- Comparing REG File Snapshots
- Comparing Registry Checker Backups
- Monitoring Access to the Registry
- Comparing Registries Across the Network
- Using Norton Registry Tracker—Not!
- Tracking the Registry with ConfigSafe

Comparing REG File Snapshots

No easier method exists for locating changes in the Registry than to compare two REG files that you export from the Registry Editor. Export the Registry to a REG file before and after performing an action that changes the Registry, and then compare both REG files using a text-comparison utility. The comparison utility will highlight the differences between each file, allowing you to determine what keys were added and removed, as well as what values were added, removed, and changed. This method is quicker than the tracking tools you'll learn about later in this chapter, and the results are often easier to read.

You can export the Registry to a REG file using the Windows-based or real mode Registry Editor. Recall from Chapter 3, "Using the Windows 98 Registry Editor," that REG files are nothing more than text files, making them ideally suitable for comparison. Each fully qualified key name is bracketed on a line by itself and is followed by each of its value entries. Each value looks like *name=value*, except for the key's default value entry, which looks like *@=value*. To export the Registry using the Windows-based Registry Editor, choose **Registry**, **Export Registry File**. Select **All** to make sure you're exporting the entire Registry, and specify the path and filename of the REG file in the spaces provided. Click **Save** to export the Registry to the REG file, a process that will take a few minutes. To export the Registry using the real mode Registry Editor, type the following command line at an MS-DOS command prompt or in the Run dialog box:

```
regedit /e filename.reg
```

The following sections describe a few text-comparison utilities you can use to compare REG files. All of them do a good job but aren't equally suitable. My preference is Norton File Compare. It's more intuitive and recognizes that you're comparing REG files, formatting its output accordingly. Norton File Compare sometimes chokes on extremely large REG files, however, and is a bit slower than WinDiff. Regardless, both programs do the same thing, so the choice is yours. If neither of these programs is available to you, you can use your word processor's comparison feature, but expect to wait a long, long time while the word processor crunches the thousands of lines found in a typical REG file. Regardless of which utility you choose, the process is the same:

1. Export the complete Registry, including both HKEY_LOCAL_MACHINE and HKEY_USERS, to a REG file. Name this file Before.reg or something similar.

2. Perform the actions that you believe change the Registry. If you want to see how a program stores options in the Registry, for example, set those options. If you want to see what values a setup program changes, install the application.

3. Export the complete Registry to another REG file. Name this file After.reg or something similar.

4. Compare both REG files, Before.reg and After.reg, using a text-comparison utility. The utility will indicate the differences between both files.

NOTE: Chapter 9, "Customizing the Windows 98 Desktop," contains dozens of ways you can customize the operating system. Don't stop there. You can find your own customizations by tracking down the settings that the operating system or any other program uses in the Registry. I found many of the customizations in Chapter 9 using the same techniques you'll learn about in this chapter.

NOTE: Breaking news! Just before this book went to the printer, I learned about a new product called RegSnap. This product completely automates the process described in this section. It takes snapshots of the Registry, compares them, and reports the changes. This program offers numerous advanced features and, best of all, compares two snapshots so fast it'll make your head spin. You can download RegSnap from the Web at http://www.webdon.com.

SEE ALSO

➤ Chapter 15, "Script, REG, and INF Files," shows you how to build REG files manually. Understanding how to create a REG file helps you better understand the results you see when comparing two files.

➤ Chapter 3, shows you how to export to a REG file using the Windows-based and real mode Registry Editor. This chapter describes all the command line options you can use with the real mode Registry Editor.

➤ Chapter 14, "Profiles, System Policies, and the Registry," shows you which User.dat file the operating system loads in different circumstances.

WinDiff

WinDiff is a classic text-comparison tool that programmers are familiar with. It comes with the software development kit that they use to write Windows programs. WinDiff comes with Windows 98; you find it on the CD-ROM under \Tools\Reskit\File. Copy Windiff.exe and Windiff.hlp to any folder on your computer. To make accessing WinDiff easier, add a shortcut to the Start menu. If you installed the Microsoft Windows 98 Resource Kit Sampler by running Setup.exe from \Tools\Reskit, you already have WinDiff on your computer under \Program Files\Win98RK; run WinDiff from the command prompt or the Run dialog box.

Tips for Creating Snapshots

If the change you're seeking is in a specific part of the Registry, don't export the entire thing; just export that specific branch. Make sure you export the exact same branch in both the before and after REG files. To export a specific branch, select the key at the top of the branch before choosing **Registry**, **Export Registry File** from Registry Editor. Select **Selected branch** instead of All.

If you enable user profiles and export the entire Registry, you might worry about whether the REG file contains all your settings as well as the default user's settings. Don't. The Registry Editor exports HKEY_USERS, which means that it exports .DEFAULT and *Username*. .DEFAULT corresponds to the User.dat file in \Windows, and *Username* corresponds to the User.dat in your profile folder. Just make sure you log onto the computer properly and don't export the Registry in MS-DOS mode. In both cases, the Registry Editor will only export the settings from User.dat in \Windows.

NOTE: If you installed the Microsoft Windows 98 Resource Kit Sampler from \Tools\Reskit on the CD-ROM, you have the Microsoft Management Console. MMC provides easy access to a plethora of Windows 98 utilities, including WinDiff. Start MMC by choosing **Start**, **Programs**, **Windows 98 Resource Kit**, **Tools Management Console**. WinDiff is under the File Tools category.

When you start WinDiff, it displays an empty window. Specify the files you want to compare by choosing **File**, **Compare Files**. Pick the first file and click **Open**, and then pick the second file and click **Open**. WinDiff displays a single line at the top of the window that indicates whether the two files are the same or different. Double-click that line to compare the files and display the comparison results. Alternatively, click the Expand button on the toolbar or choose **View**, **Expand**. Figure 12.1 shows what WinDiff looks like after the comparison of two REG files.

WinDiff combines both files, highlighting differences between each one. Press F8 to view the next difference between each file, or press F7 to view the previous difference. Lines with a white background are common to both files; WinDiff indicates differences with a red or yellow background. A red background means that the line is present in the first file but not in the second. A yellow background means that the line is in the second file but not in the first. Thus, a red background indicates lines that were removed from the second file, and a yellow background indicates lines that were added to the second file. You also see arrows beside each changed line that point left or right. They are easier to remember than the colors. An arrow pointing to the left means that the line was removed from the second file, and an arrow pointing to the right means that the line was added to the second file. When using WinDiff, refer to the following table to jog your memory about what each color and arrow means:

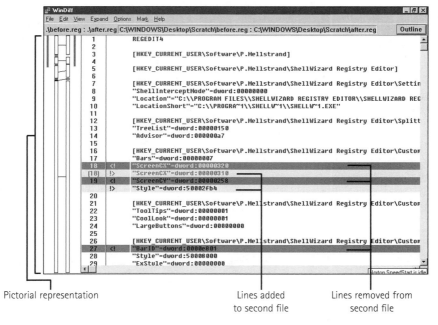

Pictorial representation · Lines added to second file · Lines removed from second file

Figure 12.1 You can't see the colors in this figure, but the darker band is red, and the lighter band is yellow.

Color	Arrow	Meaning
Red	<!	Line present in first file, not in second
Yellow	!>	Line present in second file, not in first

The bars you see along the left edge of WinDiff's window are a pictorial representation of the two files' differences. You see two columns. The first represents the first file, and the second represents the second file. You also see red and yellow bands within each column. These bands indicate differences between the two files. The two blue vertical lines on either side of the columns show what portion of the files WinDiff is displaying in the window. Click anywhere in the picture to display that portion of the files in WinDiff. Click one of the red or yellow bands in the picture to display that particular difference in the window. This is a great way to move directly to differences between both files.

Norton File Compare

Chapter 1, "Inside the Windows 98 Registry," describes where to purchase Norton Utilities and where to get an evaluation copy. Once you've installed Norton Utilities, you start File Compare by choosing **Start**, **Programs**, **Norton Utilities**, **Norton File Compare**.

After you start Norton File Compare, it prompts you for the left and right files. These correspond to the first and second files. Select new files by choosing **File**, **Open Left Pane** and **File**, **Open Right Pane**. After scanning both files for changes, File Compare them, one in each pane, as shown in Figure 12.2. When you scroll up and down, File Compare synchronizes the files in both panes. This makes it possible to compare both side-by-side as you move up and down. Note how File Compare recognizes that you're comparing REG files and formats the output accordingly. It shows Registry keys and subkeys using the appropriate hierarchy and displays the correct icons for each value's type. It doesn't change the format of each text line, however, leaving each as it appears in the REG file.

> **NOTE:** WinDiff represents changed lines by showing them deleted from the first file and added to the second. Thus, alternating red and yellow bands indicate changes rather than additions or deletions. Also note the line numbers. When WinDiff detects a changed line, it shows the line as it appears in the first file with a line number like 18. It shows the line as it appears in the second file with a line number like (18).

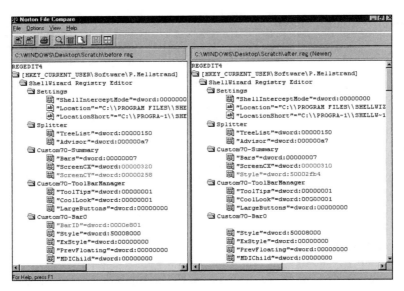

Figure 12.2 Norton File Compare shows you the path and filename above each pane. It also indicates which file is newer.

Norton File Compare indicates unchanged text with black characters and changed text with red characters. If these colors are difficult for you to see, change them by choosing **Options**, **Settings** and clicking the Display tab. You can scroll up and down to look for individual differences, or you can use File Compare's search feature to locate each difference. Choose **Options**, **Search** or press F3. Select **Non Matching Block**, and click **Search Down** or **Search Up**. File Compare brings each block of differences to the top of the window. If you only want to see the changes, choose **View**, **Show Differences Only**. This feature collapses the display so that you only see the lines that are different between each file. You won't see the changed lines in their original context, but this is the best means by which to locate changes in the Registry.

SEE ALSO

➤ Chapter 1, provides an overview of all the Registry programs that come with Norton Utilities.

NOTE: Norton File Compare is designed to work hand-in-hand with Registry Tracker. Registry Tracker uses File Compare to compare the differences between two versions of the Registry. Registry Tracker is painfully slow, however, so you're better off comparing REG files that you create yourself.

Most Word Processors

Short of using WinDiff or Norton File Compare, you can use your word processor's compare feature to find changes between two REG files. Most popular word processors such as Microsoft Word have this feature, but it's not the best choice. Using a word processor to compare two REG files is much slower than using a program designed for that purpose. Still, using your word processor might be your only choice if you don't have access to either WinDiff or Norton File Compare.

Revision tracking, as it's called in most word processors, works differently in dissimilar programs. In most cases, you open the second REG file first and compare it to the first. Opening the files in this order ensures that the word processor correctly interprets whether lines are added to, changed in, or removed from the older file.

In Microsoft Word, choose **File**, **Open** to open the second REG file. Make sure you choose **All files** from **Files of type** so that you can see REG files, not just DOC files. Select the REG file and click **Open**. Be patient, because opening a large REG file can take a long time. After Word opens the REG file, choose **Tools**, **Track Changes**, **Compare Documents**, select the first REG file, and click **Open**. Word doesn't actually open the file. It highlights the differences between the open REG file and the REG file that you chose to compare it to. By default, Word formats deleted lines using strikethrough and new lines using underline, as shown in Figure 12.3.

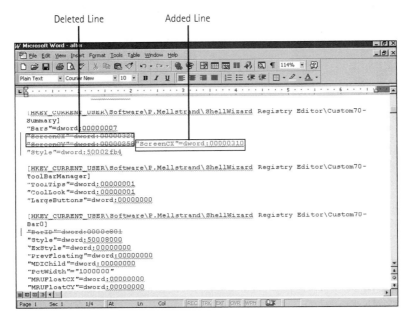

Figure 12.3 Differences between REG files aren't as easy to discern in Microsoft Word as they are in Norton File Compare.

Comparing Registry Checker Backups

You've used your computer for weeks with no problems. Without warning, it starts acting up, and you don't know why. You suspect the problem is with the data in the Registry, but you haven't taken any snapshots using ConfigSafe or exported to a REG file the contents of the Registry prior to the problem's occurring. You're out of luck, eh?

Not so fast.

Recall from Chapter 2, "Backing Up and Restoring the Registry," that Registry Checker backs up the Registry to CAB files once each day. It stores these CAB files in \Windows\Sysbckup. At the very least, you have five days of backups, but if you've followed my advice in Chapter 2, you have 10 days. Compare the Registry files in these CAB files to find the change in your configuration that's causing the problems. You can extract System.dat and User.dat using Windows Explorer or Extract.exe. Note that you must start the computer in MS-DOS mode to export the extracted System.dat and User.dat to a REG file. The Registry Editor won't properly recognize the /l and /r command line options when you're running Windows 98. Follow these instructions closely, referring to Chapter 2 for more-specific instructions about how to extract System.dat and User.dat from a CAB file:

1. In \Windows\Sysbckup, a hidden folder, locate the two CAB files that contain the Registry backups you want to compare. Remember that a higher-numbered CAB file is newer than a lower-numbered CAB file; thus, RB004.cab is newer than RB003.cab.

> **TIP:** If you must use your word processor to compare two REG files, make sure you disable its spell and grammar checkers. If they are enabled, your computer will grind to a halt, because the word processor will find spelling and grammar errors on every line of each file. Consult your word processor's documentation to learn how to disable spell and grammar checking.

Some Changes Just Don't Matter

You'll see some of the same changes repeatedly after comparing a handful of REG files. They don't mean anything. They're just normal changes that occur over time and have little to do with the changes for which you're searching. If you compare two REG files that were created before and after restarting the computer, for instance, you'll find several changes to HKEY_LOCAL_MACHINE\System. These changes just reflect the results of Plug and Play's configuring the hardware as you start the operating system. In the course of normal operation, various values change in the Registry. A variety of MRU lists will change as you run programs, open documents, or search for files. Windows Explorer will save different settings that indicate the position, size, and appearance of each Explorer window. Ignore all of these incidental changes and focus on finding the important ones.

2. Extract System.dat and User.dat from each CAB into two separate folders. Right-click the CAB file and choose **View**. Drag the file from the Explorer window to the folder you created for the file. After finishing this step, you have two folders, possibly C:\Before and C:\After, each of which contains different versions of System.dat and User.dat.

3. Restart the computer in MS-DOS mode. Step 4 won't work properly unless you do so, because it relies on the ability to redirect the real mode Registry Editor to a different set of Registry files.

4. Export the Registry files in each folder to a REG file. Assuming that you saved both sets of Registry files in C:\Before and C:\After, the following command lines will get the job done:

```
regedit /l:c:\before\system.dat
/r:c:\before\user.dat /e c:\before\before.reg
regedit /l:c:\after\system.dat
/r:c:\after\user.dat /e c:\after\after.reg
```

5. Restart Windows 98 and compare both REG files using the techniques you learned earlier in this chapter.

Listing 12.1 is a batch file that automates the preceding steps through step 4. You find it on my Web site, `http://www.honeycutt.com`. Start the computer in MS-DOS mode and run Listing 12.1. The command line is `cabreg reg1 reg2`, where *reg1* is the older CAB file and *reg2* is the newer CAB file. An example is `cabreg rb003.cab rb004.cab`. The batch file extracts System.dat and User.dat from each CAB file. It puts the first in C:\Before and the second in C:\After. Then it exports the System.dat and User.dat files in each folder to a REG file. Exporting both DAT files in MS-DOS mode takes a long time, so be patient. After restarting Windows 98, compare the REG files that this batch file generates to locate any differences between each backup. Note that this batch file depends on Extract.exe, a program that extracts files from CAB files. To learn more about using this program, type `extract /?` at the MS-DOS command prompt.

Listing 12.1   **Cabreg.bat**

```
Echo Off
if "%2" == "" goto Error

extract /y /l c:\before c:\windows\sysbckup\%1 system.dat
➥user.dat
extract /y /l c:\after  c:\windows\sysbckup\%2 system.dat
➥user.dat

regedit /l:c:\before\system.dat /r:c:\before\user.dat
➥/e c:\before\before.reg
regedit /l:c:\after\system.dat /r:c:\after\user.dat /e
```

```
➡c:\after\after.reg

Goto Finished

:Error

Echo You must specify the CAB files containing the Registry
Echo that you want to export. The command line looks like
➡this:
Echo .
Echo cabreg cab1 cab2
Echo .
Echo cab1 - Older CAB file (ex. rb003.cab)
Echo cab2 - Newer CAB file (ex. rb004.cat)

:Finished
```

SEE ALSO

➤ Chapter 3, shows you how to import and export REG files. It also shows you how to use the real mode Registry Editor in MS-DOS mode.

Monitoring Access to the Registry

Up to this point, you've learned how to compare snapshots that you take at different times. Watching how a program uses the Registry in real time might be a better means to discover how it uses the Registry, though. Registry Monitor is a program that does just that. You learn how to download and install this program in Chapter 11, "Tweak UI and Other Registry Programs." In short, you can get a free copy of Registry Monitor from http://www.sysinternals.com. It's a very small program that takes just a few minutes to retrieve.

Figure 12.4 shows Registry Monitor. The window contains six columns. The first contains line numbers. The second and third contain the name of the process accessing the Registry and the type of request the process is making. Table 12.1 describes each of the different requests you'll see in this column. These types correspond to the different API functions available to programs accessing the Registry. The remaining columns contain the Registry path, the result (success or failure), and any other data, as described in Table 12.1. Registry Monitor also divides its window into rows and adds a new line to the end of the list every time a program accesses the Registry.

NOTE: Exporting alternative System.dat and User.dat files to a REG file in MS-DOS mode is painfully slow. On my computer, the batch file in Listing 12.1 completed after two hours. You don't have any choice if you want to compare two backups of the Registry made by Registry Checker. Be patient and wait out the process.

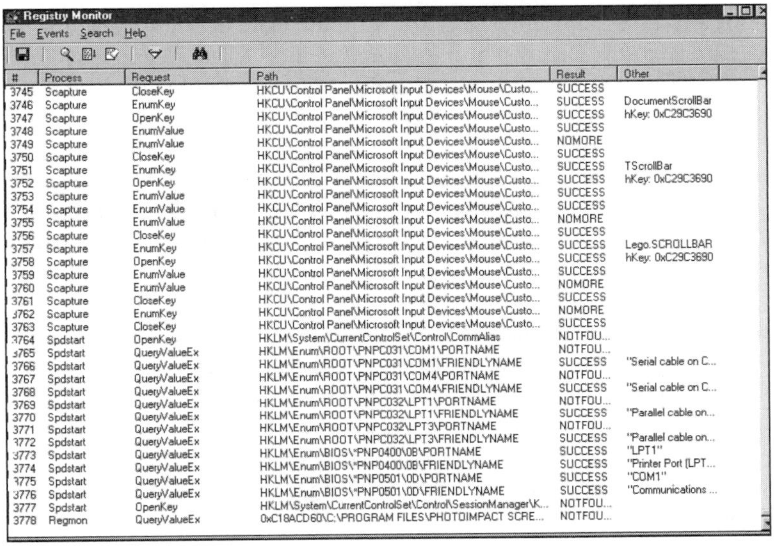

Figure 12.4 Although Registry Monitor tracks every access to the Registry, it doesn't affect your computer's performance.

Table 12.1 **Request Types in Registry Monitor**

Type	Data in the Other Column
CloseKey	Unused
CreateKey	Handle to the newly created key
CreateKeyEx	Handle to the newly created key
DeleteKey	Unused
DeleteValue	Unused
EnumKey	Name of the next enumerated subkey
EnumKeyEx	Name of the next enumerated subkey
EnumValue	Unused
FlushKey	Unused
OpenKey	Handle to the opened key
OpenKeyEx	Handle to the opened key
QueryValue	Data queried from the value entry
QueryValueEx	Data queried from the value entry
SetValue	Data stored in the value entry
SetValueEx	Data stored in the value entry

Without a filtering capability, Registry Monitor wouldn't be suitable for tracking down specific Registry changes. In the several minutes I had Registry Monitor open, it recorded over 12,000 accesses to the Registry. Pinpointing small changes is almost impossible in this case. The program does allow you to filter the lines it displays, though, so that you can focus on access by a particular process or specific types of access by any program. Choose **Events**, **Filter**; you'll see the RegMon Filter dialog box. Type the name of the process you want to watch in **Process**. You can also choose the types of access you want to observe: **Log Reads**, **Log Writes**, **Log Success**, and **Log Errors**. Note that an asterisk is a wildcard. Click **Apply** to start filtering using the criteria you chose.

Make sure you use the application's process name when filtering in Registry Monitor, not the application's proper name or EXE filename. The best way to discover the application's process name is to observe the names that Registry Monitor displays in the second column. Note that some processes will be named Run32dll, indicating that the process was a DLL file that was launched via Run32dll.exe. In this case, you won't see the name of the DLL file, and many processes might share this name.

SEE ALSO

➤ Chapter 11, contains more information about Registry Monitor and its sister program, RegMonEx.

Comparing Registries Across the Network

CompReg is on the *Microsoft Windows 98 Resource Kit* CD-ROM. Look in \Reskit\Registry. This program is not on the Windows 98 CD-ROM's Resource Kit Sampler, so you must own the full version of the Resource Kit in order to use it.

CompReg, an MS-DOS program, compares two branches of a Registry or compares the Registries from a local computer and a remote computer. The program's output looks like Listing 12.2. You can run CompReg from the Resource Kit's CD-ROM, or you can copy its EXE file to your computer. The Resource Kit's setup program copies Compreg.exe to your computer, so you might already have it. Look in \Program Files\Win98RK.

> NOTE: Most times Registry Monitor displays the correct Registry path for each line in the window. If a program opened a key before you started Registry Monitor, though, Registry Monitor won't be able to look up the key's path and thus can't display the path in the window. In those cases, Registry Monitor displays the key's handle instead of its path. The best you can do is take an educated guess at which path the handle represents.

> TIP: You can watch for hits to a specific Registry branch by filtering on it. Type the path to the branch you want to watch in **Path Include** in the Regmon Filter dialog box. Be sure to format the path just as you'd see it in Registry Monitor's window. That is, use the abbreviated root keys, such as HKLM and HKCU.

Listing 12.2 **Sample Output from CompReg**

```
1 \ShellNew
1 \ShellEx
2 \Wordpad.Document.1
2 \Word.Document.6
2 \WordDocument
2 \ShellEx
2 \Word.Document.8
1 ! REG_SZ,[Paint.Picture]
2 ! REG_SZ,[Word.Document.8]
1 !Content Type REG_SZ,[image/bmp]
2 !Content Type REG_SZ,[application/msword]
End of search : 9 differences found.
```

The following list describes CompReg's command line:

```
compreg <1> <2> [-v] [-r] [-e] [-d] [-q] [-n] [-h] [-?]
```

1	Path of the first key
2	Path of the second key
-v	Shows differences and matches
-r	Visits subkeys that exist only in *1* or *2*
-e	Sets errorlevel to the previous error code
-d	Limits output to just key names, not values
-q	Limits output to the number of differences
-n	Disables the use of color in the output
-h	Displays help
-?	Displays command line options

Some aspects of CompReg's command line bear more explanation. In particular, *1* and *2* specify the Registry paths you're comparing. The notation is *Name**Path*. *Name*, if provided, can be the name of any computer on the network. *Path* is a Registry path within that computer's Registry. If you don't provide a computer name, CompReg assumes that the path is within the local Registry. *Path* is usually a fully qualified path starting from one of the root keys. You must use one of the abbreviations shown in Table 12.2, though, not the conventional abbreviations you learned about in Chapter 1, If you specify just a computer name for *2*, CompReg compares the path specified by *1* to the same path on the machine specified by *2*. The following list shows several examples to speed you on your way:

```
compreg lm\software cu\software

compreg us\.default us\jerry

compreg lm\software \\Other

compreg \\Workstation\lm \\Other\lm

compreg \\Workstation\lm\software \\Server
```

Table 12.2 **Root Key Abbreviations for CompReg**

Abbreviation	Root Key
lm	HKEY_LOCAL_MACHINE
cu	HKEY_CURRENT_USER
cr	HKEY_CLASSES_ROOT
us	HKEY_USERS

Using Norton Registry Tracker—Not!

Norton Registry Tracker, shown in Figure 12.5, is my only disappointment with Symantec's otherwise fine suite of utilities. It seriously affects the performance of any computer on which you use it to track the Registry. The reason is that Registry Tracker continuously monitors the Registry for changes, creating a new snapshot every time it detects one. If you monitor too much of the Registry's content, Registry Tracker will take snapshots all the time, sapping the computer's resources.

If you let Norton Registry Tracker monitor the Registry in the background, you'll suffer for it. Using Registry Tracker to take occasional snapshots of the entire Registry isn't practical either. On my computer, a 233Mhz Pentium with 32MB of memory, I closed Registry Tracker via the Task Manager after giving Registry Tracker over 40 minutes to take a full snapshot of the Registry. This is not acceptable performance, given that you can export the Registry to a REG file in a matter of minutes, or that you can use ConfigSafe, covered next, to fulfill the same purpose in a fraction of the time. The only practical use for Registry Tracker is to take occasional snapshots of very specific portions of the Registry.

NOTE: If the paths you specify to CompReg contain spaces, make sure you enclose the entire path in quotation marks.

NOTE: If you want an excellent alternative to Registry Tracker, one that offers most of the same features, try ConfigSafe. You'll learn about this product in the following section.

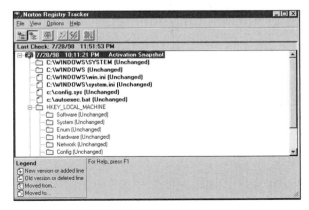

Figure 12.5 Norton Registry Tracker relies on File Compare to show the differences between two snapshots.

SEE ALSO

➤ Chapter 1, describes the other Registry programs in Norton Utilities and shows you how to get a licensed copy.

Tracking the Registry with ConfigSafe

ConfigSafe was originally designed to help hardware manufacturers better support their customers. It records the configuration of a computer when the manufacturer ships it. Then, when a customer calls in with a problem, the support person uses ConfigSafe to determine what the user has changed on his or her computer.

ConfigSafe is just as valuable to you. Use it to take occasional *snapshots* of your computer's configuration; then you can see what changed on your computer from time to time, snapshot to snapshot. For example, if you installed a program that changed your Autoexec.bat without asking, you can see exactly what the program changed. If a program messed up the Registry, you can use ConfigSafe to see exactly how. ConfigSafe is also a good program to use for tracking down changes in the Registry when you're hunting down that next great customization.

The easiest—and fastest—way to start using ConfigSafe is to download an evaluation copy. Open `http://www.imagine-lan.com`, click the **Download** button, and follow the instructions you see on the Web page. You can also order ConfigSafe directly from imagine LAN:

imagine LAN, Inc.

76 Northeastern Blvd., Suite 34B

Nashua, NH 03062-3174

(603) 889-3883

When you first install ConfigSafe, it takes an initial snapshot of the computer's configuration. After the first snapshot, you don't really have to do much. Just sit back and let ConfigSafe do its job. By default, ConfigSafe takes a new snapshot once a week. This is more than enough to protect your computer against most problems. As you can see from the following items it records in each snapshot, ConfigSafe covers all the bases:

Configuration files	Protocol.ini, System.ini, Win.ini, Autoexec.bat, Config.sys, and Msdos.sys
System information	Processor, coprocessor, memory, and Windows version
Drive information	Free space on each drive
Directory information	Files in C:\Dos and in C:\Windows and all its subdirectories
Registry information	All value entries for all keys in the Registry

Even though ConfigSafe tracks a variety of configuration data, I'll limit this discussion to how you use the program to track Registry changes. ConfigSafe's help describes the program's remaining features.

Viewing Changes

To run ConfigSafe, choose **Start, Programs, ConfigSafe, ConfigSafe**. It monitors `HKEY_LOCAL_MACHINE` and `HKEY_USERS`, which includes every key and value in System.dat and User.dat. You don't need to add any other keys to the list, since these two cover all the bases. Click the Registry Information button on the toolbar to see Registry keys that ConfigSafe is tracking and the changes to each value entry. You'll see a view similar to Figure 12.6. My only beef with this program is that it doesn't use a tabbed interface as similar programs do.

You have to tell ConfigSafe which snapshots you want to compare when building the list of changes. You can compare any two snapshots, as well as any snapshot and the current configuration. For example, you can compare a snapshot you took two weeks ago to the current configuration, represented by the word *Now* instead of a date and time. You can also compare a snapshot you took four weeks ago to a snapshot you took two weeks ago. Choose the beginning snapshot from **Changes Starting**. Choose the ending snapshot from **Changes Ending**.

To see changes to a particular Registry key and all its subkeys, select a key from the list. ConfigSafe will go away again, possibly for a very long time, so keep your fingers off Ctrl+Alt+Delete. Look under the list of Registry keys to see the actual value entries that have changed. You see a plus sign by each new Registry key and a minus sign beside each deleted Registry key. ConfigSafe displays before and after versions of changed keys with a green arrow pointing from the older value data to the newer value data. The following table describes the conventions:

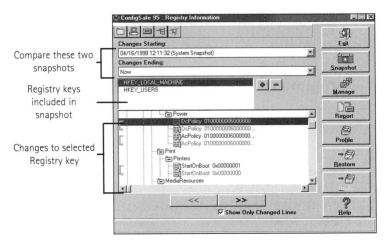

Figure 12.6 See the section "Sniffing Out Customizations" to learn how
to use this view to track down changes in the Registry.

Type	Color
Add	Blue
Delete	Red
Change	Green

Taking New Snapshots

Create a new snapshot anytime by clicking the **Snapshot** button. Type a name in the
Create Configuration Snapshot dialog box, and click **OK**.

Maybe changing ConfigSafe's snapshot schedule is what you really wanted to do.
ConfigSafe takes a configuration snapshot once every week by default. If you find
yourself taking a snapshot every morning, change ConfigSafe's schedule so that it does
so automatically. A monthly snapshot may be more suitable for users who don't use
their computers much. A daily snapshot is more appropriate for someone like me, who
toys with his configuration regularly. Follow these steps to change the schedule:

1. Click **Manage** to display the Manage Configuration Snapshots dialog box.

2. Make sure that **Enable Scheduled Snapshot** is checked.

> NOTE: Most times, you'll want to compare the most recent snapshot to your current configuration. This
> allows you to determine recent changes to your configuration. Other times, you'll want to compare two
> different snapshots that occur before and after a specific configuration change, such as installing a new
> program. This allows you to figure out what changes the program made.

3. Select **Daily**, **Weekly**, **Monthly**, or **At Windows Startup**.

4. Click **OK** to save your changes.

Sniffing Out Customizations

ConfigSafe can track down Registry settings that a program changes. Compare a snapshot after the program makes its changes to a snapshot you take beforehand. Here's how:

1. Create a new profile so that you can easily clean up your mess when you're finished. Profiles are individually named collections of snapshots. Click the **Profile** button, name the profile, and click **OK**.

2. Take a snapshot of the configuration by clicking **Snapshot**, typing a name, and clicking **OK**. This saves your current configuration. Close ConfigSafe.

3. Run the program and cause it to make the changes to the Registry that you want to uncover. You may have to set various options, move the window, and so on. The steps depend on what you're trying to discover.

4. After you're sure that the program has changed the Registry, close it. Then run ConfigSafe again and compare the previous snapshot to the current configuration.

NOTE: Missed a snapshot? If ConfigSafe misses a snapshot, either because you didn't start the computer that day or because you temporarily disabled the program, it will take the snapshot immediately at the next available opportunity.

NOTE: This chapter has shown you how to track Registry changes using ConfigSafe. You must understand that ConfigSafe is more than that. As its name implies, it's a good way to stash your configuration for safekeeping. You can restore any portion of your configuration if needed. Few problems can sneak by ConfigSafe, meaning that as long as it's protecting your computer, you can fix any problem.

D

Administering the Registry

13

Security and Remote Administration

In this chapter:

- Securing Windows 98
- Enabling Remote Administration
- Enabling Remote Administration via Setup Scripts
- Connecting to a Remote Computer's Registry

Securing Windows 98

Windows 98 is not a secure operating system. If you require serious workstation security, consider installing Windows NT Workstation instead of Windows 98. Windows NT Workstation has security features you don't find in Windows 98, such as file system security and control over user rights.

The typical example is that a user can log onto any Windows 98 workstation without providing credentials; all he has to do is press Esc at the logon prompt to bypass the validation process. As a result, Windows 98 uses the default profile for that user (a fact you can use to your advantage). Likewise, Windows 98 doesn't secure the Registry against tampering. The user can move or delete the Registry's files, for example, or make changes in the Registry Editor—Windows 98 won't prevent him from doing so. As an administrator, you can take definitive steps to improve security in Windows 98 and, more specifically, the Registry.

Most of the techniques you'll learn about in this section involve policies, but some are outside that realm. A simple method for protecting the Registry is to keep back-ups, as you learned in Chapter 2, "Backing Up and Restoring the Registry," allowing you to restore the Registry if the user tampers with it. Also make sure that you disable `AutoAdminLogon` in `Winlogon` so that Windows 98 won't automatically log the user onto the workstation without providing credentials. You learned about this setting in Chapter 9, "Customizing the Windows 98 Desktop." And if you've configured a Windows 98 workstation for remote administration, make sure you know who has permission to administer the computer's Registry. The later section "Enabling Remote Administration" shows you how to specify which users have the right to administer a Windows 98 computer.

The following sections describe a variety of polices you can use to tighten up security in Windows 98. See Chapter 14, "Profiles, System Policies, and the Registry," to learn how to use the System Policy Editor to change these settings. These sections don't cover all the available policies, just the ones that I think are most appropriate for protecting a workstation and the network.

SEE ALSO

➤ Chapter 2, "Backing Up and Restoring the Registry," has more information about backing up the Registry.

➤ Chapter 9, "Customizing the Windows 98 Desktop," shows you how to make specific customizations that affect security in Windows 98. In particular, you learn about the AutoAdminLogon setting in Winlogon.

➤ Chapter 11, "Tweak UI and Other Registry Programs," describes the Boot tab of Tweak UI, which allows you to control whether the user sees the boot menu when Windows 98 starts and whether he can use the boot keys to start in MS-DOS mode or Safe mode.

➤ Chapter 14, "Profiles, System Policies, and the Registry," shows you how to use the System Policy Editor to beef up security. Since many of the settings in this chapter come from the Shellm.adm template file, see the section "Using Custom Policy Templates."

Controlling the Default User

Use the System Policy Editor to restrict what the default user can do in Windows 98. The only require-ment is that you enable user profiles on the computer so that each user has a profile separate from the default profile. When a user bypasses the logon prompt by pressing Esc, Windows 98 uses the default profile for that user. This allows you to control what a guest user can do on the computer. The settings you apply to this default user don't apply to other users who log onto the computer as long as you enable user profiles on it.

Securing the User Interface

Windows 95 never gave the administrator much control over the shell. It was tough to remove commands from the Start menu, for example, or to disable shortcut menus in Windows Explorer. Windows 98 remedies this situation with a handful of policies found in the Shellm.adm policy template. You must specifically load this template in the System Policy Editor, as you will learn in Chapter 14, because the System Policy Editor doesn't load it by default.

All the following user policies are within the **Start Menu**, **Shell**, and **System** categories for a default or specific user. The first item, **Remove *Name* menu from the Start Menu**, isn't actually a single policy, because you see a policy for each command on the Start menu. Just replace *Name* with the submenu's name.

Remove Name menu from Start Menu

Disable File menu in Shell folders

Disable context menu in Shell folders

Hide Floppy Drives in My Computer

Disable net connections/disconnections

Do not allow computer to restart in MS-DOS mode

Draconian Security

Other security methods, while being a bit draconian, provide even more protection, particularly from a user who wants to abscond with data from your computer. Consider disabling the floppy drives in the BIOS, for instance, so that a user can't copy files to a disk and take off with them. Make sure you password-protect your BIOS settings, though. Disable the user's ability to display the boot menu or use the boot keys so that he can't start the computer in MS-DOS mode or Safe mode, circumventing all the policies you establish. You can change these settings easily using Tweak UI, as you learned in Chapter 11, "Tweak UI and Other Registry Programs."

Windows 98 allows the administrator to remove specific shortcuts from the Start menu and totally disable shortcut menus in Windows Explorer. You see one policy for each submenu on the Start menu called **Remove Name menu from the Start menu**, where *Name* is the name of the submenu. You can disable shortcut menus in Windows Explorer by enabling the **Disable context menu in Shell folders** policy. This doesn't do you much good unless you also disable the File menu using the **Disable File menu in Shell folders** policy.

Controlling Access to the Network

Policies that control network access are in the Windows.adm template file, which the System Policy Editor loads by default. You find all of these under the Access Control, Logon, Password, and Dial-Up Networking subcategories of the Windows 98 Network category, and the Programs to Run and Windows Update subcategories of the Windows 98 System category within the default computer or a specific computer's policies:

User-level access control

Require validation from network for Windows access

Don't show last user at logon

Disable password caching

Require alphanumeric password

Minimum Windows password length

Disable dial-in

Disable Windows Update

Preventing Access to the Control Panel

In some situations, you don't want the user changing system settings without your knowledge. The following policies are in the Control Panel subcategory of the Windows 98 System category for a default or specific user:

Restrict Display Control Panel

Restrict Network Control Panel

Restrict Passwords Control Panel

Restrict Printers Control Panel

Restrict System Control Panel

This policy ensures that the user can't access the workstation unless a security provider validates the user's credentials. It tightens up security considerably by preventing guest users from accessing the Windows 98 workstation unless they have an account on the network server.

Restrict Passwords Control Panel is an effective way to keep the user from changing his remote administration settings, as you'll learn later in this chapter. Set the **Hide Remote Administration Page** option so that the user can't add or remove users from this list.

Restricting the User's Activities

The following policies, all self-explanatory, are under the Restrictions subcategory of the Windows 98 System category:

Disable Registry editing tools

Only run allowed Windows applications

Disable MS-DOS prompt

Disable single-mode MS-DOS applications

Enabling Remote Administration

Remote administration lets the administrator inspect and change settings on one computer—the *target* or *remote* computer—from another computer on the network— the *administrative* computer. You can browse another computer's file system, for example, or set policies that control what the user can and can't do on the computer. Given that this book is about the Registry, this chapter focuses on the tools that allow you to inspect or change values in a remote computer's Registry.

Disable Registry editing tools is an effective policy for preventing the user from editing the Registry using the Registry Editor. Other Registry-editing tools don't honor this policy, however, so it's not a sure thing. In reality, there is no way to keep a determined user from editing the Registry unless you also specify a list of programs that the user is allowed to run using the **Only run allowed Windows applications** policy. Note that a user with access to the System Policy Editor can remove this restriction.

Microsoft Management Console

The Windows 98 CD-ROM includes the Microsoft Management Console, which you install by running the Microsoft Windows 98 Resource Kit Sampler's setup program: *d*:\tools\reskit\setup.exe, where *d* is the drive letter of the CD-ROM.

The Microsoft Management Console (MMC) provides a convenient location for accessing all the utilities in the resource kit. Microsoft calls each program in MMC a *snap-in*. You can easily add programs built as snap-ins or otherwise to MMC. Just remember that MMC doesn't actually provide any maintenance—it just provides a convenient location from which you can access all the administrative programs you use.

Macmillan Computer Publishing publishes a variety of Windows 98 books that include information about remote administration tools, such as *Platinum Edition Using Windows 98*.

You must configure Windows 98 correctly in order to use remote administration. In particular, the administrative and target workstations must meet the following requirements in order for you to administer the target computer remotely:

- **Network Protocol**   Both the target and administrative computer must use at least one common network protocol. Both computers can use TCP/IP, for example, or both can use IPX/SPX. This requirement doesn't prevent you from installing additional protocols, however, that might not be common. You install network protocols using the Network dialog box, which you open from the Control Panel. Click the **Add** button to display the Select Network Component Type dialog box, choose **Protocol** from the list, and click **Add**. Choose the manufacturer from the list on the left and the protocol from the list on the right. Click **OK** to install the protocol.

- **User-Level Security**   Even though some tools don't require user-level security, most do. In particular, you can't use the Registry Editor or System Policy Editor to edit a remote computer's Registry without it. You'll learn how to configure user-level security later in this chapter.

- **Remote Administration**   You enable remote administration in the Passwords Properties dialog box, which you open in the Control Panel. Enabling remote administration lets you specify which users or groups have the right to administer the workstation. You'll learn more about enabling remote administration later in this chapter.

- **Microsoft Remote Registry Service**   This service provides RPC support for the Registry, which allows the Registry Editor on the administrative computer to make calls to the Registry API on the remote computer. You'll learn how to install this service, which is at the heart of remote administration when it involves the Registry, later in this chapter.

- **File and Printer Sharing Service**   This is not an absolute requirement for remote administration, but some tools won't work without it. Note that you must install the File and Printer Sharing Service for Microsoft Networks or the File and Printer Sharing Service for NetWare Networks, whichever is appropriate. Installing the File and Printer Sharing service is easier than installing a protocol. Open the Network dialog box from the Control Panel and click the **File and Printer Sharing** button. Select whether you want to share files and whether you want to share printers. Click **OK** to save your changes.

Remote Administration

To enable remote administration on a computer, follow these steps on that computer:

1. Open the Passwords Properties dialog box from the Control Panel, and click the Remote Administration tab. You see the dialog box shown in Figure 13.1.

Figure 13.1   You'll see a different dialog box if this computer is using share-level security.

2. Select **Enable remote administration of this server** to enable remote administration. This enables the remaining controls in the dialog box, which are different depending on whether the computer uses user-level or share-level security:

   ■ **User-Level**   Windows 98 gives the Domain Admins group on a Windows NT network or the Admin account on a NetWare network initial rights to administer the computer. To add a new group or users to the list, click **Add**.

   ■ **Share-Level**   In the space provided, type a password that an administrator must know before Windows 98 allows him to administer the computer remotely.

3. Close the Passwords Properties dialog box to save your changes. Windows 98 doesn't require you to restart the computer.

NOTE: When you enable user-level security, Windows 98 automatically enables remote administration and adds the Domain Admins group to the list of administrators on a Windows NT network or the Admin account on a NetWare 4.0 network. Thus, computers using user-level security probably already have remote administration enabled for the network's administrators. Note that user-level security requires either an NT or NetWare server to validate credentials.

After setting up remote administration on a computer, you'll notice a few special, hidden shares. You can access any of the following shares by launching the UNC path to the share from the Run dialog box:

C$, D$, and so on	Provides shares for each non-removable drive on the workstation's computer. You can browse these with Explorer.
ADMIN$	Gives full access to the folder in which Windows 98 is installed.
IPC$	Provides a channel for inter-process communication between two computers. IPC$ remains hidden, and you can't browse it.

Microsoft Remote Registry Service

Enabling the Microsoft Remote Registry service is different from enabling remote administration. Remote administration is useful to inspect the files and shares on a remote computer, but it doesn't give you access to the other computer's Registry. Access to the Registry is required if you want to use tools such as the Registry Editor, System Monitor, or System Policy Editor. You must enable Remote Administration before you can use the Microsoft Remote Registry service, though, so I hope you didn't skip the preceding section. The Microsoft Remote Registry service has a few requirements before you can enable it:

- The network must have a security provider: NT domains and NetWare servers are equally suitable.
- Both your computer and the computer you're administering must have remote administration enabled. The preceding section describes how to enable it on each workstation.
- Both computers must use user-level security.

Shares whose names end with a dollar sign ($) are invisible. That is, they don't show up in Network Neighborhood. You can create hidden shares, which other users can connect to only if they know the exact name, by appending a dollar sign to the end of any share when you name it using the Share dialog box.

Figure 13.2   The contents of this dialog box come from the INF file contained in the folder that you pointed Windows 98 to in the previous step.

You have to install the Microsoft Remote Registry service on both the target and administrative computers. The following steps describe how to do so:

1. Open the Network dialog from the Control Panel.

2. Click **Add** to display the list of network components. Select **Service** from this list, and click **Add**. Windows 98 may pause a bit while it builds the driver information database. Then you'll see the Select Network Service dialog box.

3. Click **Have Disk** to locate the Microsoft Remote Registry service on your Windows 98 CD-ROM. The Remote Registry service isn't a part of the Windows 98 source files; thus you'll point Windows 98 to a different folder on the CD-ROM.

4. In the space provided in the Copy Manufacturer's Files From dialog box, type `d:\tools\reskit\netadmin\remotreg`, where *d* is the drive letter representing the CD-ROM. Click **OK** to continue. You see the Select Network Service dialog box, shown in Figure 13.2.

5. Select **Microsoft Remote Registry** from the list, and click **OK**.

6. Close the Network dialog box. Windows 98 copies the appropriate files to your computer. Restart your computer when prompted.

Enabling Remote Administration via Setup Scripts

Remote administration isn't practical if you're physically enabling it on each computer. A better alternative is to plan well ahead and enable remote administration as you roll out Windows 98. You do so with custom setup scripts.

The Windows 98 CD-ROM comes with a program called Microsoft Batch 98 that you use to build a script. A script is an INF file that specifies the settings that Setup uses when installing the operating system. You can specify as few or as many settings as you like. After creating the script, you can push it to the user via his logon script, or you can have the user launch the setup program with the script as its only command line argument. You'll find Batch 98 and a variety of documentation about this program in \Tools\Reskit\Deploy on the CD-ROM.

To enable remote administration using a setup script, add the lines shown in Listing 13.1 to the Msbatch.inf file that the Batch Editor creates. If the sections you see in this listing already exist within the Msbatch.inf file, merely add the settings you see in this file to those sections. Set `Security` to either `domain` or `server`, enabling user-level security, and set `PassThroughAgent` to the name of the domain or server providing validation for user-level security. `Server_Domain_Username` indicates the group or account that has administrative rights on the computer.

Listing 13.1 **Enabling Remote Administration in a Setup Script**

```
[Install]
AddReg=Remote.Admin

[Remote.Admin]
HKLM,"Security\Access\Admin\Remote",
➥%Server_Domain_Username%,1,ff,00

[Network]
Security=domain ¦ server
PassThroughAgent=provider
services=remotereg

[strings]
Server_Domain_Username="server\account"
```

SEE ALSO

➤ Chapter 15, "Script, REG, and INF Files," contains more information about creating Msbatch.inf and manually updating it to modify the Registry.

Batch 98 is one part of the automated installation process. First you use Batch 98 to create a file called Msbatch.inf. Then you copy Msbatch.inf and the Windows 98 source files to a network share accessible by everyone installing Windows 98. You can allow users to start the installation on their own, or you can push the installation to the user in his login script or via an email message. The *Microsoft Windows 98 Resource Kit*, published by Microsoft Press, contains more information about automated installations.

Connecting to a Remote Computer's Registry

Having met the requirements for the target and administrative computers, remote administration is straightforward. You use tools you're already familiar with, but you must first connect to the remote computer. The following list describes the tools you'll learn about in this section:

- **Registry Editor**   Use this tool to make changes to the remote computer's Registry directly.

- **System Policies Editor**   Use this tool to make changes to the remote computer's Registry using policy templates.

- **Performance Monitor**   Use this tool to monitor performance measurements stored in the remote computer's Registry.

- **Net Watcher**   Use this tool to monitor user and administrative shares on a remote computer.

You can access most of these tools via Network Neighborhood. Right-click any computer in the Network Neighborhood folder, choose **Properties**, and click the Tools tab. Click **Net Watcher** to open the computer in Net Watcher. Click **System Monitor** to monitor the remote computer's performance. Click **Administer** to access the remote computer's file system in Windows Explorer.

Changing Multiple Registries at Once

To administer a Windows 98 orkstation remotely, you must log onto the administrative computer using an account name that has administrative privileges on the remote computer. Your account name can be explicitly listed in the remote computer's Passwords Properties dialog box, or it can be implicitly implied by one of the groups given administrative privileges in this dialog box. In other words, the name you used to log onto your computer must jibe with a name explicitly or implicitly implied on the Remote Administration tab of the Passwords Properties dialog box on the user's computer.

Using the Registry Editor to change values on multiple computers at one time is not very convenient, particularly if you're changing values on a large number of computers at one time. Multi-Remote Registry Change is a useful program that allows you to change a value on any number of computers at one time.

Here's how it works. You select the computers you want to change from the left pane of the program's window. The program gets this list from the network's browse list. On the right side of the program's window, you specify the value you want to change. Then you turn Multi-Remote Registry Change loose as it changes that value on each networked computer you chose.

Note that this is different from using the System Policy Editor with a group of computers on the network. You use the System Policy Editor to create a Config.pol file that Windows 98 downloads from the network and loads into the user's Registry each time the user logs onto his computer. It doesn't permanently change the Registry. Also, the System Policy Editor limits you to a predefined set of Registry values you can change unless you create custom policy templates. Multi-Remote Registry Change makes permanent changes to every computer you specify, and it lets you change any Registry setting.

Does this utility sound right up your alley? If so, see Chapter 11, "Tweak UI and Other Registry Programs," which describes how to download, install, and use this program.

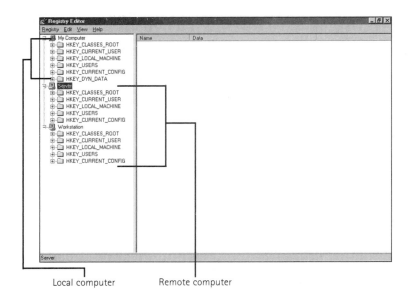

Local computer   Remote computer

Figure 13.3   You can connect to more than one Registry at a time.

Registry Editor

Browsing and making changes to a remote computer's Registry requires that you install the Microsoft Remote Registry service on both the target and administrative computers. Doing so also requires that you set up user-level security and enable remote administration on the remote computer.

To connect to a remote computer's Registry, choose **Registry**, **Connect Network Registry**. Then type the name of the remote computer or click **Browse** to select a computer on the network. You see your computer and the remote computer in the Registry Editor, as shown in Figure 13.3.

After you've connected to the remote computer's Registry, everything works as usual. For example, you can add and remove Registry keys, and you can add, remove, and change value entries. Just make sure that you're selecting keys and value entries on the proper computer. Otherwise, you might change a Registry key on your own computer when you really intended to change a key on the remote computer.

SEE ALSO

➤ For more information about using the Registry Editor, see Chapter 3, "Using the Windows 98 Registry Editor."

Changing settings in a remote computer's Registry is no less dangerous than changing settings in your own Registry. Windows 98 implements no Registry security whatsoever. Thus, the remote user's entire Registry is at your disposal. Review the precautions you learned in Chapter 1, "Inside the Windows 98 Registry," before making any changes to another user's Registry.

System Policy Editor

Since the System Policy Editor changes the Registry just the same as the Registry Editor, it has the same requirements. You must install the Microsoft Remote Registry service on both the target and administrative computers. Doing so also requires that you set up user-level security and enable remote administration on the remote computer.

To launch System Policy Editor, choose **Start**, **Programs**, **Accessories**, **System Tools**, **System Policy Editor**. Figure 13.4 shows you what the Policy Editor looks like. The background window is the Policy Editor itself. The foreground window, which pops up when you double-click one of the icons in the Policy Editor, contains the actual policies for the selected user or computer. To connect to a remote computer, choose **File**, **Connect**. Type the name of the computer to which you want to connect, and click **OK**.

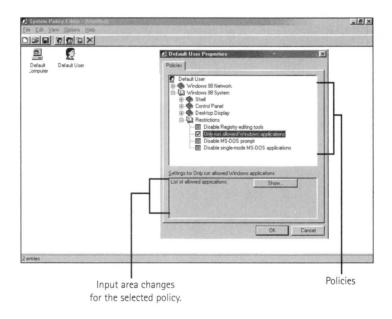

Input area changes
for the selected policy.

Policies

Figure 13.4   If the remote computer uses user profiles, you'll see an icon for each user who logs onto that computer.

The System Policy Editor isn't part of Windows 98's source files; thus the setup program doesn't install it by default. You find it on the Windows 98 CD-ROM, however, in \Tools\Reskit\Netadmin\Poledit. Chapter 14, "Profiles, System Policies, and the Registry," contains more information.

The System Policy Editor works in two modes. You can create a policy file called Config.pol that Windows 98 automatically downloads from the network. Windows 98 merges the Registry settings found in the policy file with the user's existing Registry, overriding the user's settings with the settings contained in the policy file. Alternatively, you can use the System Policy Editor in Registry mode, which allows you to connect to a remote computer's Registry and make immediate changes.

SEE ALSO

➤ See Chapter 14, "Profiles, System Policies, and the Registry," to learn more about applying system policies to groups of users, individual users, or individual computers on the network.

System Monitor

You launch System Monitor by selecting **Start**, **Programs**, **Accessories**, **System Tools**, **System Monitor**. To monitor a remote computer's performance, choose **File**, **Connect** from System Monitor. Type the name of the computer you want to monitor, and click **OK**.

You use System Monitor to monitor the target computer's performance. You can monitor dozens of variables, including file system, CPU, memory, and network-performance variables. You can also watch as many variables as you like at one time. Click the Add button on the toolbar to watch additional variables for this computer. Figure 13.5 shows System Monitor while it's monitoring a remote computer.

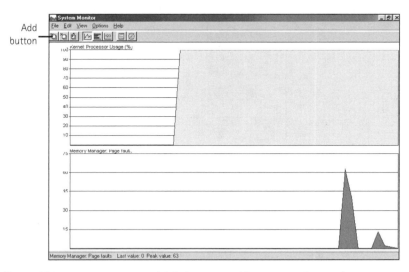

Figure 13.5   You can open multiple instances of System Monitor so that you can monitor more than one computer at a time.

Users connected
to this computer

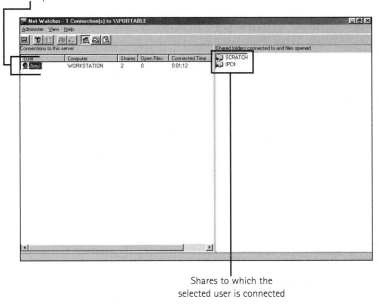

Shares to which the
selected user is connected

Figure 13.6   Net Watcher is the only tool in which you can see the hidden shares IPC$ and ADMIN$.

Net Watcher

Net Watcher has requirements similar to those of the other administration tools. You must be using user-level security and have enabled remote administration. You must also use File and Printer Sharing, but you don't have to install the Microsoft Remote Registry service.

Other Registry programs support remote administration, too. The Norton Registry Editor allows you to connect to a remote computer's Registry, for example, by choosing **Registry, Connect Network Registry**.

Launch Net Watcher, shown in Figure 13.6, by selecting **Start**, **Programs**, **Accessories**, **System Tools**, **Net Watcher**. The left pane shows you each user who is using a resource on this computer. The right pane shows you the shares to which the selected user is connected and the files he has open. Besides inspecting the shares on a remote computer, you can also add or remove shares.

Note these restrictions on using Net Watcher:

- If the administrative computer is using share-level security, it can only monitor other computers that are also using share-level security.

- If the administrative computer is using user-level security, it can monitor other computers regardless of the type of security they're using.

- If the administrative computer is using File and Printer Sharing for NetWare Networks, it can only monitor other computers that are also using the same service.

- You can't close files on a remote computer participating on a NetWare network.

If after enabling remote administration and the Microsoft Remote Registry service, you can't connect to the other computer using System Monitor, make sure that you enabled remote administration and the Microsoft Remote Registry service on both computers. That is, you must enable the Microsoft Remote Registry service on the computer from which you're administering, as well as the computer you are administering. If you've successfully administered a particular computer many times, but recently you weren't able to connect to it, realize that Remote administration works only if someone is logged on to the remote computer. Thus, make sure someone is logged on before you administer the computer.

How Remote Administration Works

RPC (Remote Procedure Calls) is the technology behind remote administration. It allows developers to build distributed applications. An application on one computer can invoke code running on another computer on the network, for example.

The Microsoft Remote Registry service uses RPC. The Registry Editor on the administrative computer calls the Registry API on the remote computer. If you use the Registry Editor to remove a key from another computer's Registry, for example, the Registry Editor running on your computer invokes code on the remote computer that carries out the task. RPC access to a remote computer's Registry is secure and gives the administrator full access to the remote computer's Registry.

Each workstation running the Microsoft Remote Registry service has an RPC client and server. In this case, the administrative computer acts as the RPC client, and each remote computer acts as an RPC server. The client invokes code on the server, and the server returns the result to the client.

Profiles, System Policies, and the Registry

In this chapter:

Understanding User Profiles

A user profile is the user-specific portion of the Registry, User.dat, as well as a number of folders such as Start Menu, Desktop, and Favorites. Storing configuration data separately for each user allows multiple users to log onto Windows 98 with their own individual settings. Enabling user profiles in Windows 98 doesn't change how it stores machine-specific settings. All that still goes in System.dat. Windows 98 provides a few twists on user profiles, too, such as roving profiles and mandatory profiles. Roving profiles make a user's configuration available no matter which machine he uses. Mandatory user profiles create a configuration for the user that he can't change. You'll learn about both twists in this chapter.

Windows 98 supports two different types of user profiles, local and network, which are characterized only by their location:

- **Local** Windows 98 stores local profiles on the workstation. You find a folder for each user in \Windows\Profiles*Name,* where *Name* is the username.

- **Network** Network profiles are also known as *roving* profiles. Windows 98 stores a network profile in the user's home or mail folder, depending on the type of network: Microsoft or NetWare.

Folders in a Profile

As I mentioned, a user profile is more than just a copy of User.dat. It includes a number of folders, too. For local profiles, you find these in \Windows\Profiles*Username*. For network profiles, you find these in the user's home or mail folder on the network:

Application Data	Applications such as the Windows Address Book, QuickLaunch toolbar, and Outlook Express Mail and News store user-specific data in this folder. It doesn't contain documents as much as it contains configuration files.
Desktop	This folder contains the contents of the user's desktop. It includes shortcuts, folders, or other files that the user puts on the desktop.
Cookies	Internet Explorer 4.0 stores cookies in this folder. Web sites use cookies to store data they need between sessions.
History	Internet Explorer 4.0 stores information in this folder about each Web site the user visits so that the user can see a list of recent sites.
NetHood	This folder contains shortcuts that the user adds to the Network Neighborhood folder.
Recent	Some applications store a shortcut for each document you open in this folder. You see these shortcuts on the Start menu's Documents submenu.
Start Menu	This folder is where Windows 98 gets the contents of the Start menu. Anything in \Start Menu is at the top of the Start menu, while anything under \Start Menu\Programs is in the Programs submenu.

SEE ALSO

➤ See Chapter 1, "Inside the Windows 98 Registry," to learn more about User.dat and System.dat.

➤ See Chapter 9, "Customizing the Windows 98 Desktop," to learn about the relationship between these folders and the Registry.

How Windows 98 Chooses Profiles

The best way to understand how user profiles work is to take a look at the process that Windows 98 uses to locate the profile each time a user logs onto the operating system. Windows 98 looks in the Registry at `HKEY_LOCAL_MACHINE\Software\Microsoft\Windows\CurrentVersion\Profile List` to determine if the user has a local profile. Then it looks for a user profile in the user's home or mail folder on the network. Which profile Windows 98 chooses depends on a number of criteria:

■ **Newer Network Profile** If the network profile is more current than the local profile, or the user doesn't have a local profile, Windows 98 copies the user profile from the network to the local profile and loads User.dat into the Registry.

■ **Newer Local Profile** If the local profile is more current than the network profile, Windows 98 uses the local profile and updates the network profile when the user logs off the operating system. This means that the user can still log onto an undocked portable computer and use the local profile, and Windows 98 will update the network profile the next time the user connects to the network.

■ **Unavailable Network Server** If the server isn't available to validate the user's credentials, Windows 98 uses the local profile, if it's available, and updates the network profile the next time the user logs onto the network.

■ **No Profile Available** If the user doesn't have a local or network profile, Windows 98 creates a new profile using the default configuration.

Windows 98 allows a user to log onto multiple workstations. With regard to user profiles, this creates some confusion. Windows 98 updates the network profile each time the user logs off. If the user logs onto two different workstations, the network profile reflects the machine on which he last logged off. In other words, Windows 98 doesn't merge changes to a user profile when the user is working on two different computers.

Note: WhenWindows 98 copies the user's profile to the network, it doesn't copy any folders or documents in the Desktop folder, but it does copy shortcuts. Documents and folders are therefore only part of the local profile, not the network profile.

Enabling Local User Profiles

You can enable user profiles individually on each Windows 98 workstation, you can enable them using a custom setup script, or you can use the System Policy Editor, which you'll learn about later in this chapter. You enable user profiles locally using the Passwords Properties dialog box. Open it from the Control Panel. As well as enabling user profiles, the Passwords Properties dialog box lets you determine how much information to include in the profile. You can choose whether to include the contents of the Desktop and Network Neighborhood folders, for example. Here's how to enable user profiles in Windows 98:

1. Open the Password Properties dialog box from the Control Panel, and click the User Profiles tab. You see the dialog box shown in Figure 14.1.

2. Select **Users can customize their preferences and desktop settings**.

3. Choose how much content you want to include in each user profile under **User profile settings**. You can choose to include the Desktop, Network Neighborhood, and Start Menu folders.

4. Close the Passwords Properties dialog box and restart the computer. Windows 98 will use the configuration data that existed before you enabled profiles to create the profile when a new user logs onto the operating system.

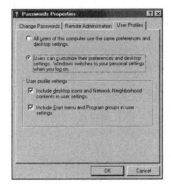

Figure 14.1   The User Profiles tab of the Passwords Properties dialog box.

TIP: If you're using network profiles, make sure that Windows 98 can accurately determine whether the network or local profile is more current by keeping the clock current. The easiest way to do so is to add the command net time *server* /set /y (where *server* is the name of a server on the network) to the user's login script. This command causes Windows 98 to synchronize the clock with the server.

TIP: When Windows 98 enables user profiles, it creates a value entry called UserProfiles under HKEY_LOCAL_MACHINE\Network\Logon and sets its value to 1.

Windows 98 provides an alternative means to enable user profiles—the Enable Multi-user Settings Wizard, which acts as a portal to Windows 98 user administration. Open the Enable Multi-user Settings dialog box by double-clicking the Users icon from the Control Panel. This wizard walks you through the process step by step. You provide the user's credentials, which are the username and password, and then you set options that indicate what the user profile contains:

- **Desktop folder and Documents menu**
- **Start menu**
- **Favorites folder**
- **Downloaded Web pages**
- **My Documents folder**

The primary differences between the Enable Multi-user Settings Wizard and the Passwords Properties dialog box are that you can use the wizard to create a new user profile during a work session, and you can customize the contents of each user profile individually. Note that you don't have to have any sort of *administrative* privileges to create profiles using this wizard. Any user can use it to create profiles as long as that capability isn't disabled via system policies.

Enabling Profiles on a Network

Enabling user profiles on a network allows users to log onto different computers with their own settings. This is called *roving profiles,* and it allows the user to log onto different computers with familiar settings. To support network profiles, Windows 98 and the network must meet certain requirements:

- **32-bit networking client**   You must use 32-bit networking clients on each Windows 98 workstation.
- **Support for long filenames**   The network must support long filenames. If it doesn't, Windows 98 copies only User.dat to the server, not the remaining folders in the profile.
- **Home folders on the network**   Each user must have a home folder on a Microsoft network or a MAIL*user*_ID folder on a Novell NetWare network.

> **TIP:** A good way to tighten security in Windows 98 is to prevent new users from logging onto the operating system. Then you use the Enable Multi-user Settings Wizard to add users individually. You must require validation from a security provider, as described in Chapter 13, "Security and Remote Administration," so that users can't circumvent the Logon dialog box.

- **Primary network logon** You must specify a primary network logon in the Network dialog box. Windows 98 stores the network version of the profile on that server.

- **Hard disk organization** Each workstation must have a similar organization if you want the user to be able to log onto multiple workstations with the same configuration. In particular, make sure you install Windows in the same folder on every machine.

The following sections provide more specific information about enabling network profiles on each type of server.

Windows NT Networks

To use profiles with a Windows NT network, you must complete the following tasks on each Windows 98 workstation:

- Install the Client for Microsoft Networks.
- Enable user profiles, as you just learned how to do.
- Set the primary network logon to Client for Microsoft Networks.
- Assign a home folder for each user on the server.

NetWare Networks

To use profiles with a NetWare network, you must complete the following tasks on each Windows 98 workstation:

- Install the Client for NetWare Networks.
- Enable user profiles, as you just learned how to do.
- Set the primary network logon to Client for NetWare Networks.
- Make sure that each user has a home folder if the user is logging onto the network with Novell Directory Services (NDS). Otherwise, if the user logs on in bindery mode, Windows 98 stores the profile in the user's mail folder.

NOTE: You can put each user's home folder in \Winnt\Profiles, but you must explicitly configure the location of each profile in the User Manager for Domains. I recommend that you store each user's home folder on a separate volume so that you don't have to worry about running short of disk space on the boot disk.

TIP: If you want to prevent a user from logging onto a computer with the network version of his user profile, you can prevent Windows 98 from using it by adding the DWORD value entry called UserHomeDirectory to HKEY_LOCAL_MACHINE\Network\Logon, leaving the value empty.

Other Networks

Windows 98 supports network profiles on other types of networks, even peer-to-peer networks. Since the network client probably won't support network profiles, however, you must use an alternative configuration to accomplish the same thing. Here's how to force Windows 98 to support network profiles even though the networking client doesn't:

1. Create a folder on the network using an arbitrary name such as Users and share it, giving all users read-only access to it. Below that, create a home folder for each user and give each person full access to his home folder. You can use the user's logon name for each folder, or you can use any arbitrary folder name, such as User0001.

2. Create a text file named Profiles.ini that looks similar to the file shown in Listing 14.1. Each line under [Profiles] is named after the user's logon name, and the value you assign to it is the UNC path to the user's home folder. Copy this file to the folder you created in step 1. If you called the top-level folder Users, copy Profiles.ini to Users on the server.

3. Disable network profiles on each workstation, as you learned how to do in the sidenote called "Disabling Network Profiles on a Workstation." That is, add the DWORD value entry called UserHomeDirectory to HKEY_LOCAL_MACHINE\Network\Logon, leaving the value empty.

4. Add a new string value entry called SharedProfileList to HKEY_LOCAL_MACHINE\Network\Logon. Assign the UNC path of Profiles.ini to this value. The path should be the root folder that you created in step 1. If you created a folder called Users and shared it using the same name, for instance, you would assign \\Server\Users\Profiles.ini to SharedProfileList, where Server is the name of the server containing the folder.

When the user logs onto Windows 98, Windows 98 looks in Profiles.ini for an entry that matches the user's logon name. If it finds one, it uses the profile indicated in the file. Otherwise, it uses the user's local profile or creates a new profile for the user.

Listing 14.1 **Profiles.ini**

```
[Profiles]
Jerry=\\server\users\jerry
Bones=\\server\users\bones
Turbo=\\server\users\turbo
Corky=\\server\users\corky
```

Enabling Mandatory User Profiles

A mandatory user profile is a configuration that Windows 98 uses every time the user logs onto the operating system. The user can change the configuration during the session, but Windows 98 doesn't save any changes to it; thus the user starts with the same configuration every time. You can create mandatory profiles for use on Microsoft or Novell networks. Here's how:

1. Enable user profiles on the workstation.

2. Create a profile on a Windows 98 computer, customizing the user preferences as required.

3. Copy the folders and files you want to include in the profile to the appropriate folder, as described in the earlier section, "Enabling Profiles on a Network." Make sure you copy User.dat, too.

4. Rename User.dat to User.man, indicating that this is a mandatory user profile.

When Windows 98 copies the profile from the network, it takes notice of User.man, copying it to the user's profile as User.dat. Windows 98 saves changes to the local User.dat, but it doesn't copy this file back to the server when the user logs off the computer. This ensures that the user starts with the same configuration every time he logs onto the computer.

Disabling User Profiles

User profiles aren't without problems. First, they affect the computer's performance ever so slightly. Second, user profiles add more complexity to Windows 98's configuration. Not only does the user have to keep track of the profile folder in which he'll find his stuff, but Windows 98 and other applications have to do this as well. Some applications don't even recognize user profiles, behaving as though user profiles aren't enabled at all.

Mandatory Profiles Versus System Policies

Mandatory profiles and system policies both let you control the user's preferences. Mandatory profiles work only with the user-specific settings you find in User.dat, and they require that you control every setting in it. System policies work with both configurations, machine-specific and user-specific, and they let you specify exactly which settings you want to control.

In most cases, using system policies to lightly enforce certain settings is the most appropriate choice. Mandatory profiles require the user to pay a performance penalty when he logs onto the computer, and they don't let the user permanently change any user-specific setting, even if it's not one you particularly care about.

If user profiles prove not to be the boon you had hoped, you can remove them, restoring your configuration to its original state. Windows 98 doesn't provide an easy way to do this, however, so you must follow these steps:

1. Restart Windows 98 without logging on. In other words, press Esc when you see the Logon dialog box.

2. Disable user profiles on the User Profiles tab of the Passwords Properties dialog box by choosing **All users of this computer use the same preferences and desktop settings**.

3. Remove `HKEY_LOCAL_MACHINE\Software\Microsoft\Windows\CurrentVersion\ProfileList` from the Registry.

4. Remove \Windows\Profiles.

Windows 98 restores the original settings it was using before you enabled user profiles. You can try copying one of the profiles to \Windows, but chances are it won't work properly, because paths to the profile are stored in User.dat.

Understanding System Policies

System policies let you override certain machine- and user-specific settings. You put policies in a file called Config.pol and place it on the network server specified in the user's primary network logon, and Windows 98 updates the Registry with the contents of this file. System policies are the most underused but most powerful administration tool that Windows 98 provides:

■ You can restrict the user in countless ways, preventing him from modifying the Active Desktop, for example, or from running certain programs.

■ You can apply policies to individual users or groups of users as defined on a Microsoft or Novell network.

■ You can use the policy templates that Windows 98 provides or create your own for any application that uses the Windows 98 Registry.

NOTE: System Policies are the most underutilized administrative tool that Windows 98 provides. Even though administrators can ease their burden considerably, to their detriment most continue to ignore this valuable resource. Enable user profiles and take charge of your organization's computing resources.

ADM, POL, and the Registry

To understand how to implement system policies, you must understand how policies work. Three different components are responsible for making them work the way they do:

- **Templates**   Templates are text files with an ADM file extension that describe the Registry values you want to set. Think of templates as scripts that define forms and relate each field on that form to a value in the Registry.

- **Policy Files**   These are binary files with a POL file extension that you create with the System Policy Editor. You open a template in the System Policy Editor, define values for one or more policies defined in the templates, and save the result as a POL file. Each item in the POL file is an ordered entry with a name and a value, just like the Registry.

- **Registry**   Each time Windows 98 starts and loads a policy file, it overwrites values in the Registry with values it finds in the policy file. The values in the policy file always supersede the values in the Registry.

How Windows 98 Loads Policies

As with user profiles, understanding how Windows 98 loads system policies helps you understand how to configure them. Here's a description of that process:

1. **User policies**   Windows 98 looks for a policy that has the same name as the user's. If Windows 98 finds a user policy, it loads the settings from it. Windows 98 always loads the default user policy.

2. **Group policies**   Windows 98 creates a list of any groups to which the user belongs and looks for policies that have the same name as each group. Windows 98 downloads groups that have the lowest priority first and the highest priority last, ensuring that higher-priority groups always overwrite lower-priority groups. Windows 98 doesn't copy group policies if it finds a user policy for the user.

3. **Machine policies**   Windows 98 looks for a policy that matches the computer's name and downloads the settings it finds in it. It always loads the default computer policies, whether or not it finds a policy for that computer.

> TIP: You can prevent users from accessing the Registry by enabling the **Disable Registry editing tools** policy. Doing so helps ensure that the policies you define stay the way you defined them.

Enabling System Policies on the Network

You must configure each workstation in order to use system policies. You can complete these tasks manually, or you can perform them as part of a setup script:

- Install the System Policy Editor on the administrator's Windows 98 workstation.

- Enable user profiles on each Windows 98 workstation with which you want to use policies. If you fail to enable user profiles, system policies will work only with machine-specific configuration data.

- Install group policy support on every Windows 98 workstation that you're configuring for policies.

- Create policy files, as you learn how to do in this chapter. The policy file can include default user and default machine, user- and machine-specific, and group policies.

- Copy the policy file, Config.pol, into the Netlogon folder of a Windows NT server or the SYS:PUBLIC directory of a NetWare server. The Netlogon share is typically \Winnt\System32\Repl\Import\Scripts, which is the same folder in which you stash login scripts.

SEE ALSO

➤ Chapter 15, "Script, REG, and INF Files," contains more information about building custom setup scripts. You do so using the Batch 98 utility that you find on the Windows 98 CD-ROM. Install it from \Tools\Reskit\Batch.

> **CAUTION:** System policies have weaknesses that allow an average user to get around them. Here are a few examples. (I'm sure a clever user could come up with more ways to circumvent policies.) The user can prevent Windows 98 from loading the policy file by booting to Safe Mode or by not logging onto the network. Here's another one: Even though you enabled the **Disable Registry editing tools** policy, users can still edit the Registry, because this policy requires the cooperation of each Registry program. A variety of shareware Registry editors are available that do not honor this restriction. Not only that, but a user can still change the Registry using INF and REG files, as described in Chapter 15, "Script, REG, and INF Files."

Automatic Downloading

Windows 98 automatically downloads the policy file from the Netlogon folder of a Windows NT server or the SYS:PUBLIC directory of a NetWare server. Make sure you put the policy file on the server chosen as the primary network logon in the Network dialog box. The following instructions show you how to configure Windows 98 so that it automatically downloads system policies from the network:

1. Set the primary network logon to Client for Microsoft Networks or Client for NetWare Networks, depending on your network.

2. Copy the policy file Config.pol to the Netlogon folder of a Windows NT server or the SYS:PUBLIC directory of a NetWare server. Make sure you copy Config.pol to the user's preferred server if you're using a NetWare network.

Manual Downloading

If you want to control the location of the policy file, or if the networking client you're using doesn't support policies, as is the case with most 16-bit clients, you must configure Windows 98 to manually download policies. You must also configure Windows 98 to manually download policies if you're using a policy file stored locally instead of on the network. Here's how to configure Windows 98 to manually download a policy file:

1. Start the System Policy Editor and choose **File**, **Open Registry**. Alternatively, choose **File**, **Connect** to configure a remote computer, type the name of the computer in the space provided, and close the Connect dialog box.

2. Open the Local Computer icon, or the icon representing the remote computer, and expand the **Windows 98 Network** item, followed by the **Update** item.

3. Select **Remote update**, and type the UNC path and filename of the policy file in **Path for manual update**.

4. Save your changes to the Registry and close the System Policy Editor.

Alternatively, you can configure a computer that's automatically downloading policies to manually download policies by following these steps:

1. Open the network copy of Config.pol in the System Policy Editor.

2. Open the Default Computer icon, and expand the **Windows 98 Network** item, followed by **Update**.

3. Select the **Remote update** checkbox, select **Manual** in **Update Mode**, and type the UNC path and filename of the system policy file in **Path for manual update**.

4. Save your changes to Config.pol and close the System Policy Editor.

Installing the System Policy Editor

As I've hinted, you use the System Policy Editor to read template files (ADM), specify settings, and create policy files (POL). The System Policy Editor isn't part of the Windows 98 source files. You have to install it from \Tools\Reskit\Netadmin\Poledit on the Windows 98 CD-ROM. Microsoft suggests that you copy these files to your computer, but I recommend that you follow these steps instead:

1. Open the Add/Remove Programs Properties dialog box, and click the Windows Setup tab.

2. Click **Have Disk**, and type the path to the \Tools\Reskit\Netadmin\Poledit folder on the Windows 98 CD-ROM. Close the Install from Disk dialog box, and you see the Have Disk dialog box, shown in Figure 14.2. This dialog box contains an entry for the System Policy Editor.

3. Select **System Policy Editor** from the list. If you want to install support for group policies, also select **Group Policies**. Click **Install**. Windows 98 copies the files to the computer. Insert the Windows 98 CD-ROM if asked to.

Start the System Policy Editor by choosing **Start**, **Programs**, **Accessories**, **System Tools**, **System Policy Editor**.

If you intend to use group policies, you must also install support for group policies on each Windows 98 workstation, including the administrator's. Use the Add/Remove Programs Properties dialog box to install group policies, which you find under **Start, Programs, Accessories, System Tools**. Windows 98 copies Grouppol.dll to \Windows\System and updates the Registry accordingly. Note that you can also install support for group policies using the preceding instructions by choosing **Group Policies** from the list.

Figure 14.2   This dialog box shows the components it finds in all the INF files contained in the folder you specified.

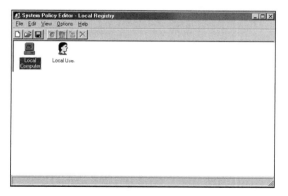

Figure 14.3 Local represents the local computer. When editing a remote computer, you see the name of the computer and user.

Using the System Policy Editor

You can use the System Policy Editor in two different modes:

- **Registry mode** In this mode, you edit a local or remote computer's Registry directly. You don't create a policy file. This is similar to using the Registry Editor, except that you're editing the Registry using a template, which causes much less concern about human error. Choose **File**, **Open Registry** to open the local computer's Registry, or choose **File**, **Connect** to open a remote computer's Registry. Figure 14.3 shows what the System Policy Editor looks like in Registry mode.

- **Policy File mode** In this mode, you create a policy file from a template. You copy the policy file (POL) to the network, as you learned earlier in this chapter. Windows 98 automatically downloads the POL file to the user's computer when he logs onto the network. Choose **File**, **New Policy** to create a new policy file, or choose **File**, **Open Policy** to open an existing policy file.

NOTE: Use Registry mode when you're using the System Policy Editor on a single computer. This is good as a customization tool, for instance. You should use policy mode if you're using the System Policy Editor on a network and you're configuring settings for one or more users on the network. You can use policy mode on an individual computer, but doing so adds needless complexity to the startup process.

Each option you see in the System Policy Editor has three states: selected, cleared, and not defined. Each time you click an option, it toggles between these three states.

- **Selected**   Indicated with a checkmark, this means that the selected policy will appear in the file and will be enabled.

- **Cleared**   Indicated with a clear checkbox, this means that the selected policy will appear in the file and will be disabled.

- **Not Defined**   Indicated with a grayed checkbox, this means that the selected policy will not appear in the file.

Be careful that you don't clear an option that you really intend to leave out of the policy. Clearing an option means that you want to include it in the policy file but disable it on the user's computer. If you clear the Enable User Profiles policy, for instance, Windows 98 won't let the user enable user profiles on that computer. To allow the user to choose, you must gray out this policy.

SEE ALSO
➤ See Chapter 13, "Security and Remote Administration," to learn how to enable remote administration, which is required in order to edit a remote computer's Registry using the System Policy Editor in Registry mode.

Policies for Default Users and Computers

Policies for the default user and default computer apply to every user and every computer. To define default policies, follow these steps:

1. Open the policy file, perhaps Config.pol, in the System Policy Editor. Create a new policy file if necessary.

Figure 14.4   Remember that the System Policy Editor stores cleared options in the policy file as disabled. If you want to omit a policy, gray it out.

2. Open the Default User icon to display the Default User Properties dialog box, shown in Figure 14.4. Select the policies you want to include in the policy file, and then close the dialog box.

3. Open the Default Computer icon. You see the Default Computer Properties dialog box, which is similar to the preceding dialog box. Select the policies you want to include in the policy file, and then close the dialog box.

Policies for Users, Computers, or Groups

Before defining policies for groups, make sure you're ready. You define policies for groups that are defined on a Windows NT or NetWare sever. You can't create new groups in the System Policy Editor; you must rely on the groups reported by the server, so plan and define your groups ahead of time. Also note that you must install support for group policies on every Windows 98 workstation, as described in the earlier section "Installing the System Policy Editor." To keep things simple, consider installing this as part of your setup script when you roll out Windows 98.

You learned how to edit policies in the previous couple of sections. Editing policies for specific users, computers, or groups is no different, except that you open a different icon. Here's how to do each:

- **User**   To add a user to a policy file, choose **Edit**, **Add User**. Type the name of the user in the space provided, and click **OK**. You can browse a list of names on the network by clicking **Browse**.

- **Computer**   To add a computer to a policy file, choose **Edit**, **Add Computer**. Type the name of the computer in the space provided, and click **OK**. You can browse a list of computers by clicking **Browse**.

- **Group**   To add a group to the policy file, choose **Edit**, **Add Group**. Type the name of the group in the space provided, and click **OK**. You can browse a list of groups by clicking **Browse**.

Windows 98 handles the situation in which a user might belong to more than one group. You prioritize groups so that the policies in a higher-priority group always overwrite policies in a lower-priority group. Choose **Options**, **Group Priority** to display the Group Priority dialog box, shown in Figure 14.5. Move groups up and down in the list to change their priority, and then close the Group Priority dialog box to save your changes.

TIP: Make your life easier by defining as much as you can for the default user and computer. Then, define user- and group-specific policies to handle specific needs. That way default policies define the rules while user and group policies define the exceptions.

CAUTION: Defining policies for a particular user prevents Windows 98 from applying any group policies to that user. This might be a nasty surprise if you think that Windows 98 still applies your group policies to a user after defining user policies.

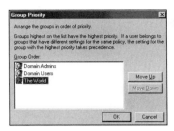

Figure 14.5 The top of the list is a higher priority than the bottom.

Using Custom Policy Templates

Policy templates define the input forms and relationships between each input field and a particular field in the Registry. Most of the policies you need are in Windows.adm and Common.adm, which Windows 98 installs in the System Policy Editor by default. (Common.adm is actually void of any policies, but Windows 98 installs it anyway.) You find these files and more in \Windows\Inf. Table 14.1 describes the remaining template files that you can use with the System Policy Editor.

Table 14.1 **Policy Templates in \Windows\Inf**

File	Description
Chat.adm	Microsoft Comic Chat
Conf.adm	NetMeeting
Inetres.adm	Internet Explorer
Inetset.adm	Internet Explorer
Oem.adm	Outlook Express
Pws.adm	Personal Web Server
Shellm.adm	Additional shell policies
Subsm.adm	Internet Explorer Channels

You can also create your own policy templates if the ADM files that Windows 98 provides don't do the job for you. For example, if you have a custom-built application that you want to control, create a template for that program. The program must rely on the Registry for its customization data, but most programs do these days. Here's how to add a custom policy template or one of the templates you learned about in Table 14.1 to the System Policy Editor:

TIP: Shellm.adm is one of the most useful policy templates. This policy file contains settings that control Internet Explorer, the Active Desktop, and even the Start menu. Windows 98 copies it to \Windows\Inf but doesn't install it in the System Policy Editor; thus, you must add it to the System Policy Editor if you want to use it.

1. Close the open policy file.

2. Choose **Options**, **Policy Template**. You see the Policy Template Options dialog box, which lists all the policy templates you've added to the editor.

3. Click **Add**, specify the template's path and filename, and close the Open Template File dialog box to add a template.

4. Close the Policy Template Options dialog box to start working with the additional template. This file doesn't replace your existing templates; it merely adds to the list of available options.

Troubleshooting System Policies

Before you assume the worst, double-check the following three items, which represent the most common reasons for policies failing to work properly:

- Make sure that Config.pol is in the Netlogon folder on a Microsoft network or in the PUBLIC directory on the SYS: volume of a NetWare server.

- On a Microsoft network, make sure that the primary network logon points to the server on which you've put the policy file. On a NetWare network, make sure that Preferred Server is set to the NetWare server on which you've placed the policy file.

- Make sure that the user can log onto the network properly and has access to the network directory that contains the policy file.

If group policies don't work for an individual user or group, check the following:

- Make sure that the user is really a member of the group for which you've defined the policies.

- Make sure that you haven't defined a user-specific policy for the user that overrides default and group policies.

- Make sure that you've installed support for group policies, as described in the section "Installing the System Policy Editor."

- Make sure that you've enabled user profiles on the user's computer. See the section "Enabling Local User Profiles."

NOTE: The *Microsoft Windows 98 Resource Kit,* published by Microsoft Press, describes how to create policy templates using the appropriate keywords. You can find an online version of the resource kit on the Windows 98 CD-ROM in \Tools\Reskit\Help.

Must-See Policies

The best way to find out what policies Windows 98 makes available is to open the System Policy Editor and browse. Some policies deserve special mention because they serve very useful purposes in most organizations. The following table is divided into sections, with each section representing a policy template. The first column indicates whether the policies in the second column are machine or user policies. The second column contains the actual policy name, whose purpose is self-evident.

Template	Policy Name
SHELLM.ADM	
User	Desktop Restrictions
	Active Desktop Items
	Start Menu
	Shell
WINDOWS.ADM	
Machine	Disable Windows Update
	Minimum Windows password length
	Require validation from network for Windows access
	Require alphanumeric Windows password
User	Hide Start Menu subfolders
	Disable Shut Down command
	Hide Drives in 'My Computer'
	Hide Network Neighborhood
	Hide all items on Desktop
	Remove 'Run' command
	Remove folders from 'Settings' on Start Menu
	Remove Taskbar from 'Settings' on Start Menu
	Remove 'Find' command
	Restrict Display Control Panel
	Restrict Network Control Panel
	Restrict Passwords Control Panel
	Restrict Printer Settings
	Restrict System Control Panel
	Disable Registry editing tools
	Only run allowed Windows applications
	Disable MS-DOS prompt

Start Menu is the most useful of all Shellm.adm's policies, fulfilling needs that I frequently hear about from administrators. In particular, this policy allows you to enable or disable individual commands on the Start menu. You can remove the **Find** and **Run** commands from the Start menu, for instance, as well as other commands. The **Shell** policy is useful, too, because it allows you to disable shortcut menus in Windows Explorer or restrict the user to using the classic Windows shell.

15

Script, REG, and INF Files

Updating the Registry with REG Files

REG files are the classic method for updating values in the Registry. The main reason is that they are so easy to create using a text editor or the Registry Editor's export feature. Importing REG files is easy, too: Just double-click the file, or right-click it and choose **Merge**.

Listing 15.1 shows a typical REG file. It makes several changes to the Registry, most of which you learned about in Chapter 9, "Customizing the Windows 98 Desktop." The first line always contains REGEDIT4, indicating that the file is a valid Registry Editor file, and the second line must always be blank. The Registry Editor won't import the file if it doesn't begin with REGEDIT4 and a blank line.

The remainder of Listing 15.1 changes various value entries, adding them if they don't already exist. The file is split into three sections, with each Registry key in its own section. The fully qualified name of the key is given between brackets, like this:

[*Keyname*]. A fully qualified key name includes the entire path to a key (such as HKEY_CLASSES_ROOT\txtfile\shell) rather than just a portion of the path (such as txtfile\shell). In this case, the three sections are for the following Registry keys:

HKEY_CURRENT_USER\MyKey

HKEY_LOCAL_MACHINE\Software\Microsoft\Windows\CurrentVersion\Winlogon

HKEY_CURRENT_USER\Control Panel\Desktop

Listing 15.1 **A Sample REG File**

```
REGEDIT4

[HKEY_CURRENT_USER\MyKey]
@="Default Value"

[HKEY_LOCAL_MACHINE\Software\Microsoft\Windows\
➥CurrentVersion\Winlogon]
"DefaultUserName"="Jerry"
"DefaultPassword"="Password"
"AutoAdminLogon"="1"

[HKEY_CURRENT_USER\Control Panel\Desktop]
"ScreenSaveUsePassword"=dword:00000000
"SmoothScroll"=hex:01,00,00,00
```

Under each key in Listing 15.1, you see a list of value entries belonging to that key. Except for default value entries, the name appears in quotation marks. Use an at sign (@) for the default value entry within a key. Obviously, you should include only one default value entry within a single section. The name goes on the left side of the equal sign, as shown, and the value you're assigning to it goes on the right side. The listing shows how to write string, DWORD, and binary values, each of which looks a bit different:

String	"This is a string value"
DWORD	DWORD:00000001
Binary	HEX:FF,00,FF,00,FF,00,FF,00,FF,00,FF,00

NOTE: You must begin every REG file with the keyword REGEDIT4 on the first line, and the second line must be blank. Thereafter, divide the file into sections, with each section containing a Registry key followed by value entries.

String value entries sometimes contain special characters. It's common to include quotes within a command line, such as `Wordpad.exe "%1"`, for example, so that WordPad can open long filenames that contain spaces. I've also seen string value entries that contain linefeeds and carriage returns. The format for REG files makes special provisions for these characters; it's called *escaping*. When you prefix a special character with a backslash, the Registry Editor knows to replace the combination with the actual character that is represented. `\n` represents the newline character, for example, which is an ASCII 10. Table 15.1 describes the special characters that the Registry Editor supports and gives examples.

Table 15.1 **Escape Characters**

Esc	Expanded	Escaped in the REG File	Expanded in the Registry
`\\`	\	`"\\\\Server\\Drive"`	\\Server\Drive
`\"`	"	`"This is \"quoted\""`	This is "quoted"
`\n`	Newline	`"First\nSecond"`	First newline Second
`\r`	Return	`"First\rSecond"`	First return Second

Creating REG Files by Hand

Creating a REG file by hand is easy enough. Create a new text file with a REG extension and follow these steps:

1. Put `REGEDIT4` at the top of the file. This must be the first line in the file. Also, make sure that you insert one blank line between `REGEDIT4` and the first section of the REG file, as shown in Listing 15.1.

2. Add a section for each key that you want to add to or change in the Registry. Put each key name in square brackets, like this: `[Keyname]`. Make sure that you use the fully qualified path to the key, beginning with the root key.

3. Put an entry under each key for each value entry that you want to add or change. Each entry has the form `"Name"=Value`, where *Name* is the name of the value entry you're adding or changing. If you're changing the default value entry, use the at sign (@) for *Name,* without the quotes. *Value* is the value to which you want to set the value entry. Make sure it follows one of the forms shown in Table 15.1.

4. Save your changes to the REG file.

> NOTE: REG files don't have separate syntaxes for adding new entries and changing them. If you specify a key or value entry that doesn't exist, the Registry Editor creates it. If you specify a value entry that doesn't exist, the Registry Editor creates and changes its value. If you specify a value that does exist, the Registry Editor merely changes the existing value.

Creating REG Files Using REGEDIT

Creating REG files by hand seems easy enough, but I don't recommend it. There are entirely too many chances for errors—especially if you're a poor typist. Thus, you should use the Registry Editor if possible. Chapter 3, "Using the Windows 98 Registry Editor," showed you how to export a branch of the Registry to a REG file. For your convenience, however, those instructions are repeated here:

1. In the left pane of the Registry Editor, highlight the key representing the branch you want to export.

2. Choose **Registry, Export Registry File**. The Registry Editor displays the dialog box shown in Figure 15.1.

3. Select **Selected branch**. REGEDIT automatically fills in the key you selected in step 1.

4. Type the filename into which you want the Registry exported in the **File name** box, and click **Save**.

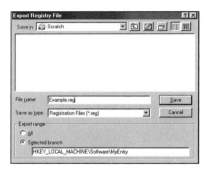

Figure 15.1   If you don't type a file extension, REGEDIT uses the default file extension (REG).

TIP: You can't use a REG file to remove a key from the Registry. If you require this capability, use an INF file or a Windows Scripting Host script. You'll learn how to do both later in this chapter.

TIP: An interesting aspect of REG files is the order in which the Registry Editor writes values under each key. Though you might expect it to write values in alphabetical order by name, it doesn't. The Registry Editor writes values in the order they were created in the Registry. This is a great way to see the order in which values were created under a key. For instance, export HKEY_CURRENT_USER\Control Panel\ Desktop to a REG file, and you can see the order in which the values in this key were created.

There are a couple of issues you should be aware of when using this technique:

- **Trimming**   When you export a key using the Registry Editor, you're exporting all of that key's subkeys and value entries. Thus, you'll need to open the file (right-click it and choose **Edit**) and remove any keys and value entries that you don't want to distribute in the REG file.

- **Editing**   You can change any of the values in the REG file. That is, if you're not satisfied with the settings that you exported from the Registry, you can alter those settings in the REG file before you distribute it. Make sure you stick to the formats you learned earlier in this chapter.

SEE ALSO

➤ Chapter 9, "Customizing the Windows 98 Desktop," describes how to prevent Windows from automatically importing REG files when you double-click them.

➤ Chapter 3, "Using the Windows 98 Registry Editor," tells you more about importing and exporting.

Editing the Registry with INF Files

Windows 98 describes INF files as "setup information" files. This is a much more generic description than Microsoft usually uses for INF files, which is that INF files contain device driver information. In fact, you can put much more in an INF file than device driver information. You can put software setup information in it. More importantly, you can put statements in an INF file that add, change, and remove Registry entries when the user installs the INF file. In that manner, INF files are like scripts, which you'll learn about in the section "Writing Scripts to Update the Registry," but they're much simpler.

Listing 15.2 shows you a complete example of an INF file that adds and removes values from the Registry. It also shows you how to remove an entire key from the Registry. You'll learn how to build INF files such as this in the following sections. For now, try out this INF file using these steps:

1. Create a new text file and type in the contents as shown in Listing 15.1. Save the file to your disk with an INF file extension.

2. Create a new subkey under HKEY_CURRENT_USER called MyKey. Add a few subkeys under this one. This helps demonstrate the line that removes this key.

3. Right-click the INF file, and choose **Install**. Open the Registry Editor to observe the changes.

Listing 15.2 **Editing the Registry with INF Files**

```
[Version]
signature=$CHICAGO$

[DefaultInstall]
AddReg=My.Add.Reg
DelReg=My.Del.Reg

[My.Add.Reg]
HKLM,Software\Microsoft\Windows\CurrentVersion\Winlogon,
➥AutoAdminLogon,0,"0"
HKCU,Control Panel\Desktop,SmoothScroll,1,01,00,00,00
HKCU,Control Panel\Desktop,ScreenSaveUsePassword,1,00,00,
➥00,00

[My.Del.Reg]
HKCU,MyKey
HKLM,Software\Microsoft\Windows\CurrentVersion\Winlogon,
➥DefaultUserName
HKLM,Software\Microsoft\Windows\CurrentVersion\Winlogon,
➥DefaultPassword
```

Creating an INF File

The first section in all INF files is the [Version] section. It's also called a header. For the purpose of editing the Registry, this section will always start with the following two lines. Note that the Class item, which you normally see in INF files, isn't required in order to create a file to edit the Registry. $CHICAGO$ indicates that the INF file is for Windows (Chicago was the code name for Windows 95).

```
[Version]
signature=$CHICAGO$
```

The remaining sections specify the Registry entries you're working with and what you want to do to them. The [DefaultInstall] section points to other sections within the INF file—the AddReg and DelReg sections. Each AddReg and DelReg section contains a list of Registry entries you want to add, change, or remove. You can think of the INF file as a tree with [DefaultInstall] as the trunk, branching out to the AddReg and DelReg sections, which in turn branch out to a list of Registry entries.

NOTE: INF files are complex. Microsoft has created a whole language for INF files, defining intricate rules that link various sections. Most of the statements and sections that programmers use in INF files are irrelevant to the topic at hand. The *Microsoft Windows 98 Resource Kit,* published by Microsoft Press, contains complete documentation for INF files. You'll also find a version of the resource kit on your Windows 98 CD-ROM in \Tools\Reskit\Help.

[DefaultInstall]

The [DefaultInstall] section has two entries: AddReg and DelReg. AddReg indicates the name of the section containing Registry entries you want to add or change. DelReg indicates the name of the section containing Registry entries you want to remove. In most cases, the [DefaultInstall] section of your INF file will look just like the following:

```
[DefaultInstall]
AddReg=My.Add.Reg
DelReg=My.Del.Reg
```

You must type the name of each item (on the left side of each equal sign) exactly as shown. Remember that the keywords AddReg and DelReg have special significance, indicating sections that include Registry entries to add or remove. You can name the section (on the right side) anything you like, however, and you can use periods in the name, as shown in the example. You can also list multiple sections for AddReg and DelReg, as shown here:

```
AddReg=Name1[,Name2[,Name3[,...]]]
DelReg=Name1[,Name2[,Name3[,...]]]
```

The **AddReg** and **DelReg** Sections

For each item you put in the [DefaultInstall] section, you have to create another section. The name of the section will be the value on the right side of each item's equal sign. Continuing the example from the preceding section, you would create two sections, called [My.Add.Reg] and [My.Del.Reg]. Windows 98 adds the items listed in [My.Add.Reg] to the Registry. It removes the items listed in [My.Del.Reg] from the Registry.

Each line within these sections has a similar format, as shown in the following list. You use all the parameters shown if you're adding a value entry. If you're removing a value entry, you use the first three. If you're adding or removing a key, you use the first two.

```
HKEY, Subkey, ValueName, Type, Value
```

HKEY	One of the abbreviations listed in Table 15.2 for the root key.
Subkey	The subkey under the root key, not including the name of the root key.
ValueName	The name of the value entry you're adding. Leaving this item blank implies that you're working with the default value entry.
Type	The type of value entry. Use 0 for a string. Use 1 for binary. Use 0x10001 for DWORD.
Value	The data for the value entry. Use the appropriate format for the type you specified. That is, strings should be in quotation marks. DWORD and binary values should be in hexadecimal notation with each byte separated by a comma.

Table 15.2 **Abbreviations for Root Keys**

Abbreviation	Root Key
HKCR	HKEY_CLASSES_ROOT
HKCU	HKEY_CURRENT_USER
HKLM	HKEY_LOCAL_MACHINE
HKU	HKEY_USERS
HKCC	HKEY_CURRENT_CONFIG
HKDD	HKEY_DYN_DATA

To make things a bit clearer, Table 15.3 shows you several examples. Notice that in a number of the examples I've completely omitted one of the parameters; you see two commas side by side, with no value between them. This has special significance in both the `AddReg` and `DelReg` sections. If you leave out the type, for example, it defaults to string. Omitting the value entry name within an `AddReg` section means you're changing a key's default value entry. Omitting the value entry name within a `DelReg` section means you're removing a key and its subkeys.

Table 15.3 **Examples for the AddReg and DelReg Sections**

Example	Description
`[My.Add.Reg]`	
`HKCU,MyKey,MyValue,0,"String"`	Adds a string value called `MyValue` to `MyKey`, if it doesn't exist, and sets its value to `String`.
`HKCU,MyKey,MyValue,,"String"`	Adds a string value called `MyValue` to `MyKey`, if it doesn't exist, and sets its value to `String`.
`HKCU,MyKey,MyValue,1,77,34,05,20`	Adds a binary value called `MyValue` to `MyKey`, if it doesn't exist, and sets its value to the binary string `77 34 05 20`.
`HKCU,MyKey,,0,"Default Value"`	Sets the default value entry of `MyKey` to the string `Default Value`.
`HKCU,MyKey,,,"Default Value"`	Sets the default value entry of `MyKey` to the string `Default Value`.
`HKCU,MyKey`	Adds the Registry key called `MyKey` without setting any values.
`[My.Del.Reg]`	
`HKCU,MyKey,MyValue`	Removes the value entry called `MyValue` from the key `MyKey`.
`HKCU,MyKey`	Removes `MyKey` and all its subkeys, deleting the entire branch.

NOTE: The order in which you list the `AddReg` and `DelReg` items within `[DefaultInstall]` has no bearing on how Windows 98 processes the INF file. Windows 98 processes the `DelReg` sections first, followed by the `AddReg` sections. You can use this to your advantage to completely remove a Registry key, clearing out all its contents, and then replacing the key with new contents.

Understanding How INF Files Work

In the previous sections, you learned how to create INF files. You'll do better by understanding how they work, however. `HKEY_CLASSES_ROOT\inffile\shell\install\ command` contains the command line that Windows 98 executes when you right-click an INF file and choose **Install**. It looks similar to the command line described in the following list:

```
C:\WINDOWS\rundll.exe setupx.dll,InstallHinfSection
➥DefaultInstall 132 %1
```

`rundll.exe`	A small program that invokes a particular routine within a DLL. You can't normally execute a DLL file, but some DLL files have special functions in them that you can execute using Rundll.exe.
`setupx.exe,...`	Setupx.dll contains a function called `InstallHinfSection` that knows how to install INF files.
`DefaultInstall`	Remember `[DefaultInstall]`? This is the name of the section that contains the `AddReg` and `DelReg` sections within the INF file.
`132`	Who knows what this means?
`%1`	Windows 98 executes this command line, substituting the name of the INF file for `%1`.

Using Setup Scripts and Msbatch.inf

The Windows 98 CD-ROM includes a utility called Microsoft Batch 98, which you can use to create setup scripts. Setup scripts allow a user to install or upgrade to Windows 98 with little user intervention, because you specify most if not all of the installation options within the setup script. You can specify options that go far beyond installation, too, such as network configuration, user profiles, and so on.

You'll find Batch 98 in \Tools\Reskit on the Windows 98 CD-ROM.

Batch 98 creates a file called Msbatch.inf that contains all the settings you specified. You start the setup program with this INF file by typing *path*\setup.exe *path*\msbatch.inf, including the paths to Setup.exe and Msbatch.inf if necessary.

Msbatch.inf includes a section called [Install] that is similar to the [DefaultInstall] section you'll learn about in this chapter. It allows you to add or remove Registry entries when the user installs Windows 98. One typical case in which you might want to do this is if you're enabling user profiles as the user installs the operating system. You can add the AddReg and DelReg items to this section if they don't already exist. Then add the appropriate AddReg and DelReg sections to the remainder of the file.

The following steps describe the process from beginning to end:

1. The user right-clicks an INF file and chooses **Install**. As a result, Windows 98 executes the command line just described.

2. Rundll.exe loads Setupx.dll, calling the function called `InstallHinfSection`. Setupx.dll passes this function the remainder of the command line as follows: `DefaultInstall 132 %1`.

3. `InstallHinfSection` loads the INF file specified by `%1` and looks for the section named on the command line. It processes each item within that section, which happens to be `[DefaultInstall]` in this case.

4. `InstallHinfSection` processes the `DelReg` item first, which leads it to the `[My.Del.Reg]` section of the INF file, removing each key or value specified.

5. `InstallHinfSection` processes the `AddReg` item second, which leads it to the `[My.Add.Reg]` section of the INF file, adding and changing each Registry entry as specified.

Using INF Files to Set DWORD Values

Many folks believe that INF files can't write DWORD values to the Registry; they're wrong. INF files can indeed write DWORD values to the Registry, but you get there via a twisted path through binary and little-endian values.

Remember that a DWORD value is a four-byte, or 32-bit, integer number. Take 52,059, for example, which is 0x0000CB5B in hexadecimal. Within memory, the computer stores DWORD values in reverse byte order (also called *little-endian*), so it stores 0x0000CB5B as 5B CB 00 00. The computer turns the bytes back around when a program loads the four-byte number from memory. The same goes for values that a program stores in the Registry. You see DWORD values represented normally in the Registry Editor only because it reads the value as a DWORD, automatically flipping the bytes around as they should be.

Therefore, the first solution to writing DWORD values to the Registry is to write them as binary strings using reverse byte order. For instance, if you want to store 21,465 in a value entry, store it as a four-byte binary value with the bytes reversed. Thus, 21,465 is 0x000053D9, so you would store the binary string D9 53 00 00 in the value entry. You must make sure to use a four-byte value, however, not three-byte and not five-byte. Note that if you're trying to change an existing DWORD value entry, you might have to remove the original value and replace it with a new binary value. If you're using a script, REG, or INF file, however, Windows 98 will automatically change the type for you.

> NOTE: The process you read about in this section describes what happens with an INF file that contains only the AddReg and DelReg sections of an INF file. INF files can contain many more sections, however, including Copyfiles, LogConfig, Renfiles, Delfiles, UpdateInis, UpdateIniFields, Ini2Reg, UpdateCfgSys, and UpdateAutoBat.

Just to make sure you understand, Table 15.4 contains a number of examples. The first two columns show a value that you might try to write to the Registry, and the third column shows the little-endian binary string you'd actually write to represent that value.

Table 15.4 **Examples of Writing DWORD Values to the Registry**

DWORD (Decimal)	DWORD (Hexadecimal)	Binary (Little-Endian)
01	0x00000001	01 00 00 00
331	0x0000014B	4B 01 00 00
4096	0x00001000	00 10 00 00
5001	0x00001389	89 13 00 00
7779863	0x0076B617	17 B6 76 00
53896313	0x03366479	79 64 36 03
2147483649	0x80000001	01 00 00 80

The second solution is to use `0x10001` as the type. This is a relatively unknown type that you can use in the `AddReg` section of your INF file that indicates the DWORD data type. Even when using `0x10001`, you must still write the value as a four-byte little-endian binary string. Thus, to write the value 2147483649 to the Registry as a DWORD value, convert it to hex, which is 0x80000001, and then to a little-endian binary string, which is 01 00 00 80. As a result, you would add a line similar to this to your INF file:

```
HKLM, MyKey, MyValue, 0x10001, 01,00,00,80
```

Writing Scripts to Update the Registry

The Windows Scripting Host is new to Windows 98. It includes two Active Scripting engines, JScript and VBScript—and more scripting engines are coming down the pike. You're probably familiar with Active Scripting, because Internet Explorer 3.0 and greater support it already. The Windows Scripting Host brings that same technology to the Windows desktop. Think of it this way: The Windows Scripting Host is to Windows 98 what batch files were supposed to be to MS-DOS.

Scripts are ideal for administrators and power users alike. Administrators can use scripts to automate complex administrative tasks such as advanced login scripts or updates to the user's Registry. Power users can use scripts to automate repetitive tasks. You might use a script to arrange your Windows 98 desktop, for example, or to perform a series of tasks that you do every day.

NOTE: *Little-endian* is an addressing scheme in which the bytes with lowest significance are stored first in memory (little end first). *Big-endian* (big end first) is an addressing scheme in which the bytes with the most significance are stored first in memory. For the most part, Intel computers use little-endian addressing.

Teaching you how to write scripts is beyond the scope of this book. Additional information is available from a variety of sources, however, all of which are close at hand. \Tools\Reskit\Scrpting on the Windows 98 CD-ROM contains more information about WSH files, which you use to set properties that control how scripts run. If you need more information about writing scripts, visit Microsoft at `http://www.microsoft.com/management/WSH.htm`. Similarly, Microsoft's Developer Network provides documentation for the object model (the operating system objects, such as network connections or the shell, that you control from scripts) at `http://www.microsoft.com/msdn/sdk/inetsdk/help/wsh/wobj.htm`.

The following sections still show you how to write scripts that work with the Registry, however. You'll learn how to create and run scripts; how to write scripts that add, remove, and change Registry entries; and how to check for errors and report them to the user.

Creating New Script Files

Scripts are text files that use the extensions listed in Table 15.5. JS stands for JScript scripts, Microsoft's incarnation of JavaScript, and VBS stands for VBScript scripts. Note that Windows 98 associates both types of files with Notepad, but I prefer to edit scripts in WordPad. If you do too, change the **Edit** command of the JScript Script File and VBScript Script File types. Don't try associating WordPad with either file type's **Open** command, however, because this prevents you from running scripts by double-clicking them in Windows Explorer. Use Windows Explorer's Folder Options dialog box, or change the default values of the following keys to `"C:\Program Files\ Accessories\Wordpad.exe" "%1"`:

```
HKEY_CLASSES_ROOT\JSFile\Shell\Edit\Command

HKEY_CLASSES_ROOT\VBSFile\Shell\Edit\Command
```

Table 15.5 **VBScript and JScript Scripts**

File Extension	Language	Sample Statement
JS	JScript	`WSHShell.RegDelete("HKCU\\MyKey\\");`
VBS	VBScript	`WSHShell.RegDelete "HKCU\MyKey\"`

NOTE: Here are some real-world examples of things you can do automatically with scripts: Back up important configuration files, control the programs running on your desktop, collect system information and post it on the server, and connect to the Internet and download files. You can, of course, use scripts to update the Registry with the customization tips you learned in Chapter 9, "Customizing the Windows 98 Desktop."

A script starts its life as an empty file. The first line you should add to this file is always the same, depending on the language you're using. The first of the following two examples shows you that first line for a JScript script. The second example shows you the same line in VBScript. Both of these statements create a shell object, which provides access to the Registry methods and assigns that object to WSHShell. You can, of course, add a few comments to the top of the file, as shown in Listing 15.3, so that the script is easier to read and understand. Note that JScript comments begin with two forward slashes (//) and VBScript comments begin with a single apostrophe (').

```
var WSHShell=WScript.CreateObject("WScript.Shell");
```

```
Set WSHShell=WScript.CreateObject("WScript.Shell")
```

The second statement in Listing 15.3 shows you how to display a message on the screen. It uses the shell object's Popup method to display whatever you pass it as a parameter. Remember that you created a shell object in the first statement and assigned it to WSHShell, so you use the syntax WSHShell.Popup to invoke the Popup method. You'll use this same approach when invoking the shell object's Registry methods, as you'll learn in the following sections.

Listing 15.3 **A Basic JScript Script**

```
// A Basic Script
//
// This example shows you how to start your script files.
// Begin each file with a brief description of what the
// script does. You might even include your name and a brief
// history of all the changes you make in order to better
// document it. Note that JScript uses two forward slashes
// to start a comment, while VBScript uses an
// apostrophe (').

var WSHShell = WScript.CreateObject( "WScript.Shell");
WSHShell.Popup( "This is a basic JScript script!" );
```

SEE ALSO

➤ Chapter 9, "Customizing the Windows 98 Desktop," shows you how to change file associations so that you can associate JS and VBS files with WordPad.

TIP: WordPad makes a better editor for scripts than does Notepad. For one thing, its search-and-replace feature is far better than Notepad's. More importantly, however, it handles tabs and indentations better than Notepad so that you can format your scripts properly. Associate the JScript Script File and VBScript Script File types with WordPad using the File Types tab in Explorer's Folder Options dialog box.

Running Scripts in Windows and MS-DOS

Double-click a VBS or JS script file to run it. Windows 98 associates the **Open** command of both file extensions with the Windows Scripting Host and makes that the default command. You can also launch a script from the Run dialog box. Select **Start**, **Run**, type the path and filename of the script in the space provided, and click **OK**.

Windows 98 includes two different script interpreters—one DOS-based and one Windows-based. The DOS-based interpreter is Cscript.exe, and it allows you to run scripts from the MS-DOS command line. The Windows-based interpreter is Wscript.exe. As you learned, you don't have to do anything special to start scripts using Wscript.exe; just double-click the script file in Windows Explorer or launch it from the Run dialog box. To launch scripts using the DOS-based interpreter, you must run Cscript.exe and pass it the path and filename of the script, like this:

```
cscript.exe myscript.vbs
```

Both the DOS-based and Windows-based interpreters allow you to specify options that change their behaviors. The DOS-based interpreter accepts a number of command line options. Note that each of these options begins with two forward slashes, not one. That's because you can pass options to the script itself, and you specify these options using a single forward slash. In general, the command line for Cscript.exe looks like this:

```
cscript filename [host options] [script options]
```

`//?`	Displays help for command line options.
`//i`	Allows the interpreter to display prompts and script errors.
`//b`	Prevents the interpreter from displaying prompts and script errors.
`//T:n`	Kills the script if it runs for longer than *n* seconds. This is good for debugging.
`//logo`	Displays an execution banner.
`//nologo`	Prevents the execution banner from being displayed.
`//H:Cscript`	Registers Cscript.exe as the default script interpreter in the Registry.
`//H:Wscript`	Registers Wscript.exe as the default script interpreter in the Registry.
`//S`	Saves the current options as the default.

You can specify options for the Windows-based interpreter, too. These are similar to the command line options for Cscript.exe. Right-click a script file, choose **Properties**, and click the Script tab. You see the dialog box shown in Figure 15.2. You'll recognize the options in this dialog box because they're similar to the command line options for Cscript.exe. Click **OK** to save your changes. Windows 98 creates a

WSH file, which looks like an INI file, in the same folder as the script file. Think of WSH files as you do PIF files, each of which contains options for running a particular MS-DOS program: They point to a particular script file and contain options for running that script. Listing 15.4 shows you what a typical WSH file looks like.

Listing 15.4 **A Sample WSH File**

```
[ScriptFile]
Path=C:\Windows\Desktop\Scratch\Listing 15-3.js

[Options]
Timeout=10
DisplayLogo=1
BatchMode=0
```

Writing Statements to Change the Registry

Before learning how to change the Registry using a script, there are a few things you should know about specifying key and value names. First, you must use a double back-slash (\\) in JScript instead of a single backslash because the backslash character has special meaning in that language. Second, a backslash at the end of a name has special significance. Ending a name with a backslash, such as HKLM\MyKey\, means you're specifying a key, while ending a name without a backslash, such as HKLM\MyKey\MyValue, means you're specifying a value entry. The last thing to note is that you can use the short or long root key names. Table 15.2 describes the abbreviations you can use for each of the root keys. In general, the short names are more manageable than the long names. Here's a summary of what you have just learned:

■ Use double backslashes with JScript, not VBScript.

■ End key names with a backslash, values without.

■ Use the abbreviations in Table 15.2 for root keys.

TIP: Right-click a script, choose **Properties,** and click the Script tab to create a WSH file for that script. The WSH file, which will have the same root filename as the script, contains all the options you specified in the script file's Property sheet. You can launch the script by double-clicking the script or WSH files.

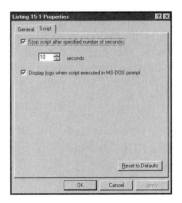

Figure 15.2   The property sheet for a script file allows you to set options similar to Csscript.exe's command line.

The following sections show you how to perform the most common tasks that you normally perform in the Registry Editor with a script. You'll learn how to add a new key or value entry, how to set a key's default value entry, how to change a value entry, and how to remove keys and value entries. You do all this with only three of the shell object's methods: `RegWrite`, `RegRead`, and `RegDelete`.

Adding a New Key

Use the `RegWrite` method of the shell object to write new keys to the Registry. The following examples show you what the syntax looks like in both JScript and VBScript:

JScript   `WSHShell.RegWrite( KeyName\\ );`

VBScript   `WSHShell.RegWrite KeyName\`

The only argument to `RegWrite` is the name of the key you're adding. Don't forget to use double backslashes in the key name if you're using JScript, and end the name with a backslash to specify that you're writing a Registry key. Here's an example that creates a key called `Test` under `HKEY_CURRENT_USER`:

`WSHShell.RegWrite( "HKCU\\Test\\" );`

Setting the Default Value of a Key

Setting the default value entry for a key isn't much different than creating a new key. You use the `RegWrite` method as well, but you specify an additional parameter: a value.

> NOTE: The result of omitting the double backslash (\\) in a key when using JScript is interesting. Windows 98 removes all the backslashes, leaving you with a long name that Windows 98 assumes is a value entry. Thus, `HKLM\My\Value` becomes `HKLMMyValue`. In this case, Windows 98 reports an error that says `The System cannot find the path specified`. If you typed `HKLM\\My\Value`, you'd end up with `HKLM\MyValue`.

The following examples show you the syntax for setting a key's default value entry in JScript and VBScript:

JScript   WSHShell.RegWrite(*KeyName*\\, *Value*);

VBScript   WSHShell.RegWrite *KeyName*\, *Value*

The difference between creating a new key and changing the default value entry is that you add the value to the parameter list. Note that this assumes that the default value entry is a string, which is usually the case. Listing 15.5 shows you a complete example that automatically changes the default command for folders to Explorer so that you can open My Computer in a two-pane Explorer window by double-clicking it.

Listing 15.5   **Changing the Default Command for Folders**

```
// Changing the Default Action for Folders
//
// This script changes the default action of folders so
// that you can open My Computer in a two-pane Explorer
// window by double-clicking it on the desktop.

var WSHShell = WScript.CreateObject( "WScript.Shell");
WSHShell.RegWrite( "HKCR\\Folder\\shell\\", "explore" );
WSHShell.Popup( "Double-click My Computer to open Windows Explorer" );
```

Adding or Changing a Value Entry

`RegWrite` strikes again: You also use it to add or change a value entry. There are a couple of differences between using `RegWrite` for keys and using it for value entries, however. First, you omit the backslash from the end of the name, indicating that you're working with a value entry. Second, you specify an additional parameter to tell Windows 98 the value entry's data type. Here's the syntax for this form of `RegWrite` in both languages:

JScript   WSHShell.RegWrite(*Key**Name*, *Value*, *Type*);

VBScript   WSHShell.RegWrite *Key**Name*, *Value*, *Type*

> **CAUTION:** The RegWrite method allows you to change the type of a key's default value entry. You can do so by specifying an additional parameter to RegWrite that indicates the type, as described in the next section. Note that you should leave default value entries as string values, because you can't predict the outcome.

If the value entry given by *Key\\Name* doesn't exist, Windows 98 adds the value entry, changes its type to *Type*, and sets it to *Value*. If the value entry already exists, Windows 98 changes it and its value. Note that if you don't specify a type, Windows 98 assumes you meant to specify REG_SZ, which is a string value entry. Table 15.7 describes the values you can assign to *Type*. REG_SZ works about as you'd expect; you must specify *Value* as a quoted string. Both REG_DWORD and REG_BINARY types allow you to use an integer for *Value*. You can optionally put the integer number in quotes if you specify REG_DWORD.

Table 15.7 **Value Types for** RegWrite

Type	Description
REG_SZ	Quoted string: "This is a string"
REG_DWORD	Integer between 0 and 2147483647
REG_BINARY	Integer between 0 and 2147483647

Listing 15.6 shows you an example that adds a new value entry and changes an existing one. First, it adds an additional command to the program identifier for text files: txtfile. Note what's going on in the second RegWrite statement. The value I'm assigning looks something like "\"C:\ ... \" \"%1\"". If you use quotes to specify the beginning and end of strings in JScript, you must have some method of writing quotes into the middle of a string; otherwise, you wouldn't be able to properly change commands in the Registry. \" is that method. In the second RegWrite method, JScript replaces each occurrence of \" with a single quote when it writes the string to the Registry.

Listing 15.6 **Adding a New Command for a File Type**

```
// Adding a New Action for a File Type
// Turning Off Windows Animation
//
// This script does two things to demonstrate changing
// a value entry. First, it adds a action to the txtfile
// type for opening a TXT file in WordPad. Second, it turns
// off window animation, just in case it annoys you.

var WSHShell = WScript.CreateObject( "WScript.Shell");

// Add the "Open in Wordpad" action to the txtfile type

WSHShell.RegWrite( "HKCR\\txtfile\\shell\\wordpad\\",
➥"Open in &Wordpad", "REG_SZ" );
```

```
WSHShell.RegWrite( "HKCR\\txtfile\\shell\\wordpad\\
➥command\\", "\"C:\Program Files\Accessories\
➥Wordpad.exe\" \"%1\"", "REG_SZ" );

// Change MinAnimate to 0

WSHShell.RegWrite( "HKCU\\Control
Panel\\Desktop\\WindowMetrics\\MinAnimate",
➥"0", "REG_SZ" );

WSHShell.Popup( "Right-click a file in Explorer and choose
➥Open in Wordpad" );
```

Removing a Key or Value Entry

Enough of `RegWrite`. It's time to move on to the `RegDelete` method, which you use to remove a key or value entry from the Registry. The following examples show you what the syntax of `RegDelete` looks like in both JScript and VBScript. The first example for each language shows the syntax for removing a key. The second shows the syntax for removing a value entry.

JScript
```
WSHShell.RegDelete( KeyName\\);
WSHShell.RegDelete( KeyName\\Value );
```

VBScript
```
WSHShell.RegDelete KeyName\[sr]
WSHShell.RegDelete KeyName\Value
```

The only argument to `RegDelete` is the name of the key or value entry you're removing. Remember to end the name with the backslash (a double backslash for JScript) if you're removing a Registry key. If you remove a Registry key, Windows 98 deletes the entire branch beginning with that key, so be careful. Listing 15.7 shows you a real-world example. It clears out the MRU history lists from the Registry as described in Chapter 9, "Customizing the Windows 98 Desktop." I wrote this in VBScript for two reasons: to demonstrate a complete VBScript script, and to take advantage of VBScript's `On Error` statement for easy error handling. Since there is a good chance that one or more of the keys we're removing in this script might not exist in the Registry, we must use the error handling illustrated here to avoid seeing error messages.

> NOTE: Even though `RegWrite` supports the `REG_BINARY` data type, it doesn't handle binary strings very well. First, it only supports four-byte binary values, not the binary strings you're accustomed to seeing in the Registry. You can get around this problem by creating a small REG file, however, and importing that REG file by launching it using the `Run` method: `WSHShell.Run( "import.reg" );`

Listing 15.7 **Removing the History Lists from the Registry**

```
' Removing the History List from the Registry
'
' This script cleans out the history lists by removing
' the following subkeys of HKEY_CURRENT_USER\Software\
' Microsoft\Windows\CurrentVersion\explorer:
'
' RecentDocs
' RunMru
' Doc Find Spec MRU
' FindComputerMRU
'
' Since the user will likely run this script at
' startup, it doesn't display a message.

Dim WSHShell
Set WSHShell = WScript.CreateObject( "WScript.Shell" )

On Error Resume Next

WSHShell.RegDelete "HKCU\Software\Microsoft\Windows\
➥CurrentVersion\explorer\RecentDocs\"
WSHShell.RegDelete "HKCU\Software\Microsoft\Windows\
➥CurrentVersion\explorer\RunMru\"
WSHShell.RegDelete "HKCU\Software\Microsoft\Windows\
➥CurrentVersion\explorer\Doc Find Spec MRU\"
WSHShell.RegDelete "HKCU\Software\Microsoft\Windows\
➥CurrentVersion\explorer\FindComputerMRU\"
```

Reading a Value from the Registry

The shell object's `RegRead` method allows you to read any value from the Registry and assign it to a variable in your script. Then you can do a variety of things with the value, such as writing it to a new location in the Registry or displaying it to the user. The following examples show the syntax for both JScript and VBScript. The first example for each language shows the syntax for reading a key's default value entry. The second shows the syntax for reading any other value entry.

> CAUTION: In the process of experimenting with these methods, I have made more than a few typos, leaving out the second backslash, typing the key's name wrong, or forgetting to provide the value entry name. The results were costly, particularly in the latter case. Windows 98 removed the entire branch instead of simply removing the value I wanted to nuke. So back up the Registry first.

JScript	`WSHShell.RegRead( KeyName\\ );`
	`WSHShell.RegRead( KeyName\\Name`
VBScript	`WSHShell.RegRead KeyName\`
	`WSHShell.RegRead KeyName\Name`

The only argument to `RegRead` is the name of the value entry you're reading. If you want to read a key's default value entry, make sure you end the name with a backslash. Don't end the name with a backslash if you're reading a normal value entry. Listing 15.8 shows you how to read both a default value entry and a normal value entry. Also notice that this script assigns the result to a variable and displays that variable so that the user can see it.

Listing 15.8 **Reading Value Entries from the Registry**

```
' Reading Value Entries from the Registry

Dim WSHShell
Set WSHShell = WScript.CreateObject( "WScript.Shell" )

CRLF = Chr(13) + Chr(10)

Dim Name, Org, Wordpad

Name = WSHShell.RegRead( "HKLM\Software\Microsoft\Windows\
➥CurrentVersion\RegisteredOwner" )
Org =  WSHShell.RegRead( "HKLM\Software\Microsoft\Windows\
➥CurrentVersion\RegisteredOrganization" )
Wordpad = WSHShell.RegRead( "HKLM\Software\Microsoft\Windows\
➥CurrentVersion\App Paths\WORDPAD.EXE\\" )

WSHShell.Popup Name + CRLF + Org + CRLF + wordpad
```

> **TIP:** In Listing 15.8, you might have noticed parentheses around the parameters to RegRead. For normal *procedure calls,* which don't return a value, you don't need to include parentheses. However, you must enclose the parameters in parentheses when calling a method that returns a value (also called a *function*), such as RegRead.

Distributing Scripts, REG, and INF Files

A good way to impress the users that you support is to distribute fixes to them without their asking. Better yet, make it as simple as possible, and they'll adore you.

If you have an intranet in your organization, you can make REG and INF files available on a Web page. Lacking an intranet, you can distribute REG files in mail messages or in the user's login script. You'll learn about each in the remaining sections.

Choosing Scripts, REG, or INF Files

Scripts are complex. Aside from access to the Registry, scripts provide access to the rest of the user's computer, including the file system. Thus, they're more appropriate if changing the Registry is part of a larger task, such as editing files on the user's computer.

If your needs are simpler, however, and all you need is to change a value or add a value to the Registry, use REG files. They're quite easy to create by hand or using the Registry Editor's export feature. The one drawback of REG files is that you can't use them to remove keys or value entries from the Registry. If that's your requirement, move on to INF files.

INF files are the ultimate method for editing the Registry, especially if you need to remove keys or value entries. They are easier to read than REG files, in my opinion, but they are harder to create. One other benefit of using INF files is that the default command for an INF file is not to install, so Windows 98 doesn't load the INF file when you double-click it, as the operating system does when you double-click a REG file.

The following table summarizes these details for your convenience:

Feature	Script	REG	INF
Accesses OS features	Yes	No	No
Adds keys and values	Yes	Yes	Yes
Changes value entries	Yes	Yes	Yes
Deletes keys and values	Yes	No	Yes
Easy to learn and use	No	Yes	Yes
Easy to read and understand	No	No	Yes
Installs on a double-click	Yes	Yes	No

On a Web Page

You can put a link to a REG file on a Web page. Then, when a user clicks that link, the browser will download the file to the user's computer and automatically apply the change it contains. This works fine for Internet Explorer users, but Netscape users will have to register a helper application for REG files. Figure 15.3 shows an example of a Web page that contains a few REG files. When you build such a Web page, it's recommended that you follow these suggestions:

- Provide clear information about who needs to apply each particular REG file. For example, if you post a REG file that affects only Microsoft Mail users, say so on the Web page.

- Provide clear information about what the REG file does to the user's computer. Some people are a bit nervous about doing something like this when they don't know exactly what's going to happen.

- Provide instructions that the user can use to download the REG file to his own computer without applying it. That way, if the user wants to, he can inspect the file before applying it.

- Provide contact information for yourself—your office number, phone number, pager number, and so on. If a user is about to panic, he'll feel better knowing that he can quickly get in contact with you.

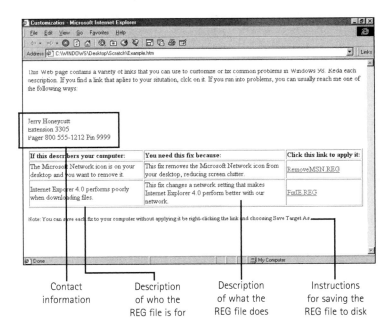

Figure 15.3 Some Web pages are simple, containing only a few REG files. Make sure that yours fits in with the overall Web site.

In an Email Message

If you don't have an intranet in your organization, the next best thing to do is distribute a REG or INF file in an email message. Attach the file to the message and instruct the user on how to apply the file. In most email programs, users have to double-click an attachment to apply a REG file or right-click an INF file and choose **Install**.

The same recommendations apply as for Web pages. Tell the recipients whether or not they need to apply the REG file, tell them what it will do to their computer, tell them how to view the file, and make sure they know how to get in contact with you. Figure 15.4 shows an example of such an email message.

In a Login Script

It takes a bit of work, but you can also put a command in each user's login script that automatically applies the REG or INF file when the user logs onto the network. If you've set up a login script for multiple users, you can slip the command into that script instead. All you have to do is put the following command in the script (*filename* is the name of the REG file):

```
start filename.reg
```

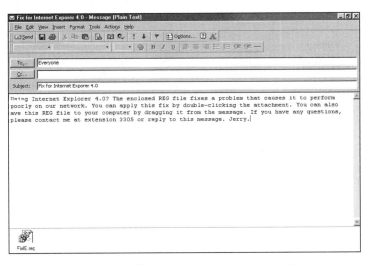

Figure 15.4   You can post a REG file on a Web page and then email a notice containing its description and URL.

> NOTE: Remember that the default Windows 98 command for a REG file is to import it. The default command for an INF file is *not* to install it, however, so you won't be able to distribute an INF file on a Web page. (You can use email or other methods, as shown later.)

The one problem with this method is that every time the user logs onto the network, the login script will apply the REG file. You can avoid this problem by putting the command just discussed in a batch file. Then the login script can check for the existence of this batch file on the user's computer. If it doesn't exist, the login script copies the batch file to the user's computer and executes it. Otherwise, it just ignores it.

The command line for INF files is a bit more convoluted. That's because the default command for an INF file is to not install it. Thus you'll actually specify the command line that Windows uses for INF files' **Install** command (see the earlier section "Understanding How INF Files Work"). *Filename* is the name of the INF file:

```
C:\WINDOWS\rundll.exe setupx.dll,InstallHinfSection
➥DefaultInstall 132 Filename.inf
```

> **TIP:** You can also distribute REG and INF files via Lotus Notes or similar groupware packages. Consult the documentation for your groupware package for more information.

Index

Symbols

∑ (wildcard character), 112

%1, 106, 200

%1 as an icon, 111

\, 29, 69

A

abbreviations for root keys, 18, 340

access
  computers, 144
  controlling for networks, 300–301
  monitoring, 286, 288
  preventing, 300
  restricting
    activities, 301
    registry, 322
    Windows 98, 317

Accessibility Options dialog box, 151

Accessibility subkey, 151

accessories, settings for, 162

ACPI (Advanced Configuration and Power Interface) subkey, 123

Activation follows mouse (X-mouse), 246

Active Desktop, 237

Active Scripting engines, 343

Active Setup, 130

ActiveSetup key, 131

ActiveTitle value, 153

ActiveX, 95

Add New Hardware wizard, 220

Add/Remove Programs dialog box, 159

Add/Remove Programs Properties list, 257

adding
  commands, 199–201
  computers, policy files, 328
  files, Emergency Repair Utility (ERU), 40
  folders, menus, 207
  groups, policy files, 328
  keys, 348
  programs, 257
  templates, 204, 256, 329, 331
  users, policy files, 328
  value entries, 349–351

AddReg entry, 339–342

addresses, formatting for Internet, 209

ADM files, 325

administration, remote. *See* remote administration

Advanced Configuration and Power Interface (ACPI) subkey, 123

aliases
  HKEY_CURRENT_CONFIG, 169
    Display subkey, 171
    Enum subkey, 171

D

I

N

O